Spirit, Resistance, and Community Formation in Luke

Biblical Hermeneutics Rediscovered

The Series as the name suggests will focus on Biblical Hermeneutics, i.e., literary works concerned with methods of interpreting the Old and New Testaments of Bible via different stream of topics like Literature & Poetry, Indigenous Philosophizing, Ethical response towards Ecology, Health & Healing, Science & Technology, Feminist Theology, Sociological approach towards Human Rights, Law & Politics, Arts, History of Ideas, Ancient Civilizations, Cultural Contiguity, Religious Cosmologies & Mysticism, Appraisal of various Theologians, World Peace & Harmony, Global Capitalism, Network Marketing, Cybertheology, Population & Demographics, Epigraphic Studies, Contextualized Education, and many others. We welcome a Mss. on any topic/s mentioned, whether they are original works, scholarly monographs, collections of conference papers, revised dissertations, or translations of historical documents. Through the Series we, the Publishers, are striving to put forward published works that may help Institutions, Academic Bodies, Researchers, Scholars and the World at large in furthering their respective knowledge and understanding on the concerned subject. We welcome your comments on our efforts and further suggestions on how we can enshrine new ray of analysing & explaining the written Texts through our upcoming books.

Biblical Hermeneutics Rediscovered - 48

Spirit, Resistance, and Community Formation in Luke

A Postcolonial Cultural Reading

Rampaukopoing Michui

Christian World Imprints

First Published in 2021 by

Christian World Imprints
Christian Publishing & Books from India
C-3, Wazirpur Industrial Area
Delhi-110052
cwidelhi2017@gmail.com
www.ChristianWorldImprints.com
Phone: +91 11 41526079

ISBN: 978-93-5148-594-0 (HB)
ISBN: 978-93-5148-595-7 (PB)

Printed in India.

For my brother Ekobe Michui

That the book in its original form is the thesis submitted to the Senate of Serampore College, towards the D.Th. degree and is published with written permission. The candidate is responsible for the title, contents and opinions expressed in it.

The original title of the thesis is, *Spirit and Community Formation in Luke's Gospel and Resistance Movement among Zeliangrong Nagas*. But for the purpose of publication with due acknowledgement and the permission required, the title of the thesis is reconstructed to the present form.

Contents

Foreword

Dr. Rampau's book "Spirit, Resistance and Community Formation in Luke: A Postcolonial Cultural Reading" is a very systematic and ground-breaking work in the field of Lukan Scholarship and postcolonial studies. The Gospel of Luke indeed documented many Charismatic tendencies in the Early Christian cult in the first century C.E. The identity of the Holy Spirit in Luke is associated with the community of Luke. It can be understood from the contextual and perspectival studies based on parallelism; function and inter-textual references.

Dr. Rampau is a systematic and serious researcher at UTC, Bangalore and I had the privilege to journey with him as his doctoral supervisor. The major strength of the work is the textual and exegetical analysis in the light of postcolonial insights and encounters.

I am delighted to recommend this book for a critical reflective study in the academy and churches for the work of the Kingdom of God. In India there are many researchers and scholars who systematically publish with scholarly contributions to enrich the New Testament research. I am sure Dr. Rampau's work will inspire many to take up the study of Lukan community and scholarship. I wish and pray that Dr. Rampau will publish many books in the near future.

Rev. Prof. Dr. C. I. David Joy
Principal
Kerala United Theological Seminary
Trivandrum Kerala

Preface

Postcolonialism has produced a creative site of bible reading — a site of resistance, a site of tracing the story of those whose voice were submerged by the weight of colonial edifice. It not only allows one to challenge and go beyond the 'given' meaning of text and interpretation but also allows one to attempt to recover and bring to the fore the voices of the silenced other, who fought the Empire in their time, and to imagine the possibility of a better future. As one who come from a community that once resisted the colonial formation of British Raj and one that continues to struggle to come to term with the legacy of colonial violence, the theme of resistance from the margins in an imperial situation gained impetus in my thought formation as I read the bible from the vantage point of postcolonial subject. It is this interest that I endeavoured to do my doctoral research on the resistant discourses of the margins taking Lukan text and context of Roman Empire.

Thus, this work on the Spirit, Resistance, and Community Formation in Luke's Gospel is a postcolonial cultural reading of selected Lukan texts that emphasise the activity of the Spirit in inspiring protest voices and empowering countercultural actions to the marginalised for counter social formation in the context of empire. This work is therefore, an attempt to underscore the political dimension of the Spirit of God, which has not received adequate attention in the pneumatological debates surrounding Lukan writing. Lukan departure from the Synoptic Gospel portrait of the Holy Spirit shows a turn to the political, in that Luke emphasises the Spirit as a political entity actively breathing life into the community. (The Old Testament and Second Temple traditions, which Luke inherited, show parallel functions of the Spirit of resistance in several charismatic circles). In this work, the selected texts which showed the vivid Spirit's activity in the social formation of the community in Luke's Gospel is analysed in the light of postcolonial insights.

Postcolonial and cultural reading of selected passages delve into a careful detail exegetical analysis of Lukan canticles such as the Magnificat and the Benedictus; Jesus' Nazareth proclamation (4:16-30); Jesus' exorcism (4:31-37) and healing (5:17-26); Lukan Passion Narrative (ch. 23) and the Resurrection

Narrative (ch. 24). It probes colonial mimicry and hybridity in Lukan narrative and highlights how the Spirit empowers the margins to subvert colonial discourse of power with resistant adaptation of colonial languages that destabilises the imperial hegemony and open up space for the margins a faithful resistance to empire. Also, drawing insights from postcolonial and cultural theories the research probes the countercultural actions of the Spirit-anointed Jesus' healings that disrupts the status quo maintained by the establishment. The passion and resurrection narratives are examined to see its subversive power that counters the finality of colonial penal liturgy that forecloses the lives of those who challenge the empire. And in the light of Lukan Spirit, the native resistance movement among the Zeliangrong Nagas against the British Empire during the second quarter of the twentieth century, is analysed as extra textual reference to explore parallel functions of the Spirit of God.

This work has impacted my own understanding of the Spirit of God. The Spirit of God is not always with the powerful but it is always *with* the weak and frustrated community, those who are victims of the violence eviscerated by the dominant power or the empire of the day. And the Spirit empowers faithful resistance to the colonial forces of domination and exploitation. A clear picture of the Spirit's solidarity with the margins emerges in this study of Luke's Gospel. And, in short, this work explores the political activity of the Spirit of God among the margins in Luke's Gospel.

Acknowledgement

As research is always a collective endeavor, I am indebted to many individuals, institutions, church and groups of people who contributed to this work with different resources. At the risk of leaving out many, I want to acknowledge here some few, whose contribution and support was paramount to the success of this work.

My single greatest debt is to C. I. David Joy, my supervisor who has taken deep interest in my work with prompt, detailed and rigorous reading of my manuscript. His expert guidance and generosity with sharing knowledge has inspired me throughout my research. The tutorial group fellowship and dinners at his place provided a soft cushion to eat well and laugh from time to time, for which I am thankful to his family for the kind hospitality. Professor David Joy must share in any success this work may merit, (except for the shortcomings that is my own).

I am thankful to United Theological College, Bangalore for giving me all the essential facilities making my stay in the campus pleasant the entire period of research. In this regard, I want to thank the principal of the college, John Samuel Raj, the esteemed faculty members, the library staff, student friends for their kind help and support in different capacities. In particular, I am grateful to the college for granting me an international exposure to participate in the Bridging Gaps 2016 programme at the Vrije University (VU) University and Protestantse Theologische Universiteit (PThU), Amsterdam, which especially enabled me to avail the VU library resources for my research. I acknowledge the help and support of Peter Ben Smith, Klass Spronk, Arie Zwiep, Willemien van Berkum, the Bridging Gaps members and the VU library staff and the PThU library staff for their assistance. Big thanks also to Keyigum Thou for aiding me in library sources, and Ipetlung for assisting me in several errands and office works to place my work in the calendar timeline.

It has been a joy studying with the companionship of many doctoral students friends Biju C., Saju Thomas, Mayang Lonkumer, Wilson Cherian, Among Jamir, Zubeno Kithan, Zubenthung Humtsoe, Hetoho Achumi, Alfred Chiru, Hiapierai — the 11 am tea break outside the library and the several fellowship meals truly added fun to the nature of our work. I must add the dinner chats fellowships with Chenijan, Jian, Ania, Yajen, later joined by Ngater, Imidau.

I am indebted to Jalukie Town Local Baptist Church for funding my fees and for the moral support throughout my research project. And in this regard, I must thank my friend Pastor Mongzeung Mpom, who, as the Pastor of my sponsoring church, would come all the way from Jalukie Town to pay a visit every year. My gratitude would not be complete without acknowledging the love, care, and the prayers Baptist Church New Poilwa, Zeme Christian Fellowship, Bangalore and UTC Naga Fellowship. I have received much lively support from all of them.

My family members were always my strength. As always my deepest gratitude is to my mother (who is no more today) and father for years of love and prayers who shared my success more than anyone. Big thanks to my Uncle Heluibe, pui-Kelalie, ti-Nchanglie, pui-Asako and Ekobe (who left us in between my study), Paihem and Asape, Ramyi and Namheu, Chising and Suiyisi, and my wonderful younger siblings Gwesy, Samgwam, Kongsing and Dima for their love and support. Especially during my stay in Bangalore the intermittent visit of Samdibe, Radi and then Kongsing with their stories was remarkably refreshing in many ways. I am grateful to my wife Pauria for the support and encouragement in preparing this modest work for publication. And finally, all glory and honor to God for all His gracious blessings and for His faithfulness in my life.

Rampaukopoing Michui

List of Abbreviations

AB	Anchor Bible
ABD	*Anchor Bible Dictionary*
ACNT	Augsburg Commentary on the New Testament
AOT	*The Apocryphal Old Testament.* Edited by Hedley F. D. Sparks. Oxford: Clarendon, 1984.
ASTI	Annual of the Swedish Theological Institute
AYB	Anchor Yale Bible
BAGD	Bauer, Walter, William F. Arndt, F. Wilbur Gingrich, and Frederick W. Danker. *Greek-English Lexicon of the New Testament and Other Early Christian Literature.* 2nd ed. Chicago: University of Chicago Press, 1979.
BECNT	Baker Exegetical Commentary on the New Testament
Bib	*Biblica*
BJRL	*Bulletin of the John Rylands University Library of Manchester*
CBQ	*Catholic Biblical Quarterly*
EGL & MWBS	Eastern Great Lakes and Midwest Biblical Society
ExpTim	*Expository Times*
HKAT	Handkommentar zum Alten Testament
HTR	*Harvard Theological Review*
ICC	International Critical Commentary
IDB	The Interpreter's Dictionary of the Bible
Int	Interpretation
ISPCK	Indian Society for Promoting Christian Knowledge
JAAR	*Journal of the American Academy of Religion*
JBL	*Journal of Biblical Literature*
JBPR	*Journal of Biblical and Pneumatological Research*
JETS	*Journal of the Evangelical Theological Society*
JPTSup	Journal of Pentecostal Theology Supplementary Series

JQR	*Jewish Quarterly Review*
JSNT	*Journal for the Studies of New Testament*
JSNTSup	Journal for the Studies of New Testament Supplement
JSOT	*Journal for the Study of Old Testament*
JSOTSup	Journal for the Studies of Old Testament Supplement
JSS	*Journal of Semitic Studies*
JSTJSup	Supplements to the Journal for the Study of Judaism
JTS	*Journal of Theological Studies*
L	Lukan Special Source
LCL	Loeb Classical Library
LNTS	Library of New Testament Studies
LXX	The Septuagint
MT	Masoretic Text
NAB	New American Bible
NAC	New American Commentary
NCBC	New Century Bible Commentary
NIB	*New Interpreters Bible*
NICNT	New International Commentary on the New Testament
NIDNTT	*New International Dictionary of New Testament Theology*
NJBC	*The New Jerome Bible Commentary*
NovT	*Novum Testamentum*
NRSV	New Revised Standard Version
NTS	*New Testament Studies*
OBT	Overtures to Biblical Theology
OTL	Old Testament Library
PTMS	Princeton Theological Monograph Series
Q	*Quelle* (A Hypothetical common source for Matthew and Luke)
RevQ	*Revue de Qumran*
RSV	Revised Standard Version
RTR	*Reformed Theological Review*
SBJT	*Southern Baptist Journal of Theology*
SBL	Society of Biblical Literature
SBLDS	Society of Biblical Literature Dissertation Series
SBLSS	Society of Biblical Literature Symposium Series
SCSS	Septuagint and Cognate Studies Series
SNTSMS	Society for New Testament Studies Monograph Series
SPCK	Society for Promoting Christian Knowledge

TDNT	*Theological Dictionary of the New Testament*
TDOT	*Theological Dictionary of the Old Testament*
TLNT	*Theological Lexicon of the New Testament*
TLOT	*Theological Lexicon of the Old Testament*
TPI	Theological Publications in India
VTSup	Vestus Testamentum Supplementary Series
WBC	Word Biblical Commentary
WTJ	*Wesleyan Theological Journal*
WUNT	Wissenschaftliche Unterschungen zum Neuen Testament

Ancient Sources

1 En.	1 Enoch (Ethiopic Apocalypse)
2 Bar.	2 Baruch
4 Ezra	4 Ezra
Pr. Azar.	Prayer of Azariah
Pss. Sol.	Psalms of Solomon
Mart. Ascen. Isa.	Martyrdom and Ascension of Isaiah
T. Ab.	Testament of Abraham

Rabbinic

B. Bat.	Baba Batra
Num. Rab.	Numbers Rabbah
Sanh.	Sanhedrin
T. Is.	Targum Isaiah
t. Sotah	Tosefta Sotah

Josephus

Ag. Ap.	*Against Apion*
Ant.	*Antiquities of the Jews*
J.W.	*Jewish War*

Tacitus

Agri.	*The Life of Gnaeus Julius Agricola*
Ann.	*Annales*
Hist.	*History*

Philo

Alleg. Interp.	*Allegorical Interpretation*
Drunkenness	*On Drunkennes*
Good Person	*That Every Good Person is Free*

Unchangeable	*That God is Unchangeable*
Worse	*That the Worse Attacks the Better*
Ep.	Seneca, *Epistles*
Hist. eccl.	Eusebius, *Ecclesiastical History*

Dead Sea Scrolls

1QH	Hodayot or Thanksgiving Hymns
1QM	Milhamah or War Scroll
1QS	Serek Hayahad or Rule of the Community
CD	Cairo Genizah copy of the Damascus Document
1QpHab	Pesher Habakkuk
4QPBless	Patriarchal Blessing
4QFlor	Florilegium, also Midrash on Eschatology
11Q13	11QMelchizedek
1QapGen	Genesis Apocryphon
11QTemple	Temple Scroll

Chapter 1

Introduction

1.1. Introduction

Empire building is a perennial enterprise in human history both ancient and modern with sophisticated discourses of power, but it also breeds resistance from the ground. The victims of empire fights back with counter discourses of power, dislodging the official truth claim with their subjectivity emerging from their experience of marginality. The bible is one that witnesses the counter discourse of those who lived under the shadow of empire. Luke's Gospel shows colonial imprints of domination as well as resistance to such domination with theological-ideological discourse on the role of the Spirit as a political entity actively breathing life into the community. This study examines the role of the Spirit in community formation in Luke's Gospel.

1.2. Rationale of the Study

This study is motivated by a clear indication in Luke's Gospel's departure from the Synoptics' eschatological moorings of the Spirit's activity and Luke's emphasis on the role of the Spirit as the driving force for the social formation of the Jesus' movement that resists the domination system of the empire. This aspect of resistance is evident in the Spirit-inspired proclamations of God's liberative work for the oppressed through the voices from the margins of the empire (Luke 1:46–55; 67–79; 4:14–20), and in the powerful healings of Jesus (4:31–37; 5:17–26) — discourses which engage the dominant discourse and the fixed authority of the ruling powers. At the same time, the Gospel is set within the larger political landscape of the Roman Empire and narrates the subversive activities of the Spirit anointed-Jesus that attracted opposition from client rulers of Rome. Therefore, this study explores the activities of the Spirit in empowering resistance that engenders social formation of marginal community in the context of empire.

Previous studies on Lukan pneumatology have significantly noted that the Spirit in Luke's writing is the Spirit of prophecy with varied emphases on its role as the Spirit of empowering mission. However, there is an apparent lack of adequate attention among interpreters to study the political dimension of the Spirit of God in Luke's Gospel. This study has attempted to fill this gap. Further, this study takes up one native resistance movement — the Zeliangrong Movement, which resisted the British Raj during the second quarter of the twentieth century — as an extra text to appraise the Spirit of resistance in people's movement in the light of the Spirit in Luke's Gospel. This study advances the understanding that the Spirit of God in Luke's should be appreciated as a Spirit of resistance that empowers the social formation of the marginal communities.

1.3. The Spirit in Luke's Gospel

The Synoptic Gospels regard the Spirit as the power of God[1] manifesting the authoritative (ἐξουσία) words of the awaited Old Testament-Jewish spirit-anointed son of God and elect servant[2] Jesus (Matt 3:11–13 // Mark 1:9–11 // Luke 3:21–22 cf. Is 42:1 and Ps 2:7).[3] However, Luke takes a detour and goes beyond Matthew and Mark in emphasising the powerful operation of the Spirit in the life and work of Jesus. *Firstly*, Luke emphasises that, "full of the Spirit" (Luke 4:1) Jesus was led by the Spirit into the wilderness to combat the διάβολος and returned to Galilee "filled with the power of the Holy Spirit"[4] (Luke 4:14). Luke claimed that Jesus was "anointed" with the Spirit quoting Isa 61:1–2a at the beginning of Jesus' work to drive home the point that his entire life and work was carried out with the power of the Spirit (cf. Acts 10:38).

---

1 Eduard Schweizer, "πνεῦμα," *TDNT* 6: 397, 404. For footnote, bibliography, and abbreviations of works related to biblical studies this work has followed *Society for Biblical Literature Handbook of Style*, 2nd ed. (Atlanta, GA: SBL, 2014).

2 C. K. Barrett, *The Holy Spirit and the Gospel Tradition*, (London: SPCK, 1958), 41; Eduard Schweizer, *The Spirit of God*, Bible Key Words from Gerhard Kittel's Theologisches Wörterbuch zum Neuen Testament, trans. A. E. Harvey (London: Adam and Charles Black, 1960), 30.

3 Instances of Jesus' authoritative statements are "Be silent and come out of him" (Mark 1:25/ Luke 4:35b); "Blessed are the poor" (Matt 5:3ff // Luke 6:20ff.); "But I say to you" (Matt 5:22); "Go and tell John what you hear and see" (Matt 11:4 // Luke 7:22). Jesus' powerful deeds especially exorcisms are explicitly attributed to the Spirit/finger of God (Matt 12:28 // Luke 11:20). That an exorcism was carried out with the power of the Spirit of God is implicit in Mark 3:28–30.

4 The Holy Spirit in Luke's Gospel is interchangeably used as Lukan Spirit.

Secondly, In Luke's Gospel, the πνεῦμα (as the Spirit of God) and δύναμις (power) are indissolubly related and are used as synonyms[5] whereas it is not the case in Matthew and Mark. In many places, Luke collocates power and the Spirit (Luke 1:17; 1:35; 4:14; 24:49 cf. Acts 1:5, 8; Acts 10:38). Especially in Luke 4:14, δύναμις (power) is explicitly said to be the power of the Spirit. Luke 24:49 shows a clear substitution of πνεῦμα with δύναμις since for Luke "power from on high" refers to the outpouring of the Spirit (Acts 1:8). Luke 1:17 and 35 are further hints that Luke is using δύναμις and πνεῦμα as synonymous parallels.

Thirdly, it is also notable that Luke has added δύναμις in several places where Matthew and Mark do not, so as to emphasise the power of the Spirit (Luke 4:36 cf. Mark 1:27; Luke 5:17 cf. Mark 2:1–12; Matt 9:2–8; Luke 6:19 cf. Mark 1:35–39; Matt 4:23–25; Luke 8:46; Mark 5:30 cf. Matt 9:21; Luke 9:1 cf. Mark 6:7; Matt 10:1). What is striking in some of these noted instances is that Luke collocates δύναμις (power) and ἐξουσία (authority) especially in the context of exorcism and healing (4:36; 9:1 cf. 10:19). Presumably, Lukan Jesus has his power in the Holy Spirit, which anointed him (Luke 4:18 cf. Acts 10:38) and his power is expressed in his authority (ἐξουσία). Luke emphasised several times that Jesus was "mighty in deed and word," an expression unmistakably linked to the anointing of Jesus with the Holy Spirit and with power (Luke 24:19; Acts 2:22; 10:38; cf. Luke 4:18; 36). Thus for Luke, power is inextricably linked to the Spirit, and has its referent to the Spirit when Jesus is the subject. Thus, Luke apparently presents the Spirit as the "power of resistance."

Equally important here is to note the earthly powers in the physical and temporal space specific to Lukan world against which Lukan community engages. In *Naming the Powers*,[6] Walter Wink spells out several terms that were employed by Luke with reference to earthly political powers and structures of authorities, such as, ἀρχιερεῖς (chief priests) and ἄρχοντες (rulers) in Luke 24:20; ἀρχας (rulers) and ἐξουσίας (authorities) in Luke 12:11; ἀρχῇ (authority), ἐξουσία (jurisdiction) and ἡγεμόνος (governor) in Luke 20:20; ἄρχοντας (rulers) in Luke 23:13 and so on. Notably, Luke also uses ἐξουσία in reference to the power of Satan (12:5) and to human authorities (12:11). According to Wink, the New Testament's use of the pervasive language of "principalities and powers" (ἀρχαι και ἐξουσίαι) is "a generic category referring to the determining forces of physical, psychic, and social existence."[7] The Gospel sketch a narrative of how the community engages these "principalities and powers" with the numinous power of the Spirit.

5 Walter Grundmann, "δύναμαι, δύναμις," *TDNT* 2:301; Schweizer, *TDNT* 6:407; R. E. Brown, *The Birth of the Messiah: A Commentary on the Infancy Narratives in Matthew and Luke* (Garden City, NY: Double Day, 1977), 290.

6 Walter Wink, *Naming the Powers: The Language of Power in the New Testament*. Philadelphia: Fortress Press, 1984), 7–9.

7 Walter Wink, *Unmasking the Powers: The Invisible Force that Determine our Existence.* Philadelphia: Fortress Press, 1986. 4.

Thus, unlike the imminent eschatological tension in Mark and Q, Luke tones down the eschatological language (Mark 1:15; Matt 4:17 cf. Luke 17:20; Acts 1:7–8), which in turn is reflected in some of the Spirit passages. *Firstly*, Luke altered the "Spirit of God" saying in Matt 12:28 into the "finger of God" (cf. Luke 11:20)[8] and transposed the saying on the "unpardonable sin against the Holy Spirit" (Mark 3:29; Matt 12:32 cf. Luke 12:10). This suggests that Luke dissociated the term πνεῦμα from the imminent eschatology, even though it is construable that the "Spirit of God" and the "finger of God" equally mean "the power of God."

Secondly, Luke placed the teaching about the "help of the Holy Spirit before authorities" (Luke 12:11–12) along with various teachings. However, in Q it is placed in the context of preaching the imminent coming kingdom of God (Matt 10:18–20 cf. ἤγγικεν ἡ βασίλεια των οὐρανῶν, Matt 10:7) and Mark places it in the context of the apocalyptic tribulation of the end time (Mark 13:11).

Thirdly, in Q, John the Baptist differentiates his "water baptism" from the baptism with the "Holy Spirit and fire" of the "one" who comes after him (Matt 3:11; Luke 3:16) which suggest that the fire is meant to be a fire of judgment[9] as the following verse indicates (Matt 3:12; Luke 3:17). However, Luke excluded "fire" when the resurrected Jesus differentiates the Baptist's water baptism from the baptism of the Holy Spirit, which the disciples will receive (Acts 1:5). Rather, Luke links the baptism of the Holy Spirit with the receiving of "power from on high" (Luke 24:29 cf. Acts 1:8). Luke also excluded "the day of vengeance of our God" (Isa 61:2b) in the Spirit-anointed preaching of Jesus about salvation and liberation that quotes Isa 61:1–2a.

Since Luke's primary purpose was to strengthen the identity of the community, as it comes to term with the realities of the marginal experience

---

8 The arguments are: (1) it is more likely that Luke deleted the reference contained in Q than Matthew added it. Matthew never omits a reference to the πνεῦμα which is contained in Mark or Q, but follows his source carefully with reference to the Spirit, but Luke feels free to add or delete πνεῦμα to his sources (cf. Luke 20:42 // Mark 12:36). (2) The presence of the phrase the "kingdom of God" instead of Matthew's favourite phrase the "kingdom of heaven" in the Q version of Matthew 12:28 suggests that Matthew retained the Q version without modifying it as he normally would have done in other instances (cf. Matt 4:17; 5:3). (3) The statement that follows after the Beelzebub controversy, which is about blasphemy against the Holy Spirit (Matt 12:32 // Luke 12:10) also supports that Matthew's "Spirit of God" formed part of the text of Q. (4) J. D. G. Dunn argues that, it is unlikely that Matthew would have altered the "finger of God" to the "Spirit of God," since he draws a careful parallel between Moses and Jesus, but his interest in the motif of the spirit is less prominent. See J. D. G. Dunn, *Jesus and the Spirit: A Study of the Religious and Charismatic Experience of Jesus and the First Christians as Reflected in the New Testament* (London: SCM Press, 1975), 45–46. Robert P. Menzies, *The Development of Early Christian Pneumatology with Special Reference to Luke-Acts* (Sheffield: Sheffield Academic Press, 1991), 185–189.

9 Rudolf Bultmann, *The History of the Synoptic Tradition,* trans. John Marsh (Oxford: Basil Blackwell, 1963), 246.

under the shadow of Roman rule, he seems to have taken a detour from the pneumatology of Mark and Q to inform and transform the community's self-understanding of the experience of the Spirit. Luke apparently presents the Spirit of God as that power which inspires and empowers to resist in word and deed the forces, whether "demonic" or "human institution," which oppress and silence the powerless. Luke sees the entire life of Jesus as one empowered by the Spirit, whether it is in the exorcisms of the demon possession, proclaiming the messages of liberation or in challenging the authorities centred at Jerusalem that executed him.

Given the distinctiveness of purpose, Lukan pneumatology is significantly different not only from the Synoptic Gospels but from Pauline,[10] Johannine[11] and other New Testament writings, though there are common grounds as well. It is notable that the New Testament writings agree that the Spirit is the Spirit of prophecy. However, for Luke the Spirit of prophecy is not a phenomenon of the past but a present experience. Yet, it is not a community-edifying Spirit of prophecy as in Paul, but an instigating power that inspires prophetic voice and action of the community in the world. The Petrine "Spirit of God" which rests upon the persecuted believers (1 Pet 4:14) is consolatory, whereas, the Spirit in Luke empowers the people in the midst of persecution, though one can draw a parallel experience of the persecution of the communities of these two works. In the book of Revelation, the Spirit is the "Spirit of vision" (17:3; 21:10), which leads a person into visions which the natural *man* does not perceive and the "Spirit of prophecy" (19:10) that admonishes and encourages the church. However, the Spirit in Luke is not the power of seeing visions as such but the power that enables

10 For Paul, the Spirit is definitely power, but not simply a source of miraculous power (1 Cor 12:10a; Gal 3:5). For Paul, πνεῦμα is that power which operates within a person as an inner, religious, moral principle of the life, which transforms the believers' consciousness and conduct of life (Rom 5:5; 8:9, 14; 1 Cor 1:4–9; 6:9–11; 12:13; 2 Cor 1:21f.; 3; Gal 3:1–5; 4:6f.; Col 2:11f.; 1 Thess 1:5f). The Spirit is the fundamental dynamic, which shaped the believers life. Cf. O. Pfeiderer, *Paulinism: A Contribution to the History of Primitive Christian Theology*, vol. 1, trans. E. Peters (London: William & Norgate, 1877), 200. For Paul, the Spirit is given to the church for the edification of the communal life. For Luke, the Spirit gives voice and empowers actions to the community.

11 Johannine Spirit has a regenerative function, which gives new birth that enables a person "to enter into the kingdom of God" (3:5). "The *how* of the process remains a mystery (3:8), but the *fact* is perfectly clear. It is the spirit that gives life (6:68)." William Ross Schoemaker, "The Use of רוח in the Old Testament, and of πνεῦμα in the New Testament," *JBL* 23 (1904): 50. The most distinctive feature of Johannine pneumatology is the description of the Spirit as the (another) Paraclete (14:16–26; 14:26; 15:26–27; 16:7–15) obviously implying that Jesus is the first Paraclete (1 John 2:1). R. E. Brown, *The Gospel According to John*, AB 29A, (Garden City, NY: Doubleday, 1970), 1140. The Spirit-Paraclete of John is a personal figure that guides, teaches and reveals truth to the community (14:16–17, 26; 16:13). However, neither the Synoptics nor Acts sees the Spirit in terms of a figure like the Fourth Gospel.

the community to envision new socio-political praxis; not a Spirit that speaks *to* a community but one that speaks *through* the active community.

The distinctiveness of Lukan pneumatology from other New Testament writings is its political nature of operation in the community life. However, a brief survey on the history of research on Lukan pneumatology would reveal that the previous researches were occupied with historical and theological questions but lack attention to the political activity of the Holy Spirit[12] (see discussion below).

Luke, more than any other evangelist showed interest to narrate the movement of Jesus and his followers within the broader context of Roman/Judean geo-politics. The time prior to the birth of Jesus was dated to "the days of King Herod" (Luke 1:5a) and Jesus' birth was placed in the time of the first census bill passed by Caesar Augustus when Quirinius was the Governor of Syria (Luke 2:1–2). Jumping a chronological gap of some three decades, Luke presented a still more elaborate power configuration in Roman Palestine in introducing the preaching of the Baptist and the ministry of Jesus. "In the fifteenth year of the reign of Emperor Tiberius, when Pontius Pilate was governor of Judea, and Herod was ruler of Galilee ... during the high priesthood of Annas and Caiaphas" (Luke 3:1–2).[13] As much as it may be an imitation of the Greco-Roman historical writing, the chronological markers were intended to inform the readers of the political climate and the sociocultural and economic conflicts of the early first

12 Herman Gunkel's work, *Die Wirkungen des heiligen Geistes nach der papulüren Anschauung der apostolischen Zeit und nach der Lehre des Apostels Paulus*, 1888; (English Translation) *The Influence of the Holy Spirit: The Popular Teaching of the Apostolic Age and the Teaching of the Apostle Paul*, trans. Roy A. Harrisville and Philip A Quanbeck II (Philadelphia: Fortress, 1979), set the agenda for pneumatological exploration of the New Testament though one can note the preceding works by B. Weiss (*Lehrbuch der biblischen Theologie des Neuen Testaments*, 1868) and O. Pfleiderer (*Der Paulinismus*, 1873; English Translation, *Paulinism: A Contribution to the History of Primitive Christian Theology*, 1877) that have identified the distinctiveness of Pauline pneumatology from the *Urgemeinde*. Gunkel concurs with his predecessors that the *Urgemeinde* viewed the Spirit as power which wrought wonders and spectacular deeds, and concludes that "Paul found ready-made the concept of the πνεῦμα as a wonder-working power, but on the basis of his experience, by which the Christian himself appeared to be the greatest miracle, he described the Christian life as an activity of the πνεῦμα in a completely original way" (ET, 102). The discussion on the evolution of pneumatology of the New Testament was taken further by Friedrich Büchsel (*Der Geist Gottes im Neuen Testament*, 1926) and Heinrich von Baer (*Der heilige Geist in den Lukaschriften*, 1926). Heinrich von Baer identified the Spirit as the driving force of Lukan salvation history, which he divides into three epochs. Lukan studies begin to treat Luke as a theologian with the work of Hans Conzelmann's on Luke's theology in 1961; ET, Hans Conzelmann, *Theology of St. Luke*, trans. Geoffrey Buswell (Philadelphia: Fortress, 1982). Conzelmann regards the Spirit as the connecting link between Jesus and the church that guarantees the hope of the future (184, 230).

13 All the Bible quotations are from NRSV unless otherwise specified.

century Palestine.[14] Given this colonial context, a fresh reading that attends to the political nature of the Spirit-inspired voices and actions of the community seem legitimate.

For instance, the Magnificat heralds the hope of the ταπείνωσις[15] (lowly) against the ὑπερηφάνους (proud) who are scattered in the thought of their heart, the δυνάστας (powerful) who are brought down from their thrones, the πλυτοῦντας (rich) who are sent away empty as they do not care for the poor (cf. Luke 16:19; 18:23). However, it is noted that traditional interpretations have often ignored the "the thunder and tenor of her song,"[16] by spiritualising and eschatologising its transformative message[17] while there is nothing specifically spiritual or eschatological about the song in the Lukan context.[18] Joel B. Green observes that, setting the Benedictus against the background of a "grossly oppressive militaristic, economic, and political foreign presence will lead us to read in Zechariah's song the expression of deep-seated revolutionary hopes held by a people thrust violently to the margins of society."[19]

The Spirit-anointed Jesus' Nazareth proclamation challenges a society characterised by inequality, sickness, suffering, oppression and exclusion with visions of an alternative egalitarian society (Luke 4:18–19), as do the Beatitudes and Woes (Luke 6:20–26). As the Gospel unfolds, the anointing of the Holy Spirit sets in motion Jesus' mighty words and deeds which subverts the religious and political spaces of the Jewish nation such as the synagogue and the Jerusalem Temple. Hence, the pneumatological significance of the mighty word and deed of Jesus and the community formed around him must be given adequate attention in the study of Lukan pneumatology.

---

14 Virginia Burrus, "The Gospel of Luke and Acts of the Apostles," in *A Commentary on the New Testament Writings*, ed. Fernando F. Segovia and R. S. Sugirtharajah (London: T&T Clark, 2007), 134.

15 In the New Testament this word which is rendered "lowliness," is not merely "humility"—humbleness as a state of being or as an attitude but also "humiliation as an experience" or "afflicted state" describing an objective, unfavourable condition. Luke Timothy Johnson, *The Gospel of Luke*, Sacra Pagina, vol. 3 (Grand Rapids: Eerdmans, 1991), 42. ταπείνωσις in the latter sense, afflicted state might be used with reference to the humiliation of the oppressed people of God (cf. Deut 26:7; 1 Sam 9:16; 1 Macc 3:51).

16 Green borrows the line, "the thunder and the tenor of her song" from the poet Thomas John Carlisle whose poetic construction speaks of the song as a "revolutionary beat." Joel B. Green, *The Theology of the Gospel of Luke* (Cambridge: Cambridge University Press, 1995), 1 cf. Thomas John Carlisle, "Revolutionary Carol," in *Beginning with Mary: Women of the Gospel in Portrait* (Grand Rapids: Eerdmans, 1986), 4.

17 For instance, Robert C. Tannehill, "The Magnificat as Poem," *JBL* 93 (1974): 275; John Nolland, *Luke 1–9:20*, WBC 35A (Dallas: Word, 1989), 64.

18 Richard A. Horsley, *The Liberation of Christmas: The Infancy Narratives in Social Context* (New York: Crossroad, 1989), 113.

19 Joel B. Green, *The Gospel of Luke*, NICNT (Grand Rapids: Eerdmans, 1997), 114.

In this light a few pertinent questions can be raised. What is the significance of the Spirit in the Lukan community? Does the Spirit create a "site of resistance" that engenders the identity formation of the community? How much does Luke reflect the colonial scars and imprints in the text, indicating the socio-political conflicts of the Roman occupied Palestine? What are the socio-cultural, economic, political, and religious issues of the postcolonial condition that helps in re-reading the pneumatology of Luke? Can the resistance movement of the (contemporary) people's struggle be seen as the activity of the Spirit in the light of the Lukan Spirit?

1.4. Importance of the Research

This study is important for at least three reasons. Firstly, studies on Lukan pneumatology have not given (adequate) attention to the Holy Spirit as a Spirit/power of resistance and its role in engendering the social formation of the marginalised. Secondly, such a pneumatology of resistance will broaden the traditional pneumatology of the church from its dogmatic structure towards a holistic understanding of the Holy Spirit as the spirit that is not limited to any established ecclesiastical circle but is active in the socio-political struggle of the marginalised communities. Thirdly, a pneumatological/hermeneutical paradigm is necessary in a postcolonial context like India in order to listen and understand the groans and cries emerging from the margins as the voice of the spirit that calls upon the church and the society to forge together in realising a better world.

1.5. Limitations of the Research

The Gospel of Luke and Acts of the Apostles are considered as a single work in two volumes and hence the legitimacy to treat them together. However, the *Sitz im Leben* of the community in the Gospel is decisively that of Palestine, while Acts of the Apostles encompass the circum-Mediterranean. Therefore, this study is limited to the Gospel of Luke. There are thirty-six references of πνεῦμα in the Gospel out of which seventeen refers to the Spirit of God.[20] However, the texts for a detail study are chosen with a thematic focus. Firstly, the Magnificat (1:46–55), the Benedictus (1:67–79) and the Nazareth proclamation (4:16–30) are chosen to explore the role of the Spirit in a prophetic protest that emanates from the margins. Secondly, the exorcism of the demoniac at Capernaum (4:31–37) and the healing of the paralytic (5:17–26) are chosen to study the Spirit-anointed Jesus' exorcism and healing as modes of socio-political resistance against the system of domination and oppression. And thirdly, the Lukan passion narrative (ch. 23) and resurrection narrative (ch. 24) are taken to study the role of the

20 The occurrences of πνεῦμα in the Gospel can be classed in the following manner: (1) Breath 8:55; 23:46, (2) anthropological spirit 1:17, 47, 80, (3) angelic spirit 24:37, 39, (4) evil spirit 4:33, 36, 6:18; 7:21; 8:2, 29; 9:39, 42; 10:20; 11:24, 26; 13:11, and (5) divine Spirit such as τὸ ἅγιον πνεῦμα 12:10, 12, τὸ πνεῦμα τὸ ἅγιον 2:26; 3:22; 10:21, πνεῦμα ἅγιον 1:15, 35, 41, 67; 2:25; 3:16; 4:1a; 11:13, and simply πνεῦμα 2:27; 4:1b, 14, 18.

Spirit in Lukan Jesus passion and resurrection account. The Spirit is not explicitly mentioned in all of these selected texts but the role of the Spirit is implicit in the selected texts.

1.6. Previous Research

A significant step in the study on Lukan pneumatology appeared in Eduard Schweizer's article on "πνεῦμα," which delineated how the Lukan Holy Spirit is different from the other New Testament writings. He opines that owing to the influence of Judaism, Luke limits the activity of the "Spirit of prophecy" to inspired proclamation such that Luke never ascribed the Spirit as the source of miraculous activity.[21] However, Schweizer's strict theological lexicographic study of the term could not enter into conversation with the Lukan ideological language and its subversive implication. The work of J. D. G Dunn, which came out of his uneasiness with the Pentecostal and the sacramental interpretation of the Holy Spirit in the New Testament,[22] tackled Lukan pneumatology as a theological doctrinal issue. His conclusion against the doctrine of subsequence ignited the debate on the reception of the Holy Spirit. What followed after Dunn's work was the rigorous debate on whether the spirit is a *sine qua non* of Christian existence or a *donum superadditum* in the subsequent works of Roger Stronstad, Max Turner, Robert Menzies and so on, anchoring their arguments on the baptism of Jesus in Jordan and the Pentecost accounts.[23]

Roger Stronstad's *The Charismatic Theology of St. Luke* is a targeted response to Dunn's *Baptism in the Holy Spirit* and to a great extent a consolidation of the Pentecostal theology of the Spirit. Stronstad accuses Dunn (and others) for interpreting Luke in the light of Paul thereby devaluing Luke's independent theology.[24] Stronstad argues that Luke's understanding of the Spirit-reception is devoid of the soteriological connotations; it is given to those who are already Christians that is to his disciples (19:1) and believer (8:12; 19:2) to equip them for vocational purpose.[25] The church described by Luke becomes a charismatic

21 Schweizer, *TDNT* 6: 407.

22 J. D. G. Dunn, *Baptism in the Holy Spirit: A Re-examination of the New Testament Teaching on the Gift of the Spirit in Relation to Pentecostalism Today* (London: SCM Press, 1970), 1–7.

23 Roger Stronstad, *The Charismatic Theology of St. Luke* (Peabody: Hendrickson, 1984); Max Turner, *Power from on High: The Spirit in Israel's Restoration and Witness in Luke-Acts* (Sheffield: Sheffield Academic Press, 1996); Robert P. Menzies, *Empowered for Witness: The Spirit in Luke-Acts.* JPTSup 6 (Sheffield: Sheffield Academic Press, 1994).

24 Stronstad specifically pointed out that the twelve references to the two phrases by Luke ("filled with the Holy Spirit" [9X] Luke 1:15, 41, 67; Acts 2:4; 4:8, 31; 9:17; 13:9; 13:52 and "baptism in the Holy Spirit" [3X]: Luke 3:16; Acts 1:5; 11:16) do not carry the same meaning with Paul's singular use of the phrases "baptism in the Spirit" (1 Cor 12:13) and "filled with the Spirit" (Eph 5:18). See *Charismatic Theology of St. Luke*, 11.

25 Stronstad, *Charismatic Theology of St. Luke*, 63–69. In the manner of the transfer of the charismatic Spirit from Moses to his elders (Num 11:14–17, 25) and subsequently to Joshua

community, called and empowered for mission through the Spirit. Stronstad concludes, "Luke relates the gift of the Spirit to service and witness; that is, to vocation."[26]

Robert Menzies reconstructs the development of the concept of the Spirit from Judaism to early Christianity and identifies Lukan Holy Spirit as the Jewish "Spirit of prophecy," which was given to the disciples as a prophetic *donum superadditum* (additional gift—of divine grace) which empowers them for missionary enterprise. Thus, he validates the Pentecostal distinctive characteristic of the doctrine of subsequence, arguing that "Spirit-baptism, in the Pentecostal sense, is distinct from (at least logically, if not chronologically) conversion"[27] *contra* Dunn. Menzies thinks that Luke differs from the primitive church pneumatology that included the miraculous function (as in Mark and Q), and shows a reluctance to associate the Spirit with the miraculous works (cf. Luke 11:20, 12:10). Menzies privileges the Jewish spirit of prophecy as the background of Lukan pneumatology and writes, "Luke retained the Jewish understanding of the Spirit as the source of special insights and inspired speech."[28] However, Lukan pneumatology is also indebted to the Old Testament spirit's tradition in which the Spirit comes as an invasive force and empowers the community in crisis (e.g., Moses, Judges, Elijah-Elisha) and helps their social formation over against the dominant power structure.

Max Turner's *Power From on High: The Spirit in Israel's Restoration and Witness in Luke-Acts* tackles the two unreconciling position of J. D. G. Dunn, for whom the Spirit is a new covenant life and sonship and Robert Menzies, for whom the Spirit is the Spirit of prophecy given almost exclusively for mission.[29] Turner takes a mediating position in this debate. Turner agrees that Luke indeed understand the Spirit as the "Spirit of prophecy" promised by Joel (3:28–32) and reflected in the pre-Christian Judaism. But unlike Menzies, Turner did not think that the role of the Spirit is limited to missional role in Luke-Acts. He also insists that the Spirit is also the source of miraculous phenomena (Luke 1:35; 4:14; Acts 1:38) and that these are vital for Jesus to carry out his messianic role. Contrary to Dunn, he maintains that Jesus' reception of the Spirit at his baptism was not an archetypical entry into the experience of a new covenant life, but an empowering factor to bring about Israel's liberation. For Turner, Luke's portrait of the Spirit

---

(Num 27:16–20; Deut 34:9), the same Spirit rests upon Jesus (Luke 4:18–21) and empowers Jesus' entire mission which is then transferred by Jesus to the disciples at Pentecost (45, 52).

26 Stronstad, *Charismatic Theology of St. Luke*, 81.

27 Menzies, *Empowered for Witness: The Spirit in Luke-Acts*, 236.

28 Menzies, *Empowered for Witness: The Spirit in Luke-Acts*, 227. Thus, Menzies maintains that, Lukan "prophetic pneumatology" can be differentiated from the more "charismatic pneumatology" of the primitive church (Mark and Q) and the "soteriological pneumatology" of Paul (226–227).

29 Turner, *Power From on High*.

"is dominated by his broader intention to portray the ministry of Jesus, and the Church which results, as the fulfillment of God's promises to restore his people Israel to make her a light to the nations."[30] However, these works were theological-doctrinal in orientation. It shows little or no attention to the implications of the Spirit empowered mighty works and inspired voices upon the community life of the Lukan community.

James B. Shelton's *Mighty in Words and Deeds* provides a redactional analysis of Luke-Acts that differentiates Lukan pneumatology from other New Testament writers. Shelton argues that in Luke-Acts, the Spirit's role cannot be limited to inspired speech alone but must include the mighty deeds. Shelton writes, "Luke's main point is that Jesus is the Spirit-anointed Messiah and that he both spoke and performed wonders by the power of the Holy Spirit."[31] "Thus, in Luke-Acts the recipients of the Holy Spirit are like Moses, 'mighty in … words and deeds' (Acts 7:22), even as Jesus himself was 'mighty in deed and word' (Luke 24:19)."[32] However, Shelton too does not see the Spirit's empowered mighty words and deeds as protest voices and actions of the margins subverting the power structure of the empire.

William Shepherd and Ju Hur take up narrative analysis of Lukan Spirit. Shepherd takes the "Spirit of prophecy" as the starting point to investigate the "Spirit's function as guarantor of the prophetic word."[33] Shepherd's main thesis is that "in Luke-Acts the character of the Holy Spirit signals narrative reliability, and that ultimately the Spirit's presence and action is that of God."[34] In other words, for Shepherd, Luke presented the Holy Spirit as a character who acts as an onstage representative of God and its fundamental function was to provide "narrative reliability" for the reader.[35] For instance, in her treatment of the Pentecost narrative, Shepherd argues that the presence of the Holy Spirit establishes not only the reliability of Peter's speech, but the narrative itself, in that what was promised came to fulfillment in the Pentecost.[36] Like Shepherd, Ju Hur also employs a narrative critical approach by describing his method as a "dynamic biblical narrative criticism."[37] Hur explores the extra-text of Luke-Acts especially the Old Testament or Hebrew Bible, LXX, Old Testament Apocrypha,

30 Turner, *Power From on High*, 188–201.

31 James B. Shelton, *Mighty in Words and Deeds: The Role of the Holy-Spirit in Luke-Acts* (Peabody, MA: Hendrickson, 1991), 74.

32 Shelton, *Mighty in Words and Deeds*, 6.

33 W. H. Shepherd, *The Narrative Function of the Holy Spirit as a Character in Luke-Acts*, SBLDS, 147, (Atlanta: Scholar Press, 1994), 2.

34 Shepherd, *Narrative Function of the Holy Spirit as a Character in Luke-Acts*, 101.

35 Shepherd, *Narrative Function of the Holy Spirit as a Character in Luke-Acts*, 247, 255.

36 Shepherd, *Narrative Function of the Holy Spirit as a Character in Luke-Acts*, 167.

37 Ju Hur, *A Dynamic Reading of the Holy Spirit in Luke-Acts* (Sheffield: Sheffield Academic Press, 2001), 34.

and selected Qumran literature and argues that Lukan Holy Spirit is rooted in this extra-text, but that Luke redefined the Spirit in terms of Jesus so that in Acts the Spirit of God is channeled through Jesus and God's will is defined in terms of Jesus' life, death, and resurrection on the one hand and the Spirit of God which operates exclusively within the God's faithful Jews past, present and future, now incorporates even the non-Jews into God's eschatological people.[38] He concurs with Shepherd that in Luke-Acts, Holy Spirit is used in the service of legitimating narrative reliability so that both the narrator and the protagonist are associated positively with the divine frame of reference.[39] This is aimed at encouraging the reader to understand that not only the Holy Spirit but also the characters are themselves God's reliable agents in the unfolding narrative of Luke-Acts.[40] Except that Hur employs a narrative reading, like Stronstad, Menzies and Turner he comes to the conclusion that Lukan narrative plot is aimed at "empowering and guiding main characters to bear witness to God's Kingdom and the risen Jesus by inspiring them to speak and perform mighty deeds in accordance with the plan of God."[41]

In recent years, there is a growing interest in looking at the Spirit and community in Luke-Acts. For instance, Matthias Wenk's *Community Forming Power*[42] calls into question assumptions that earmarked the function of the Spirit in Luke-Acts to almost exclusively in inspired speech or empowerment for witness. He has shown how the Spirit functions to bring about ethical transformation in a manner consistent with the Spirit-inspired prophetic tradition of the Hebrew Scriptures. But, Wenk's concern was limited to the role of the Spirit in socio-ethical transformation of the community. He did not venture into the community-forming role of the spirit from the vantage point of socio-political concerns. Martin William Mittelstadt's *The Spirit and Suffering in Luke-Acts: Implications for a Pentecostal Pneumatology* (2004) also challenges the simple notion of Spirit-empowerment for witness and points out the neglected element of the Spirit and its relation with the theme of suffering within the context of Luke-Acts.[43] He argues that for Luke the ministry of the Spirit is not free from opposition and suffering, but rather is a "pathway to conflict with those who oppose Jesus and his message."[44] Strikingly, Mittelstadt did not venture to explore the role of the Spirit

38 Hur, *A Dynamic Reading of the Holy Spirit in Luke-Acts*, 282.

39 Hur, *A Dynamic Reading of the Holy Spirit in Luke-Acts*, 88.

40 Hur, *A Dynamic Reading of the Holy Spirit in Luke-Acts*, 114.

41 Hur, *A Dynamic Reading of the Holy Spirit in Luke-Acts*, 278.

42 Matthias Wenk, *Community Forming Power: The Socio-Ethical Role of the Spirit in Luke-Acts*. Sheffield: Sheffield Academic Press, 2000).

43 Martin William Mittlestadt, *The Spirit and Suffering in Luke-Acts: Implications for a Pentecostal Pneumatology* (London: T&T Clark, 2004).

44 Mittelstadt, *Spirit and Suffering*, 65.

in the passion narratives, which constitute the most explicit case of suffering and conflict as Jesus engages with the colonial and sacerdotal authorities.

Aaron Kuecker's *The Spirit and the "Other": Social Identity, Ethnicity and Intergroup Reconciliation in Luke-Acts* (2011) is another work, which argues that the Spirit is central in the formation of a new social identity. He takes the reconciling work of the Spirit as the major focus of his study arguing that the Spirit generated a new identity for the early Christians making it possible for the reconciliation of diverse social identities. According to Aaron Kuecker, Luke was convinced that "the transformative power of the Spirit creates a concern for the 'other' expressed by the willingness to leverage privileged identity for the sake of 'other.'"[45] This is an important work which brings to the fore the role of the Spirit in the formation of a community which is open to the other. However, the formation of such countercultural community is an act of protest not least against the cultural-religious norms but against the very fixity of social order. This subversive or resistant aspect of the Spirit is important feature of the spirit in Luke's Gospel.

A review of literature shows that, for a long time, study on Lukan pneumatology was occupied with the Spirit-empowering function for mission and witness. Only recently few works have shown interest in the role of the Spirit in community formation. While Luke definitely intends to legitimise the success of church expansion as the work of the Holy Spirit, with the same yardstick he legitimises the very formation of the church as the work of the Holy Spirit. As his primary purpose was to boost and strengthen the identity of the church, the Spirit functioned not so much as a Spirit of mission or of prophecy but as the Spirit that calls into existence an alternative community, inspiring and empowering the subjectivity of the marginal community to become a potent force to rally with the empire of the day. In this case, it is also important to revisit Luke's literary repertoire as well as the socio-political universe of pneumatology from which Luke developed his pneumatology. This would call into question a monolithic conception that Luke is dependent on the Jewish Spirit of prophecy as noted by some of the scholars. The Spirit in Luke functions like the Spirit that empowers the community in the margins of the society in the Old Testament and also in some movements of the Second Temple Judaism, a point which is taken up in the next chapter. Therefore, it is pertinent to explore Lukan pneumatology against this background and see how Luke presents the role of the spirit in relation to Jesus' movement in Luke's Gospel.

1.7. Method of Research

The researcher intends to employ socio-cultural and postcolonial biblical criticism in this study. However, in the contemporary biblical studies, methodologies are

---

45 Aaron Kuecker, *The Spirit and the "Other": Social Identity, Ethnicity and Intergroup Reconciliation in Luke-Acts*, LNTS 444, (London: Bloomsbury, 2011), 217.

not mutually exclusive and any responsible interpretation cannot ignore the historical, literary, socio-cultural and ideological lenses of reading the text. Hence, a preference for a particular methodology does not necessarily negate other ways of reading nor does it exclude the interdisciplinary integration of the gains of other ways of reading. Nevertheless, to be precise, historical criticism will be employed since, the Gospel according to Luke, being one of the Synoptic Gospels, entails the conventional mode of seeing them together.

1.7.1. Socio-cultural Criticism

Sociological criticism is an exegetical enterprise that analyses the social and cultural dimensions of the text, its author(s), recipients, and their relations, its social context, and its intended impact through the utilisation of the perspectives, theory, models, and research of the social sciences to gain an understanding of texts as meaningful social communication.[46] It goes beyond the historical question of asking what-is-it to a search for a sociological explanation of why, how and what-for to understand the text within the contours of its own sociocultural context.[47] The premise is that New Testament was written within a social system, and hence, in order to understand them, the political, economic, social religious, educational, institutional, and cultural systems must be given attention.[48]

The preference for the term socio-cultural lies in that, the Gospel is a cultural document, produced in a specific cultural context. Despite the fact that "culture" is a broad concept and not easily defined, all human societies have cultures, though "the particular pattern of culture differs among all."[49] Hence, an inquiry into the cultural influences—the political, religious, social, economic—upon the Gospel is valid and important. According to Clifford Geertz, culture "denotes an historically transmitted pattern of meaning embodied in symbols, a system of inherited conceptions expressed in symbolic forces by means of which men communicate, perpetuate, and develop their knowledge about and attitude towards life."[50] However, the important point is, "culture" is not a static monolithic entity. Lucian Legrand makes this point in his *Bible on Culture* and insists that the "cultural world of Jesus" be given importance to uncover the culture and

46 John H. Elliott, "Social Scientific Criticism of a Biblical Text: 1 Peter as an Example," in *Social Scientific Approaches to New Testament Interpretation*, ed. David G. Horrell (Edinburgh: T&T Clark, 1999), 340. ibid, *What is Social-Scientific Criticism?* (Minneapolis: Fortress, 1993), 18.

47 Elliott, *What is Social-Scientific Criticism*, 10–14.

48 M. Robert Mulholland, "Sociological Criticism," in *New Testament Criticism & Interpretation*, ed. David Alan Black and David S. Dockery (Grand Rapids: Zondervan, 1991), 307–308.

49 Lucian Legrand, *The Bible on Culture: Belonging or Dissenting* (Bangalore: Theological Publication of India, 2008), xiv citing J. Bennett and M. Tumin, *Social Life* (New York: Knopf, 1948), 209.

50 Clifford Geertz, *The Interpretation of Culture* (London: Fontana Press, 1993 [1973]), 89.

subcultures operating not only in Hellenism but even within the Jewish Culture of Jesus. He maintains that

> cultures are not consistent wholes. The apparent consensus in a given culture hides internal struggles for power and domination. A dominant culture is too often the privilege of dominating classes of a society. Vast sections of the population are left deprived of the benefit of this 'culture.' Eitherthey remain voiceless or they give expression to their protest through subcultures, and countercultures which the 'dominant culture' will try to silence by open or covert violence.[51]

This fact is true not only of the historical past but of the present as well. The present study will engage in a "cultural exegesis" to attend to the "subcultures" and "countercultures" which protest against the dominant culture traceable in the text. In this, what Anthony Thiselton called "socio-critical hermeneutics" will be helpful. According to Thiselton, socio-critical hermeneutics is an "approach to texts (or to traditions and institutions), which seeks to penetrate beneath their surface-function *to expose their role as instruments of power, domination or social manipulation* (emphasis original)."[52] Such a critical hermeneutics will not only liberate people from the pre-existing prejudices, traditions and social relationship effected by "certain ways reading and using the bible," but also lead to liberation of biblical texts.[53]

1.7.2. Postcolonial Biblical Criticism

Postcolonial hermeneutics investigates and interrogates the colonial discourse of knowledge and power and brings to the fore the material effects of colonialism. There is a growing awareness among biblical scholars about the effects of colonialism and imperialism upon the production and interpretation of the Bible.[54] It is now widely acknowledged that the Roman Empire had widespread

51 Lucian Legrand, *The Bible on Culture*, xiv.

52 Anthony C. Thiselton, *New Horizons in Hermeneutics* (Grand Rapids: Zondervan Publishing House, 1992), 379.

53 Thiselton, *New Horizons in Hermeneutics*, 379.

54 Susan VanZanten Gallagher, ed., *Postcolonial Literature and Biblical Call for Justice* (Mississippi: University Press of Mississippi, 1994); Laura E. Donaldson ed., "Postcolonialism and Biblical Reading," *Semeia* 75 (1996); R. S. Sugirtharajah ed., *The Postcolonial Bible* (Sheffield: Sheffield Academic Press, 1998); ibid, *Asian Biblical Hermeneutics and Postcolonialism: Contesting the Interpretations* (Sheffield: Sheffield Academic Press, 1998); ibid, *Postcolonial Criticism and Biblical Interpretation* (Oxford: Oxford University Press, 2002); Stephen D. Moore and Fernando F. Segovia eds., *Postcolonial Biblical Criticism: Interdisciplinary Intersections* (London: T&T Clark, 2005); C. I. David Joy, *Overlooked Voices* (Borderless Press, 2015).

influence upon the early Christian movement[55] as well as on the production of Luke's Gospel.[56] Equally important is the realisation that biblical interpretations went hand in hand with modern western colonialism and imperialism. In "Postcolonialism and Scriptural Reading," *Semeia* 75 (1996), which can be said to mark the beginning of postcolonial biblical criticism, Laura Donaldson conceives postcolonial criticism as oppositional reading—a "reading like Canaanites."[57] Similarly, R. S. Sugirtharajah describes postcolonialism as a tool that "enable us to question the totalizing tendencies of European reading practices and interpret the texts on our own terms and read them from our own specific locations."[58] However, despite the initial impulse of an oppositional reading strategy, critics have come to emphasise that the "relationship between the ruler and the ruled is complex, full of cross-trading and mutual appropriation and confrontation."[59] Thus, there is no one set of going about in postcolonial criticism.[60] Fernando Segovia cautioned that postcolonial critics should be aware of the intricacies introduced by culture, race, class, and gender in the colonial situation; the complexities of colonial contacts; and to move beyond binarism into hybridity.[61] He suggests postcolonial biblical criticism should

---

55 Peter Oakes, ed., *Rome in the Bible and Early Church* (Carlisle: Paternoster, 2002); Richard A. Horsley, *Jesus and Empire: The Kingdom of God and the World Disorder* (Minneapolis: Fortress, 2003); J. D. Crossan, *God and Empire: Jesus Against Rome, Then and Now* (New York: HarperCollins, 2007).

56 Allen Brent, "Luke-Acts and Imperial Cult in Asia Minor," *JTS* 48 (1997): 427–433; Steve Walton, "The State They Were in: Luke's View of the Roman Empire," in *Rome in the Bible and Early Church*, ed. Peter Oakes (Carlisle: Paternoster, 2002); Burrus, "The Gospel of Luke and Acts of the Apostles"; Kazuhiko Yamazaki-Ransom, *The Roman Empire in Luke's Narrative* (London T&T Clark, 2008); Amanda C. Miller, *Rumors of Resistance: Status Reversal and Hidden Transcripts in the Gospel of Luke* (Minneapolis: Fortress, 2014); Pyung Soo Seo, *Luke's Jesus in the Roman Empire and the Emperor in Luke's Gospel* (Eugene, OR: Pickwick Publishers, 2015).

57 Laura E. Donaldson, "Postcolonialism and Biblical Reading: An Introduction," *Semeia* 75 (1996): 1–12.

58 R. S. Sugirtharajah, "Biblical Studies after the Empire: From a Colonial to a Postcolonial Mode of Interpretation," in *The Postcolonial Bible*, (Sheffield: Sheffield Academic Press, 1998), 16.

59 R. S. Sugirtharajah, "A Brief Memorandum on Postcolonialism and Biblical Studies," in *Postcolonial Perspectives on the New Testament and Its Interpretation*, Special Issue, *JSNT* 73 (1999): 3.

60 Sugirtharajah stressed that postcolonialism "is not a homogenous project, but a hermeneutical salmagundi, consisting of extremely varied methods, materials, historical entanglements, geographical locations, political affiliations, cultural identities, and economic predicaments." Sugirtharajah, *Asian Biblical Hermeneutics and Postcolonialism*, 15.

61 Fernando F. Segovia, "Postcolonial Criticism and the Gospel of Matthew," in *Methods for Matthew*, ed. Mark Allan Powell (Cambridge: Cambridge University Press, 2009), 207.

> foreground throughout the unequal domination and subordination at work; address the imperial as well as the colonial spaces, the centre and the periphery; examine both cultural production and material matrix; make room for pursuing the colonial in its own terms; and opt for diversity in recording the encounter between the imperial and the colonial.[62]

This study will investigate the selected texts in the light of current studies in postcolonialism in order to trace the articulation of resistance in terms of identity formation and the (post)colonial conditions in Luke's Gospel. For this purpose, a very specific definition of postcolonialism is employed—postcolonialism as a critical lens that situates colonialism at the heart of the Bible and its interpretation and investigates the text looking for domination, resistance, and re-presentation to offer an interpretation from the vantage point of postcolonial concerns and conditions. In this endeavour, Bhabha's notion of mimicry and hybridity will be used to analyse the Lukan ideological discourse embedded in the selected texts.

Homi K. Bhabha has mapped the complicated ways in which power operates in human relationships particularly in context of the empire formations. Bhabha writes, "[C]olonial mimicry is the desire for a reformed, recognizable Other, *as a subject of a difference that is almost the same, but not quite*. Which is to say, the discourse of mimicry is constructed around an *ambivalence* (emphasis original).[63] Thus, for Bhabha, colonial discourses are not the product of self-contained (and all powerful) colonial masters but are the result of a hybridisation process caused by the encounter between colonialist and native traditions. He defines hybridity as

> the name for the strategic reversal of the process of domination through disavowal (that is, the production of the discriminatory identities that secure the 'pure' and original identity of authority). Hybridity is the revaluation of the assumption of colonial identity through the repetition of discriminatory identity effects. It displays the necessary deformations and displacement of all sites of discrimination and domination. It unsettles the mimetic or narcissistic demands of colonial power but reimplicates its identification in strategies of subversion that turn the gaze of the discriminated back upon the eye of power.[64]

Bhabha writes, "The ambivalence at the source of traditional discourses of authority enables a form of subversion, founded on the undecidability that

62 Fernando S. Segovia, "Mapping the Postcolonial Optic in Biblical Criticism: Meaning and Scope," in *Postcolonial Biblical Criticism: Interdisciplinary Intersections*, ed. Stephen D. Moore and Fernando F. Segovia (London: T&T Clark, 2005), 75.

63 Homi K. Bhabha, *Location of Culture*, (New York: Routledge, 1994), 86.

64 Bhabha, *Location of Culture*, 112.

turns the discursive conditions of dominance into the grounds of intervention."[65] Thus, for Bhabha colonial mimicry "is at once resemblance and menace,"[66] in that "mimicry marks those moments of civil disobedience within the discipline of civility: signs of spectacular resistance.... [W]ords of the master become the site of hybridity."[67] And this is evident in Luke's Gospel as it often mimics the colonial discourse of Roman Empire (e.g. kingdom, saviour, salvation, peace) with an ambivalent narrative and thus destabilises the popular assumptions of power and hierarchy. "Bhabha's observation on the ambivalence of power and the practices of colonial discourse ... offers a poignant view of the chances and challenges of Christian tradition, its complicities with established power structures, as well as its subversiveness and resistance to them."[68] The effects of mimicry and hybridity allows a discourse of liberating resistance; it enables the critic to transcend the simple binaries and attend to the liberating practice, which in turn allows liberating "anticolonialism without eviscerating oppositional stances."[69]

1.8. The Structure of the Study

This study is divided into seven chapters. The first chapter presents the rationale of the study and defines the methodology. The second chapter explores the development of the concept of the Spirit of God in the Old Testament and Second Temple Judaism, in the light of imperial formations and its impact on the life and thought of the people of Israel. The third chapter appraises group formations within Judaism in the Hellenistic-Hasmonean period and resistance/renewal movements within Judaism in the Roman-Herodian period to foreground Jesus' movement as a resistance movement and highlight how Luke's Gospel reflects the social formation of Luke's own community under the shadow of the Roman Empire. The following three chapters study the text with postcolonial and socio-cultural criticism. The fourth chapter studies the Magnificat (1:46–55), the Benedictus (1:67–79), and the Nazareth proclamation (4:16–30), as Spirit-inspired prophetic protests against the socio-political structure of the empire. The fifth chapter studies Jesus' exorcism and healing events as acts of Spirit-empowered socio-political resistance against the imperial domination and religio-cultural establishment politics of exclusion with the exorcism of the demoniac at Capernaum (4:31–37) and the healing of the paralytic (5:17–26) as

65 Bhabha, *Location of Culture*, 112.

66 Bhabha, *Location of Culture*, 86.

67 Bhabha, *Location of Culture*, 121.

68 Marion Grau, "Divine Commerce: A Postcolonial Christology for the Times of Neocolonial Empire," in *Postcolonial Theologies: Divinity and Empire*, ed. Catherine Keller, Michael Nausner and Mayra Rivera (St. Luois, Missouri: Chalice, 2004), 167.

69 Cf. Mark Lewis Taylor, "Spirit and Liberation: Achieving Postcolonial Theologies in the Untied States," in *Postcolonial Theologies: Divinity and Empire*, ed. Catherine Keller, Michael Nausner and Mayra Rivera (St. Luois, Missouri: Chalice, 2004), 46.

the sample texts. The sixth chapter studies the role of the Spirit in Lukan passion and resurrection narratives by underlining the relationship between the Spirit and suffering in Luke's Gospel and also the role of the Spirit in the formation of the Easter community of witness. The seventh chapter appraises the resistance movement among the Zeliangrong Nagas during the second quarter of the twentieth century against the British colonial rule in the light of the Spirit of resistance of Luke's Gospel. The work is summed up with a conclusions, which provides the gist of the study, its implications, its limitations and direction for further research in this line.

Chapter 2

The Development of the Concept of the Spirit of God in Judaism

2.1. Introduction

It is striking to note that a majority of investigations into the background of Lukan Spirit have concluded that the sole influence rests on the Jewish Spirit of prophecy. But, the privileging of the Second Temple Jewish literature over the Old Testament to locate the background for Lukan Spirit misses an important aspect, that is, the political nature of the Spirit, which finds much resonance in the Old Testament. Therefore, it is pertinent to investigate the origin and development of the activities of the Spirit of God in the life and witness of the people Israel in the various stages of their history as well as in the development of their understanding of the Spirit of God in relation to the community. This chapter begins with a brief analysis of the Hebrew word רוח (*ruah*) and its meaning to foreground the study of the Spirit of God in Judaism.

2.2. The Spirit of God in the Old Testament

2.2.1. Meaning and Occurrences of רוח in the Old Testament

The Hebrew word in the Old Testament for spirit is רוח. The basic meaning of the Hebrew word רוח is "air in motion" — the blowing of the wind or respiration and therefore "wind" and "breathe."[1] In the Old Testament, רוח at least has three references—the meteorological wind, the breath of life or the human spirit, and the Spirit of God. Since breathing is a sign of life רוח also took on the meaning

1 David Hill, *Greek Words and Hebrew Meanings: Studies in the Semantics of Soteriological Terms* (Cambridge: Cambridge University Press, 1967), 205–206; R. Albertz and C. Westermann, "רוח ruah spirit," *TLOT* 3:1203; S. Tengström, "רוח ruah," *TDOT* 13:368.

spirit and life.[2] The term in general occurs 378 times in the Old Testament and in addition 11 times in the Aramaic portion of Daniel. The word occurs 107 times approximately in relation to God. The number includes the phrase "Spirit of Yahweh" (twenty-seven times) and "Spirit of God" (fifteen times in Hebrew and five times in Aramaic).[3] However, it is not always clear between the meanings "spirit" and "wind." For instance, Ezek 37:9 summons the four winds to make alive the dry bones.[4] Thus, it is often the immediate context of the text that provides whether רוח refers to the meteorological wind or anthropological meaning or to the divine Spirit. But in many instances, רוח in the sense of wind is associated directly with God's action (cf. Gen 1:2; Exod 14: 21; 15:8, 10; 1 Kings 18:12).[5]

Strikingly, though scholars like Llyod Neve,[6] Tengström[7] and others try to find its origin in the wind/breath phenomenon, (philologically) there is no consensus among scholars concerning the origin of Spirit of God.[8] However, from the word רוח most scholars points to the power and mysterious element of God's activity to define the Spirit of God. Llyod Neve asserts that in the Old Testament, "*ruach* is only used to express God's activity *as he relates himself* to his world, his creation, his people" (emphasis original).[9] Arguing from the vantage point of רוח as wind, Walter Eichrodt defines the Spirit of God as "the mysterious nearness and activity of the divine."[10] The above two views suggest that the Spirit of God is the manifestation of divine power and/or presence experienced by the people of God. However, the multiplicity of Spirit traditions present in the Old Testament complicates any attempt to trace the origin of the Spirit of God to a single notion. At least the notion of the wind is not present in kingship, prophecy, and "soul" to which the Hebrew רוח is related.[11] Wonsuk Ma attempts a broader definition stressing not only God's activity but the representative function of God's being as well. He writes,

2 Tengström, "רוח ruah," *TDOT* 13:368.

3 Wilf Hildebrandt, *An Old Testament Theology of the Spirit of God* (Peabody, MA: Hendrickson, 1995), 18.

4 Tengström, *TDOT* 13:374. It is possible to think figuratively of the four winds (רוח) in Ezek 37:9 as the divine breathe/Spirit (רוח) that gives life. In this text, the four winds that is summoned came into the lifeless as a life giving breathe/Spirit so that the lived and stood on their feet.

5 Tengström, *TDOT* 13: 382.

6 Llyod Neve, *The Spirit of God in the Old Testament* (Tokyo: Seibunsha, 1972), 7, 13.

7 Tengström, *TDOT* 13: 368–72.

8 Wonsuk Ma, *Until the Spirit Comes: The Spirit of God in the Book of Isaiah*, JSOTSup 271 (Sheffield: Sheffield Academic Press, 1999), 26–27.

9 Neve, *The Spirit of God in the Old Testament*, 2.

10 Walther Eichrodt, *Theology of the Old Testament*, vol. 2, trans. J. A. Baker (London: SCM, 1967), 46.

11 Ma, *Until the Spirit Comes*, 27.

> The spirit of God is an element or aspect of the divine being, or an instrument at the divine disposal, manifested as God relates himself to human beings, nature, and later the nation. This divine element is present among humans, as in Gen. 6.3, or carries out God's will, as in Exod. 15.8, or 'invades' human agents, as among the 70 elders, the judges, the kings, Joseph and the prophets.[12]

Perhaps, an investigation of the evolution of the concept of רוח will provide a clear understanding of the Spirit of God. In this regard, scholars like William Ross Schoemaker, Charles Briggs, and Llyod Neve have attempted a breakdown of the use of רוח into chronological and semantic classification and studied how in various periods of Israel's history the concept of the Spirit of God underwent changes.[13] However, Tengström cautions that any strict classification remains a challenge because of the lack of a clear chronology of texts and the semantic fecundity of the term.[14] Nonetheless, while conceding such valuable caution it is inevitable to look into how the concept underwent changes in the faith history of Israel for a fruitful study of the Spirit of God. It can be noted that, many scholars have identified in the Old Testament, the role of the Spirit of God in relation to four major themes: the Spirit in creation; the Spirit and the people of God; the Spirit and leadership (and later messianic leadership); and the Spirit and prophecy.[15]

2.2.2. The Spirit and the Formation of the People of God in the Pre-Monarchical Period

The Spirit of God is integral to the social formation of Israel as a covenanted people of God. One of the earliest references to the רוח of Yahweh is found in the Song of the Sea (Exod 15 cf. 2 Sam 22:16). This song is placed in the context of Israel's liberation from Egypt and the birth of a covenanted community. The Song of the Sea (Exod 15) exalts Yahweh for saving the people of Israel. Exodus 15:8 can be translated as "at the blast of your nostrils" the waters piled up. And v. 10 can be translated as "You blew with your breath"[16] and the sea covered the enemies. רוח manifested here as the saving power of Yahweh,[17] and this decisive

---

12 Ma, *Until the Spirit Comes*, 29.

13 Schoemaker, "The Use of רוח in the Old Testament," 13–67; Charles Briggs, "The Use of רוח in the Old Testament," *JBL* 19 (1900): 132–145; Neve, *Spirit of God*.

14 Tengström, *TDOT* 13: 373.

15 See Neve, *Spirit of God*; Hildebrandt, *An Old Testament Theology of the Spirit of God*; Wonsuk Ma, *Until the Spirit Comes*.

16 Frank Moore Cross, *Canaanite Myth and Hebrew Epic* (Cambridge: Harvard University Press, 1973, 131ff.; B. S. Childs, *The Book of Exodus*, OTL (Philadelphia: Westminster, 1974), 221ff.

17 Neve, *Spirit of God*, 11.

action of Yahweh in the Exodus event established Israel as God's people.[18] Lloyd Neve opines in this early text, רוח as wind and breath developed into the Spirit of God in the Old Testament owing to Israel's understanding of God's saving power revealed in the wind or in God's breath (cf. Exod 15:8, 10; 2 Sam 22:16)[19] in the forming of the covenant people Israel.[20] In this early usage of the term in the Song of the Sea, the רוח of God played a decisive role in the formation of the people of Israel.

The activities of the Spirit of God in the social and political foundation comes clearly in view of the deuteronomistic history (Joshua to 2 Kings), which traces the origin of Israel beginning with the occupation in Canaan, the tribal confederation to the formation of monarchy. Within the deuteronomistic history, Judges narrates how the Israelites forged together as a nation in the hostile environment of Philistine oppression. For the first time, references to the power of רוח יהוה as an enabling and empowering Spirit occur in this formative period of Israel as a people.[21] The leaders who mobilised and motivated the community were invested with the רוח יהוה and led the people successfully "until further political development became imperative and monarchy was established."[22]

According to the account of the judges, in a situation of collective powerlessness and helplessness when the people of Israel experienced threat and oppression from the enemies, God's Spirit came upon an individual and equipped

---

18 Hildebrandt, *An Old Testament Theology of the Spirit of God*, 69.

19 Neve, *Spirit of God*, 13. Llyod Neve noted that there existed the concept of divine wind and divine breath in the world into which Israel was born. Firstly, in the pre-Israelite environment, wind was intimately related to the world of the deities, serving as divine agencies and in some instances; it is sometimes considered as an independent deity. Secondly, wind was also conceived of as the breath of gods, which had creative and life sustaining power that resides in each living creatures as the breath of life. He considers the early poetic texts Exod 15:8, 10; 2 Sam 22:16 as transitional texts that allows the transformation of divine wind and life giving breath to the concept of the Spirit of God (7 [n. 2]–13).

20 Covenant plays a significant role in the national life of Israel politically, socially and religiously. The foundation of this covenant relationship is the deliverance of Israel from Egypt. That Israel shall be God's people and God shall be the God of Israel (cf. Exod 6:7) provides Israel's history with a meaning. For the community aspect of covenant see Walther Eichrodt, *Theology of the Old Testament*, trans. J. A. Baker, vol. 1 (London: SCM, 1961), 36–44.

21 F. W. Horn, "Holy Spirit," *ABD* 3:262 cf. Albertz and Westermann, *TLOT* 3:1213. Tengström, *TDOT* 13:391 maintains that apart from the late comment in Deut 34:9 that Joshua was full of the "spirit of wisdom," in the Pentateuch only Gen 41:38 and Num 24:2–3 speaks of a charismatic gift of the Spirit. The association of רוח with Moses in Num 11: 4–33, a thematic text of the Spirit, may well be for the purpose of legitimating an institutional office since appointment of judges to their office in Exod 18 does not mention רוח.

22 Baruch A. Levine, "Religion in the Heroic Spirit: Themes in the Book of Judges," in *Thus Says the Lord: Essays on the Former and Later Prophets in Honor of Robert R. Wilson*, ed. John J. Ahn and Stephen L. Cook (London: T&T Clark, 2009), 27.

him to bring deliverance. With the touch of רוח יהוה, the judge(s) inspires a small group of people against a formidable opponent to victory (Judg 3:10; 11:29; 13:25; 1 Sam 11:6).[23] However, this victory does not happen all at once in a miraculous manner. It rather reports a stirring of community capacity for action; "a renewal of the people's power of resistance," in a time of despair.[24] This new capacity for action and the "power of resistance" is traced back to an individual who receives the empowerment of God's Spirit, who was chosen irrespective of status, age or sex.[25] For instance, before the rise of the judge Gideon, the Israelites were impoverished and oppressed by the Midianites so that they "cried to the Lord" (cf. Judg 6:1–7). Gideon was "beating out wheat in the wine press, to hide it from the Midianites" (Judg 6:11)—a hidden transcript of peasants in the context of domination. Gideon's response to God's commission—"how can I deliver Israel, My clan is the weakest in Manasseh, and I am the least in my family" (Judg 6:15)—also tellingly describes the helplessness of the people. However, when the Spirit of God took possession of Gideon (Judg 6:34), he inspires the Israelites to come out and fight against the Midianites.

Of the many judges, at least four of them were invested with the רוח יהוה in their leadership, such as Gideon (Judg 6:34), Othniel (3:10), Jepthah (11:29, 32) and Samson (13:25; 14:6, 19; 15:14). Despite the "archaic and magical" connotations of the Spirit in the stories, the eruptive force is understood as derived from Yahweh.[26] While the activities of the Judges were political and military, Israelites recognised the activity of a higher power in their leadership of the judges, and thus designated this power as the רוח. It is the power of the Spirit, "which is the real force behind those acts of redemption that preserves the national life of the nation."[27] Apparently, the close association of military and political activity with the Spirit of Yahweh emphasises that the socio-political formation of Israel is not an isolated human endeavour. The presence of Yahweh in the military actions of the judges was so strong that R. Smend has called these events as Yahweh's war.[28] The Spirit of God comes to the oppressed community instigating and empowering them to find their way to liberation from socio-political oppression and domination.

---

23 Horn, "Holy Spirit," 3:263.

24 Michael Welker, *God the Spirit*, trans. John F. Hoffmeyer (Minneapolis: Fortress, 1994), 53.

25 W. J. Dumbrell, "Spirit and Kingdom of God in the Old Testament," *RTR* 33 (1974): 4; Hildebrandt, *An Old Testament Theology of the Spirit of God*, 117.

26 Joseph Blenkinsopp, *A History of Prophecy in Israel* (Louisville: Westminster John Knox, 1996), 53.

27 Eichrodt, *Theology of the Old Testament*, 308.

28 R. Smend, *Yahweh War and Tribal Confederation*, trans. Max Gray Rogers (Nashville: Abingdon, 1970), 26ff. However, one should be cautious not to see God's Spirit as a spirit of war. There is no evidence that the Spirit of God immediately or directly causes a war. Cf. Welker, *God the Spirit*, 56.

Mark S. Smith argues that a study on the older layer of Judges 5 shows "lack of a clear, original picture of an Israelite social or religious coherence."[29] It is plausible in the early tribal confederacy that the judges emerge from different locations asserting only regional authority. It is also plausible that the stories are not necessarily in chronological schema and at least the careers of some of the judges were concurrent.[30] What is notable about the movements of the judges was that their movements were integrally tied to the material cultural background of the people. Norman Gottwald in his *The Tribes of Yahweh* asserted that, Yahwism is "the symbolic expression of the Israelite socioeconomic revolution," a religion which is deeply embedded in "praxis and ideology of an actual social community."[31] Thus he argues that, Israel took back a world—of the Ancient Near East, which mirrored a legitimating cosmic religio-political discourse of "the stratified world of class inequality, to the dependence of the many on the few for physical sustenance and for human identity"—and " 'freshly filled' a world with the realities and meanings of free and equal human beings."[32] What is notable in the socio-political and religious formation of Israel over against the hostile nations, narrated in Judges, is the active intervention of the Spirit of God in the formation of a resistant community for liberation from oppression. In Judges, the Spirit of God functions as a Spirit of resistance and community formation enabling the oppressed community to stand on their own feet for freedom.[33]

The transition from the time of the judges to monarchy saw the charismatic leadership of Samuel, Saul and David who were empowered by the Spirit of God in their leadership. Samuel appeared as a prophet and a judge in Israel and played a decisive role in the institution of the monarchy.[34] What is notable in the

29 Mark S. Smith, "What is Prologue is Past: Composing Israelite Identity in Judges 5," in *Thus Says the Lord: Essays on the Former and Later Prophets in Honor of Robert R. Wilson*, ed. John J. Ahn and Stephen L. Cook (London: T&T Clark, 2009), 58.

30 Levine, "Religion in the Heroic Spirit: Themes in the Book of Judges," 30.

31 Norman Gottwald, *The Tribes of Yahweh: A Sociology of the Religion of Liberated Israel 1250–1050 B.C.E.* (Maryknoll, NY: Orbis Books, 1979), 700.

32 Gottwald, *The Tribes of Yahweh*, 701.

33 The Spirit's tradition in Judges is significantly unique from the Pentateuch (and Joshua), in that, in the former, the charismatic individual and their actions are shaped by the overarching narrative trajectory, whereas in the latter, individuals and their actions are connected to the broader chain of events. In Judges, the Spirit's endowment is temporary and there is no tendency to institutionalise the Spirit's endowment in a permanent office, which suggests that, it did not originate from the Deteronomistic redactor but stems from original traditions. Tengström, *TDOT* 13:392; Albertz and Westermann, *TLOT* 3:1214.

34 For biblical reference and discussion of the identity of Samuel see William F. Albright, "Samuel and the Beginning of the Prophetic Movement," in *Interpreting the Prophetic Tradition*, ed. Harry M. Orlinsky (New York: Ktav, 1969), 158–159. He is portrayed as a judge in both military (1 Sam 11:11) and judicial sense (7:15–17), a priest (7:10; 13:8–15), a seer (9:11, 19), a man of God (9:3–10), and paradigm of prophetic opposition to royal throne (13:8–15; 15:1–31), Blenkinsopp, *Prophecy in Israel*, 52.

prophetic leadership of Samuel is that, he is identified as the head of the "band of prophets" (1 Sam 19:20). The Old Testament first mentions the movement of the prophets in 1 Sam 10:5–13. Samuel J. Deane attributed Samuel to be the founder of this "college of prophets" aimed at providing a flow of prophetic leadership.[35] The Spirit-empowered resistive activities of the band of prophets were intriguing as it is recorded in the narrative of the rise of Saul (cf. 1 Sam 9:1–10:16). They carry their musical instruments and go about in a prophetic frenzy. When Saul met them (after being anointed as ruler over Israel by Samuel), the Spirit fell upon him and he was caught in a prophetic frenzy and prophesied with them (1 Sam 10:10–11), so that the people were astonished and said "Is Saul also among the prophets" (1 Sam 10:10–11)? A similar ecstatic phenomenon of the band of prophets with Samuel as its head is recorded in 1 Sam 19:20–24. The presence of the Spirit of God among the "band of the prophets" (1 Sam 10:10) is assumed.[36] But the ecstatic frenzy of the early prophetic communities was not a search for mystical union with God; Israel knows nothing of the prophet's ability to force his way into the divine world. Rather, it is derived from the sudden irruption of God's power, namely רוח, which overpowers a person. Ecstasy "seeks to subject the most exalted religious experiences of religious feeling to the service of the divine Lord."[37] Probably, this prophetic ecstasy plays a certain function in the socio-political life of Israel. Albert C. Knudson observed that,

> As good a suggestion as any is that it was due to the intense feeling created by the subjection of the Israelites to the Philistines and the growing desire for independence. This took a religious turn and resulted in the formation of bands of "inspired" men, who went through the country with the more or less definite purpose of stirring the people up to the point where they would be willing to make whatever sacrifice was necessary in order to throw off the yoke of the hated enemy.[38]

Walther Eichrodt observes, "[I]t can hardly be denied that the emergence of groups of ecstasy precisely in that frightful time of crisis was no accident, but the result of an inner logic of events, even if this is not made explicit by the Old Testament narrators."[39] The prophetic frenzy of the band of prophets displays peripheral form of ecstasy. Robert R. Wilson contends that, "any study of prophetic behavior in Israel must take into account the role of social groups

35 W. J. Deane, *Samuel and Saul: Their Lives and Times* (London: James Nibet and Co., 1886), 70.

36 Ma, *Until the Spirit Comes*, 31.

37 Eichrodt, *Theology of the Old Testament*, 1:318.

38 Albert C. Knudson, *The Prophetic Movement in Israel* (New York: The Methodist Church Book Concern, 1921), 21.

39 Eichrodt, *Theology of the Old Testament*, 1:317.

in creating prophets and in shaping their behavior.... Divergent behavioral patterns will imply different social situations and support groups, and this social complexity must be taken into account in analyzing biblical prophecy."[40] In other words, it is vital to know the social location of prophetic activity—whether they are located in the periphery or within the central social structure. Probably the band of prophets functioned as support groups to leaders like Samuel and Saul in the periphery of the society.

Anthropological studies suggest that ecstatic practices are often attested among the marginalised periphery that are dispossessed or deprived. Their ecstatic practices are a kind of "ritualised rebellion against the power structure" of the society of which they are a part. This kind of group ecstatic behaviour seems to correlate with situations of social, political military stress such as that of foreign invasion and occupation. Furthermore, drawing insights from I. M. Lewis' *Ecstatic Religion* for a case study of peripheral and central form of ecstasy, John R. Levison argues that peripheral possession frequently arises not only in contexts of oppression but is "thought to occur chiefly during times of transition, and 1 Samuel 10 clearly reflects a difficult transition from intermittent leaders to an established monarchy."[41] Joseph Blenkinsopp states, "it is no surprise that so much prophetic activity of this kind is attested in Israel during the life-and-death struggle with the Philistines in the eleventh and tenth centuries."[42] Probably this prophetic movement took on a distinctive social form of resistance against foreign domination under the leadership of Samuel. What is notable is that, the Spirit of God inspires this prophetic movement that seemed to function as the popular base for the charismatic leadership of Samuel.

In summation it can be noted that, Israel first encountered the רוח (the Spirit of God) in the blast of Yahweh's breath that saved them and constituted them into a nation. The Spirit of God continuously intervenes in the formation and preservation of Israel in the socio-political contexts of the nation's fight against the expanding oppressive suzerainty of the neighbouring nations. In the context of despair and hopelessness in the community life, the Spirit of Yahweh came as an eruptive force upon the charismatic leaders (Judges), which in turn enabled the charismatic leaders to inspire the Israelite tribes to rally in unity against the opponents of Israel. The transitional period from the time of judges to monarchy saw the rise of early prophetic community empowered by the Spirit of God, in which Samuel was the foremost. The phenomenon of the ecstatic frenzy of the band of prophets into which Saul was dragged into illustrates the stirring power of the Spirit of God to foment resistance and counter socio-political formation in the context of Philistine oppression. The Spirit also descended upon David

40 Robert R. Wilson, *Prophecy and Society in Ancient Israel* (Philadelphia: Fortress, 1980), 87.

41 John R. Levison, "Prophecy in Ancient Israel: The Case of the Ecstatic Elders," *CBQ* 65 (2003): 512 notes 23.

42 Blenkinsopp, *Prophecy in Israel*, 37.

who succeeded Saul as king. In short, prior to monarchy, Israel experienced the Spirit of God as a divine power that enabled the formation and preservation of the nation.

2.2.3. The Spirit of God and Prophetic Protests in the Monarchical Period

During the monarchy, the Spirit of God was dominantly associated with the Israelite prophets who confronted the oppressive regime of Israelite kings with the word of the Lord. Though the prophets came from diverse social location and backgrounds, one unifying feature of the prophets was their exclusive loyalty to Yahweh from whom they received revelation. As spokespersons of Yahweh, they exemplified a strong self-conscious awareness of Yahweh speaking to them within history as an objective event. Divine inspiration seemed to be the only prerequisite that makes a person a prophet and a legitimate spokesperson for God.[43] Some were prophets in the royal court, and many prophets came from the fringes of the society. Among the early monarchical prophets, the favoured terminology (to describe the prophet) was that "the word of the Lord came to" the person (1 Sam 15:10; 2 Sam 24:11 cf. 1 Kings 13:1). In some instances, "thus says the Lord" (1 Kings 14:7; 20:13) is employed. In the case of Micaiah, "hear the word of the Lord" (1 Kings 22:19) is employed. In fact, "the word of the Lord" occurs approximately about 240 times in the Old Testament that it is taken as "a technical term for the prophetic word of revelation."[44] Of course, it is not explicit that the "word of Yahweh" is the same as the Spirit's inspiration.[45] Samuel A. Meier points out that such technical term as "the word of X" is a commonplace for an "authoritative communication" within the Old Testament (1 Sam 4:1; 2 Kings 18:28) and elsewhere in the ancient Near East.[46] However, in the Old Testament, the prophets were those who acted and spoke with divine impulse. There is no question whether their words and actions emanated from the Spirit's empowerment; they always were.[47]

---

43 John J. Schmidt, "Preexilic Hebrew Prophecy," *ABD* 5:482.

44 W. H. Schmidt, "דבר dabar," *TDOT* 3:111.

45 Wilson, *Prophecy and Society*, 144–145, advanced a thesis that the special emphasis on the "word of Yahweh" characterised the Ephraimite prophetic tradition, and attempted to tie "spirit possession" with such expression. Wilson contends that the use of such expression as "word of Yahweh" expresses a prophet's self-understanding of רוח-possession, though רוח is not mentioned necessarily. However, it is not that such typical expression as the "word of X" is not uncommon in ancient Near East. A the same time, Wilson did not clearly point out "the difference between Ephraimite and Judean traditions with regard to רוח-inspiration." Cf. James Robson, *Word and Spirit in Ezekiel* (New York: T&T Clark, 2006), 32.

46 Samuel A. Meier, *Speaking of Speaking: Making Direct Discourse in the Hebrew Bible*, VTSup 46 (Leiden: Brill, 1992), 315–316.

47 Edmond Jacob, *Theology of the Old Testament*, trans. A. W. Heathcote and P. J. Allock (London: Hodder & Stoughton, 1958), 125, observes that it is the "word" that qualifies the prophets for their ministry "because only the word creates between the prophets and God a

The prophets appeared to perform cultic function, in that they were connected to particular sanctuaries; performed religious duties such as anointing of kings or intercession.[48] However, the prophetic institution was not homogenous. Some were stationed in the royal court, while some emerged from the margins of the society.[49] Both Nathan and Gad were court prophets and they gave the king moral guidance. They challenged the king by calling him to repent based on Israel's ancient religious and ethical traditions (2 Sam 11–12; 24:10–14). There were several other prophets who confronted the king such as the unnamed man of God from Judah (1 Kings 13), Ahijah (1 Kings 14:1–18), Jehu (1 Kings 16:1–4) and Micaiah (1 Kings 22). These prophets mediated the "word of the Lord" without fear of the consequences of their prophetic pronouncement since the "word" came to them and they were compelled to speak. Apparently, with the rise of the monarchy, a split between the prophetic function of message and action developed. Though Samuel was both a messenger of God and a charismatic leader, the prophet Nathan appeared to be only a messenger of God while the political leadership was strongly established in Davidic kingship. Notably, the great eight and seventh century prophets such as Amos, Isaiah, Hosea, and Jeremiah were rather messengers pronouncing the oracles of God. However, the covenantal traditions and social forms of early Israel were not completely suppressed by monarchy. The tradition of Elijah-Elisha circle "indicate that prophets as both messengers and leaders of movements continued long into the monarchical period in the Northern kingdom of Israel, if not in the kingdom of Judah."[50]

Elijah-Elisha circle offered unrelenting prophetic opposition to the royal throne. The time of Elijah occasioned the onslaught of baalism in Israel and socio-economic abuses by the Omride dynasty that included the *latifundalisation* of free Israelites land. The Omrides set up Samaria as their capital and embark on building projects, which also includes a "house of Baal" (2 Kings 16:32). The prophets of Baal held official status whereas, the prophets of Yahweh flee persecution and sought refuge (1 Kings 18:4).[51] There is probably a connection between the changing allegiance to Baal and the royal house incursion into the

relationship of person with person. But the word presupposes the spirit, the creative breathe of life, and for the prophets there was such evidence of this that they thought it unnecessary to state it explicitly."

48 Aubrey R. Johnson, *Cultic Prophet in Ancient Israel* (Cardiff: University of Welsh Press, 1962), 2 writes, "both in general and particularly as regards the Jerusalem Temple, the … 'prophet' originally filled a cultic role of at least equal, if not greater, importance."

49 For instance, Elisha's station in life was obviously quite different from Elijah's; and both these prophets are clearly different again from such a man as Nathan.

50 Richard A. Horsley and John S. Hanson, *Bandits, Prophets, and Messiahs: Popular Movements in the Time of Jesus* (San Francisco: Harper & Row, 1985), 139.

51 Jerome T. Walsh, "Elijah," *ABD* 2:464.

patrimonial land of the individual Israel.[52] A severe drought in Israel compounded the problem of these domestic and religious affairs. It was in this social-religious context Elijah entered the scene. Norman Gottwald maintains that, Elijah-Elisha stories also reflect religious formations at the margins of the society away from the "history making" royal court that "functioned as rescue stations and advocacy groups."[53]

C. F. Keil and F. Delitzsch noted that "[a]s the Lord raised up prophets for His people at the times when apostasy had become great and strong, that they might resist idolatry with almighty power; so did He also create for himself organs of His Spirit in the schools of the prophets, who united with their spiritual fathers in fighting for His honor."[54] Notably, in the socio-political circumstances of religious apostasy and social distress, the Spirit of God empowered Elijah and the sons of the prophets to foment popular resistance to the establishment. It is natural that when Elisha makes a final request to Elijah before the latter was taken up, he asked for a double portion of Elijah's רוח (2 Kings 2:9, 15), which is best understood as "a metonymic figure of speech for 'the Spirit of Yahweh which resides upon Elijah.'"[55] That the רוח in 2 Kings 2:9, 15 which rests upon Elisha refers to the Spirit of Yahweh is supported by Elisha's prophetic career that ushered in a regime change in the monarchy of Israel. What began as a small movement of Elijah-Elisha and fifty sons of prophets (cf. 2 Kings 2) in the margins of the society transpired into a regime changing movement of liberation. Horsley and Hanson observe, "[I]t is significant that it was not the new messiah Jehu but Elijah (2 Kings 2:11–12) and Elisha (2 Kings 13:14) who were associated with the heavenly armies and the great saving acts by which Yahweh liberated his people

52 Scholars like Mendenhall, Gottwald and Chaney posit that the emergent Israelite society was somewhat the polemical obverse of the Canaanites city-states. The arable land of Canaanite city-states belong to the king or warlord who let out the land to peasant producers and extracts the largest possible surplus from the peasant majority. This socio-economic system of a sharp stratification was endorsed and legitimated by the official Canaanite religion at the time Israel emerged as a separate society in the adjacent hill country. However, for Israel, the lands belong to Yahweh. Premonarchic Israel understood Yahweh to distribute this economic base to peasant vassals in a manner, which sought to assure secure and sufficient access to arable land and thereby to livelihood. See Marvin L. Chaney, "Systemic Study of the Israelite Monarchy," *Semeia* 37 (1986): 61.

53 Norman K. Gottwald, *The Hebrew Bible: A Socio-Literary Introduction* (Philadelphia: Fortress, 1985), 352.

54 C. F. Keil and F. Delitzsch, *Biblical Commentary on the Books of Samuel* (Grand Rapids: Eerdmans, 1950), 205.

55 Daniel I. Block, "Empowered by the Spirit of God: The Holy Spirit in the Historiographic Writings of the Old Testament," *SBJT* 1 (1997): 46. A different view is found in Ze'ev Weisman, "The Personal Spirit as Imparting Authority," *ZAW* 93 (1981): 225–234, which maintains that the spirit of Elijah refers to neither the human spirit of Elijah nor the Spirit of Yahweh but a "personal" spirit that acts by "imparting authority"—a spirit which is also seen in Num 11 in the seventy elders.

anew."[56] It is significant to note that the Spirit of God is the force behind the movement of emancipation from oppression.

The episode of Micaiah ben Imlah recorded in 1 Kings 22[57] provides a significant example of peripheral prophetic opposition against the royal throne. This text has sparked a great deal of scholarly discussion with scholars bringing in different issue into the text.[58] The episode concerns the contests between the royal court prophets, who endorse King Ahab's military campaign against the Syrian on the one hand, and Micaiah ben Imlah, who warned the doom ahead of such military campaign on the other. The narrative shows that Zedekiah, the leader of the court prophets, has no doubt the Spirit of Yahweh spoke with them (cf. v. 24b). Micaiah too does not negate that רוח-inspiration of the court prophets when he speaks of his vision, except that it is "a lying spirit" though commissioned by Yahweh.[59] In this context, Lyod Neve comments, "the belief that the word is inspired by a spirit, even in the case of the 'weal' prophets, is left standing."[60] However, the voice of opposition from the peripheral prophet Micaiah must be taken seriously. Undoubtedly, the common people would pay for the king's expansionist ambition. And probably, it is in view of the negative socio-political and economic impact such a war would fall upon the common people, the peripheral prophet opposed the establishment with the word from God. Levison opines that, unlike the court prophets who serve to legitimate status quo, Micaiah's prophesying subverts the status quo with an alternative "that differed radically from the one Zedekiah's hierarchically organized prophets had promised them."[61] Micaiah's prophecy subverts thus the theological legitimation of the court prophets and dissent to the potential negative socio-economic and political implications of offensive war.[62]

The classical prophets were deeply engaged in the socio-political and economic issues of their day. Often they were partisan figures and advocated social justice and right worship of God that constituted an alternative to the status quo

56 Horsley and Hanson, *Bandits, Prophets, and Messiahs*, 141.

57 This text posed compositional, historical as well as theological complexities for scholars. See Simon J. DeVries, *1 Kings*, WBC 12 (Waco: Word Books, 1985), 265–266; Steven J. McKenzie, *The Trouble With Kings: The Composition of the Book of Kings in the Deutoronomistic History*, VTSup 42 (Leiden: Brill, 1991), 88–93.

58 For a history of interpretation of this passage see Wolfgang Roth, "The Story of the Prophet Micaiah (1 Kings 22) in Historical-Critical Interpretation," in *The Biblical Mosaic Changing Perspectives*, ed. Robert. M. Polzin and Eugene Rothman (Philadelphia: Fortress, 1982), 105–137.

59 Cf. Robson, *Word and Spirit in Ezekiel*, 144.

60 Neve, *Spirit of God*, 40.

61 Levison, "Prophecy in Ancient Israel," 518.

62 For the significance of Micaiah's episode, which illuminates the classical prophets' conflicts false prophets, see Mordechai Cogan, *1 Kings*, AYB 10 (New Haven: Yale University Press, 2008), 497.

of social relations and religion. Though they were not royal court prophets, they brought the oracles of God with power irrespective of their social background. Therefore, notwithstanding a minimum reference to the Spirit-inspiration to prophesy in the classical prophecy, it is untenable to place undue emphasis to the extent of stating that "the spirit cease to operate"[63] in the classical prophets.[64] The רוח-inspiration is obviously not prominent in the classical prophets; however, there are substantial indications that the classical prophets did not negate the רוח (cf. Hos 9:7; Mic 3:8; and Jer 5:13; Isa 30:1–2).

In the case of Hos 9:7, Sigmund Mowinkel argues that, it is a castigation of the נביאים since Hosea himself would not accord himself a "fool" or "mad."[65] Hans Wolff maintains that, the people spoke these words and hence, "Hosea does not speak of himself as a person filled with the spirit."[66] However, though Hosea does not plainly claim to be "a man of spirit," he does not distance himself from this title. According to Robson, Hosea is נביא and a "man of the spirit" like Elijah (1 Kgs 18:12 cf. 1 Kgs 22; 2 Kgs 2:9), except that he was not at ease to use the term, and this explains that he does not repudiate such a reference.[67] James L. Crenshaw maintains that, distinction of true prophets as transmitters of the word of God, and false prophets as those who emphasised the spirit cannot be maintained without doing "violence to the Hebrew text at crucial junctures

63 Cf. Gerard von Rad, *Old Testament Theology*, vol. 2, trans. D. M. G. Stalker (Edinburgh: Oliver and Boyd 1965), 57.

64 There are at least four positions that express that the prophets do not have any רוח consciousness in their prophecy. *Firstly*, Sigmund Mowinkel S. Mowinkel, "The 'Spirit' and the 'Word' in the Pre-exilic Reforming Prophets," *JBL* 53 (1934): 199, 207, argues that the classical prophets repudiated רוח probably owing to the embarrassment caused by the abuses of the spirit by the enthusiast who boast of their vocation. Also see Albertz and Westermann *TLOT* 3:1215. *Secondly*, Gerard von Rad, *Old Testament Theology* 2:57, expressed a "historical" position and argued that the "spirit ceased to operate" during the classical prophets. *Thirdly*, the absence of רוח is caused by the loss of confidence in prophetism arising out of false prophecy (cf. 1 Kgs 22). Eichrodt, *Theology of the Old Testament*, 2:56. Thus for practical or rhetorical reasons, classical prophets were reticent to speak of רוח in their own inspiration "since it had come to disrepute." Robert Koch, *Der Geist Gottes im Alten Testament* (Frankfurt: Lang, 1991), 59. *Finally*, a theological view opines that the prophets are "so directly constrained by the message of Yahweh that they simply do not reflect the notion of a mediating spirit." Walther Zimmerli, *Old Testament Theology* in Outline, trans. D. E. Green (Edinburgh: T&T Clark, 1978), 102. In other words, the strong theocentric orientation of the prophets explains the absence of רוח. Johannes Lindblom, *Prophecy in Ancient Israel*, (Oxford: Blackwell, 1962), 178.

65 Mowinckel, "The 'Spirit' and the 'Word' in the Pre-Exilic Reforming Prophets," 204–205.

66 Hans Walter Wolff, *A Commentary on the Book of the Prophet Hosea*, trans. Gary Stansell, Hermeia (Philadelphia: Fortress, 1974), 157.

67 Robson, *Spirit and Word in Ezekiel*, 149.

(Mic 38, for example)."[68] In other words, it is erroneous to deny the רוח-inspiration in the classical prophets on the basis that they give prominence to the word and maintained relative silence on speaking of the רוח.

The use of רוח in the theological sense is remarkably absent from the book of Jeremiah except there may be a word play present in 5:13.69 Here Jeremiah lashed out at the false prophets as "winds" and "nothing." If a word play is intended here, the prophets of Jeremiah's time claimed inspiration of the רוח in their prophecy although there was no evidence of Jeremiah doing it unambiguously. But many scholars maintain that Jeremiah's silence about his own (רוח) inspiration should not be taken as ill-disposed towards רוח.[70] Probably, as Robert Koch suggests, "an indirect witness for the ruach Yahweh as the source of prophetic inspiration may lie in this word of mockery."[71]

Isaiah also opposes the political leadership of Judah which ignores Yahweh's political decisions in Isa 30:1–2 with a woe oracle, which spells Yahweh's displeasure with Israel's embassy to Egypt that is deemed not according to Yahweh's רוח. Some scholars try to define the use of the רוח here in terms of divine qualities.[72] But, it is likely that רוח is used here as the prophetic Spirit.[73] This understanding takes v. 2a as explaining v. 1b, which implies that "the רוח of Yahweh is the source of prophetic counsel," though the weakness of this interpretation lies in that Proto-Isaiah nowhere claims "the spirit of Yahweh as his prophetic message."[74] Seeking counsel from Yahweh was an ancient practice (cf. Josh 9:14; Judg 1:1; 20:18; 1 Sam 13:41), which after the setting up of monarchy involves "an utterance by a prophets."[75] Thus, not to seek the counsel of Yahweh from the prophets is not to

68 James L. Crenshaw, *Prophetic Conflict: Its Effect upon Israelite Religion* (Berlin: Walter de Gruyter, 1971), 55.

69 Robert P. Caroll, *Jeremiah: A Commentary* (Philadelphia: Westminster Press, 1986), 183.

70 Peter C. Craigie, Page H. Kelly and Joel F. Drinkard, *Jeremiah 1–25*, WBC 26 (Dallas: Word Books, 1992), 92; Arvid S. Kapelrud, "The Spirit and the Word in the Prophets," *ASTI* 11 (1977–78): 43.

71 Koch, *Der Geist Gottes im Alten Testament*, 59–60 cited by Robson, *Spirit and Word in Ezekiel*, 156.

72 For instance, Baumgärtel thinks that it refers to the "inner nature of God." Friedrich Baumgärtel, "πνεῦμα," *TDNT* 6:364. However, Albertz and Westermann, *TLOT* 3:1216 rejected such concept as foreign to Old Testament. They in turn assert that "*ruach*" refers to the power of Yahweh or "the effect of Yahweh's might." Some scholars have understood this to mean the "mind of Yahweh." Isaiah's point is that, the embassy sent to Egypt is not in accordance with the will of Yahweh. See Neve, *Spirit of God*, 54; Mowinckel, "Spirit and Word," 201; Tengström, *TDOT* 13: 379–308.

73 Jacob, *Theology of the Old Testament*, 126; Ma, *Until the Spirit Comes*, 49; John N. Oswalt, *The Book of Isaiah Chapters 1–39*, NICOT (Grand Rapids: Eerdmans, 1986), 545.

74 Ma, *Until the Spirit Comes*, 48.

75 Otto Kaiser, *Isaiah 13–39: A Commentary*, trans. R. A. Wilson (London: SCM, 1974), 285.

hear what the Spirit says that is implicitly assumed to be inspired by the Spirit.[76] Wonsuk Ma opines that this interpretation makes good sense since the context concerns the "conflict between the prophet and the court politicians."[77]

Finally, in the pre-exilic monarchy, there is a significant pointer to the future role of the Spirit of God in relation to the rise of an ideal messianic leader (Isa 11:1–2) and socio-ecological regeneration (Isa 32:15a).[78] Probably, it was in the context of the failures of monarchy and the socio-political and economic degeneration that the Spirit of God was invoked to construct a future reality of God's just rule. However, the longing for a future Davidic king was not peculiar of Isaiah. Jeremiah (and Ezekiel) also looks to a new order in which the ruler appointed by Yahweh will have become a theocratic ruler very different from the political and military king (Jer 23:25f. cf. Ezek 37:24).[79] However, the uniqueness of Isaianic eschatological ruler is the investiture of the Spirit of God that will enable him to establish justice and righteousness in his rule (Isa 11:1–10).

The reference to the "stump of Jesse" in Isa 11:1 is a point of debate for dating this text.[80] But the activity of the Spirit in a messianic figure, who is to come

---

76 Robson, *Spirit and Word in Ezekiel*, 158.

77 Ma, *Until the Spirit Comes*, 49 cf. Robson, *Spirit and Word in Ezekiel*, 158.

78 Isaiah 11:1–2 and 32:15a fall within the block of Proto-Isaiah (Isaiah 1–39), which is generally considered pre-exilic, though there are voices that claim that the text in consideration could be post-exilic as well. Randall Heskett, *Messianism within the Scriptural Scrolls of Isaiah* (New York: T&T Clark, 2007), 122 writes, "Isaiah 1–39 has been so reworked that one cannot determine with certainty which layer of editing governs the later formation of the book."

79 Eichrodt, *Theology of the Old Testament*, 1:451.

80 Those who espoused a post-exilic origin of Isa 11:1–2 argue that the "stump of Jesse" assumes that Davidic dynasty has been terminated. And the reference to the Spirit resting on individuals, the paradisical and the eschatological elements of the text reveals concepts that emerged at a later date. See Heskett, *Messianism within the Scriptural Scrolls of Isaiah*, 122 cf. Bernhard Duhm, *Das Buch Jesaja: Übersetzt und eklärt*, HKAT 3 (Göttingen: Vanderhoeck & Ruprecht, 1902), 104–105; Sigmund Mowinkel, *He that Cometh*, trans G. W. Anderson (New York: Abingdon, 1954), 17; Otto Kaiser, *Isaiah 1–12*, OTL, trans. John Bowden (Philadelphia: Westminster, 1983), 254–255; Walter Brueggemann, *Isaiah 1–39*, Westminster Bible Companion (Louisville: Westminster John Knox, 1998), 99; R. E. Clements, *Isaiah 1–39*, NCBC (Grand Rapids: Eerdmans, 1980), 121–22. On the other hand, a good number of scholars argue for a pre-exilic date. Marvin A. Sweeney, *Isaiah 1–39: With an Introduction to Prophetic Literature*, FOTL 16 (Grand Rapids: Eerdmans, 1996), 203–205 maintains that the setting reflects 2 Kgs 22:19–26, the assassination of Amon, the abortive coup, and the restoration of the throne of the eight-year boy Josiah. Similarly, he argues that the imagery is consistent with the tree/forest imagery found both in ch. 10 and elsewhere in 5–12, in that, the stump-like condition of Judah can be descriptive of situations other than the aftermath of 587. See Thomas L. Leclerc, *Yahweh is Exalted in Justice: Solidarity and Conflict in Isaiah* (Minneapolis: Fortress, 2001), 68. Albeit the political condition of eight century proposed by a majority of scholars is different from Sweeney's convincing argument for a seventh-century setting, the overall pre-exilic social condition of Judah is evident.

according to the prophecy of Isaiah, has a very different emphasis from that of the early charismatic judges and kings of Israel. In Isa 11:2, the prophet points out six gifts of the spirit of Yahweh which the messianic king will be endowed with to discharge his duties: a spirit of wisdom and understanding; a spirit of counsel and power; a spirit of knowledge and fear of the Lord. It outlines further the messianic king's "commitment to the defence of the poor and the weak, and his efforts on behalf of justice and righteousness" (Isa 11:3–5).[81] Probably, it was in the context of a morose monarchy that the role of the Spirit of God was invoked to construct a future ideal ruler who would rule in the "fear of the Lord" (Isa 11:2).

Similarly, the date of the text Isa 32:15a is not provided, whether pre-exilic or post-exilic. But a pre-exilic date is plausible.[82] It is significant to note that in Isa 32:15a, for the first time in the Old Testament, one encounters the Spirit of God as the agent of transformation in a nostalgic tone: "Until the spirit is poured upon us from on high." According to Gary V. Smith, "It is difficult to determine what Isaiah or his audience understood about the coming of God's Spirit, since the amount of information revealed at this time about the work of the Spirit is somewhat limited."[83] However, he reasoned since one of the fundamental changes that the new king (Isa 32:1) and the Spirit will inaugurate with was the rule of righteousness and justice, "the spiritual transformation of the hearts and behaviour of the people is at the center of what God desires to accomplish on earth."[84] But the new creation or regeneration envisioned in the text is not limited to the religious sphere alone but encompasses the socio-political and even ecological spheres.

---

81 Marie-Theres Wacker, "The Spirit of God in the Public Sphere of Christian Communities: The Inspiration of the Hebrew Bible," *Concilium*, 2011/4 (2011): 35.

82 Clements, *Isaiah 1–39*, 259–261, hypothesises that a later post-exilic redactor inserted Is 32:15–20 after the fall of Jerusalem in 587 to Isaianic prophecy. However, Oswalt, *The Book of Isaiah Chapters 1–39*, 583, posits the authenticity of the passage and rejects the position that it is the work of a redactor. B. S. Childs, *Isaiah: A Commentary* (Louisville, Kentucky: Westminster John Knox, 2001), 237, also claims that positing a redactional scheme is unsatisfactory. According to Blenkinsopp, since there have been many occasions of natural and military disaster in Palestine during the biblical times, positing a specific event may not settle the issue, however, in the context of chs. 28–33, Sennacherib's assault on Jerusalem (701–700) is the most likely date of this text (Isa 32:15–20). Thus, he considers Isa 32:15–20 a continuation of the preceding lament (32:1–8). Joseph Blenkinsopp, *Isaiah 1–39: A New Translation with an Introduction and Commentary*, AYB 19 (New Haven: Yale University Press, 2000), 433–434.

83 Gary V. Smith, *Isaiah 1–39*, NAC 15A (Nashville: Broadman & Holman, 2007), 545. Smith notes that the people did know about the Spirit of God as the source of strength and skills (Judg 14:5–6; Exod 31:3–5), lead the people (Numbers 11:16–17, 25) and the source of prophecy (Mic 3:8). The Spirit will also be endowed in the ideal ruler for a righteous rule (Isa 11:1–2).

84 Smith, *Isaiah 1–39*, 545.

Blenkinsopp considers Isa 32:15–20 as a continuation of 32:1–8 that projects "a new political and social order" and sees the outpouring of the transforming spirit as the turning point, "which brings about reversal of fortune characteristic of eschatological and apocalyptic thinking" (cf. Isa 65:13-14; Ezek 37:5, 9–10; Joel 2:28).[85] Walter Brueggemann maintains that the Spirit here is the "force of God" that enlivens and transforms God's creation. The Spirit gives new life, transforming nature and humankind. The power of the Spirit will effect justice and righteousness in the community. In the same way it will rejuvenate the creation, transforming wilderness into a fruitful land.[86] Thus, already in the pre-exilic period there is an insipient concept that the Spirit of God would be the agent of transforming the socio-political and thus even the creation towards God's reign of righteousness and justice.

The establishment of the monarchy saw the active role of the Spirit in the prophetic office. During the early monarchy, the prophets confronted the kings with the moral and ethical standards of Israelite religious traditions. Especially, the Elijah-Elisha cycle fomented opposition to the royal house with the regime-changing programme by the empowering of the Spirit of God. But monarchy also saw the institutionalisation of the prophetic office in the royal court and the concomitant domestication of the רוח-inspiration, which in turn provided the occasion for the conflict of the royal court prophets and peripheral prophets (cf. 1 Kgs 22). The prevalence of such situation probably answers why the classical prophets of the eight-century were not so keen to state their רוח-inspiration. But it is clear that the Spirit of God empowers the prophets (cf. Mic 3:8) to boldly criticise the rulers of day. In the late monarchy, the prophet came to an understanding that the monarchy incorrigibly stood in violation of God's sovereign rule over Israel. And this provided an eschatological expectation of the Spirit of God for the socio-political transformation and even ecological regeneration of the land of Israel. This eschatological expectation includes the coming of the Spirit-endowed ideal ruler, who would champion social justice in the fear of God (Isa 11:2).

2.2.4. The Spirit of God and Religio-Socio-Political Transformation in the Exilic Period

The problem of a strictly chronological division of the study of the Spirit of God is already noted above. However, there are notable shifts in the concept of the Spirit of God in the literary documents of the exilic, post-exilic periods, and beyond. Thus, a chronological division is preferred here for an instructive purpose to understand the shift in the concept of the Spirit of God. The devastating experience of the Babylonian exile provided Israel with a movement inward, and reappropriation of

85 Blenkinsopp, *Isaiah 1–39*, 433.

86 Brueggemann, *Isaiah 1–39*, 258; Smith, *Isaiah 1–39*, 546.

their religious heritage through which they achieved a renewed sense of identity.[87] Exile also provided Israel with the understanding of God's transcendence, but the Spirit provided the medium by which God could mysteriously make himself present to the nation transcending time and space.[88] Ezekiel addressed the exiles in the name of the Lord, "I will never again hide my face from them, when I pour out my spirit upon the house of Israel, says the Lord." (Ezek 39:29 cf. 36:26; 37:14). But most prominently, the exile provided Israel with the understanding that God is the creator who creates not only the universe but also the nation. This understanding perhaps paved the way to express the רוח of God as the reviving and recreative power that can revive the down-spirited exiles.

The book of Ezekiel conspicuously portrays the Spirit of God as the animating power that supplies life energy to the disheartened prophet and the subjugated people. Ezekiel employs רוח concept both to legitimise his prophetic career as "it is rooted in the traditional explanation for extraordinary physical movement (1 Kgs 18:12) such as the exiles experienced, and also because the Spirit is the source for vitality which they (exiles) needed."[89] רוח occur several times in Ezekiel, but their semantic domain is fluid and ambiguous whether deliberate or unintended. Given this fact, Daniel I. Block made a point concerning the opening chapter:

> The precise connection among this *rûahi*, the stormy *rûahi* that had borne the apparition to the prophet (v. 4), the *rûahi* that would later enter and energize him (2:2; 3:24), and the *rûahi* that would lift him up and carry him away (3:12, 14) is not clear. However, the reference serves as a harbinger of the role that the *rûahi* will play in Ezekiel's ministry."[90]

According to Moshe Greenberg, in 2:2 רוח is "vigor or even courage … infused into the prophet by the address of God."[91] Here, the רוח that comes from Yahweh revitalises the stunned (discouraged exiled) prophet. As the Spirit enters, it lifted him on his feet.[92] In the same manner, Schüngel-Straumann sees here the

87 Richard J. Sklba, "Until the Spirit from on High is poured out on Us (Isa 32:15): Reflections on the Role of the Spirit in the Exile," *CBQ* 46/1 (1984): 3.

88 Schoemaker, "The Use of רוח in the Old Testament," 27; Sklba, "Until the Spirit from on High," 13.

89 Sklba, "Until the Spirit from on High," 14. Ezekiel was moved back and forth by the רוח from the River Chebar, and made to stand (3:12; 8:3), and speak (11:5). Ezekiel claims that he speaks and acts under the control of the Spirit and it is from the Spirit that he receives both the message and the power to proclaim it (2:2; 3:24; 11:5). Hill, *Greek Words and Hebrew Meanings*, 208.

90 Daniel I. Block, *The Book of Ezekiel Chapters 1–24* (Grand Rapids: Eerdmans, 1997), 101.

91 Moshe Greenberg, *Ezekiel 1–20*, AB 22 (New York: Doubleday, 1983), 62.

92 Helen Schüngel-Straumann, *Rûah bewegt die Welt: Gottes schöpferische Lebenskraft in der Krisenzeit des Exils*, Stuttgarter Bibelstudien 151 (Stuttgart: Katholisches Biblewerk, 1992),

רוח giving the prophet vim where his own was lacking, and hence she thinks that the translation should be rather vitality instead of spirit.[93] Zimmerli also regards the רוח in 2:2 and 3:24 as enabling the prophet "capable of speech," as the רוח enters into him in his state of collapse.[94] In short, רוח in these references refers to the agency of animation.[95] The fresh upsurge of the Spirit in 11:5 that includes the divine authority to speak the word should be also seen as Spirit's power to animate the prophet.[96]

There are three references in Ezekiel in which Yahweh speaks in terms of "my breath/Spirit" (36:26, 27; 37:14; 39:29). Block opines that the Spirit used in Ezek 36:26, 27 refers to the "animating" power that brings about "radical spiritual revitalization of the nation."[97] He sees a "significant shift in meaning" of רוח in 37:14, in that for him the רוח here is not the natural life breath but the Spirit of God itself. Woodhouse prefers the meaning Yahweh's breath to Spirit. He opines that there is an unmistakable link between Jer 31:31–34 and Ezek 36:27 and notes that "there is little obvious difference between God writing his law on the heart, and placing his (speaking) breath within. Any difference seems to fade when the consequence of the latter act is to be obedience to the law (Ezek 36:27b)!"[98] Strikingly, Ezek 39:29 goes further to state that Yahweh will "pour out" his Spirit upon the house of Israel and will not hide his face again. Notably, the emphases that Yahweh will give a new רוח to his people, put his רוח within them, and pour out his רוח upon them indicate that God will be present with the people through רוח. This will enable Israel's obedience and fidelity to God that will bring religious and ethical transformations as well as the socio-political transformation of the down-spirited exiles.

The clearest picture of the role of רוח in regenerating the lifeless exile is seen in Ezekiel's vision of the dry bones. This vision is also one of the most compact yet has varied expressions of the activity of רוח.[99] The force that moved him was

40.

93 Schüngel-Straumann, *Rûah bewegt die Welt*, 44.

94 Walther Zimmerli, *Ezekiel 2: A Commentary on the Book of the Prophet Ezekiel Chapters 25–48*, trans. J. D. Martin, Hermeia (Philadelphia: Fortress, 1983), 566. The six occurrences of רוח in chs. 1 and 10 (1:4, 12, 20a, 20b, 21; 10:17) connected with the living creatures' movement with the throne can also be construed as "the vitalizing principle of life that comes from God himself." Daniel I. Block, "The Prophet of the Spirit: The Use of *RWH* in the Book of Ezekiel," *JETS* 32 (1989): 36. Also see Robson, *Word and Spirit in Ezekiel*, 88.

95 Robson, *Word and Spirit in Ezekiel*, 85.

96 Cf. Walther Eichrodt, *Ezekiel: A Commentary*, trans. Cosslett Quin (London: SCM, 1970), 137–138.

97 Block, "The Prophet of the Spirit," 39. Robson, *Word and Spirit in Ezekiel*, 92.

98 John Woodhouse, "The 'Spirit' in the Book of Ezekiel," in *Spirit of the Living God Part One*, Explorations 5, ed. B. G. Webb (Sydney: Lancer, 1991), 17 cited in Robson, *Word and Spirit in Ezekiel*, 92.

99 Cf. Helen Shüngel-Straumann, *Ruah Bewegt die Welt*, 51–66.

the hand of God or the spirit/wind (רוח) which appears to be a kind of a mediator of Yahweh's activity (37:1). Here one also finds the רוח as the breath of life which revives those in fatal despair as is evident in the רוח reviving the dry bones into dynamic living (37:14).[100] As commanded by God, Ezekiel summons the four winds to enter into the lifeless bodies, and they enter as a revivifying Spirit that made them alive and they stood on their feet (37:9–10). Block claims that the רוח that "will revitalize Israel is not the ordinary, natural life breath that is common to all living things; it is the spirit of God himself."[101] According to Marie-Theres Wacker, Ezekiel 37:1–15 also became a major text on which to base the hope of resurrection of the death, for God's breath is more enduring than dead.[102] In the socio-political context of exile, the revitalising power of the Spirit of God provides the power of resistance to the exilic community to challenge the lifelessness and hopelessness of the exilic situation.

A resistant discourse is also found in Deutero-Isaiah, a document that emerged in the late Babylonian period, with messages of comfort, new creation, and promises of God. Especially, the theme of (new) creation is strongly pronounced in Deutero-Isaiah (Isa 42:9; 43:18–19). Deutero-Isaiah opens with good news of comfort to the disheartened exiles with the message of Yahweh as the creator of the universe (Isa 40). R. N. Whybray observes that this passage is probably a counter to the salvation tradition that claimed that the counselor-gods counsel Marduk the plan of creating the world.[103] The incomparability and transcendence of Yahweh as creator is emphasised in the rhetorical question, "Who has directed the spirit of the LORD (רוח יהוה), or as his counselor instructed him?" (40:13). The rhetorical question suggests that the creator God planned and implemented the design for creation by the רוח יהוה. For Hildebrandt, this reference, "is a précis to the creation theme as developed in Isaiah 40–66."[104] The motif of creation and recreation has to be seen in the context of exile. It is a claim that Israel's God Yahweh is the creator of the universe, the God who is incharge of Israel and the universe. And this God is "about to do a new thing" (43:19). Notably, the discourse on creation speaks of the socio-political foundation of Israel as God's work just the same way the creation of the universe is God's work (40:26; 43:1; 44:24–28).

Deutero-Isaiah also constructs a new socio-political order that will be inaugurated by the Spirit-anointed chosen servant of Yahweh in the four servant songs (Isa 42:1–9; 49:1–13; 50:1–11; and 52:13–53:12). In these songs, the concern for social justice constitutes the main thrust of the mission of the Spirit endowed Yahweh's servant. Isaiah 42:1cd appears like a modified version of

100 Albertz and Westermann, *TLOT* 3:1219.

101 Block, "The Prophet of the Spirit," 38.

102 Wacker, "The Spirit of God in the Public Sphere of Christian Communities," 36–37.

103 R. N. Whybray, *Isaiah 40–66* (London: Oliphants, 1975), 53–54.

104 Hildebrandt, *An Old Testament Theology of the Spirit of God*, 19.

Isa 11 with investiture of the רוח upon Yahweh's servant: "I have put my spirit upon him; he will bring forth justice to the nations." Sklba opines that here the prophet is authenticating his prophecy by resorting to the Spirit of God in the exilic context of prophecy in crisis, asserting God's Spirit as the source of his mission to bring justice, that is, a just order in society to the nations (Isa 42:1 cf. 61:1).[105] Authenticating one's special calling with the investiture of the רוח is not uncommon in the Israel's heritage.[106] However, the question of the identity of the servant is not easily answered. A case for an individual identity and corporate identity abounds with reasoned arguments.[107] Not only that, some interpreters think the servant in some places refers to an individual while in some places refers to a collective group.[108] At any rate, the servant songs herald hope to comfort the post-exilic community that God will carry our justice through his Spirit-anointed chosen servant.

The major tasks of the Spirit-empowered servant are to resists injustice and bring justice (vv. 1d, 3c, 4b), open the eyes that are blind (v. 7a) and bring out prisoners from the dungeon (v. 7b). The threefold emphasis on משפט (justice) in 41:1c, 3c, 4b is significant. But this justice is marked by the concern for the weak—"a bruised reed he will not break, and a dimly burning wick he will not quench, he will faithfully bring forth justice" (42:3). The presence of the servant amidst the brokenhearted will become a source of "strength and hope that is not their own."[109] The Spirit-endowed servant will not grow "faint or be crushed" (42:4) but will have the resilience against opposition until he brings forth justice on earth, because the Spirit of God is resting upon him,[110] which empowers him

105 Sklba, "Until the Spirit from on High," 14. In fact there were disputes and infighting among prophets in exile. Jeremiah 23:34–40 is an exilic attempt to forbid new oracles in the classical style. The repeated references of Ezekiel to his fellow exiles as "rebellious" and "contradictory," almost like dealing with scorpions (2:3–8), indicates another type of polemics within the exilic communities. P. D. Hanson sees in the exile an origin of the gulf and quarrel between the priestly aristocrat and the visionary eschatological prophets. See. P. D. Hanson, *The Dawn of Apocalyptic* (Philadelphia: Fortress, 1965), 29.

106 Whybray, *Isaiah 40–66*, 72. The servant is empowered by the Spirit in a manner of divine appointments of kings (1 Sam 10:6, 10; 16:13; cf. Isa 11:2; 61:1) and prophets (Ezek 2:2; 3:24; Mic 3:8; 2 Chro 15:1; 20:14).

107 For a history of interpretation of the identity of the "servant" in Isaiah see C. R. North, *The Suffering Servant in Deutero-Isaiah* (London: Oxford University Press, 1948), and H. H. Rowley, *The Servant of the Lord and Other Essays on the Old Testament* (Oxford: Basil Blackwell, 1965).

108 See Peter Wilcox and David Patton-Williams, "The Servant Songs in Deutero-Isaiah," *JSOT* 42 (1988): 79–102; John D. W. Watts, *Isaiah 34–66*, WBC 25 (Waco: Word Books, 1987), 117.

109 George A. F. Knight, *Servant Theology: A Commentary on the Book of Isaiah 40–55* (Edinburgh: Handsel, 1984), 47.

110 Knight, *Servant Theology*, 47.

for the work of resistance. The Spirit endowment was to enable the servant to cause justice to go out to the nations (42:1b).[111]

During the exilic period, the understanding of God as the creator who creates through the רוח (Isa 40:13) became firmly rooted. Thus, the Spirit of God is also seen as the driving force for spiritual and socio-political transformation of Israel from the lifeless situation of exile. In other words, it occurred to Israel that only God's Spirit could empower the quest for a new socio-political space from the hopeless situation of exile. A significant pneumatological emphasis in the exilic period is also the construction of a new and just moral community in which the Spirit anointed Yahweh's servant (individual or community) would play a major role to maintain social justice. In other words, social justice is integrally connected to the work of the Spirit of God.

2.2.5. The Spirit of God in the Post-exilic Period and the Democratisation of the Spirit

The return of the exile was certainly a new age, the age of fulfillment of the promise of restoration, but one that is only partially fulfilled, strictly speaking in terms of the historical circumstances. The time was "evidently a lively moment, beset by hopes and frustrations."[112] The returnees had to deal with social strife from within the community, political uncertainties, economic difficulties, and religious challenges that were posed to them.[113] Each of the major groups that returned after a long time of exiles brought "a distinctive notion of the function and effect of the Spirit in their experience."[114] But there is a clear transition from the previous understanding, in that the Spirit is now understood as the primary force of history. In the words of Sklba, "That Spirit's work gradually extended to all so that what once had been viewed as a physical and transitory phenomena ... became, through reflections of the exiles and those who returned to establish a new order, a permanent moral power infusing the entire community and preparing it for the future. The transformation occurred during exile."[115]

According to J. Lindblom, the increased importance of the Spirit of God in the postexilic period is caused by the "double tendency" to emphasise the immanence and transcendence of God. The immanence of God is expressed by the expectation of God dwelling in Zion in the midst of his people. However, God becomes "far off" from human and hence a need arises to bridge the gap between God and humans and it is here the Spirit comes in as an intermediary.[116]

111 Gary V. Smith, *Isaiah 40–66*, NAC 15B (Nashville: Broadman & Holman, 2009), 161.

112 P. R. Ackroyd, *Israel under Babylon and Persia* (Oxford: Oxford University Press, 1970), 172.

113 Lindblom, *Prophecy in Ancient Israel*, 404; Ackroyd, *Israel under Babylon and Persia*, 172–173; Ma, *Until the Spirit Comes*, 141.

114 Sklba, "Until the Spirit from on High," 16.

115 Sklba, "Until the Spirit from on High," 16.

116 Lindblom, *Prophecy in Ancient Israel*, 413–414.

The Spirit of God was frequently invoked in the post-exilic writings, to prophesy (cf. Isa 61:1); to motivate the building of the new Temple (Zech 4:6), to invoke God's presence in the post-exilic community (Hag 2:5); to express God's guidance and leading in the past (Isa 63:10, 14 cf. Neh 9:20, 30). This "recurring invocation of the Spirit to achieve harmony and new vitality seems to be one of the theological treasures brought back from exile."[117]

Post-exilic work both prophetic and historical stress the role of the Spirit in the history and religious traditions of Israel in order to assert the presence of God in the post-exilic community. Isaiah 63:7–14 recounts the crossing of the sea and tells that Yahweh was the one who placed in the midst of Israel τὸ πνεῦμα τὸ ἅγιον (the Holy Spirit LXX 63:11) and πνεῦμα παρὰ κυρίου (Spirit from the Lord, LXX 63:14) which guided them like cattle in the valley. Such remembering is not merely recalling to mind but also "an appeal to that gracious will which once upon a time wrought these deeds, and is now entreated to perform them afresh."[118] Wonsuk Ma contends that, "the text gives a strong impression that the real hero is the spirit of God," expressing an expectation that even the "second exodus will come to its completion through the leading of the same spirit."[119] Similarly, Zech 7:12 speaks of the prophetic guidance.[120] A penitent prayer in Neh 9:30 also noted that God instructs and warned Israel by his Spirit through the prophets. In other words, it occurred to Israel that God's Spirit was the motive force of their history.[121] This paradigm shift also allowed the transformation of the dynamic significance of the רוח to the static character most vividly expressed in the phrase Holy Spirit (Isa 63:10; Ps 51:11).[122]

---

117 Sklba, "Until the Spirit from on High," 14.

118 Westermann, *Isaiah 40–66*, 387.

119 Ma, *Until the Spirit Comes*, 153.

120 Zechariah 7:12 associates the Spirit of God with prophecy. Carol L. Meyers and Eric M. Meyers, *Haggai, Zechariah 1–8: A New Translation with Introduction and Commentary*, AB 25B (New York: Doubleday, 1987), 403.

121 The important stress on the role of the Spirit in the history and religious traditions of Israel during the post-exilic period shows Israel's deepening understanding of the Spirit of God. The chronicler also demonstrates an increased inclination to ascribe the past events to the influence of the Spirit. In repeating the book of Kings, new legends were added wherein the Spirit absent in the deuteronomist accounts cropped in. For instance, in Chronicles, the Spirit envelope Amasai during Ziklag campaign (1 Chro 12:18), but in the parallel account in 1 Sam 30 both reference to the Spirit or Amasai was missing. In 2 Chro 15:1, the Spirit came upon Azariah and led him to support Asa's removal of idols, but in this case too both Azariah and the Spirit is not mentioned in the parallel version of 1 Kgs 15. Similarly, in 1 Kgs 22, there was no mentioned of Jahaziel or the Spirit, but in 2 Chro 20:14, the Spirit came upon Jahaziel to aid Jehoshaphat in war. Sklba, "Until the Spirit from on High," 16.

122 Albertz and Westermann, *TLOT* 3:1219, opine that Holy Spirit is actually an oxymoron expression given that it combines the static character of holy (*qādôš*) with the dynamic character of רוח.

However, strikingly, apart from the nostalgia for the Spirit of prophecy in the past, Trito-Isaiah 61:1 claims the Spirit of God as the power that gives voice to the prophet. Here the prophet claims the Spirit's anointing and proclaimed good news to the poor, release to the captives, and the favourable year of the Lord. Sklba maintains that the invocation of the Spirit points to the prophet's personal legitimation.[123] Without any reference to vision or dream, the prophet bluntly claims that the רוח of Yahweh is upon him through the anointing of God (61.1).[124] However, there is also a movement from the circumscribed prophetic inspiration to a single prophet (cf. Isa 61:1) to the democratisation of the Spirit of God to all people to prophesy. One finds an incipient pointer in Isa 59:21 and a full unreserved democratisation of the Spirit in Joel 2:28–29.

A number of scholars agree that Isa 59:21 does not belong to the larger section of 59:1–20, because it diverges so much "both in style and subject matter."[125] However, given that this passage links the preceding passages with the following, the writer would not just intend a disjunction of the meaning of the word and Spirit other than the meaning used in chs. 60–62. Hence, Wonsuk Ma argues, this verse concerns "God's revelation communicated through his word, which has been placed in the mouth of his people."[126] Kendall asserts, "v. 21 says that as long as Israel exists, (active) prophecy will never cease to be. It is an aspect of the longed for salvation. The people are the bearers of the prophetic gift, though the nation as a whole is not considered Yahweh's spokesman."[127] Similarly, Lindblom argues that the intimate relationship between prophecy and Spirit is evident in this verse. "The people as a whole are here thought of as being in possession of the prophetic spirit and the prophetic word, in virtue of the presence of the prophet among them."[128] Given that, in Israel, the absence of prophets was seen as a sign

123 Sklba, "Until the Spirit from on High," 14.

124 Ma, *Until the Spirit Comes*, 152.

125 Claus Westermann, *Isaiah 40–66*, OTL, trans. D. M. G. Stalker, (London: SCM, 1969), 352; Duhm, *Das Buch Jesaja*, 446, Mowinkel, "The 'Spirit' and the 'Word,'" 204. Elisabeth Achtemeier, *The Community and Message of Isaiah 56–66: A Theological Commentary* (Minneapolis: Augsburg, 1982), 72 thinks that this verse concludes the first part of the book (chs. 56–59) assembled by the "Levitical-prophetic" community. On the other hand, John L. McKenzie, *Second Isaiah*, AB 20 (New York: Doubleday, 1968), 171 views this as an expansion of the preceding passage by a later hand. However, Westermann, *Isaiah 40–66*, 352, 427 opines that the text fits in between 66:20 and 22. In this prose form, God is the speaker, and promises a wider circle than a single prophet (*contra* 61:1–3) that the word and the prophetic Spirit will be found in "the mouth of your children" and "the mouth of your children's children." Duhm, *Das Buch Jesaja*, 447 contend that the word is not of the prophet, but the presentation of the ideal of nomism. The Spirit is not the Spirit that is at work in the Servant, nor the prophetic Spirit, nor the Spirit that leads Israel. It is probably the Spirit of obedience.

126 Ma, *Until the Spirit Comes*, 134.

127 D. J. Kendall, "The Use of *Mispat* in Isaiah 59," *ZAW* 96 (1984): 404.

128 Lindblom, *Prophecy in Ancient Israel*, 176 cf. Kendall, "The Use of *Mispat* in Isaiah 59," 404.

of punishment and judgment, and God's distancing of himself from his people (Amos 8:11-12; Ezek 7:26; Ps 74:9; Lam 2:9),[129] "the coming age of salvation is envisaged as a time when prophecy is given to everyone in the community."[130]

A promise of unreserved democratisation of the Spirit is seen in Joel 2:28–29 (LXX 3:1–3).[131] This promise occurs in the reassuring words of God's saving presence among his people even in the midst of the epic catastrophes (cf. 2:27, 32). According to Hans Walter Wolff, the outpouring of the Spirit "on all flesh" in Joel emphasises in general "the weak, the powerless and the hopeless," as "recipients of new life with God."[132] According to Michael Welker, the promise of the Spirit of God in Joel's prophecy extends "beyond imperialistic monocultures" that no specific group of people or tradition or culture can claim for itself the exclusive monopoly of "God's presence, reception of God's Spirit, prophetic testimony, and true definitions of reality."[133] Every person who participates in the outpouring of the Spirit will attain prophetic knowledge of God and help others perceive "*what God is doing in and on the ruptured members of God's people not only to heal them for themselves, but to bind them together for each other and to revitalize them*" (emphasis original).[134]

2.3. Spirit of God in the Second Temple Judaism

There were both evolution and vibrancy of the Spirit of God in the various streams of writings of the Second Temple Judaism. It should be noted that several literatures of this period respond to the *cultural imperialism* of Hellenism and thus gave rise to the transformation of the concept of the Spirit, which should be studied in this context. A brief discussion of the theme as found in the apocalyptic literature, diaspora Judaism, and in the Palestinian Judaism are in order.

129 Lindblom, *Prophecy in Ancient Israel*, 203.

130 Ma, *Until the Spirit Comes*, 135.

131 Lindblom, *Prophecy in Ancient Israel*, 176 cf. Kendall, "The Use of *Mispat* in Isaiah 59," 404.

132 Hans Walter Wolff, *Joel and Amos: A Commentary on the Books of the Prophets Joel and Amos*, trans. W. Janzen, S. D. Macbride, Jr. and C. A Muenchaw, Hermeia (Philadelphia: Fortress, 1977), 67. "The promise regarding 'manservants and maidservants,' added by way of intensification, unmistakably introduces into the hope an element of social revolution. The ancient law of God in Israel had already accorded special attention to the rights of male and female slaves, providing that they, too, should freely share the joy to be found in the presence of Israel's God. Beginning with Amos, prophecy had raised its voice on behalf of all who were oppressed and unfree (cf. especially Jer 34:8–22). In the coming age they shall be incorporated fully into the community of the free, by being deigned worthy of the highest distinction along with all the rest" (67).

133 Welker, *God the Spirit*, 155.

134 Welker, *God the Spirit*, 155.

2.3.1. Apocalyptic Literature

The appearance of the apocalyptic literature is one of the most notable developments of the Second Temple Judaism. A majority of scholars sees apocalypticism as a "child of prophecy."[135] In the Second Temple period, Shaye J. D. Cohen claims, there was the transformation of prophecy into apocalypse. This transformation is part of the outcome of the canonisation of the Tanak. He finds that Zechariah already demonstrates that such a transition was already underway in the Persian period. Zechariah refers to "the former prophets" three times (1:4, 7; 7:12), which indicates a cognisance that "one era has passed and another is about to begin."[136] Haggai, who is a contemporary of Zechariah can still use the classical formula "Thus says the Lord of hosts" (Hag 1:2). However, in Zechariah, it is the angel, not the prophet who says, "Thus says the Lord" (Zech 1:16). Cohen argues that, "prophecy did not cease so much as it was transformed," but by the middle of second century BCE this transformation was complete. Thus, "[p]rophecy became apocalypse, and prophets became apocalyptic seers. Other heirs of the prophetic tradition were 'holy men,' miracle workers, 'charismatic' healers, foretellers of the future, and mystics."[137]

It is significant to ask what socio-political and religious context propelled apocalypticism and the production of the apocalypses.[138] H. H. Rowley thinks that apocalyptic though is the child of prophecy, it owes more to the circumstances of the Maccabean age.[139] Otto Plöger concurs with Rowley but goes further to assert that its pre-history dates back to the Persian period. For him, Joel, Trito-Zechariah, Isa 24-27 and Daniel constitute the literary deposits of the Hasidim who opposed the priestly theocratic party.[140]

Martin Hengel maintains that the earliest real apocalypse comes from the Hasidim, and it emerged as a by-product of the Jewish struggle against the onslaught of the Hellenistic spirit.[141] Robert R. Wilson who found the evolution of the socio-political condition that produced the book of Daniel, concludes,

---

135 Cf. Paul L. Redditt, "The Vitality of Apocalyptic Vision," in *Passion Vitality, and Foment: The Dynamics of Second Temple Judaism*, ed. Lamontte M. Luker (Harrisburg PA: Trinity Press International, 2001), 84. But Gerhard von Rad, *Old Testament Theology*, 2:302–306, claims that apocalypticism is the child of wisdom literature.

136 Shaye J. D. Cohen, *From the Maccabees to the Mishnah* (Philadelphia: Westminster Press, 1987), 199.

137 Cohen, *From the Maccabees to the Mishnah*, 200.

138 For formal definition of 'Apocalypse' see Redditt, "The Vitality of Apocalyptic Vision," 81 cf. J. J. Collins, "Introduction: Towards the Morphology of a Genre," *Semeia* 14 (1979): 9.

139 H. H. Rowley, *The Relevance of Apocalyptic*, 2nd ed. (London: Lutherworth Press, 1952), 41.

140 Otto Plöger, *Theocracy and Eschatology*, trans. S. Rudman (Richmond: John Knox, 1968).

141 Martin Hengel, *Judaism and Hellenism: Studies in their Encounter in Palestine during the Early Hellenistic Period*, vol. 1, trans. John Bowden (Philadelphia: Fortress, 1974), 94–95, 175–180.

"apocalyptic groups may develop wherever the required social conditions are present and that the *shape* of a particular group's religion and literature will depend on the group's social and religious background" (emphasis original).[142] In other words, the crucial matter is that when a group perceives itself to be deprived and powerless in certain social circumstances, caused by external or internal factor, they produce a resistance discourse from the periphery. Such a group produces new discourses about power and construct an alternative social order.[143] For instance, Daniel and Enochic writings can be considered as products of such social circumstances.

It can be asked, what is the connection between the Spirit of God and apocalypticism? In the apocalyptists, revelations were received through angelic messengers or visionary experiences, and רוח does not appear in the fashion that comes upon the pre-exilic charismatic leadership or ecstatic prophets. Like the classical prophets, which mention little of the Spirit of God, in the apocalytptic writings too, "little mention is made of the spirit as a strictly inspirational agency." However, D. S. Russell asserts, "the belief is strongly expressed in the accessibility of man's nature to the invasive forces sent from God as a means of inspiration."[144] In the manner, the classical prophets legitimised their prophecy with the conventional phrase "thus said the Lord," the term "vision" came to have a conventional use both in prophecy and apocalyptic.[145] It can be granted here, that just as "thus said the Lord" presupposes the inspiration (of the Spirit) of God for the prophets; "vision" too can be granted as the activity of the Spirit of God.

Though the Spirit of God is not prominent as the source of inspiration or prophecy in apocalyptic literature, 1 En. 49.3 and 1 En. 62.2 make a strong connection between the Spirit and a future messianic figure.[146] M. Black rightly sees an unmistakable correspondence between the noted Enochic texts Isa 11:2 and 4.[147] The Isaianic text (Isa 11:2) reverberates again in Pss. Sol. (17:37; cf. 18:7) stating that the royal messiah receives his power through the Holy Spirit,[148] and

142 Robert R. Wilson, "From Prophecy to Apocalyptic: Reflection on the Shape of Israelite Religion," *Semeia* 21 (1981): 93.

143 Reddittt, "The Vitality of Apocalyptic Vision," 88.

144 D. S. Russell noted that the use of רוח is limited to 1 En. 68:2; 70:2; 91:1; Mart. Ascen. Isa. 1:7; 5:14; T. Ab. 4; 2 Bar. 6:3; 7:2; 2 Esdras (4 Ezra) 14:22. D.S. Russell, *The Method and Message of Jewish Apocalyptic* (London: SCM, 1964), 160.

145 Russell, *The Method and Message of Jewish Apocalyptic*, 161.

146 1 Enoch 49.3 speaks of the qualities of the son of man upon whom, "dwells the spirit of wisdom, the spirit which gives understanding, the spirit of knowledge and of power, and the spirit of those who sleep in righteousness" (*AOT*). Again in 1 En. 62.2 the power of the elect one is extolled: "And the Lord of the Spirits has sat on the throne of his glory, and the spirit of righteousness was poured out on him [the Elect One], and the word of his mouth kills all the sinners and all the lawless, and they are destroyed before him" (*AOT*).

147 M. Black, *The Book of Enoch* (Leiden: Brill, 1985), 212.

148 Fabry, "רוח ruah," *TDOT* 13:400.

that the priestly messiah is endowed with the Spirit of understanding and holiness (Ps. Sol. 18:7). Notably, the development of the concept of the Spirit in the exilic period that speaks of a coming messiah who would be anointed with the Spirit continues to find expression in the apocalyptic literature.

2.3.2. The Spirit in Diaspora Judaism

2.3.2.1. The Septuagint

The LXX's rendering of the Hebrew רוח by πνεῦμα added new dimensions to the term. Though πνεῦμα does not have a wide range of meanings, following the Hebrew word רוח, πνεῦμα in LXX covers the concepts such as wind, breath, anthropological spirit, evil spirit and the divine Spirit.[149] Two significant theological aspects of πνεῦμα that become conspicuous in the LXX are its association with divinity and prophetic inspiration. Apart from Stoicism, other Greek schools of philosophy and religion did not accord any importance to the role of πνεῦμα nor usually associate πνεῦμα with divinity.[150] Given the lack of satisfactory equivalence of רוח in Greek writings, the LXX rendering of πνεῦμα for רוח cast the word (πνεῦμα) a new dimension. Isaacs states, "In faithfully translating the Hebrew term *ruach* as πνεῦμα, when applied not only to wind, breath, and life, but also to God, the LXX plays a significant part in the development of its meaning in subsequent Greek literature."[151] According to David Hill, the transformation of πνεῦμα as the Spirit of God in LXX provided a perceptible tendency to view the Spirit as "some kind of power or personality separate from God" since Greek usage consistently understands πνεῦμα in terms of substance.[152] Hill argues that the definite article in the LXX translation of Ps 51:13 καὶ τὸ πνεῦμα τὸ ἅγιόν σου could point to hypostatization.[153] Similar change is seen in Isa 63:10. He observes that in 1 Sam 16:14 and 1 Kgs 22:21f., what is implicit in the Hebrew concerning the Spirit under Yahweh's control become explicit in Greek text (cf. Num 16:22;

149 Schoemaker, "The Use of רוח in the Old Testament," 36; Hill, *Greek Words and Hebrew Meanings*, 217–218; Werner Bieder, "πνεῦμα, πνευματός," *TDNT* 6:368–375. For the most part when it means wind, the LXX render it πνεῦμα, but it also used ανεμος some 50 times suggesting that the two words are synonymous. When the Hebrew רוח means breath, the LXX normally translate it πνεῦμα, but occasionally used ανεμος (Jer 5:13) as well as πνοη (Isa 38:16 Ezek 13:13; Prov 1:23). At the same time LXX also used πνεῦμα to translate נשמה indicating that it used πνεῦμα to mean breath. However, when רוח refers to human emotions and inner force, it used a variety of Greek words cf. Marie E. Isaacs, *The Concept of the Spirit: A Study of Pneuma in Hellenistric Judaism and its Bearing on the New Testament,* Heythorp Monographs (London: Heythorp College, 1976), 11–12.

150 Isaacs, *The Concept of the Spirit*, 17; Menzies, *Empowered for Witness*, 50.

151 Isaacs, *The Concept of the Spirit*, 17.

152 Hill, *Greek Words and Hebrew Meanings*, 218.

153 Hill, *Greek Words and Hebrew Meanings*, 219 cf. Tengström, *TDOT* 13:395.

27:16; Ps 104:4).[154] However, Isaacs cautions such postulation of a separate hypostasis based on the text that are more of poetic imagery.[155]

In LXX, πνεῦμα is also usually depicted as the Spirit of prophetic inspiration. Two instances where πνεῦμα is conspicuously absent in the MT but appears in the LXX are cited here as the case in point. In Num 23:7, LXX inserts the phrase καὶ ἐγενήθη πνεῦμα θεοῦ ἐπ' αὐτῷ (and the Spirit of God came upon him) to suggest that Balaam spoke by the inspiration of the Spirit of God whereas, in the MT this phrase appears only in Num 24:2 and not in Num 23:7. The LXX translators pick up the formula phrase from Num 24:2 and inserted it into 23:7 showing a predilection to attribute prophecy to the Spirit of God. Similarly, in Zech 1:6 God spoke to Zechariah saying "But receive ye My words and My statutes—all that I, by My spirit [ἐν πνεύματί μου], give in charge to My servants the prophets" (trans. Charles Thompson). The MT does not have the phrase ἐν πνεύματί μου. This shows that the LXX translators associated the prophetic inspiration with the Spirit.[156]

2.3.2.2. Wisdom of Solomon

The Wisdom of Solomon is a document that emerged as a response to the invading cultural imperialism of Hellenism and uses wisdom to help the Jews to resist the forces of pagan culture. In the Wisdom of Solomon, πνεῦμα is employed as breath (Wis 2.3; 11.20), as wind or air (5.11, 23), and also as a permeating force that "fills the world" and holds all things together (1.7).[157] But Wisdom used πνεῦμα as the Spirit of God in two senses. Firstly, it is the source of physical life that is granted to every human and creation as a permanent gift by God (Wis 12.1). Thus, he rebukes the idol makers, "because they fail to know the one who formed them and inspired them with active souls and breathed a living spirit [πνεῦμα ζωτικόν] into them" (15.11). Secondly, Wisdom identifies the Spirit of God with the wisdom of God (cf. 1.4–7 and 9.17). The author of wisdom also speaks of the Spirit as the Spirit of wisdom (7.7) and describes wisdom as "a breath of the power God [ἀτμὶς ... τῆς τοῦ θεοῦ δυνάμεως]" (7.25). It is also notable that in other diaspora literature, the Spirit is the source of special insights to select persons but in Wisdom this role is taken over by wisdom. For instance, wisdom brought up Joseph to become the ruler of Egypt (10.14) and enabled Moses to withstand Pharaoh (10.16), which in turn brought socio-political transformation in the life of the people of God. So also prophecy elsewhere associated with the Spirit is now associated with wisdom (7.27; 11.1).[158]

---

154 Hill, *Greek Words and Hebrew Meanings*, 219.

155 Isaacs, *The Concept of the Spirit*, 14.

156 Menzies, *Empowered for Witness*, 50.

157 Menzies, *Empowered for Witness*, 57.

158 Menzies, *Empowered for Witness*, 57.

For the author of Wisdom, the Spirit of wisdom does not dwell with the impious (1.5). It is given only to those who ask in humble prayer (7.7 cf. 8.20–21; 9.4). Solomon's prayer gives the purest expression of the gift of the Spirit: "Who have learned your counsel, unless you have given wisdom and sent your holy spirit from on high? And thus the paths of those on earth were set right, and people were taught what pleases you, and were saved by wisdom" (9.17–18). For Wisdom, discerning the will of God "depends entirely on revelation, which comes in the form of sophia or the holy spirit,"[159] apparently suggesting the synonymy of the terms. However, Robin Scroggs allows a distinction of the two terms stating, "Σοφία is more of the content of revelation, while πνεῦμα is the means by which this content is revealed."[160] The new paradigm of the Spirit in Wisdom is that the wisdom given by the Spirit is placed in contrast to human ability to know with its natural state. This is probably an ideological negation of the high cultural intellectualism of Hellenism.

2.3.2.3. Philo

Philo, an Alexandrian Jew of the Hellenistic synagogue of the Diaspora attempts to square the Stoic-Platonic philosophy with the biblical faith in order to dispel the assumption that the Hebrew faith is not averse to Greek philosophies. In Philonian writings, πνεῦμα is used to refer to the higher elements of the air (*Drunkenness* 106), an immaterial force that permeates cohesion material elements (*Unchangeable* 35), the rational soul of humankind, which has the impress of the divine power, and the Spirit of God, which is also the prophetic Spirit.[161] The discussion here is confined to the latter two aspects of Philonian πνεῦμα. Philo distinguishes the non-rational soul, which the human has in common with animals, and the rational soul, which differentiates human from animals. Philo equated the rational soul of the human with πνεῦμα (*Worse* 80–84), which has the impress of divine power, not the material substance as the Stoics posits. But to be distinguished from πνεῦμα as the impress of divine power is the πνεῦμα θεῖον, the Spirit of God, which is breathed into the human.[162] This enables the rational mind capable of knowing God.[163] Robert Menzies surmises that, like the author of Wisdom, Philo affirms the necessity to receive the gift of πνεῦμα in order to know God's will, but in contrast to the author of Wisdom, Philo places a unique emphasis on the universality of the gift of the Spirit that enables him "to affirm the centrality of divine grace without forfeiting human responsibility."[164]

---

159 Robin Scroggs, "Paul: ΣΟΦΟΕ and ΠΝΕΥΜΑΤΙΚΟΕ," *NTS* 14 (1967): 50.

160 Scroggs, "Paul: ΣΟΦΟΕ and ΠΝΕΥΜΑΤΙΚΟΕ," 50.

161 Bieder, "πνεῦμα," *TDNT* 6:372–374.

162 Bieder, *TDNT* 6:373.

163 *Alleg. Interp.* 1.31–38.

164 Menzies, *Empowered for Witness*, 60.

Philo also used πνεῦμα as the charismatic prophetic Spirit, which abides with all wise persons (παντὶ δὲ ἀστείῳ) that is not limited by ethnic boundaries.[165] However, Philo maintains a distinction between the rational aspect of the soul and the prophetic Spirit.[166] The prophetic Spirit, for Philo is the supreme divine Spirit, which confers knowledge that the mind cannot acquire. The rational man meets God in and with the rational mind, but the man inspired by God is lifted up into a plane inaccessible to rationality. The two worlds of rational enlightenment and divine prophecy converge in the wise men. Prophecy for Philo, constitute the highest form of knowledge that points to the revelation of a transcendent God.[167] The Philonic notion that, prophetic Spirit represents the highest gift derives from both Hellenistic and Old Testament-Jewish notions of Spirit.[168]

The Spirit of God in the diaspora literature is dominantly the Spirit of prophecy. The Septuagint has given emphasis to the Spirit as the Spirit of prophecy. For Philo, the highest gift of the Spirit is the Spirit of prophecy. The author of Wisdom of course associates the law as the locus of wisdom but in this the highest sapiential achievement is attributed to the gift of the Spirit.

2.3.3. The Spirit of God in Palestinian Judaism

2.3.3.1. Ben Sira

Jesus ben Sira draws on the traditions of Israel to give wisdom istruction to the young people in the context of the cultural imperialism of Hellenism. Martin Hengel maintains that, Ben Sira is rooted in the wisdom and prophetic tradition though it goes beyond them. In Sirach, there appears an inner transformation of the scribal office who with the "spirit of understanding" enters the heritage of the prophets to protect the holy scriptures of Israel in the onslaught of Hellenism. Hengel maintains that this development was significant for further development of (Rabbinic) Judaism that institutionalised exegesis and primitive Christianity (Essenism and Zealots movement) which took on inspired interpretation of the law and the prophets.[169]

Sirach 1.1 gives a programmatic expression of the main theme of the work that all wisdom is from God and with him it remains forever. For Ben Sira, the locus of wisdom is the law thus wisdom comes from the study of the law (1.26;

165 Finny Philip, *The Origins of Pauline Pneumatology*, WUNT 194 (Tübingen: Mohr Siebeck, 2005), 112–113.

166 Philip, *The Origins of Pauline Pneumatology*, 113.

167 Bieder, *TDNT* 6:374–375.

168 Harry Austryn Wolfson, *Philo: Foundations of Religious Philosophy in Judaism, Christianity, and Islam,* vol. 2, (Cambridge: Harvard University Press, 1948), 26.

169 Hengel, *Judaism and Hellenism,* 135–136.

3.22; 6.37).[170] But Ben Sira makes a connection between acquiring nomistic wisdom with the Spirit in Sirach 39.6. Sirach 39.6–8 states,

> If the great Lord is willing, he will be filled with the spirit of understanding; he will pour forth words of wisdom of his own and give thanks to the Lord in prayer. The Lord will direct his counsel and knowledge, as he meditates on his mysteries. He will show the wisdom of what he has learned, and will glory in the law of the Lord's covenant.

Up until 39.1–4, Ben Sira speaks about human diligent efforts to gain wisdom. But in Sir 39.5, the perspective changes as though it is gained by divine response to prayer and supplication. And in Sirach 39.6, Ben Sira underline that it is a matter of divine response to such diligent effort that one is filled with the spirit of understanding. In other words, for Ben Sira, wisdom is embodied in the law, yet it is to be searched by studying diligently. But the full comprehension of its meaning presupposes the aid of the Spirit of understanding (39:6).[171] The Spirit of understanding in Sirach 39.6 refers to the wisdom that comes from the Spirit of God. The frequent collocation of Spirit and understanding in the LXX with reference to wisdom imparted by the Spirit of God (Exod 31:3; Deut 34:9; Isa 11:2) also gives credence that here "the Spirit of understanding is given in accordance with the will of the Lord."[172] James Davis writes, "By placing verse 6 in between the descriptions of 39.1–5 and 39.7–11 then, Ben Sira has given added importance to the point made within the verse, namely that the quest for wisdom is only brought to fulfillment and completion by the entrance of a 'spirit of understanding', that is, by an experience of divine, spiritual inspiration."[173]

In the context of the cultural imperialism of Hellenism, Ben Sira produced a counter discourse with the sacred tradition of Israel. Ben Sira is not ignorant about the problem of suffering (2.1–6), but he is a firm believer of God's justice (15.11–16.23). Thus, he personified wisdom with the law or Torah, and made Torah the locus of wisdom. But it is the Spirit of God that will enlighten wisdom.

2.3.3.2. Qumran Scrolls

The Qumran scrolls were a product of a resistant community who opposed the Jerusalem Temple establishment as polluted and retreated into the desert near the Dead Sea to constitute an alternate holy community during the time of Hasmonean

170 James A. Davis, *Spirit and Wisdom: An Investigation of 1 Corinthians 1.18–3.20 Against the Background of Jewish Sapiential Traditions in the Greco-Roman Period* (Lanham, MD: University Press of America, 1984), 17.

171 So, Hengel, *Judaism and Hellenism*, 135.

172 Menzies, *Empowered for Witness*, 64.

173 Davis, *Spirit and Wisdom,* 20.

rule.[174] The community considered themselves as a remnant community formed by the guidance of the Holy Spirit (cf. CD 2.12). Thus, although there is a conception in Second Temple Judaism that the Spirit was quenched in Israel with the passing away of the last prophets, that is, Haggai, Zechariah, and Malachi (cf. t. Sotah 13.2–4),[175] Qumran community departs from this conception and acknowledges the activity of the Spirit in their community life.[176]

The Spirit plays a central role in the formation of the Qumran community. The community's self understanding of constituting an alternate community is deeply rooted in their reception of the Spirit of God. The community has the strong conviction that they constitute a holy community purified from sin by the Holy Spirit (1QS III, 7; IV, 21; 1QH XVI, 12). Alex Deasley argues that, more than the consciousness that the Spirit at work in their midst, "[t]he sect believed itself to be a community of the spirit in the further sense that in and through it, and through it alone, the spirit could be received ... The community was the community of the spirit in the sense that to it the spirit had been given."[177] He maintains that the crucial text, which describes the meaning of membership in the community (1QS III, 6–9), the Holy Spirit is referred to as "the holy spirit of the community" (III, 7).[178] This idea is expressed again in CD II, 12, while in

174 For a brief history of the Qumran community, see Florentino García Martínez, *The Dead Sea Scrolls Translated: The Qumran Text in English*, trans. Wilfred G. E. Watson, 2nd ed. (Leiden: Brill, 1996), lv–lvi.

175 For a balance view on the cessation of the Spirit refer to Erik Sjöberg, "πνεῦμα, πνευματός," *TDNT* 6:385–386. Joachim Jeremias, *Theology of the New Testament*, vol. 1, (London: SCM, 1971), 80–81; John R. Levison, "Did the Spirit Withdraw from Israel? An Evaluation of the Earliest Jewish Data," *NTS* 43 (1997): 35–57.

176 It should be noted here that Qumran pneumatological reflection includes a "treatise on the two spirits" found in the *Rule of the Community* (1QS III, 13–IV, 26) can be equated with the Holy Spirit. According to 1QS the two spirits is seeded in every person and exerts influence on the person—the spirit of truth, which emanated from the prince of light and the angel of truth (1QS III, 18, 20, 24) and the spirit of perversion, which originated in darkness and is equivalent to the angel of darkness (1QS III, 19, 21; IV, 12). However, it is not clear whether the good spirit can be equated with the Spirit of God. P. Wernberg-Møller, "A Reconsideration of the Two Spirits in the Rule of the Community (1 Q Serek III, 13–IV, 26)," *RevQ* 3 (1961): 422, claims that since the two spirits dwell in man as created by God, they are not something of metaphysical cosmic dualism, but human dispositions similar to the rabbinic good and evil impulse. M. Treves, "The Two Spirit of the Rule of the Community," *RevQ* 3 (1961): 449, also opines that two spirits are "simply the tendencies or propensities which are implanted in every man's heart."

177 Alex R. G. Deasley, "The Holy Spirit if the Death Sea Scrolls," *Wesleyan Theological Journal* 21 (1986): 60.

178 Deasley argues that the textual problem discussed by B. E. Thiering does not effect the meaning whichever way it is translated. Deasley, "The Holy Spirit in the Dead Sea Scrolls," 71 note 68 cf. B. E. Thiering, "Inner and Outer Cleansing as a Background to New Testament Baptism," *NTS* 26 (1980): 267 note 5.

the 1QH receiving the Spirit is interpreted in terms of community membership (IQH XI, 9–14; XIV, 13).[179]

The authors of the scrolls envisage that the reception of the Spirit privileges the community to access to the mystery of God's wisdom. There are many sapiential propensities characteristic of the wisdom tradition in the scrolls, and the writers of the scrolls also identify wisdom with the law.[180] Nonetheless, like Wisdom and Sirach, the scrolls are pessimistic about human ability to gain wisdom without the aid of the Spirit of God. Human cannot understand the ways of God (1QH XV, 32)[181] because they are dust and creatures of clay (1QH XIX, 3). As flesh humans cannot understand God's wisdom (1QH V, 19). But the hymns in 1QH also assert that through the reception of the Spirit, the members of the community have drawn close to understanding the wisdom of God.[182] Menzies writes, "As an essential element of initiation into the community, the gift of the Spirit reveals the previously hidden wisdom of God to the recipient. Sapiential achievement at every level is dependent upon the reception of this gift. Indeed, reception of the gift enables one to know God and live within the community."[183]

The Qumran community also ascribed to the Holy Spirit the attributes of the Spirit, which reveals God's revelation. 1QS VIII, 15–16 states: "This is the study of the law which he commanded through the hand of Moses, in order to act in compliance with all that has been revealed from age to age and according to what the prophet has revealed through his holy spirit." In the same measure, CD II, 12–13a declares that God raised a remnant (the community) and "taught them by the hand of the anointed ones through his holy spirit and through seers of the

179 However, the Qumran sects maintains a distinction within the sect between provisional members (who are admitted but on probation) and full members and the basis of this distinction is the spirit, in that a new member is examined seriously "concerning his spirit and his deeds" by the Council of the Community (1QS 4:14, 18). A new member is fully accepted only when the person is proved worthy. Deasly, "The Holy Spirit in the Dead Sea Scrolls," 60.

180 Eckhard J. Schnabel, *Law and Wisdom from Ben Sira to Paul: A Tradition Historical Enquiry into the Relation of Law, Wisdom, and Ethics* (Tübingen: Mohr Siebeck, 1985) 206–226.

181 All English translations of the scrolls (unless otherwise specified) are from Florentino García Martínez, *The Dead Sea Scrolls Translated: The Qumran Text in English*, trans. Wilfred G. E. Watson, 2nd ed. (Leiden: Brill, 1996).

182 According to the 1QH XIV, 12b–13, it is the gift of the Spirit that enables the community members to approach the intelligence of God: "But I, I have known, thanks to your insight that in your kindness towards man you have enlarged his share with the spirit of your holiness. Thus, you made me ***approach*** your intelligence." 1QH XII, 11b–13 also declares that wisdom is attained through the reception of the Spirit of God: "And I, the Instructor, have known you, my God, through the spirit which you gave me, and I have listened loyally to your wonderful secret through your holy spirit. You have opened within me knowledge of the mystery of your wisdom the source of power.

183 Menzies, *Empowered for Witness*, 79.

truth." There are two aspects of revelation in these texts. First, it acknowledged that the Spirit was associated with the law and the prophets. Second, the Qumranites believed the same Spirit who inspired prophetic writers was at work in themselves as the true interpreters of the Law and the Prophets.[184] However, the sectarian group is not the source of revelation but interpreters of revelation.[185] An important corollary to the claims of inspired exegesis is the central role of the teacher of righteousness, who was raised by God for the community, so that "he (the teacher) guide(s) them (the community) in the way of his (God's) heart" (CD I, 11). The teacher's function is more precisely defined in Habakkuk Commentary (IQpHab. VII, l–5a).[186]

For a community that separated itself from the mainstream society to constitute an alternate community, the invocation of the Spirit involves both the community's self-understanding of the experience of the Spirit and a self-legitimating discourse for counter social formation from the margins of the empire. Thus, there is a paradigm of resistance in the pneumatological reflection of the Qumranites, in that the community understood their own identity formation in the margins of the empire as the work of the Spirit.

2.3.3.3. Rabbinic Judaism

In Rabbinic Judaism, the Spirit is predominantly the Spirit of prophecy. This is evident in the insertions of the "Spirit of prophecy" in various places in the Targumim where the Hebrew Bible does not mention.[187] But the most debated issues concerning the Spirit in Rabbinic Judaism is whether the Spirit is withdrawn from Israel? The notion of the withdrawal of the Holy Spirit which was active in

---

184 A. A. Anderson, "The Use of 'Ruah' in 1QS, 1QH and 1QM," *JSS* 7 (1962): 302; Deasley, "The Holy Spirit if the Death Sea Scrolls," 54.

185 Geza Vermes, "The Qumran Interpretation of Scripture in Its Historical Setting," in *Post-Biblical Jewish Studies*, ed. Geza Vermes (Leiden: E.J. Brill, 1975), 39–41.

186 "And God told Habakkuk to write down that which would happen to the final generation, but He did not make known to him when time would come to an end. And as for that which He said, that he who runs may read it speedily, interpreted this concerns the Teacher of Righteousness, to whom God made known all the mysteries of the words of His servants the Prophets" (IQpHab. 7:l–5a).

187 *According to Targum Pseudo Jonathan, the Spirit given to the seventy elders (Num 11:25) refers to the Spirit of prophecy. So also the Spirit that was given to Samuel (1 Sam 10:6) and to Balaam (Num 24:2) is the Spirit of prophecy.* An explicit example of this tendency is found in *Targum Onqelos* Isa 11:2 where the phrase "Spirit of the Lord" is replaced by "the Spirit of prophecy from God." Isa 63:10f. can be taken as a further example where the "spirit of holiness" is rendered by "the words of his holy prophets." This change also reflects the rabbinic estimation of the patriarchs in the category of God's prophets, which is not explicit in the Hebrew bible. The rabbis holds that all devout and righteous person of the former generation such as Moses, David, Solomon, priests, patriarchs and their wives, were inspired by the Spirit, an considered the past prophetic activity as a great era of the Spirit. See Hill, *Greek Words and Hebrew Meanings*, 227–228.

the tannaitic period as the source of prophecy was built upon such texts as Ps 74:9; 1 Macc 4:46; 9:27 and 14:41; Josephus, *Ag. Ap.* 1:37–41; 2 Bar. 83:3; Pr. Azar. 15; and t. Sotah 13:2–4.[188] The most significant text is t. Sotah 13.2–4 which states,

> When the last prophets died, that is, Haggai, Zechariah, and Malachi, the Holy Spirit came to an end in Israel. But even so, they caused them to hear through an echo. Sages gathered together in the upper room of the house in Guria in Jericho, and a heavenly echo came forth and said to them, "There is a man among you who is worthy to receive the Holy Spirit, but this generation is unworthy of such honor." They all set their eyes upon Hillel the elder…Then another time they were in session in Yabneh and heard an echo saying, "There is a man among you who is worthy to receive the Holy Spirit, but this generation is unworthy of such honor." They all set their eyes upon Samuel the Small.[189]

Sjöberg concedes "a widespread theological conviction" about the withdrawal of the Holy Spirit from Israel on the basis of several texts that suggest the absence of prophecy.[190] Several scholars acknowledge the cessation of the Spirit in Israel in the Second Temple Judaism.[191] Jeremias summed up the popular view that "with the death of the last writing prophets, Haggai, Zechariah and Malachi, the spirit is quenched because of the sin of Israel. After that time, it was believed, God still spoke only through the 'echo of his voice' … a poor substitute."[192] J. D. G. Dunn also supported the view that "with the rabbis the belief becomes very strong that Haggai, Zechariah and Malachi were the last of the prophets and thereafter the spirit had been withdrawn."[193]

However, Levison argues that t. Sotah 13.2–4 should be interpreted according to a principle that is introduced t. Sotah 10.1.[194] "When a righteous person comes into the world, good comes into the world … and retribution departs from the world; and when the righteous person leaves the world, retribution comes into the world and goodness departs from the world" (t. Sotah 10.1). Levison argues, "Interpreted within its literary context t. Sotah 13.2–4 is an affirmation that, with

188 Levison, "Did the Spirit Withdraw from Israel?" 35.

189 Cited from Jacob Neusner, *Tosefta: An Introduction* (Atlanta: Scholars Press, 1992), 258–259.

190 Sjöberg, *TDNT*, 6:385.

191 Barrett, *The Holy Spirit and the Gospel Tradition*, 108–109; David Hill, *New Testament Prophecy* (London: Marshall, Morgan & Scott, 1979) 21. G. W. H. Lampe, "Holy Spirit," *IBD* 2:630.

192 Jeremias, *New Testament Theology*, 81.

193 J. D. G. Dunn, *Christology in the Making: A New Testament Inquiry into the Origins of the Doctrine of Incarnation* (London: SCM, 1980), 135.

194 Levison, "Did the Spirit Withdraw from Israel?" 47–49.

the presence once again of the righteous in the first century CE, the Holy Spirit could reappear following its temporary withdrawal after the death of the latter prophets."[195] Levison further asserts that the placing of Hillel in t. Sotah 13:3 as a disciple of Ezra, squares Hillel in the line of the prophets mentioned in Avot 1:1: "Moses received the law from Sinai, and committed it to Joshua, and Joshua to the elders, and the elders to the prophets, and the prophets committed it to the Great Synagogue." R. Meyer thinks that the restriction of the Holy Spirit is linked to legitimate prophecy to an ideal classical period with "the development of the Synagogal concept of Canon."[196] Still others see the relation of the Spirit to the past as a rabbinic polemic against the claims of the Spirit's activity in other's circle (for example, Christianity).[197]

While the rabbinic literature do not say much about the presence of the Spirit in the present time, but tended to relegate the activity of the Spirit to the past, it nevertheless sustained a strong hope for the future outpouring of the Spirit in the future. The Tg. Isa. 11:2 reiterates the hope and Tg. Isa. 42:1 ff. makes God saying about the servant messiah, "I will make my spirit rest upon him." In the last age, the righteous also would receive the Spirit as an agent of regeneration, and for this expectation of national revival Ezek 36:26–7 and 37:14 were the foundational texts.[198] Hill notes that the rabbis also believe, "The evil impulse will be taken out of Israel's heart in the Age to come, and the Spirit, as power for moral renewal, would rest upon her (Pesik. 165a)."[199] In Num. Rab. 15:25 it states, "The Holy One, blessed be He, said: In this world the individuals were given prophetic power, but in the world to come, all Israel will be made prophets, as it is said (Joel 2:28), 'I will pour out my Spirit on all flesh.'"[200]

2.4. Conclusion

There is always the paradigm of social justice and freedom in the concept of the Spirit of God in the Old Testament. Therefore, in the life and witness of Israel as the people of God, the Spirit of God intervenes at any given situation of domination, through charismatic leaders and prophets, and resists the system of domination and brings socio-political and religious transformation. Even the understanding of the Spirit of God as the Spirit of new creation and the anticipation for the Spirit-anointed ideal ruler as well as the future out pouring of the Spirit upon all flesh must be seen in the light of God's program of transforming socio-political and religious life of the people of God through the power of the Spirit of God. The Spirit of God is not prominent as the source of inspiration in apocalyptic

195 Levison, "Did the Spirit Withdraw from Israel?" 57.

196 Rudolf Meyer, "προφήτης," *TNDT* 6:816.

197 Refer to Levison, "Did the Spirit Withdraw from Israel?" 55.

198 Sjöberg, *TDNT* 6:232.

199 Hill, *Greek Words and Hebrew Meanings*, 232–233.

200 Hill, *Greek Words and Hebrew Meanings*, 233.

literature, except that it makes a strong connection between the Spirit and a future messianic figure of Isaiah (Isa 11:2). However, in many of the Second Temple literatures discussed above, the Spirit is prominently identified as the Spirit of prophecy. It should be noted that the emphasis on the law and wisdom and the ascription the enlightening role to the Spirit of God to gain wisdom in such works as Ben Sira, Wisdom, Qumran Scrolls must be seen as an ideological resistant discourse that emerged in the context of cultural imperialism of Hellenism. The rabbis are rather silent about the activity of the Spirit in the present time but anticipate a time when God's Spirit would be poured upon all flesh. The next chapter will attend to the background of Luke's Gospel and sketch the various socio-political developments in the Second Temple Judaism especially the various group formations that responded to the Hellenistic-Hasmonean hegemony and the resistance/renewal movements that responded to the Roman-Herodian hegemony in Palestine as it constituted the background and foreground of Jesus' movement which Luke accounted for his contemporaries.

Chapter 3

Lukan Community
Forging a Community in the Midst of Conflict and Resistance

3.1. Introduction

The land of Israel is a strategic highway that connects the east and the west in antiquity and hence it remained perennially a contested zone for neighbouring great empires for political and economic advantage.[1] The destruction of Solomon's temple and the exile of the cultural elites to Babylon in 587 BCE saw the demise of Israelite monarchy. While the construction of the Second Temple under the Persians brought hopes of restoration, it ended up becoming the political and economic powerhouse under the shadow of foreign empire with the high priest as the political and religious representative of the Judeans.[2] The Jews responded to the political and cultural imperialism of the empires, which threatened ever intensely the identity of the Jewish nation, with counter social formations for survival and representation. Most of the movements emerged with a sense of divine guidance to re-enact God's rule over the people based on the Israelite tradition. Jesus' movement is one of the resistance movements that offer an alternative to the empire system of domination. This chapter firstly appraises the Jewish group formations during the Hellenistic-Hasmonean period, since the political and socio-religious legacy of that time continues to

1 Hengel, *Judaism and Hellenism*, 6–7. Seàn Freyne, *Galilee: From Alexander the Great to Hadrian 323 BCE to135 BCE* (Edinburgh: T&T Clark, 1980), 27.

2 Helmut Koester, *Introduction to New Testament*, vol. 1, *History, Culture, and Religion of the Hellenistic Age* (Philadelphia: Fortress, 1980), 205, 207; Horsley and Hanson, *Bandits, Prophets, and Messiahs*, 9–10.

reverberate in Jesus' time. Secondly, it evaluates the various Jewish resistance movements contemporaneous to Jesus' movement. Thirdly, it discusses how Luke appropriates Jesus' traditions by insinuating the role of the Spirit of God in initiating and empowering Jesus' movement with the purpose to forge an inclusive community in the context of conflict and resistance of the late first century Roman Empire.

3.2. Jewish Socio-Political Formation Behind Luke's Gospel

In the Gospels one comes across distinguishable social groups such as Pharisees, Sadducees, Samaritans and so on. However, there are many more groupings in early Judaism than one finds in the Gospels or in Josephus.[3] The political and cultural imperialism of Hellenism, despite its appeal to the aristocracy, resulted in a crisis that had lasting impact upon Judaism and birthed many movements right down to the Bar Kochba revolt.[4] The Hasidim (also Hasidean) and the Maccabean movement emerged as a counter-movement during the Hellenistic reform. Essenes-Qumran, Pharisees, Sadducees,[5] the priestly group of Oniads

---

3 Josephus, *Antiquities of the Jews* (2.11–22), introduced "three sects of philosophy peculiar to themselves," the Essenes, the Sadducees, and the Pharisees, and adds a "fourth sect of Jewish philosophy" (2.23–25).

4 Hengel, *Judaism and Hellenism*, 56.

5 They are one of the major groups in early Judaism (*Ant.* 18.11), though their history is obscure. They first appear as an organised group and as an opponent of the Pharisees during the Hasmonean rule (*Ant.* 13.293, 297) and ceased to exist after the destruction of the temple in 70 CE. Cf. Joachim Jeremias, *Jerusalem in the Time of Jesus*, trans. F. H. Cave and C. H. Cave (Philadelphia: Fortress, 1969), 243; W. D. Davies, *Introduction to Pharisaism* (Philadelphia: Fortress, 1967; 19; Samuel Sandmel, *The First Christian Century in Judaism and Christianity: Certainties and Uncertainties* (New York: Oxford University Press, 1969), 58; John Bowker, *Jesus and the Pharisees* (Cambridge: Cambridge University Press, 1973), 10. The Sadducees have theological differences with the Pharisees. Especially they rejected the "oral law" popular among the Pharisees and refused to accept theological ideas that has no explicit basis in the "written law" (*Ant* 13.297). Koester, *History, Culture, and Religion of the Hellenistic Age*, 229–230. Geoffrey Wigoder *et al.* eds., "Sadducees," *The Encyclopedia of Judaism* (New York: MacMillan, 1989), 618. Lester L. Grabbe, "Sadducees and Pharisees," in *Judaism in Late Antiquity*, vol. 2, ed. Jacob Neusner and Allan J. Avery-Peck (Boston: Brill Academic Publishing, 2001), 60. Many scholars see the connection between the Sadducees and priesthood, owing to their name *saddukim* which many connects it with Zadok, however, one scholar noted, none of ancient sources "equates the Sadducees with priestly party; the most they claim is that certain priest were Sadducees," cf. Gary G. Porton, "Diversity in Postbiblical Judaism," in *Early Judaism and its Modern Interpreters*, ed. Robert A. Kraft and George W. E. Nickelsburg (Atlanta: Scholars, 1986), 66. At any rate, the Sadducees constituted a major party till the destruction of the Second Temple, who cannot be simply categorised as an anti-Pharisaic movement, but a movement with a strong Jewish nationalistic colour. Cf. S. W. Baron, *A Social and Religious History of the Jews*, vol. 2, *Christian Era: The First Five Centuries* (New York: Columbia University Press, 1952), 36.

(IV) who founded a Jewish temple at Leontopolis in Africa,[6] and probably the Samaritanism[7] emerged during the Hasmonean rule. One can also mention the "Fourth School of Philosophy,"[8] which Josephus mentioned and the Theurapeutae, which Philo mentioned as a quietist group.[9] There could be other Jewish circles "whose identity remain obscure."[10] However, the Hellenistic reform and its repercussion alone cannot explain group formations within the Jewish society. One must account for the politics of empire, how it operated, and how it adversely affected the socio-economic and political foundation of Israel.

---

6 Koester, *History, Culture, and Religion of the Hellenistic Age*, 222. According to Hengel, the temple at Leontopolis seems like a rival sanctuary to that of Jerusalem cf. Hengel, *Judaism and Hellenism*, 12, 100.

7 Being disenfranchised in Samaria by Alexander for an abortive rebellion against his power, the Samaritan went to Shechem and rebuilt the old city and also built their temple on Mount Gerizim. This Samaritan sanctuary was probably an independent activity and not a schism with Jerusalem. However, the razing down of the temple at Mount Gerizim (in 128 BCE) and the annexation of Samaria into the Hasmonean kingdom accompanied by a forceful subjection to the religious policies of Jerusalem birthed the Samaritan schism. Cf. James D. Purvis, *The Samaritan Pentateuch and the Origin of the Samaritan Sect* (Cambridge: Harvard University Press, 1968), 109–118; Hengel, *Judaism and Hellenism*, 13; Koester, *History, Culture, and Religion of the Hellenistic Age*, 248. Following the schism, the Samaritan began to define their identity by resorting to archiving their identity as the true descendent of Israel. The Samaritan Pentateuch privileges the theological legitimacy of Shechem/Gerizim as the divinely ordained centre of Israel cultic life. Purvis "The Samaritans and Judaism," 89, writes, "It was this contention, not simply the existence of Samaritan temple, which drove the permanent wedge between the Samaritans and the Jews."

8 The fourth school of philosophy that Josephus talks about has been generally more or less identified as the Zealots and the Sicarii by older scholarship. Cf. Gary G. Porton, "Diversity in Postbiblical Judaism," 72–73. However, Smith critically reviewed scholarship on Zealots and Sicarii and argue that, the Zealots as an organised resistance movement only late in the first Jewish revolt against Rome. He also noted that there is no indication that the Sicarii and the Zealots were related. Morton Smith, "Zealots and Sicarii, their Origins and Relation," *HTR* 64 (1971): 11, 19.

9 Scholars have tried to draw a similarity between the Essenes and the Theurapeutae but both are not the same. Cf. Porton, "Diversity in Postbiblical Judaism," 65–66.

10 George W. E. Nickelsburg, *Ancient Judaism and Christian Origins: Diversity, Continuity, and Transformation* (Minneapolis: Fortress, 2003), 178, used "circles" in two ways: those with "actual established and organised communities" like the Essenes and those more or less "loosely associated groups" whose common life is relatively obscure such as the Pharisees, Sadducees and the Hasidim. Nickelsburg advance his argument by noting the vast amount of Apocrypha, Pseudepigrapha, and scrolls found at Qumran but not written there, as the work of variety of circles. For instance, he maintains that, the communities who authored the *Jubilees* were on the one hand different from the Enochic writers though they stood in the Enochic chain of transmission, and on the other hand different from the Qumranites, though *Jubilees* found a special place at Qumran (179–180).

To digress briefly at this point, Gerhard Lenski categorises Greco-Roman Empire as an "advanced agrarian empire,"[11] which on the one hand is post-horticultural and on the other hand pre-industrial. In such societies, agriculture constituted the backbone of economy, but the distribution of resources lay in the controlling power of small ruling class. Political power was centralised in the city and centrally executed. As a consequence, a steep socio-economic inequality with differential power, privilege and control of resources in the hands of a small elites marked the agrarian empires.[12] The Greek Empires, as an advanced agrarian empire, impacted Palestine adversely beginning with the rule of the Ptolemies. The Ptolemies who preferred a "tightly centralised administration" in which the king managed the empire as a Greek would manage his own household.[13] Good information about the economic situation of Palestine during the Ptolemaic rule is found in the so-called Zeno papyri. Apparently, latifundalisation began since the Ptolemaic rule. There were probably royal estates in Palestine,[14] which was very significant in the Roman times[15] as it is characteristic of agrarian empires.

Under the Greek Empires, Judea with Jerusalem as the centre was like a temple state, but did not have any political independence.[16] The high priest raised land tax from the populace and paid tax to the Ptolemies like in the Persian period.[17] The presence of a *prostates* (2 Macc 3:4) and *gerousia* suggest that the

---

11 The following works provides a good ingress to understand the fundamental features of "agrarian empires." Gerhard E. Lenski, *Power and Privilege: A Theory of Social Stratification* (New York: McGraw-Hill Book Company, 1966); John H. Kautsky, *The Politics of Aristocratic Empires* (Chapel Hill: University of North Carolina, 1982). Gideon Sjoberg, *The Preindustrial City* (New York: Free Press of Glencoe, 1960).

12 Lenski, *Power and Privilege,* 146–176.

13 Hengel, *Judaism and Hellenism*, 18–19.

14 The *dioketes* Appolonius had an estate in Beth Anath in Galilee, which was probably a royal *dorea.* See Hengel, *Judaism and Hellenism*, 39. S. Applebaum maintains that Hephtziba inscription indicates the presence of large estates in the eastern Plain of Esdraelon and in the plains of Beth-Shean that belong to the royal house of Ptolemy. See, S. Applebaum, "Economic Life in Palestine," in *The Jewish People in the First Century: Historical Geography, Political History, Social, Cultural Life and Institutions*, vol. 2, *Compendia rerum Iudaicarum ad Novum Testamentum: Section 1*, ed. S. Safrai and M. Stern (Philadelphia: Fortress, 1976), 633.

15 Hengel, *Judaism and Hellenism*, 22. Hengel also conjectures that there were probably royal estates of balsam plantation in the area of Jericho and Engedi since the Ptolemaic time. These estates would have been transferred to the Hasmonean after the Maccabean successful revolt and then to the Herodians. Roman and rabbinic sources indicate that they were imperial estates in the Roman period (44–45).

16 Hengel, *Judaism and Hellenism*, 24. Jerusalem was described by some ancient writers as 'Heirosolyma', contrary to the actual wording which indicates that it was assumed as a temple cities of Syria and Asia Minor, which term themselves *heiropolis.*

17 H. Jagersma, *A History of Israel from Alexander the Great to Bar Kochba*, trans. John Bowden (London: SCM, 1985), 26.

authority of the high priest was checked by these offices. Towards the end of the Third Syrian War (246–241 BCE), conflict between the high priest and the Ptolemies erupted as Onias II refused to pay tribute. This conflict provided Joseph Tobiads to intervene the realpolitik and earned the *prostasia*, that is, representative of the Jewish ethnos to the royal administration. He was also given the right to levy general taxation throughout Syria-Phoenicia.[18] Thus while, the high priest remained in office, the *de facto* political, social and economic power now shifted from the high priesthood to the Tobiads.[19] When the power over Palestine shifted from the Ptolemies to the Seleucids, the latter initially gave tax relaxation to Jerusalem (*Ant.* 12.138–144) but did not change any of the economic situations of Palestine. On the other hand, the aggressive cultural imperialism of Hellenism under Antiochus Epiphanes IV who politicised and commercialised the Jerusalem temple's high priesthood office that adversely impacted the socio-political and religio-cultural foundation of the Jews. The predicament of what to do with the inescapable reality of the politics of the empire propelled the formation of resistance groups among the Jews. The Hasidim and the Maccabean movements must be set against this background. So also sectarianism within Judaism must be set against the political conundrum surrounding the Hasmonean dynasty and the Greco-Roman Empire.

3.2.1. Hasidim Movement

By around 200 BCE, a segment of Palestinian Jewish community from the aristocracy felt that it was to their advantage "to exchange their Jewish 'barbarism' for the 'civilized' Greek way of life (1 Macc 1:11)."[20] When Antiochus IV ascended to the Seleucid throne in 175 BCE, Jason ousted his brother Onias III with the help of the pro-Hellenistic reform group and obtained the high priest's office and also obtained permission to build Jerusalem as a model Greek city (2 Macc 4:9–11). But the crisis that transpired following the reform was not only cultural; it was "part political (pro-Seleucid or Ptolemaic), part social (priestly aristocracy and the lay nobility represented by the Tobiads) and part religious (the hellenisers and the *Hasidim*)."[21] When the reform began, a gymnasium was built in the temple precincts and Greek culture began to penetrate the lifestyle of even the priest

18 Hengel, *Judaism and Hellenism*, 27. The income that the king received from Coele Syria seems to be enormous. Since, the tax farmers too made profit apart from paying to the king, the population were oppressed by a heavy burden. Cf Jagersma, *History of Israel*, 25–26.

19 Jagersma, *History of Israel*, 29.

20 George W. E. Nickelsburg, "1 and 2 Maccabees – Same Story, Different Meaning," in *George W. E. Nickelsburg in Perspective: An Ongoing Dialogue of Learning*, vol. 2, JSTJSup 80, ed. Jacob Neusner and Alan J. Avery-Peck (Leiden: Brill, 2003), 660.

21 Freyne, *Galilee*, 36.

(2 Macc 4:12, 14–15). Most of the Judean population saw this Hellenistic reform as a threat to their very traditional way of life and identity (2 Macc 4:11).[22]

The Hellenistic reform reached a crisis when Menalaus, a non-Zadokite, ousted Jason (a Zadokite) and assumed the high priest. As the popular resistance against the non-Zadokite high priest took its toll, Antiochus IV in 168 ruthlessly crushed the popular rebellion against him and his puppet high priest Menalaus (2 Macc 5:12–14).[23] Following this, Jerusalem was made a *katoikia* in which the soldiers, veterans and other colonists formed the citizenry. Subsequently, the Jerusalem temple cult of Yahweh was transformed into the Hellenised Syrian god, Zeus Baal Shamayim. In 167 BCE the imperial edict was promulgated that outlawed the practice of Jewish religion in Jerusalem and Judea.[24] Opposition to the imperial edict was penalised with death.

Against this backdrop, there emerged Hasidim (the "pious ones"), who found their identity in the faithful observance of the Torah, over against the Hellenisers. The Hasidim are mentioned in 1 Maccabees as ἰσχυροὶ δυνάμει (mighty warriors, 2:42) and the πρῶτοι (first among [the Israelites], 7:13) and again in 2 Macc 14:16 in connection with the Maccabean rebellion. Based on these references, Victor Tcherikover and John Kampen opine that the Hasidim belonged to an influential group with position of authority and high social standing.[25] But Hengel thinks that Hasidim were rather "a relatively self-contained group," a "penitential movement," which emerged as a Jewish party at the time of Hellenistic reform during 175–170 BCE[26]—a group probably responsible for the origins of Jewish *apocalyptic* literature.[27]

However, Stegemann and Stegemann argue that it is problematic to connect the apocalyptic, the scribal and the Pharisaic in this group. They argue, Hasidim as "mighty warrior" could simply refer to their military importance rather than their social status. Furthermore, the Hasidim in 2 Macc 14:6 (as opposed to 1 Macc 2:42 and 7:13) were probably simply a "collective designation."[28] Anthony Saldarini expresses a similar view that Hasidim were "a broad spectrum of Jews who actively resisted Hellenization and defended piety, that is, their way of life, against

22 Horsley, *Bandits, Prophets, and Messiahs*, 13.

23 Freyne, *Galilee*, 36.

24 Koester, *History, Culture, and Religion of the Hellenistic Age* 213; Freyne, *Galilee*, 36.

25 Victor Tcherikover, *Hellenistic Civilization and the Jews* (Philadelphia: Jewish Publication Co., 1959), 126; John Kampen, *The Hasideans and the Origin of Pharisaim*, SCSS 24 (Atlanta: Scholars Press, 1988), 107, 113–114.

26 Hengel, *Judaism and Hellenism* 175.

27 Hengel, *Judaism and Hellenism*, 250.

28 Ekkehard W. Stegemann and Wolfgang Stegemann, *The Jesus Movement: A Social History of Its Frist Century*, trans. O. C. Dean, Jr. (Minneapolis: Fortress, 1999), 149.

attack from Antiochus rather than the name of a well defined group."[29] However, a gross generalisation that "All opponents of Hellenization were Hasideans"[30] cannot explain the potency of opposition to Hellenisation unless one posits at least an organised movement that refuse to cooperate with the establishment as if nothing were at stake.[31] John Kampen argues that the association of Judas Maccabeus with Hasidim in 2 Macc 14:6 has to be understood in the light of the rest of 2 Maccabees, because it is intentional. Given that the Hasidim were leading citizens devoted to the law, "The writer of this letter thought that by citing the Hasideans, the regard for and the prestige of Judah Maccabee would be enhanced."[32] Thus, it is likely that the Hasidim were not just a collective designation or people who separated themselves from the affairs of the nation but "an influential group, leading citizens of Israel, who bore some weight in matters concerning the Jews of Judaea."[33]

Second Maccabees presents the hasidic martyrs as the real heroes who stood against the imperial inquisition. The martyrdom of Eleazar and the seven brothers and their mothers (6:18–31; 7:1–42) occupies central importance. Eleazar, a scribe in high position was executed for refusing to eat swine's flesh. Seven brothers and the mother were tried, tortured, and executed one after the other, as they refused to submit to the emperor's wishes. At the execution of the third brother, Antiochus himself and those with him "were astonished at the young men's spirit, for he regarded his suffering as nothing" (7:12). When the turn of the mother came, she was filled with a noble spirit (7:21). She encouraged her last son "Do not fear this butcher, but prove worthy of your brothers" (7:29). The mother was executed after the seven brothers. Each one spoked with authority cursing the oppressors and expressing hope in the Lord of mercy as they met their death. Such courage and confidence of the faithful community in God in the cruel fate of death evokes the enabling power of God. According to Nickelsburg, the Hasidim chose to die than transgress their ancestors' law and "As the roll of the martyrs lengthens, the expectation increase that God must soon act to avenge the blood of the righteous."[34] Later the Hasidim take a turn from non-violent active resistance to militant resistance by joining hands with the Maccabean. Their resilience to keep the Torah even in the face of death with confidence in God's intervention is notable. The praxis of such a political theology evokes divine motivation for self-preservation

29 Anthony J. Saldarini, *Pharisees, Scribes and Sadducees in Palestinian Society: A Sociological Approach* (Grand Rapids: Eerdmans, 2001), 253.

30 Saldarini, *Pharisees, Scribes and Sadducees in Palestinian Society*, 253.

31 Cf. Koester, *History, Culture, and Religion of the Hellenistic Age*, 212.

32 Kampen, *The Hasideans and the Origin of Pharisaim*, 149.

33 Kampen, *The Hasideans and the Origin of Pharisaim*, 150.

34 George W. E. Nickelsburg, "1 and 2 Maccabees – Same Story, Different Meaning," 661.

3.2.2. Maccabean Movement

The events that led up to the Maccabean revolt were not simply a religio-cultural reactionary rebellion against Hellenism. The situation was more complex. According to Koester, though the "political infighting of leading (priestly) families" preceded the revolution, the turmoil that erupted in Jerusalem strikingly "coincides with the humiliation of the Syrian king Antiochus IV Epiphanes by the Romans ... and is closely related to the increasing financial difficulties of the Seleucid Empire" and hence, the traditional view that Jewish insurrection as a reaction to religious persecution is simplistic and untenable.[35] Freyne rightly notes the conglomeration of social, political, religio-cultural factors that caused the upheaval.[36]

Jason (the Zadokite high priest) initiated a Hellenistic reform, though he was not accused of setting aside the "laws of the fathers."[37] But the Syrian King Antiochus IV domesticated the Jewish high priest's office by installing Menelaus who was a non-Zadokite by ousting Jason to secure fund for his war campaign. However, there was opposition to Menelaus. Antiochus repressed opposition against Menelaus and also raided the temple's treasury in 169 BCE on his return from campaign against Egypt. When Antiochus left Jerusalem, the conservative Jews took possession of the city and locked up Menelaus in the Acra, the fortified Hellenistic quarter. Antiochus struck back a second time, who then captured Jerusalem, made it into a Greek city, transformed Yahweh's cult with a pagan cult,[38] and annulled the "laws of the fathers." Koester writes that Antiochus "forced the population to participate in the new pagan cult and he outlawed circumcision. The eating of pork became a test of loyalty.... It cannot be doubted that many Jews who were unwilling to deny their faith were cruelly executed and martyred."[39]

The Maccabean movement sparked out when a country priest Mattathias, from the Hasmon family, butchered an imperial agent who came to impose the imperial religious policy in a certain town Modein (1 Macc 2:15–30). The Maccabeans soon found alliance with the Hasidim who were loyal to the Torah (1 Macc 2:42), and opposed the Hellenistic reformers.[40] But as noted above, the Maccabean movement was not simply a religio-cultural reactionary movement. It also involved the issue of economic exploitation and the loss of social and

35 Koester, *History, Culture, and Religion of the Hellenistic Age*, 210, 212.

36 Freyne, *Galilee*, 36.

37 Koester, *History, Culture, and Religion of the Hellenistic Age*, 211.

38 Eduard Loshe, *The New Testament Environment*, trans. John E. Steely (Nashville: Abingdon, 1976), 25; Koester, *History, Culture, and Religion of the Hellenistic Age*, 212.

39 Koester, *History, Culture, and Religion of the Hellenistic Age*, 213.

40 Koester, *History, Culture, and Religion of the Hellenistic Age*, 213.

economic status, owing to the imperial policy.[41] The economic aggrandisement policy of the Seleucids was clear in the plan to confiscate the land of those faithful to Mosaic law, sell them off into slavery and resettle foreigners in the confiscated land in order to raise funds to pay war indemnity to the Romans (1 Macc 3:35–36, 41).

The Maccabeans had successes (1 Macc 3:27–4:35). And in their success they expropriated the spoils of the Hellenistic aristocracy "to those who had been tortured and to the orphans and widows, and also to the aged," sharing thus equally to their own (2 Macc 8:30). Finally, the Maccabees under Judas recaptured Jerusalem in 164 BCE and immediately purified the temple and celebrated Hanukkah, which later became an annual festival (1 Macc 4:36–59). However, the new high priest Alcimus (an Aaronide) of the rededicated temple was a sympathiser of Hellenism. In a turn of events, Alcimus seized sixty Hasidim and killed them (1 Macc 7:12–18), which dented the initial success of the Maccabeans. Judas himself was defeated and killed by the Seleucid. Nevertheless, the Judean peasantry and the Maccabee brothers continued their resistant guerrilla warfare and later achieved politically independent Jewish state.[42]

The political ambition of the Hasmoneans certainly derailed the egalitarian ideals of the early resistance movement. Especially, when Jonathan achieved a semi-autonomous temple-state, he also assumed the office of the high priest that caused some segment of Hasidim to break away from the temple cult of Jerusalem. Nevertheless, this episode of Jewish history is an episode of pride for the Jews who were volleyed from one empire to the other for centuries.

The First Maccabees is a work under royal patronage to defend the Hasmonean legitimacy to high-priestly dynasty (2:23–26; cf. Num 25:6–12), recounting Mattathias' heroic act that subsequently brought political independence, possibly against its Pharisaic and Essene opponents.[43] However, notwithstanding this ideological orientation, the book portrays the basic conviction of the people that it was God who preserved Israel. Judas began his battles with

41 Cf. Gerd Theissen and Annette Merz, *The Historical Jesus: A Comprehensive Guide*, trans. John Bowden (London: SCM, 1998), 132.

42 However, the course of the Maccabees shows, they move away from their primary support base, the Jewish people and the Hasidim, and built a Hasmonean Dynasty in the manner of a Hellenistic Kingdom albeit their initial anti-Hellenistic rebellion. By the time of Hyrcanus son of Simon, the Hasmonean kingdom stretched out to Jaffa. Alexander Jannaeus succeeded Hyrcanus and extended the boundaries of the kingdom to the Galilee, Samaria, and the entire Palestine. However, the power struggle between his two sons Hyrcanus II and Aristobulus II opened the way for Roman intervention. Pompey himself led his army towards Jerusalem and seized the city in 63 BCE. This signifies the end of the independent Jewish state, which lasted for about a century.

43 George W. E. Nickelsburg, *Jewish Literature Between the Bible and the Mishnah: A Historical and Literary Introduction* (Philadelphia: Fortress, 1981), 114; ibid, "1 and 2 Maccabees – Same Story, Different Meaning," 662.

prayer (1 Macc 3:46–47; 4:30–33; 5:33); praising the Lord, the "Savior of Israel" after battle is won (4:24, 33, 55). Victory came not from military prowess but from God. This conviction was evident in Judas' address to his fainting comrades: "It is easy for many to hemmed in by few, for in the sight of Heaven there is no difference between saving by many or by few. It is not on the size of the army that victory in battle depends, but strength comes from Heaven" (3:18–19).[44] The Maccabean movement shows counter social formation of the subjugated from the margins of the empire. The movement and its counter discourse of power must be seen in the light of the people's struggle for freedom from colonial domination and exploitation of the land and the people. It is significant that this resistance movement from the periphery invokes the power of God and pledges their confidence in God the Saviour of Israel.

3.2.3. Qumran Movement

The Maccabean triumph was not a straightforward victory of godliness and justice over idolatry and tyranny. It was accompanied by serious upheavals, which had lasting social and religious implications. A deep-seated conflict emerged between the Hasidim and the Hasmonean when Jonathan Maccabeus, a priest but not a Zadokite, usurped the priestly office in 153–152 BCE under the aegis of the Syrian king Alexander Balas. For the faithful, it was an illegitimate usurping of power. But when Jonathan was executed by the Syrian general Tryphon in 143–142 BCE, Simon Maccabee was again appointed high priest and "hereditary leader of the people by means of a decree passed by a Jewish national assembly."[45] The Qumranites were most possibly a group who were bewildered at the high handedness of the Hasmonean for power.

Given the strong similarities of the Essenes as described by the writers of late antiquity[46] and the Qumran community as attested by the Dead Sea Scrolls, there is a general consensus that the Qumranites were one group of Essenes who settled at Khirbet Qumran.[47] Some scholars opine that the Wicked Priest found

44 Jonathan who succeeded Judas Maccabeus was also a mighty warrior. Like Judas, he too recognises that his help comes from God (1 Macc 9:43–46; 11:71; 12:15). However, it is notable that, the ideological discourse of 1 Maccabees accused the Aaronide high priest Alcimus as a Hellenist and endorsed Jonathan's high priesthood. Historically, this event did not go down very well with the Hasidim who supported the Hasmonean in the revolt against the colonial regime.

45 Geza Vermes, *The Dead Sea Scrolls: Qumran in Perspective*, rev. ed. (London: SCM, 1994), 123.

46 Reports about the Essenes are also found in Philo, *Good Person,* 75–91, *J. W.* 2. 119–161 and Hippolytus, *Refutation of All Heresies* 9.18–28, as well as occasional remarks in the writings of Pliny and Dio Chrysostom. Koester, *History, Culture, and Religion of the Hellenistic Age*, 234.

47 Koester, *History, Culture, and Religion of the Hellenistic Age*, 235. Nickelsburg cautions an uncritical identification of the Essenes and the Qumranites. He cites that there are three arguments against such identification. First, some Qumran scrolls reflect Sadducean halakah.

in the Qumran text refers to Simon (or less probably to Jonathan).[48] But it is most likely that the Wicked Priest in Qumran literatures evokes all the Hasmonean high priests who have illegitimately arrogated themselves the office.[49] Against the backdrop of Zadokites losing their legitimate high priesthood in Jerusalem temple, the Teacher of Righteousness (CD I, 9; plausibly a deposed Zadokite high priest) moved to the Judean desert and formed an alternative community as a substitute temple for the Jerusalem cult, which in his eyes had been profaned. Among the Qumran scrolls, 1QS, CD and the Halakic Letters present the core theological orientation and rules governing the community.[50] The Qumran understood itself as the elect people of God, "the people of the renewed covenant of the last days"[51] (1QS V, 7–8, 21), "the eschatological community of God's people."[52] Nickelsburg writes, "Believing that the cult of Jerusalem was defiled, the Qumranites understood their community to be the temple of God, where they sacrificed and effected atonement for the Holy Land through their prayers and observance of the Torah (1QS 9:3–7; cf. 1QH 14[6]:22–29)."[53] They based their life according to the interpretation of the Torah that had been revealed to the Righteous Teacher, the Zadokite priest and the founder of the community.[54]

Qumranites believed that the community was being constituted in the spirit of holiness (1QS IX, 3), to offer atonement for the land "until there shall come the prophet and the messiahs of Aaron and Israel" (1QS IX, 11). The Community Rule (1QS) IV, 20–21 stated: "and then God will purge by his truth all the deeds of man…to cleanse him through a holy spirit from all wicked practices, sprinkling upon him a spirit of truth as purifying water." Also 1QS III, 7b–8a stated, "He shall be cleansed from all his sins by the spirit of holiness uniting him to His truth, and his iniquity shall be expiated by the spirit of uprightness and humility." The

---

Secondly, not all details of Philo, Josephus and Hippolytus description of Essenes coincide with the community rule (1QS). Thirdly, early Judaism was more complex than Josephus four categorical groups can circumscribe. Hence, Qumranites need not be forced into one of these four groups. See Nickelsburg, *Ancient Judaism and Christian Origins*, 168, 175. Despite this caution, the Qumran-Essene identification has been strongly argued recently by Kenneth Atkinson and Jodi Magness. Cf. Kenneth Atkinson and Jodi Magness, "Josephus Essenes and the Qumran Community," *JBL* 129 (2010): 317–342.

48 Nickelsburg, *Jewish Literature Between the Bible and the Mishnah*, 123; Koester, *History, Culture, and Religion of the Hellenistic Age*, 235.

49 Cf. Jerome Murphy-O'Connor, "The Judean Desert," in *Early Judaism and Its Modern Interpreters*, eds., R. A. Kraft and George W. E. Nickelsburg (Philadelphia: Scholars, 1986), 140.

50 Nickelsburg, *Ancient Judaism and Christian Origins*, 168.

51 Koester, *History, Culture, and Religion of the Hellenistic Age*, 236.

52 Nickelsburg, *Ancient Judaism and Christian Origins*, 169.

53 Nickelsburg, *Ancient Judaism and Christian Origins*, 169.

54 Nickelsburg, *Ancient Judaism and Christian Origins*, 169; Koester, *History, Culture, and Religion of the Hellenistic Age*, 236.

community believed that they were purified by the Holy Spirit so as to maintain a righteous community vis-à-vis the outside world. The passion and vitality of the Qumran community was shown by their continued existence for over 200 years until they were destroyed by the Roman legions at the end of the Jewish war in 70 CE.

The Qumran formation of an alternative pious community was not simply a quietist religious-spiritual formation of a group disenchanted by the politics of the outside world; it was political as well. In the context where the Hasmonean inverted the theocratic political foundation with the Zadokite high priesthood to a form of semi-Hellenised oriental state with the king as the high priest, the Qumranites dissented the distortion of the political and religious life of Israel. Their retreat to the Dead Sea was a protest against the incumbent political establishment that gave way to the status quo of the empire. The Qumranites forged to preserve and maintain an Israelite identity pure and unpolluted from the forces of political and cultural imperialism of the empire. Their passion and vitality shows a will to order their lives according to the traditions of their own against the tide of colonial domination and its cultural production.

3.2.4. Pharisaic Movement

The origin of the Pharisees[55] is obscure, though a majority of scholars place it at the time of the Hasmoneans.[56] The Pharisees (like the Essenes) seemed to bear the basic currents that influenced the Torah-loyal Hasidim, the supporters of Maccabean revolt in the second century. Jacob Neusner cautions that, a historical quest about the Pharisees "promises modest results," since the three sources (Josephus, New Testament and rabbinic literature), that tell about them were shaped by ideological interests, beliefs and concerns.[57]

Josephus portrays the Pharisees as a strong political force in the Jewish state (Josephus, *J.W.* 1.88–98; *Ant.* 13.372–373, 379–383, 401–404). The Pharisees had a strong mass support such that whatever they said gained credence (*Ant.* 13.288). The Sadducees had the support only of the rich, but the Pharisees had

---

55 Ancient witnesses about the Pharisees are found in three sources: Josephus, Gospels of the New Testament and rabbinic tradition, especially in the Mishnah. Each of the sources presents a biased picture of the group though in different ways. Jacob Neusner, *From Politics to Piety: The Emergence of Pharisaic Judaism* (New Jersey: Prentice-Hall, 1973), 1; Koester, *History, Culture, and Religion of the Hellenistic Age*, 239. Anthony J. Saldarini, "Pharisees," *ABD* 5:289.

56 M. Simon thinks that the Pharisees originated "either at Hyrcanus or Janeaus time." M. Simon, *Jewish Sect at the Time of Jesus*, trans. J. H. Farley (Philadelphia: Fortress, 1967), 21. R. Meyer, "Pharisees," *TDNT* 9:13 maintains that the Pharisees began "to organise themselves firmly" at the beginning of the first century CE. S. Zeitlin has dated it to the postexilic time of Ezra and identified with the *perushim* who refused to follow the rule of the Zadokite. Cf. S. Zeitlin, "The Pharisees: A Historical Study," *JQR* 52 (1961): 97–128.

57 Neusner, *From Politics to Piety*, 2.

the multitude on their side (*Ant.* 13.298). The New Testament also speaks of the power of the Pharisees as sitting on the seat of Moses (Matt 23). Cohen argues that, the power of the Pharisees was not in the control of the state as such but it consisted in the soft power of their piety and in the knowledge of sitting on Moses' seat.[58] Though, the origin of Pharisaism is not clear, the political significance of the Pharisees during the Hasmonean rule has been widely acknowledged by scholars.[59] Especially during the reign of Alexandra Salome (76–67 BCE), the Pharisees dictated the state policies. The Pharisees also seem to have had political leverage during the initial rule of Herod, but in a turn of events involving a court intrigues Herod repressed the Pharisees and executed several of the leaders, and thus they lost political significance to influence the state as an organised group, though individual Pharisees appears to be actively political in the first century.[60] In the changed political situation, the Pharisees' turned to define what living Judaism in a time of powerlessness.

Jacob Neusner maintains that, the Pharisees evolved themselves "from politics to piety" during the Herodian period only to enter politics again in the post 70 CE. He writes,

> The Pharisees determined to concentrate on what they believed was really important in politics, which was fulfillment of all the laws of Torah, even ritual purity and tithing, to achieve elevation of the life of all the people, at home and in the streets, to what the Torah had commanded: *You shall be a kingdom of priests and a holy people*.... The Temple altar in Jerusalem would be replicated at the tables of all Israel (emphasis original).[61]

However, Anthony Saldarini opines that the Pharisaic agenda of holiness was not as such a shift from "politics to piety" but a sign of political will for self-preservation. Saldarini writes, "These [Pharisaic] laws set out an agenda of holiness for the land and people which was a fitting response for a powerless people dominated by the Romans because these laws pertain to the parts of domestic life which can be controlled by people out of power in their own society: food, sex and marriage."[62] The Pharisaic investment of profound meaning to the mundane activities of the daily realm of life was a mode of resistance against the political and cultural imperialism of the empire. Hence, the Pharisees in fact turned to the "politics of piety" by defining the private space of the people which

---

58 Cohen, *From the Maccabees to the Mishnah*, 148.

59 Neusner, *From Politics to Piety*, 45–66, 146; Ellis Revkin, *A Hidden Revolution* (Nashville: Abingdon, 1978), 31–50, 211–45; Cohen, *From Maccabees to the Mishnah*, 144–46.

60 Jacob Neusner, *From Politics to Piety*, 65–66. Also see Koester, *History, Culture, and Religion of the Hellenistic Age*, 241.

61 Neusner, *From Politics to Piety*, 146.

62 Saldarini, *Pharisees, Scribes and Sadducees in Palestinian Society*, 213.

will have lasting significance for Jewish identity preservation at a time when Jews were weak and could not maintain their independence and were hence forced to reconcile themselves to the new situation of powerlessness. Ellis Rivkin is partly right in calling Pharisaism as a "hidden revolution," though his preponderance on the Pharisees as a group of religious scholars and intellectuals is problematic.[63]

Saldarini argues that the Pharisees were political interest groups actively seeking to influence the society and hence they are best understood as a reform movement with a web of network of social relations filling many social roles as retainers.[64] They "were not a simple group with a limited, concrete goal but a long, well-connected, voluntary, corporate organization which sought to influence Jewish society and entered into many mutual relationships to accomplish their aims."[65] Neusner argues that, in the context of Roman domination, they "invested powerlessness with such meaning that ordinary folk living everyday lives, might still regard themselves as a kingdom of priests and a holy people."[66] The resilience of Pharisaic movement, which metamorphosed into Rabbinic Judaism in the absence of the temple, deserves critical appreciation. The Pharisees like any other Jewish social groups attempted to make sense of what is living Judaism for the weak Jewish nation in the late Second Temple period.

Jon L. Berquist writes, "[i]mperialization is a strong and momentous force in human history, but it always breeds resistance."[67] After the end of the monarchy, the Jews experienced living under different imperial powers. As a subjected people, resistance and accommodation went hand in hand as they responded to the material cultural melting pot of (Hellenistic) empire(s) with new imaginations to assert their identity. In order to move beyond the immediacy of colonial atrocities upon their culture, economy, religion and politics, several movements and group formations emerged, each with a divine sense of guidance, and tried to woo their fellow Jews to respond to their movements. Some groups were certainly quietist and some were reformist, however, each grouping has to be seen in the light of colonial resistance to empire.

3.3. Jewish Resistance Movements Against Roman Imperialism in Palestine

The group formations within Second Temple Judaism antecedent to Jesus' movement have highlighted how the Jewish society mostly from the upper strata responded to the politics of empire formation. Popular resistance movements that emerged against Roman imperialism formed the immediate background and the

---

63 Revkin, *Hidden Revolution*, 211–251.

64 Saldarini, *Pharisees, Scribes and Sadducees in Palestinian Society*, 281.

65 Saldarini, *Pharisees, Scribes and Sadducees in Palestinian Society*, 284.

66 Neusner, *From Politics to Piety*, 154.

67 Jon L. Berquist "Resistance and Accommodation in the Persian Empire," in *In The Shadow of Empire*, ed. Richard A. Horsley (Louisville: Westminster John Knox, 2008), 54.

foreground of Jesus' movement.[68] In the immediate period of Jesus' mission and the first generation of Jesus' movements, Jewish peasants and ordinary people in Palestine mounted popular resistance violently and non-violently against the political domination, economic exploitation and cultural imperialism of the Roman rule and its client rulers in Jerusalem. According to Richard Horsley, the ideology underpinning Jewish resistance movements was anchored on to the "central social memories of the origin and formation of Israel as an independent people"[69]—liberated from the foreign rule of Pharaoh and covenanted on Sinai with God as their true king that excludes oppressive human rulers. But to explicate why there were so many resistance movements and why it emerged mostly from the lower stratum, one has to view how the Roman Empire operated from the vantage point of the colonised.

The impact of the Maccabean revolt[70] must have brought relief to the Jewish peasantry economically (2 Macc 8:30)[71] as it gained temporary political independence from the Seleucids by forging alliance with the Romans.[72] However, the Jewish political independence was short lived as the Roman hegemony cast its shadow over Palestine in the political vacuum created by the decline of the Seleucids and the Ptolemaic Empire. Rome took over Palestine in 63 BCE and became the colonial master of the Jews. The Romans continued the legacy of the political and economic administration of the Hellenistic Empires that was extractive and exploitative.[73] John Kautsky identifies that Roman empire is not purely an aristocratic empires like Egypt, Mesopotamia and early medieval Europe

---

68 For detail reading of popular resistance movements in Roman Palestine, refer to Horsley and Hanson, *Bandits, Prophets, and Messiahs.*

69 Richard A. Horsley, *Jesus in Context: Power, People, and Performance* (Minneapolis: Fortress, 2008), 38.

70 For a detailed reading see Louis H. Feldman and Meyer Reinhold, *Jewish Life and Thought among Greeks and Romans: Primary Readings* (Minneapolis: Fortress, 1996), 147–148; Koester, *History, Culture, and Religion of the Hellenistic Age*, 210–215. For ancient sources refer to *Ant.* 12.265–326, I and II Maccabees.

71 It is possible that the Maccabean freed the Jewish peasants from the imperial taxation and distributed land among the people, though part of the liberated land become royal property leased to tenants. The later Hasmonean annexed extensive territories, which most probably became royal property or distributed to Jewish notables as estates. Cf. Applebaum, "Economic Life in Palestine," 635.

72 The Hasmoneans were encouraged by their alliance with Rome in the wake of waning Seleucids power to enhance their territory. They expanded their territory to Samaria, destroying the Temple on Mount Gerezim in 122 BCE and destroying the city of Samaria in 109 BCE. To the South, the Hasmoneans annexed the territory of the Arab tribe of the Idumeans and forcibly converted them to Judaism. See John Stambaugh and David Balch, *The Social World of the First Christians* (London: SPCK, 1994), 22.

73 M. Rostovtzeff, *The Social and Economic History of the Hellenistic World*, vol. 2 (Oxford: Clarendon, 1941), 1000; K. C. Hanson and Douglas E. Oakman. *Palestine in the Time of Jesus: Social Structures and Social Conflicts.* Minneapolis: Fortress, 1998), 114.

but as partly "commercialised," in that, there existed a significant merchant class, private ownership of land apart from the aristocrats who controlled the agriculture economy. Nevertheless, the vast majority of the population, the peasants were not free to farm and marketise their products for their gains.[74] Dominic Crossan tersely summarises what this commercialism means in Roman Empire:

> Put bluntly: in a traditional agrarian empire, the aristocracy takes the (agricultural) surplus (of the land) from the peasantry; in a commercializing agrarian empire, the aristocracy takes the land (itself) from the peasantry. The former devours the industry and productivity of the peasantry; the latter their very identity and dignity. Commercialization moves (… the peasant) in increasing numbers down the terrible slope from small freeholder to tenant farmer to day-laborer to beggar or bandit.[75]

With the coming of the Roman rule, the Jewish peasantry, which had been virtually free of fiscal exactions since the liberation of Judea by Simon Maccabeus, was crushed by the extractive exaction of Pompey and his successors that was compounded by the client king Herod.[76] The drastic land re-organisation following Pompey's conquest of Palestine must have meant "the creation of a very considerable class of landless Jewish peasants."[77] More and more land was controlled by the elites and, conversely, more and more Palestinian Jews came under tenancy arrangement. According to Applebaum, Ezechias' struggle was part of the conflicts that followed the drastic land reorganisation by the Romans, and such a conflict found its initial expression in marginal areas where Jews and non-Jews intersected.[78] The parable of the tenants (Luke 20:9–19 cf. Matt 21:33–46) illustrates the sharp antagonism of the tenants and the landlord to the extent that the tenants were ready to kill the heir of the landlord and take over the property.

Since the elites controlled the land, production became elite centred, who wanted crops that filled their estate storehouse (Luke 12:18) or had commercial

---

74 John Kautsky, *The Politics of Aristocratic Empires*, 20.

75 Crossan, *The Birth of Christianity*, 157–158.

76 Applebaum, "Economic Life in Palestine," 661.

77 Applebaum, "Economic Life in Palestine," 637. It is striking to note that every Hasmonean rebel found ready support from the peasantry, especially from the dissatisfied landless folks, in their opposition against the Romans (*J. W.* 1.153 cf. *Ant.* 14.334). In fact the activities of Ezechias, the father of Judas the Galilean showed signs of things to come in Palestine. He led struggle against the villages of the area of Tyre, till he was caught and executed by Herod while the latter was the governor of Galilee (47 BCE, *Ant.* 14.159; *J. W.* 1.204).

78 Applebaum, "Economic Life in Palestine," 638. A precise estimate of average land holding at this period is difficult. The two kinsmen of Jesus of Nazareth held 39 plethra or 4.78 hectares which supported two families in Western Samaria (Eusebius, *Hist. eccl.* 3. 20. 1–2). The Mishnah and Bar Kochba contracts show that some units measured as little as 0.3 – 0.1 hectares (Mishnah, B. Batra 1.6). Applebaum, "Economic Life in Palestine," 657.

value.[79] Hanson and Oakman have pointed that during the time of Jesus even fishing which was an important part of the Palestinian economy was not a free enterprise but state-run enterprise, and involved a complex web of financial relationship.[80] Besides food products, essential commodities such as pottery, metal working, clothe weaving, leather working, wood craft, oil and wine making were produced by specialised artisans. But these specialties also tended to be monopolised by families who nurtured a trade secret. That means, powerful families controlled the production and distribution of specialised commodities.[81]

Herodian collaboration with the Romans puts intense economic pressure upon the Jewish peasantry for several decades by several layers of tax, tributes and tithes.[82] Herod confiscated the estate of his opponents (*Ant.* 17.305, 307). Probably Herod considered the whole land under his rule as his personal possession like a Hellenistic king.[83] Herod undertook extensive building projects and indulged in astounding munificence to foreign cities and imperial family members. He completely rebuilt the city of Samaria and renamed it Sebaste (*Ant.* 15. 292–298) in honour of Augustus. He also built a completely new port Caesarea (*Ant.* 15.331). He also greatly extended and refurnished the Jerusalem temple, which became a wonder for anyone to see (Luke 21:5 cf. John 2:20). His descendants continued Herod's legacy of massive building. Herod Antipas built two Hellenistic cities Sepphoris and Tiberias (*Ant.* 18.27, 36–38). Agrippa I too tried to imitate his predecessors.[84]

---

79 K. C. Hanson and Douglas E. Oakman. *Palestine in the Time of Jesus: Social Structures and Social Conflicts* (Minneapolis: Fortress, 1998), 106.

80 In Roman Palestine fishing was highly regulated, taxed and hierarchical. At the top, the emperor received port taxes, the Herods (client ruler, tetrarch) control the sea, harbors and sales fishing right to brokers. Fishing families or cooperatives bid for fishing contracts or leases from the brokers and they employ hired laborers in catching the fish. Fish processors' workshops were also taxed, and in marketing, carters and shippers could also be taxed for use of roads, bridges, ports, and crossing of Roman boundaries. The whole point is that, there are multiple and repeated taxes involved in fishing. Hanson and Oakman, *Palestine in the Time of Jesus*, 106–107, 109.

81 Hanson and Oakman, *Palestine in the Time of Jesus*, 110–111.

82 F. C. Grant, *The Economic Background of the Gospels* (London: Oxford University Press, 1926), 87–91; Applebaum, "Economic Life in Palestine," 661–664.

83 He probably treated the major part of Perea, Hulata, Bashan, Golan and the Trachonitis as crown domain. His family held land in Idumea (*Ant.* 16.291), in the western plain of Esdraelon (Josephus, *Life* 119) and round Jabneh (*Ant.* 18.32). He settled and allocated of fruitful land to veterans at Sebaste (*J.W.* 1.403; *Ant.* 15.296), which would naturally effect a total land distribution. Cf. Applebaum, "Economic Life in Palestine," 658.

84 Compare *Ant.* 19.335–337 and 351–352 with 19.328–331. See Richard A. Horsley, "Popular Prophetic Movements at the Time of Jesus: Their Principal Features and Social Origins," in *New Testament Background: A Sheffield Reader*, ed. Craig A. Evans and Stanley E. Porters (Sheffield: Sheffiled Academic, 1997), 142.

Roman rule subjected the Jewish peasants to three layers of rulers and their respective demands for revenues such as tribute to Rome, taxes to Herod, and tithes and offerings to the temple and priesthood. Direct taxes included the *tributum agri*, levied on agricultural products, and the *tributum capitis*, a tax on each person living within a territory or province of which one denarius was collected. Indirect taxes were market taxes (cities), transit tolls, port tax, access rents—city controlled resources,—labor for state projects such as building of aqueducts, roads etc.[85] It is estimated that Herod the Great claimed 25–33 percent of the Palestinian grain and 50 percent of the fruit from trees.[86] Jerusalem temple had its own exaction of resources from the people in the form of tithe (for support of priest), head tax (half-shekel per year), agricultural products and animal offerings as well as material goods vowed to the temple.

The heavy and competing taxation of the Roman taxation system and the temple ensured that debts would increase.[87] Rising indebtedness and loss of land led to the breakdown of the traditional village based social structure as well as the economic structure.[88] Direct evidences of debt crisis come from Josephus' description of the burning of the debts archives by the rebels at the beginning of the Jewish revolt (66–73 CE; see *J.W.* 2.426–427) and the *prosbul* measure attributed to Hillel.[89] Luke 12:58–59 (cf. Matt 5:25–26) pictures a situation where it is better to settle disputes informally than to opt for official justice. The temple oligarchy controlled not only the Great Sanhedrin, which interpreted the Law, but also the local courts through the elders. The firm enforcement of debt contracts through the courts led to the expansion of large estates, while tenancy and landlessness increased to a high scale in the time before the first

---

85 Richard J. Cassidy, *Jesus, Politics, and Society: A Study of Luke's Gospel* (Maryknoll, NY: Orbis Books, 1978), 96; Hanson and Oakman, *Palestine in the Time of Jesus*, 114.

86 Hanson and Oakman, *Palestine in the Time of Jesus*, 114.

87 Josephus records that a Judean delegation was sent to Rome to complain the over taxation of Herod I, when he died (*Ant.* 17.304–308). Yet in another occasion, ten years after Archelaus was banished, another delegation from Judea and Syria made a long trip to Rome to protest the excessive taxes that were being levied by the Roman Governors of Syria and Judea. However, the system seemed to have remained the same because in 37 CE the tax rates in Judea was so high that the Roman governor of Syria made a special intervention to abolish the market taxes for Jerusalem (*Ant.* 18. 90–95). Cf. Cassidy, *Jesus, Politics, and Society*, 96–97.

88 Richard A. Horsley, "The Imperial Situation of Palestinian Jewish Society," in *The Bible and Liberation: Political and Social Hermeneutics*, ed. Norman K. Gottwald and Richard A. Horsley. Maryknoll, NY: Orbis Books, 1993), 401.

89 The *prosbul* measure attributed to Hillel evaded the prescription of Deut 15:1–2 and permanently turned debtor over to the creditor through the agency of courts. Whether understood as collection guarantee by the judge or as of the court-forced confiscation of security land, the debtor could be evicted from patrimonial land or legally redefined as a tenant. In the Mishnah, Sanh. 3.6 shows that court situations typically involved debt disputes. Hanson and Oakman, *Palestine in the Time of Jesus*, 152.

Judean Revolt.[90] It is in this matrix of redistributive imperial economy, popular resistance movements as well as Jesus' movement emerged.

3.3.1. Popular Messianic Movements

Jesus of Nazareth was not the only person executed on the charge of being "king of the Jews." Both before and after Jesus of Nazareth, there were several popular leaders, mostly from the peasantry, who, according to Josephus, laid claim to the kingdom, donned the "diadem," or were proclaimed "king," as they succeed temporarily in seizing power (*Ant.* 17.271–274). According to Horsley, this "messiahing" was rooted in the Israelite cultural traditions of enthroning popular kingship in Israel (e.g., David) which had three characteristics: "Kingship was constituted by *popular* election or *anointing*; it was *conditional* on the king's maintenance of a certain social policy and the anointing of a new king was generally a *revolutionary* action" (emphasis original).[91] The expectation of a royal Davidic future king was much cultivated in the prophets. However, during the Persian and the Hellenistic Empires (Sir 47:11, 22; 1 Macc 2:57) and even in the time of Maccabean revolt, messianic expectation remained dormant.[92] The resurgence of messianic expectation began to show in the Dead Sea Scrolls and Ps. Sol. 17 which are dated to the Hasmonean rule. Most probably, the illegitimate and ineffective political leadership of the Hasmonean dynasty catalysed the revival of messianic expectation and later the same aggravated by the brutal Roman conquest and Herod's unpopular kingship. It is against this background the Lukan hymn, "He has raised up a mighty savior for us in the house of his servant David" (Luke 1:69) would properly be heard.

The events that led up to the Jewish war saw widespread popular expectation of an anointed king. Josephus puts it plainly that, "what more than all else incited them to the war was an ambiguous oracle, likewise found in their sacred scriptures, to the effect that at that time someone from their country would become ruler of the world" (*J.W.* 6.312 [Thackeray, LCL]).[93] Tacitus wrote about a momentous

---

90 Hanson and Oakman, *Palestine in the Time of Jesus*, 153.

91 Richard A. Horsley, "Popular Messianic Movement Around the Time of Jesus," *CBQ* 46 (1984): 477. Horsley and Hanson make a distinction between popular kingship and official royal ideology of kingship. Israelite traditions show that anointing of a king from Saul and David to the later kings by people or prophet was a revolutionary act. Anointing king in its origin was to secure and centralise political-military power against foreign domination by the Philistines. The designation of Jeroboam as king (1 Kgs 11:26–40; 12:16–20) and the anointing of Jehu (2 Kgs 9:1–13) was a revolutionary act to overthrow an oppressive incumbent regime. In contrast, royal ideology viewed Davidic monarchy along with the temple, as a guarantee for the nation, regardless of the justice and injustice of royal rule. Horsley and Hanson, *Bandits, Prophets, and Messiahs*, 94–98.

92 Horsley and Hanson, *Bandits, Prophets, and Messiahs*, 101.

93 All the quotations of Josephus in this work, unless otherwise specified, are from *Josephus*, trans. Henry St. J. Thakeray et al. 10 vols, LCL (Cambridge: Harvard University Press, 1926–1965).

vision[94] that appeared at the peak of Jewish war stating, "Some few put a fearful meaning on these events, but in most there was a firm persuasion, that in the ancient records of their priests was contained a prediction of how at this very time the East was to grow powerful, and rulers, coming from Judea, were to acquire universal empire" (*Hist.* 5.13).[95] However, for the subjugated Palestinian Jews, there was no ambiguity in rallying hope on a new David who would defeat the foreign rule and establish justice for the nation.[96] Five messianic claimants surfaced in two different episodes around the time of Jesus: once after the death of Herod I in 4 BCE and then during the Jewish revolt against Rome. Except for the Sicarii Menahem, who was from a retainer class, the rest were "men of humble origins."[97]

When Herod the Great died in 4 BCE, a number of revolts erupted led by popular figures acclaimed as kings by the followers. First, Josephus records about Judas, son of Ezechias, who organised at Sepphoris in Galilee a big number of desperate men and stormed the royal armories and armed his followers with an "ambition for royal rank" (*Ant.* 17.271–272 cf. *J.W.* 2.56). Second, Simon, a slave of Herod plundered the royal palace in Jericho, set fire on many of the royal houses in several places of the country and allowed his followers to take the spoils (*Ant.* 17.273–276). He put a "diadem on his head" and his followers declared him to be "king" (*Ant.* 17. 273–274). Third, in Judea, Athronges and his brothers attacked the Romans and managed to maintain the people's independence in the Judean hill-country for quite sometime (*Ant.*17.278–285). However, the Roman army mercilessly crushed all these revolts with temerity. Nonetheless, these revolts provided a momentous event of celebration for the poor over the rich, in which the powerful were being pull down from their pedestal and common folks rose to prominence, and the spoils of the rich being shared by the poor peasants (cf. Luke 2:52–53). The description of charismatic qualities of Simon recalls Saul and David.[98] Similarly, Athronges was a shepherd, which resembles David's legend. The movements show some oragnisational pattern of armed bands for military purpose.[99]

---

94 At the zenith of Jewish war, it was said that, there appeared a vision of armies in conflict in the sky, followed by a sudden lightning flash that lit up the Temple, abruptly opening the temple doors, and a voice from heaven (cf. Tacitus, *Hist.* 5.13).

95 All the quotations from Tacitus in this work are taken from Tacitus, *The Complete Works of Tacitus: The Annals, The History, The Life of Gnaeus Julius Agricola, Germany and Its Tribes, A Dialogue on Oratory*, trans. Alfred John Church and William Jackson Brodribb (New York: Random House 1942).

96 Horsley and Hanson, *Bandits, Prophets, and Messiahs*, 110.

97 J. D. Crossan, *The Historical Jesus: The Life of A Mediterranean Jewish Peasant* (New York: HarperSan Francisco, 1991), 198.

98 Stegemann and Stegemann, *Jesus Movement*, 178.

99 Horsley and Hanson, *Bandits, Prophets, and Messiahs*, 116.

There were two notable figures such as Menahem son Judas the Galilean from the group known as the Siicari, and Simon bar Giora from the Judean countryside who appeared in the scene as "king" in the climactic epoch of Jewish war against Roman rule. According to Horsley, Menahem was the only known example of a "king" or messianic pretender from any of the sects or parties, that is, the Pharisees, Essenes, Sadducees, or Fourth Philosophy/Sicarii.[100] Prior to the war, Menahem was not identified as the leader of the Sicarii.[101] But when the war broke out, Menahem probably led the Sicarii to capture Herod's arsenal at Masada to arm the group for the war (cf. *J.W.* 2. 433). Having armed his group, "he returned like a veritable king to Jerusalem, became the leader of the revolution, and directed the siege of the palace" (*J.W.* 2.434 [Thackeray]). The intense excitement over the liberation of Jerusalem from Roman control by a spontaneous popular uprising[102] provided an opportunity to Menahem to posture like a messiah and ruler. However, owing to his tyranny, Jerusalem revolutionaries opposed Menahem, killed him and drove out his followers.

Simon bar Giora of Gerasa was apparently a social bandit leader who robbed and plundered the rich (*J.W.* 2.652). As the Jewish revolutionaries struggled for power in the city, Simon bar Giora was expanding his group and influence throughout the Judean and Idumean countryside (*J.W.* 4.503–513). Strikingly, one sees Simon's social mindedness in his freeing the slaves and proclaiming liberty in the Judean country (*J.W.* 4.508).[103] Simon's rise to prominence to a great extent follows the model of David. Josephus reports that in Idumea, Simon first took Hebron, the city of David before his kingship (2 Sam 2:1–3; 5:3–5). When he was invited to enter the city by the opponents of John of Gischala, the people made "joyful acclamation to him, as their savior and preserver" (*J.W.* 4. 575). The messianic symbol was also reflected in the minting of coins with the inscription "Year 4" and "for the redemption of Zion" by Simon.[104] Simon preserved his royal claim till the last. When the Romans overpowered the revolt, he came out wearing a purple robe (*J.W.* 7.29). He was taken to Rome and executed there (*J.W.* 7.154–155).

3.3.2. Prophetic Resistance Movements

In addition to the main currents of group formation whose origin goes back to the Hellenistic-Hasmonean period, several religious phenomena and/or movements emerged during the Roman-Herodian period that can be interpreted as "indirect protest reactions to the socioeconomic and religio-political chaos in the land of

100 Richard A. Horsley, "Menahem in Jerusalem: A brief Messianic Episode among the Sicarii—Not 'Zealot Messianism,' " *NovT* 27 (1985): 340.

101 Horsley, "Menahem in Jerusalem," 338.

102 Horsley, "Menahem in Jerusalem," 345.

103 Martin Hengel, *The Zealots: Investigation into the Jewish Reform Movement in the Period from Herod I Until 70 A.D.*, trans. David Smith (Edinburgh: T&T Clark, 1989), 375.

104 Hengel, *The Zealots*, 297.

Israel."[105] Unlike the mainline sectarian group formations, these groups drew their supporters from the lower stratum and the underprivileged in the society. The movements in mind here were the so-called sign prophets,[106] individual prophetic figures some of which were wonderworkers, as well as that of John the Baptist (and Jesus). Stegemann and Stegemann distinguish "individual thaumaturgical and prophetic figures" from "prophetic-charismatic protest movements." They opine that, individual prophetic figures were charismatically gifted. But they did not organise a mass following or a close circle of followers. On the other hand, prophetic-chialistic movement mobilised large mass following and in the case of John the Baptist and Jesus both a larger following and a close circle of followers. They write, "[i]f the thaumaturgists (miracle workers) represented one answer to individuals distress, then the prophetic charismatic movement develops a liberation concept ... they had ... messages connected, not coincidentally, with the salvation-historical events of the people of Israel and venerated charismatic-prophetic figure of the past like Moses, Joshua, and Elijah."[107]

3.3.2.1. Thaumaturgical and Prophetic Figures

Albeit healers and exorcists were not limited to Palestine; two wonder workers such as Honi the "circle drawer" and Hanani ben Dosa were popularly known whose activities, in some respect corresponded to the presentation of Jesus in the Synoptic Gospels. Honi's tradition is found in Josephus (*Ant.* 14.22–24) and in the Mishnah (m. Ta'an. 3.8; cf. t. Ta'an. 2.13). He was a simple peasant, probably from Galilee, who had successfully prayed for rain in the manner of Elijah (1 Kgs 17:1) in a time of persistent drought shortly before the seize of Jerusalem by Pompey. Hanani ben Dosa apparently lived in dire poverty before 70 CE in Galilee near Sepphoris. Rabbinic tradition credits him with prayer miracles and healing miracles. Especially, he was ascribed to have the power of distant healing, like Jesus.[108] It is significant to note that both these figures functioned as miracle workers in a social circumstance of stress.

105 Stegemann and Stegemann, *Jesus Movement*, 163.

106 Horsley and Hanson classed two types of popular prophets at the time of Jesus such as action prophets (who leads movement like Moses) and oracular prophets (including John the Baptist) who were in the line of classical prophets. Horsley and Hanson, *Bandits, Prophets, and Messiahs*, 160–186. But Robert Webb criticises Horsley and Hanson arguing that though this classification implies action prophets did not pronounce oracles, but their action of calling people together would have involved some oracles. At the same time, just because John the Baptist had pronounced oracles it does not mean he is an oracular prophet and not an action prophet. Robert L. Webb, *John the Baptizer and Prophet: A Socio-Historical Study*, JSNTSup 62 (Sheffield: Sheffield Academic, 1991), 315, 353.

107 Stegemann and Stegemann, *Jesus Movement*, 163.

108 Stegemann, and Stegemann, *Jesus Movement*, 164–165.

3.3.2.2. Prophetic Protest Movements (Sign Prophets)

There were several "sign prophets" after Jesus of Nazareth who gathered huge crowds and led them to a significant locale anticipating a sort of eschatological deliverance from God. P. W. Barnett studied the intentions and origin of the Jewish sign prophets (40–70 CE) and ruled out several assumptions about them in scholarship.[109] Barnett argues that these signs prophets were neither Zealots/Sicarii nor pious charismatics, nor did they claim messiahship except for the Egyptian prophet, who was a self-styled prophet-king. He further inquired the common pattern of these prophetic movements, and strikingly found that Jesus too belonged to this pattern. "Each clearly was a *prophet.* A '*Sign*' was attempted by each man. A significant *locale* was involved on each occasion and a crowd of people was present" (emphasis original).[110]

Of the prophetic movements, the first perhaps was among the Samaritans (ca. 36 CE). A prophet led a crowd up to Mount Gerezim, the most sacred place, promising that they would recover the holy vessels from the tabernacle of the formative exodus-wilderness experience of Israel, buried at the spot where Moses had put them. Pontus Pilate, dispatched cavalry as well as infantry, killed some, took many prisoners, and executed the leaders (*Ant.* 18.85–87). The mass response to the prophet's call suggests that the people's yearning for liberation had reached a high pitch and their trust in the prophets' message of deliverance.[111]

About two decades later (56 CE), a similar movement emerged led by a Jewish prophet from Egypt at the time of the procurator Felix, who is mentioned in Josephus (*Ant.* 20.169–72; *J. W.* 2. 261–63) as well as in Acts 21:38. The "Egyptian" rallied many thousands up to the Mount of Olives, opposite Jerusalem.[112] The Roman Governor Felix, with heavily armed cavalry and infantry, killed hundreds of them, before the prophet himself and the others escaped (*Ant.* 20.169–72; *J. W.* 2. 261–63). Josephus presupposes that the Egyptian was a former Maccabean, who wanted to enter Jerusalem, take control of the temple mount, and claimed himself as ruler over the people. Luke also presented him as one who stirred up revolt with four thousand assassins (Acts 21:38).[113]

Josephus does not hold in high esteem these sign prophets. He callously describes these movements as "Deceivers and impostors, under the pretence of divine inspiration fostering revolutionary changes, they persuaded the multitude to act like madmen" (*J. W.* 2.259 [Thackeray]). However, Horlsey and Hanson argue that in the ordinary Palestinian Jewish context, the prophets were "filled

---

109 P. W. Barnett, "The Jewish Sign Prophets—A.D. 40–70—Their Intentions and Origins," *NTS* 27 (1980–81): 679–697.

110 Barnett, "The Jewish Sign Prophets," 689.

111 Horsley and Hanson, *Bandits, Prophets, and Messiahs*, 164.

112 According to Acts 21:38 there were 4000 assassins. Josephus numbered them as 30000 men.

113 Stegemann and Stegemann, *Jesus Movement*, 167.

with the Spirit."[114] Thus, the mass movement, however poorly organised, should be seen as people's liberation movement for a new order. Barnett surmises that these movements likely "looked for 'liberation' from their current political bondage and a re-acquisition of the land."[115]

3.3.2.3. John the Baptist Movement

The Baptist's movement is taken separately for study, as it is the precursor of Jesus' movement in the Gospels. The Baptist's movement is not simply a religious phenomenon. It has cultural, economic and political implications. For sure, John was said to come from a rural priestly family, which means that he belonged to the lower retainer stratum.[116] The Baptist's movement was not directly directed against the Romans, but against Herodians who were the client rulers. His preaching expressed criticism against the moral depravity of the ruling house, privileged identity of the elites,[117] and the socio-economic injustice perpetuated by the colonial rule. Theissen and Merz note that, "there is no mistaking the fact that the Baptist's movement, too, belongs in the series of renewal movements within Judaism which sought to preserve and redefine Jewish identity in the face of the Hellenistic pressure towards assimilation."[118]

The Gospel reports that Herod's arrest and execution of the Baptist occasioned in the latter's sharp denunciation of Herod Antipas divorcing his own wife and marrying his brother's wife. However, Horsley and Hanson observe that, John's denunciation of Antipas' second marriage was an occasion that provided Herod to arrest and execute John. The bigger issue was to do with the rising popularity of John that had potential political implications. Thus, the preaching of John in the Gospel about eschatological judgement and morality must not be taken as anything to do with politics of his day.[119] According to Josephus' account, Herod Antipas eliminated John the Baptist for fear of rebellion purely on the basis of suspicion (*Ant.* 18.116–119). Josephus writes about the Baptist as a good man who exhorted the Jews to lead righteous lives, administering justice to others with reverence to God. But when many joined the Baptist because they were aroused by his speeches, Herod became alarmed because the movement

114 Horsley and Hanson, *Bandits, Prophets, and Messiahs*, 161.

115 Barnett, "The Jewish Sign Prophets," 687.

116 Stegemann and Stegemann, *Jesus Movement*, 170.

117 Horsley and Hanson, *Bandits, Prophets, and Messiahs*, 179, argue that those who presume to claim, "We have Abraham as our father," (3:8) must be the priestly aristocracy. This is supported by the ambiguous position taken by the chief priest and the elders before Jesus on the question of the Baptist's baptism (Mark11:27–30). This suggests that the priestly aristocracy knew that the Baptist's preaching was a direct challenge to their power and authority.

118 Theissen and Merz, *Historical Jesus*, 144.

119 Horsley and Hanson, *Bandits, Prophets, and Messiahs*, 180.

might lead to some form of sedition and cause an uprising. And therefore, Herod imprisoned the Baptist and executed him (*Ant.* 18.116–119). Apparently, John the Baptist movement was a highly charged movement that challenged the ruling dispensation with warnings of its overthrow.

Charles Scobie thinks, "that John's Messianic preaching must have been completely *non*-political,"[120] except that when he condemned Antipas on moral grounds, the political implication of such condemnation became inevitable. On the other hand, Robert Webb claims that to relegate John the Baptist to the religious sphere alone is an inadequate view of "what a prophet is" and also "separates the realm of religion from the social and political issues."[121] Webb studied the prophetic activity of the Second Temple Judaism and identified three categories of prophets: clerical, sapiential and popular prophets. For him, John's ministry clearly has a socio-political orientation and John belongs to the category of popular prophets who leads a prophetic movement.[122] Paul W. Hollenbach posits that John emerges at a time of relative prosperity for the privileged in the society but impoverishment of the mass, and thus he claims that John the Baptist can be called a social rebel, "in so far as he leads a movement which sharply attacks the legitimacy of the current social structures."[123] Hollenbach contends that, through his preaching, John was stirring a social revolution, which in the eyes of Herod Antipas, was perhaps a sign of political revolution. It is clear that the Baptist's movement had a political face, but it would be saying too much to ascribe him as a rebel, since his movement was markedly non-violent. The non-violent nature of the Baptist's movement and Jesus' movement distinguishes them from all the other contemporary popular resistance movements that took on a militant face to rid the Roman rule.

3.3.3. Militant Revolutionary Movements: Sicarii and Zealots

The prophetic resistance movements, despite their socio-political overtones, did not subscribe to armed resistance. However, there were militant revolutionary movements that wanted to overthrow the Roman rule by means of direct armed resistance. The Fourth School of Philosophy (founded by Judas the Galilean during the census), the Sicarii, and Zealots that emerged during Jewish war are cases in point. Older scholarship has generally identified the Fourth School of Philosophy more or less as the Zealots and the Sicarii.[124] But later scholars have questioned this gross misunderstanding by noting the independent origin the

120 Charles H. Scobie, *John the Baptist* (Philadelphia: Fortress, 1964), 184.

121 Webb, *John the Baptizer and Prophet*, 349.

122 Webb, *John the Baptizer and Prophet*, 354.

123 Paul W. Hollenbach, "John the Baptist," *ABD* 3:897.

124 Cf. Gary G. Porton, "Diversity in Postbiblical Judaism," 72–73.

Sicarii and the Zealots had from the Fourth School of Philosophy.[125] Nonetheless, despite their independent contingent point of origins, the ideological convergence of these groups will be clear in the following discussion.

3.3.3.1. The Sicarii

The Sicarii appeared in Jerusalem when Felix was governor (*J.W.* 2.254–255). They were called Sicarii because they carried daggers (*sica*) hidden in their clothes for their terrorist act.[126] According to Josephus, they used to go about the city during the festivals and mixed with the crowd and struck down their opponents with small daggers, which they concealed under their clothes (*Ant* 20.165 cf. 20.187). They were specially known to target Jewish elites who collaborated with the Romans (*J.W.* 2.264–265). Their activities were distinguishable from social bandits, in that, they operated not in the countryside but in the urban centre Jerusalem.[127] It is noteworthy, that Josephus considered the leaders of the Sicarii, Menahem and Eleazer ben Jair as related to Judas the Galilean (*J.W.* 2.433; 7.275) who was the founder of the Fourth Philosophy of the Judeans and leader of the opposition against Roman census in 6 CE (cf. *Ant.* 18.4–7, 23). In *J.W.* 7.254 Josephus also calls the followers of Judas the Galilean "Sicarii." There are obvious connections between the religio-political legitimation and programs of the Sicarii and Judas the Galilean.[128] Judas the Galilean teaches the "sole rule of God" with the aim of freedom for Israel, because of which many had committed themselves and even died as martyrs.[129] This commitment is also ascribed to Eleazer ben Jair and to the sicarii who fled to Egypt.[130]

The Sicarii were ready to fight and die instead of submitting to any power than God. They also exhibit a program of social equality and equitable distribution of resources, probably based on Deuteronomy 15 and Leviticus 25.[131] Josephus tells that their activities were intended to cause a rising of the poor against the rich (*J.W.* 2.426–429). As the Jewish revolt began, the Sicarii entered Jerusalem with Manehem as their leader garbed like a "king." However, this royal pretension earned the scorn of other revolutionaries in Jerusalem, who considered the brash Galilean to be far below their standard. They killed him and drove his followers out of the city (*J.W.* 2. 443–448). The Sicarii fled to Masada under the leadership of Eleazer ben Jair and put up a long fight until

125 Smith, "Zealots and Sicarii," 11, 19. Horsley and Hanson, *Bandits, Prophets, and Messiahs*, 197.

126 S. Zeitlin, "Zealots and the Sicarii," *JBL* 82 (1962): 395.

127 Stegemann and Stegemann, *Jesus Movement*, 179.

128 Hengel, *The Zealots*, 49 cf. 93. Cf. Smith, "Zealots and Sicarii," 18; Zietlin, "Zealots and the Sicarii," 396.

129 *J.W.* 2.117–118, 433.

130 Cf. *J.W.* 7.323, 327, 341, 372.

131 David Rhoads, "Zealots," *ABD* 6:1048.

74 CE. However, they did not make any significant contribution to the actual Jewish revolt against the Romans. Rather, they became predators attacking and robbing neighbouring villages for supply of food. Nevertheless, their resolve was firm to the sole lordship of God. When the Romans entered Masada in 74 CE after a long siege, they found the Sicarii had already committed mass suicide rather than submit to Rome (*J. W.* 7.304–306).

3.3.3.2. Zealots

Scholars disagree about the origin and goals of the Zealots. It is not tenable to combine all the resistance fighters for religious and political freedom in the Roman-Herodian period under the rubric "Zealot," since for Josephus the party named Zealot does not designate the totality of those in revolt,[132] but only a group in the wider resistance movement. In Josephus' account, they first appeared as an armed group along with the Sicarii, when Menahem (the royal pretender) entered Jerusalem in the midst of civil war in the city (*J. W.* 2.444), and then in connection with power struggles among the Jewish revolutionaries (*J. W.* 564).[133] Noting the absolute use of the term in Josephus and drawing inferences from rabbinic and Christian sources, Hengel argues that, Zealots were most probably a "party" or "a definite group of men" in existence during the time of Jesus.[134] However, other scholars opine that Zealots as a party came into existence only in 68 CE during the war in Jerusalem.[135] According to Smith, the Zealots as a party emerged in Jerusalem, during the Jewish war, a result of the common interest of the rural resistance group who were averse to the city rich, the upper priesthood, and the foreign rulers. They played an important and determined role in the defense of the city, and were finally involved in its destruction.[136]

---

132 Hengel, *The Zealots*, 64.

133 Civil war broke out in Jerusalem when some lower priests led by few upper priests and supported by laypeople, stopped the twice-a-day sacrifice offered on behalf of Caesar in the temple (*J. W.* 2.418–456). As the war ensued, the revolutionaries joined by other insurgent groups gained sufficient control of the city and formed a provisional government. However, Eleazer son of Simon, a priest, who played a significant role in routing the Romans, was kept out of position to regional posts. The identity of the Zealots as a distinct party became clear when Eleazer ben Simon (*J. W.* 5.5), who being excluded from the provisional government, with his forces rallied bandit groups, local militia, and other refugees (who fled to Jerusalem from the devastating repression of Vespasian) and took over the temple (*J. W.* 4.138–150). Cf. Rhoads, "Zealots," *ABD* 6:1049.

134 Hengel, *Zealots*, 67–70. Hengel maintains that, Josephus wanted to blame the Jewish war as caused by robbers rather than zealous freedom fighters, thus he avoided the use of Zealots both before and after the war, but employed it only when he needed to differentiate the group from other rebel groups at the peak of Jewish War (66).

135 Smith, "Zealots and Sicarii, their Origins and Relation," 15 cf. Horsley and Hanson, *Bandits, Prophets, and Messiahs*, 220–229.

136 Smith, "Zealots and Sicarii, their Origins and Relation," 19.

At any rate, a section of revolutionaries adopted the title to describe their zeal for God and their attitude to the conflict with Romans.[137] Their major goal was political independence from the Romans. They opposed Jews with power and privilege, set up their headquarters in the temple, and established an alternative egalitarian government.[138] They selected the high priest by a lot and thus chose a country priest named Phineas who was from one of "pontifical tribes, which is called Eniachin" (*J.W.* 4.155).[139]

3.3.4. Non-Violent Resistance and Mass Protests

There were many mass protests organised by the Galileans and Judeans, around the time of Jesus of Nazareth, against the extremes of Roman cultural imperialism. Horsley argues that, the mass movements against the Roman imperial rule had a distinctive Israelite character. They were "rooted in the Israelite tradition of resistance to oppressive rule and was attempting to restore the traditional Israelite way of life that had been so severely disrupted and disordered by Roman imperialism."[140] Just before the death of Herod, taking a calculated risk at the prospect of Herod's impending death, two teachers, Judas, son of Sepphoraeus and Matthias son of Margalus, instigated their students to pull down the golden eagle from the temple gate daring possible execution, which later became their lot (*J.W.* 1.648–50; *Ant* 17. 149–154). When those responsible young men were brought before Herod, the young men confessed that they had removed the golden eagle in faithfulness to the "law of their fathers." When Herod asked, "'And why so exultant, when you will be shortly put to death?' [they replied] 'Because, after our death, we shall enjoy greater felicity'" (*J.W.* 1.653 [Thackeray]).

On one occasion, Pilate allowed the field emblems with their images of emperors to be brought into Jerusalem, which was strongly detested by the Jews. The people of Jerusalem and the rural Judeans protested in mass at the governor's residence in Ceasarea. Pilate was surprised that the Jews were willing to let their head be chopped off rather than relent from their demand (*J.W.* 2.169–174; *Ant.* 18.55–59). At last Pilate relented. But in a disciplined mass protest, the Judean protestors demonstrated the depth of their commitment to live by their traditional ways of life. Probably, the most remarkable non-violent mass protest was against Caligula's attempt to install his statue in the Jerusalem temple (*J.W.* 2.185–198).[141] All the sources indicate that it was the Galilean farmers in particular, who put up a huge protest before the Syrian Governor Petronius, the officer commissioned to carry out the plan. The protest of the Jews stretched into weeks and took on a

---

137 E. Mary Smallwood, *The Jews Under the Roman Rule: From Pompey to Diocletian* (Leiden: Brill, 1981), 299.

138 Rhoads, "Zealots," *ABD* 6:1048.

139 Stegemann, *Jesus Movement,* 182.

140 Horsley, *Jesus and Empire*, 45.

141 Also see Josephus, *Ant.* 18.261–272; Philo, *Embassy* 203ff.

form of agrarian agitation (*Ant.* 18.272). Petronius cancelled the mission at the risk of facing the emperor's anger and the mass protest won the day. These non-violent resistances illustrate not only Jewish sensitivity to the preservation of their religious identity, but also point to profound structural problems in the Roman ruled Palestine.[142]

A brief analysis of the different Jewish resistance movements against the Roman rule contemporaneous to Jesus shows that they were caused not by one single factor but by the accumulated effect of multiple factors over a long period of foreign domination. Rhoads has rightly observed that Jewish resistance movements were social revolutions; peasants' rebellion; clash of cultures; quest for holiness; as well a national war for freedom.[143] Some resistance movements were non-violent while others took on armed resistance. But, each resistance movement responded to Roman domination with the ideology of Israelites' formative tradition that demanded absolute loyalty to God and independence from foreign domination. Jesus' movement was one of the movements that responded to the empire with an alternative vision of a world free from domination and oppression. Luke's Gospel narrates how Jesus' movement challenged and subverted the colonial discourse of Roman Empire from the underside of the empire. A discussion on the salient features of Luke's Gospel will reveal the conflictual character of Luke's Gospel.

3.4. Lukan Community: Forging a Community in the Midst of Conflict and Resistance

One major emphases of Luke's Gospel is the role of the Spirit of God in the formation of a resistant community in the context of domination and oppression. In order to visualise the reality of the empire, Luke carefully paints the imperial power configuration that runs through the central axis of Rome and the provincial peripheries as well as hints at the various colonial imprints of domination and oppression that coloured the lives of the subordinate groups. And having drawn the political and geographical landscape of Roman hegemony, Luke narrates how Jesus carried out his activities in the world dominated by Rome with the anointing of the Spirit of the Lord, and how Jesus called into being a community of disciples to resist the system of domination and oppression that characterised the empire. In the following analysis, Luke's use of older sources, the world of Rome and resistance to Rome in Luke, the author of the Gospel and his reading communities, and the purpose of the Gospel is in order.

3.4.1. Luke and Its Sources

Gospel studies have more or less established that Lukan sources include Q, (which Luke shares with Matthew not found in Mark), Mark and special Lukan materials (L). To a great extent, the theology and ideology of the sources will inform Luke's

142 Stegemann and Stegemann, *Jesus Movement*, 172.

143 Rhoads, "Zealots," *ABD* 6:1052.

theological and ideological discourse. How Luke adapted his sources in retelling the story of Jesus will further shed light on the ideological stance of the Gospel.

3.4.1.1. Luke's Use of Q

Q is considered to be a written saying gospel (like the *Gospel of Thomas*) as the extensive verbatim agreement of Luke and Matthew indicates (e.g. Luke 3:7–9 par Matt 3:7b–10).[144] It is assumed that Luke preserved the sequence of Q (more) faithfully as he inserted Q material chiefly in two sections (6:20–7:35; 9:57–13:34), while Matthew has scattered it over his entire work.[145] It is also recognised that Q reached back into the Palestinian primitive church. It predates the canonical Gospels, as it shows no cue about the destruction of Jerusalem in 70.[146] There is a consensus in recent discussion on the source of Q that, the sayings within it were in circulation at least by 35 CE.[147] The names of most places in Q are from northern Galilee or western Syria, which indicates that Q may have originated in or near Galilee.[148] It is possible that there was correspondence between Mark and Q.[149]

The community of Q might be a Hellenistic Christian community located in Galilee, which was guided by the "wisdom and apocalyptic thinking of the Jesus movement."[150] Joy summarises the following factors, which supports such assumption offered by Verbin:[151]

(a) the ethnic complexities and ethnographic borders of Galilee;
(b) evidence of the attitudes of Galileans toward the principal Judean political and political-religious institutions;
(c) the presence of urbanization;
(d) the presence of priest and priestly concern;
(e) general economic and political climate.

---

144 John S. Kloppenborg, et al., *Q-Thomas Reader* (Sonoma, CA: Polebridge, 1990), 4.

145 W. G. Kümmel, *Introduction to the New Testament*, trans. A. J. Mattill, Jr. (Nashville: Abingdon, 1966), 54.

146 Kloppenborg, et al., *Q-Thomas Reader*, 5.

147 Bruce Chilton and Jacob Neusner, *Types of Authority in Formative Christianity and Judaism* (New York: Routledge, 1999), 41.

148 In Q, Jerusalem is mentioned only twice (Q 4:9; 13:34) and the region around Jordan only once (3:3). On the other hand, the names of Galilean towns occurred several times: Chorazin and Bethsaida (10:13); Capernaum (7:1; 10:15); the Gentile city Tyre and Sidon, located in western Syria is also mentioned (10:13).

149 C. I. David Joy, *Mark and Its Subaltern: A Hermeneutical Paradigm for a Postcolonial Context* (London: Equinox, 2008), 88.

150 Joy, *Mark and Its Subaltern*, 88–89.

151 Joy, *Mark and Its Subaltern*, 88 cf. J. S. K. Verbin, *Excavating Q: The History and Setting of the Q Gospel* (Edinburgh: T&T Clark, 2000), 170.

Leif E. Vaage who has analysed the socio-cultural background of the Q community, argues that they were the bearers of the good news from village to village (Q 10:13–16 cf. Mark 6:7–13) with resistance strategies to dislodge the official truth claims.

> Like Cynics, the "Galilean upstarts" whom Q's formative stratum represents conducted in word and deed a form of "popular" resistance to the official truth and virtues of their day. Registered in their unorthodox ethos, ethics, ideology and ad hoc social critique as well as the sparse but vivid memory maintained of certain "anti-heroes" of the recent past (John and Jesus) was both a decisive "no" to the typical habits and aspirations of their immediate cultural context.[152]

Some Q researchers have argued that Q is a collection of sayings (J. M. Robinson) or a wisdom gospel (Helmut Koester). Koester maintains that, the apocalyptic eschatology in Luke is a secondary layer of redaction of an earlier wisdom book.[153] On the other hand, Eugene Boring and Werner Kelber has argued that Q sayings are prophetic in nature with a strong *Tendenz* of contemporising the life of Jesus.[154] Kelber, who argues that Q represents "oral genre" imagines Q as a document that was enacted in oral performance within the community, an enactment that evoked the presence of the exalted Lord.[155] F. G. Downing opines that Q resembles *bios* of a cynic teacher seen from the socio-cultural context.[156] Though consensus on the genre is not conclusive, these pointers are suggestive of Q as a document critical of the given order of the society. While Lukan redaction of Q can at best be conjectural, in certain places Luke has heightened the tenor of Q. For instance, Luke has probably emphasised the immediacy of "now" in Q 6:21: "Blessed are you that hunger now, for you shall be filled," where as it is absent in Matthew.[157] Luke's reuse of Q in his Gospel suggests that, Luke was no reluctant writer, but critiqued the ideology of the empire system.

---

152 Leif E. Vaage, *Galilean Upstarts: Jesus First Followers According to Q* (Pennsylvania: Trinity Press International, 1994), 106 cited by Joy, *Mark and Its Subaltern*, 90.

153 Helmut Koester, "Apocryphal and Canonical Gospel," *HTR* 73 (1980): 113.

154 M. Eugene Boring, *Sayings of the Risen Jesus: Christian Prophecy in the Synoptic Tradition* (Cambridge: Cambridge University Press, 1982), 137–179; Werner H. Kelber, *The Oral and Written Gospel: The Hermeneutics of Speaking and Writing in the Synoptic Tradition, Mark, Paul and Q* (Philadelphia: Fortress, 1983), 201.

155 Kelber, *Oral and Written Gospel*, 201.

156 F. G. Downing, "A Genre for Q and a Socio-cultural Context for Q: Comparing Sets of Similarities with Sets of Differences," *JSNT* 55 (1994), 16, 20.

157 Matthew 5:6 reads: "Blessed are they that hunger and thirst for righteousness, for they shall be filled." The typical Matthean concern for righteousness may be seen in the emphasis added. Cf. Kloppenborg et al., *Q-Thomas Reader*, 5.

3.4.1.2. Luke's Use of Mark

Scholarly consensus on Luke's use of Mark is firmly established though a few voices persist against this view.[158] Studies on Mark have highlighted that, the Gospel was written at the backdrop of the Roman Empire with a critical stance towards it from the vantage point of the margins and the oppressed.[159] That is the reason a majority of the healing miracles in Luke is drawn from Mark. Particularly notable is that Luke retained all the traditions on exorcisms found in Mark.[160] It has been pointed out that Jesus' exorcisms are the symbolic portrayal of the conflict between established authorities and the authority of God as represented by Jesus and his followers.[161] Ched Myers maintains, healings and miracles are "symbolic actions," and exorcism, "political repudiation."[162] Luke had also used enormous materials from Mark that deals with power politics and the wider implications it issues out in the material relations of the established power structure and the oppressed groups (Mark 11:27–33 par Luke 20:1–8; Mark 12:1–12 par Luke 20:9–19; Mark 12:13–17 par Luke 20:20–26). Luke has faithfully reproduced Mark though he amends certain features towards corrections, clarity, and orderliness.[163]

However, it may be noted that the Markan milieu is dominantly assumed to be that of Galilee. Luke Timothy Johnson notes, "Mark's peculiar emphasis on Galilee was a theological symbol."[164] In the Markan context, Galilee is a significant political space both in terms of colonial domination and resistance to domination. Galilee was consistently resistive to the Roman rule. Resistance movement flourished in Galilee led by rebels with the support base of the peasant, even though the local elites classes of Galilee continued to co-opt with Rome in terms of culture, economics, and politics.[165] Albeit, Luke's Gospel betrays a Hellenistic city setting of the Mediterranean east, (Luke's Hellenistic features are discussed below), Luke's reuse of Mark naturally issues out the ineluctable conflicts of power embedded in its source. Conflict and resistance remain integral

---

158 For argument against Marcan priority refer to William R. Farmer, "Modern Development of Griesbach's Hypothesis," *NTS* 23 (1976–1977): 283–289.

159 Ched Myers, *Binding the Strong Man: A Political Reading of Mark's Story of Jesus*, (Maryknoll, NY: Orbis Books, 1988); Joy, *Mark and Its Subaltern*.

160 Mark 1:21–28 par Luke 4:31–37; Mark 5:1–20 par Luke 8:26–39; Mark 9:14–28 par Luke 9:39–43a cf. Mark 3:20–30 par Luke 11:14–23 and Mark 9:38–41 par Luke 9:49–50.

161 Myers, *Binding the Strong Man*, 143; Paul W. Hollenbach, "Jesus, Demoniacs, and Public Authorities: A Socio-Historical Study," *JAAR* 49 (1981): 581. Wink, *Unmasking the Powers*, 43–47.

162 Myers, *Binding the Strong Man*, 146, 192.

163 Luke Timothy Johnson, "Luke-Acts, Book of," *ABD* 4:408.

164 Luke Timothy Johnson, *The Writings of New Testament: An Interpretation* (Bangalore: TPI, 2009), 160.

165 Joy, *Mark and its Subaltern*, 72.

to Luke's Gospel. Thus, although older scholarship predominantly sees Luke's Gospel as favourable towards Roman rule, many recent works have highlighted that Luke's Gospel is critical of the Roman Empire.

3.4.1.3. Lukan Special Source (L)

Given the vast amount of Lukan special materials in the Gospel, coupled with not only the long infancy narratives, peculiar to Luke, but a substantial differences of Lukan passion narratives over against Mark, have led scholars to propose the term L to designate this Lukan materials. However, the use of the term L is ambiguous to a great extent. Since, the materials peculiar to Luke are heterogeneous, "it is difficult to argue for one single source as the wellspring of all his special material."[166] In this case L best stands for Luke's "special material" rather than his "special source." There are scholars who strongly argue for a pre-Lukan source behind Luke's gospel in varying degrees. Lyod Gaston presents the synoptic situation of Mark, Q, and L in Luke's Gospel following Jeremias' scheme in the following manner:[167]

Q and L materials	Markan materials
(1) Luke 1:5–4:30	
	(2) Luke 4:31–6:11 // Mark 1:21–3:6
(3) Luke 6:12–8:3	
	(4) Luke 8:4–9:50 // Mark 4:1–9:40 (except 4:26–34; 6:45–8:26)
(5) Luke 9:51–18:14	
	(6) Luke 18:15–43 // Mark 10:13–52
(7) Luke 19:1–48	
	(8) Luke 20:1–21:4 // Mark 11:27–12:44
(9) Luke 22:14–24:53 (with Markan insertions).	

Proto-Luke hypothesis was the foremost to explain the material peculiar to Luke.[168] According to this thesis, Luke would have first combined Q and L, and created a gospel with 3:1 as the beginning (the so called Proto-Luke), after

166 Helmut Koester, *Ancient Christian Gospels: Their History and Development* (London: SCM, 1990), 336–337.

167 Lloyd Gaston, *No Stone on Another: Studies in the Significance of the Fall of Jerusalem in the Synoptic Gospels* (Leiden: Brill, 1970), 25 cf. Joachim Jeremias, *The Eucharistic Words of Jesus*, trans. Norman Perrin (New York: Charles Scribner's Sons, 1966), 98–99.

168 B. H. Streeter is the first to popularise Proto-Luke hypothesis in his work *The Four Gospels: A Study of Origins, Treating of the Manuscript Tradition, Sources, Authorship, and Dates* (London: Macmillan, 1924), 208–222. Vincent Taylor, *Behind the Third Gospel: A Study of the Proto-Luke Hypothesis* (Oxford: Clarendon, 1926) further elaborated this thesis. But it should be noted that the works of P. Feine, B. Weiss, E. D. Burton, A. M. Perry and others provided the foundation for the thesis of Proto-Luke. Cf. Gaston, *No Stone on Another*, 244–245.

which he inserted Markan materials into it, and finally, before 3:1 placed the chps. 1 and 2 and gave form to the canonical Third Gospel.[169] But Proto-Luke theory tended to operate with a very hypothetical genesis of Luke's writing[170] so that the statistical evidence for the existence of a non-Markan source is lost in a novelistic explanation.[171] Moreover, Proto-Luke considers 3:1 as its beginning so that the infancy narrative that provides the best support for a distinct theological conception were deleted from the explanation. Thus, it has received varied responses—from acceptance with some variations[172] in details to total rejection.[173] Thus, it is difficult to conclude definitely on the Proto-Luke hypothesis. Albeit the academic climate does not favour so much the general Proto-Luke theory, several scholars have expressed the possibility that Luke may have had an independent passion source.[174]

Notwithstanding the continuing debate, there are at least three distinguishable blocks of L materials: the infancy narratives, the L materials in chs.

169 Kümmel, *Introduction to the New Testament*, 92 cf. Streeter, *The Four Gospels*, 208.

170 Gaston, *No Stone on Another*, 246. The proponents of Proto-Luke claim to know too much of Luke's literary activities by assuming that the travelling companion of Paul kept a personal diary of travel—"we-sections" which was incorporated in the final production of Luke-Acts—and also collected the traditions of Jesus which he joined with Q while he was with Paul in Caesarea—producing a first draft of a gospel. Cf. Streeter, *Four Gospels*, 218–219.

171 Gaston, *No Stone on Another*, 246. H. W. Montifiore, "Does 'L' Hold Water?" *JTS* 12 (1961): 59–60, has maintained that Luke would have lost his document in the shipwrecked while travelling from Caesarea to Rome.

172 One scholar (P. Winter) would like to distinguish between the author of Proto-Luke and Luke. Some scholars maintain that only passion narratives can be said to have a narrative basis of the account, while still others supposes a Hebrew special source or Hebrew-Aramaic "Proto-Luke" extending from Luke 1:5–Acts 15. Cf. Kümmel, *Introduction to the New Testament*, 92.

173 J. M. Creed, "'L' and the Structure of the Lucan Gospel: A Study of Proto-Luke Hypothesis," *ExpTim* 46 (1934–1935): 101–107; S. M. Gilmour, "A Critical Examination of Proto-Luke," *JBL* 67 (1948): 143–152. For a detail argument against Proto-Luke hypothesis refer to Kümmel, *Introduction to the New Testament*, 92–95; Joseph Fitzmyer, *The Gospel According to Luke I–IX: Introduction, Translation, and Notes,* AB 28 (Garden City, NY: Doubleday, 1981), 90–91.

174 Joseph B. Tyson, "The Lukan Version of the Trial of Jesus," *NovT* 3 (1959): 249–258; C. H. Dodd, *Historical Tradition in the Fourth Gospel*, (Cambridge: Cambridge University Press, 1963), 50–52. Vincent Taylor, *The Passion Narrative of Luke* (Cambridge: Cambridge University Press, 1972). Those who reject an independent Lukan passion narrative think that Luke would have simply weaves independent special traditions that he had into the Markan framework. See Gilmour, "A Critical Re-examination of Proto-Luke," 143–152. Fitzmyer, *Luke X–XXIV*, 66–71; R. E. Brown, *The Death of the Messiah: A Commentary on the Passion Narratives in the Four Gospels*, vol. 1 (New York: Doubleday, 1994), 66–67; F. J. Matera, "The Death of Jesus According to Luke: A Question of Sources," *CBQ* 47 (1985): 469–485. Jay M. Harrington, *The Lukan Passion Narrative. The Markan Material in Luke 22:54–23:25: A Historical Survey:* 1891–1997 (Leiden: Brill, 2000).

3–19 and the passion narrative. The ideology of these materials shows that the early communities who treasured these traditions must have used these traditions to forge their marginal identity in the context of the empire.

It is striking to note that the Lukan infancy narrative insinuates the pervasive presence of Roman power in the world in which Jesus was born by naming the Emperor (2:1), the provincial governor (2:2), the client king (1:5), during whose reign census was undertaken. But against this background, Luke narrates the birth of the Saviour Jesus, the bringer of peace. This suggests that Luke's community was apparently a community that was in tension with the Roman imperial theology that claim Caesar as Saviour and the bringer of peace. Especially, the Lukan canticles in the infancy narratives have close affinity with the Old Testament psalmody and passages from the Second Temple writings attested in the literature such as 1 Maccabees, Judith, 2 Baruch, 4 Ezra, the Qumran psalms (IQH), and the Qumran War Scroll,[175] not only in style, but also in the religious outlook, that of dependence on God as saviour.[176] Despite its Jewish tone, the canticles express status reversal with a resistant strain against the rich and the powerful who crushed the poor as such that it reflects a community in tension with the hierarchical status quo and domination of the vulnerable by the powerful.

The L materials in the middle section (Luke 3–19) embody many boundary-breaking traditions of Jesus. In the Nazareth scene (4:16–30), the Lukan Jesus deliberately extolled gentile healing stories of Elijah and Elisha that transgresses the fixed Jewish map of community. The L materials clearly have a special interest in the Samaritans as they speak positively of the Samaritans (10:30–37; 17:11–19).[177] The L materials also show concern for the social outcasts (cf. 15:11–32), especially the publicans (18:9–14; 19:1–10). The parables in ch. 16 form a united polemic against the rich with a deliberate concern for the poor. While Proto-Luke theory continues to linger in abeyance, considering the vast materials of L in the middle section of Luke's Gospel with a certain theological orientation, Kim Paffenforth who studied the L materials in chs. 3–19,[178] proposes an early date of L composition in a Palestinian setting. He writes,

> the community finds the center of Jesus' message in seeking and bringing back the 'lost' who are welcomed joyously and have their

175 For a table of comparison refer to Brown, *Birth of the Messiah*, 358, 386.

176 Brown, *Birth of the Messiah*, 349.

177 Gaston, *No Stone on Another*, 317.

178 Kim Paffenroth, *The Story of Jesus According to L*, JSNTSup 147 (Sheffield: Sheffeild Academic, 1996). Paffenforth proposed an examination of a much smaller body of material to determine how much of L material is pre-Lukan, how much is probably from a single source. He argues that such an inquiry will enable one to hear the "many" predecessors whom Luke acknowledges in 1:1. Thus, in contrast to the Proto-Luke hypothesis, Paffenroth excluded the infancy narrative and the passion narrative and studied vast amounts of L material in chs. 3–19.

> status as 'children of Abraham' reaffirmed ...they believe all boundaries are negative and should be broken down: the boundaries between Jews and Samaritan, men and women, rich and poor, clean and unclean. They therefore see their Jewish opponents, with their strict law of exclusion, as particularly abominable, and often portray them as bitter opponents to Jesus' (and their own) inclusivity.[179]

How far an academic consensus on L community can be arrived is a matter of debate.[180] However, the Lukan special emphases on the motifs of rich and poor, purity and pollution, man and women reflects the socio-cultural world of Luke's Gospel that shows binarism of socio-economic, racial, cultural, and gender categories. And at the same time the socio-cultural situation of Luke's Gospel reflects how the community is forging an inclusive community irrespective of class, race, culture, gender and so on.

The peculiarity of Lukan passion narrative is the heroic death of Jesus. It probably comes from a community who were forging their identity in conflict with the colonial powers and authorities. It is striking that Lukan tradition attests Jesus being accused on the charge of teaching "no tax" to Caesar and leading a movement starting from Galilee (23:2–4). And unlike in Matthew's and Mark's Gospels, in Luke's Gospel Jesus was tried by the Sanhedrin, the client king Herod, and Roman procurator, indicating how the rulers colluded to rid Jesus. Lukan Jesus' conflict with the colonial authorities in the passion narrative probably reflects the socio-political and cultural world of the audience.

In contemporising Jesus' movement to forge an inclusive community in the context of the Roman Empire, Luke draws resources from the archives of Jesus' traditions and narrates how Jesus' proclamation of the good news of the kingdom of God was conflictual with the claims of Rome and its allies. A brief analysis on Rome, resistance, and Luke is in order to underline domination and resistance inscribed in the Gospel.

3.4.2. Colonial Imprints in Luke's Gospel

3.4.2.1. Roman Imperial Theology and Colonial Mimicry

Luke is the only Gospel, which is properly set in the chronology of the Roman Empire, noting the historical markers such as the census (Luke 2:1–2; 3:1), and the only Gospel to refer to the emperor by name. It is often observed that the reference to Caesar Augustus and the census is a chronological indicator on the

179 Paffenroth, *The Story of Jesus According to L*, 157–158.

180 Cf. Robert A. Derrenbacker, review of *The Story of Jesus According to L*, by Kim Paffenforth, *CBQ* 61 (1999): 375–376; Christopher Tuckett, review of *The Story of Jesus According to L*, by Kim Paffenforth, *NovT* 91 (1999): 191–192.

part of Luke the historian.[181] However, as Yamazaki-Ransom observes, "it cannot be said that Luke was viewing the empire as merely a stage for the early Christian drama."[182] The Gospel narrates the story of Jesus and his community proclaiming the kingdom of God — and not Roman Empire! — with resistant adaptation of imperial languages and thus, hybridising the metanarratives of the empire.

In order to appreciate Lukan discursive mimesis of colonial discourse, it is pertinent to highlight Roman imperial theology, which is the ideological power that held together the Roman Empire. Ramsay Macmullen states:[183]

> Roman civilization eventually appeared everywhere, as one single thing, so far as it was ever achieved ... a thing of wonder, familiar to everyone.... The natives would be taught, if it was not plain enough on its face, that they could better rise into the ranks of the master race by reforming themselves—by talking, dressing, looking, and in every way resembling Romans. They would and did respond as ambition directed. They pulled Roman civilization to them—to their homes, their families, their world.

The imperial power is not so much a thing in itself but the combined force of the interaction of four types of power: "*military power*, the monopoly or control of force and violence; *economic power*, monopoly or control of labor and production; *political power*, the monopoly or control of organization and institution; and *ideological power*, the monopoly or control of meaning and interpretation" (emphasis original).[184] The fourth is the most crucial power and can be properly called the "Roman imperial theology." According to Crossan, it is "the glue that held Roman civilisation together."[185] Philip Esler also argues that Roman imperium was akin to European colonialism in three ways: "first, political control over subject peoples backed up by overwhelming military forces; second the voracious extraction of economic resources; and third, an *ideology legitimating these processes conveyed by discourse of various kind*" (emphasis added).[186] Thus,

181 I. Howard Marshall, *The Gospel of Luke: A Commentary on the Greek Text* (Grand Rapids: Eerdmans, 1978), 97–98.

182 Kazuhiko Yamazaki-Ransom, *The Roman Empire in Luke's Narrative* (London: T&T Clark, 2008), 3.

183 Ramsay MacMullen, *Romanization in the Time of Augustus* (New Haven: Yale University Press, 2003), ix, 134.

184 J. D. Crossan, "Roman Imperial Theology," in Horsley *In the Shadow of Empire*, 60. Crossan here takes the lead of Michael Mann, The *Sources of Social Power*, 4 vols. (Cambridge: Cambridge University Press), vol. 1: *A History of Power From the Beginning to A.D. 1760*, (1986).

185 Crossan, "Roman Imperial Theology," 59.

186 Phillip F. Esler, "Rome in Apocalyptic and Rabbinic Literature," in *The Gospel of Matthew in Its Roman Imperial Context*, JSNTSup 276, ed. John Riches and David C. Sim (London: Continuum, 2005), 10.

empire produces ideological discourse of power. Walter Wink maintains that empires, ancient one like Rome or modern ones, "can maintain cohesion across racial, ethnic, linguistic, and national lines only by creating a bogus solidarity. This they achieve by demanding the worship of the spirituality of empire."[187] For the Roman Empire, the spirituality of the empire was not just the worship of the seated emperor *per se*, but the institution of surpassing power that change little no matter whoever occupies the throne of Caesar.[188] He writes, "The Roman Empire had made itself the highest value and the ultimate concern, arrogating itself the place of God."[189] But since the power of the empire lies in its ability to legitimise its ideology, "They can not exist for a moment without the spiritual undergirding of a persuasive ideology."[190] Thus, the most potent threat to the empire were not those militant revolutionaries, who internalised the system of domination and desire power for themselves, but those who saw the "atmospherics of imperial legitimation,"[191] like Jesus who denounced it at the cost of his life.

Religious rituals and words were instruments for the emperor and his officers to articulate the relationship between the Roman emperor and the gods and impose a definition of the world.[192] Literature, decorated gates, arches, columns, statues, buildings, coins, images and various inscriptions advertised the theological claims, creating and sustaining the relationship of the coloniser and the colonised.[193] When Octavius emerged as the victor in the battle of Actium in 31, for the first time after a long period of conflicts, he brought peace and order in the Mediterranean world. The empire he established was "salvation" and he was (ac)claimed as the "saviour,"[194] who established peace and prosperity, fulfilling the hopes and longings of all humankind.[195] In 27 BCE, Octavius became Augustus.[196] Since, he was the heir of Julius Caesar, who was deified after his death, Octavius had the ground of claiming to be the "son of God." Strikingly, Octavius Caesar was deified while he was still alive while none of his predecessors were given that honour. The poet Horace in his *Epistle to Augustus* around 15 CE wrote, "upon you [Augustus], however, while still among us, we bestow honours betimes, set up altars to swear by in your name, and confess that nought like you will hereafter

187 Wink, *Engaging the Powers*, 300.
188 Cf. Wink, *Engaging the Powers*, 81.
189 Wink, *Engaging the Powers*, 300.
190 Wink, *Engaging the Powers*, 300.
191 Wink, *Engaging the Powers*, 300.
192 Carter, *Matthew and Empire*, 20.
193 Crossan, "Roman Imperial Theology," 59–73.
194 Horsley, *The Liberation of Christmas*, 26.
195 Horsley, *Jesus and Empire*, 23; N. T. Wright, *Paul: In Fresh Perspectives*, 63.
196 Green, *The Gospel of Luke*, 122.

arise or has arisen ere now." (Horace, *Epistles* 2.1.15–17, H. Rushton Fairclough, LCL).[197]

Ethelbert Stauffer observes that though Octavius refused to be anything other than a *princep senatus* (though it is a political pretence), the senate and the people found ways to express his unique authority in metaphysical categories.[198] In Virgil's *Aeneid*, he was exalted as the son of God who established the Golden Age: "Lo! Under his auspices, my son, that glorious Rome shall bound her empire by earth, (and) her pride by heaven.... This, this is he whom thou so oft hearest promised to thee, Augustus Caesar, son of a god, who shall reign again set up the Golden Age" (6.780–93). *Pax Romana* makes use of theological claims and religious practices to legitimise and maintain the existing position of the elite's military and economic power in disregard of the experience of the subaltern or marginalised who do not celebrate it.[199] The cruel nature of Roman peace can be inferred from Virgil's *Aeneid*: "You O Roman, remember to rule the nations with might. This will be your genius—to impose the way of peace, to spare the conquered and crushed the proud" (6.850–53).

In the Mediterranean east, Christopher Kelly maintains that, "for many in the provinces Roman dominance was most felt in its strengthening of the ability of existing oligarchic cliques to exercise unrivalled control in their localities."[200] Thus, elites competed for government offices, imperial favour and public honor and in the process legitimised their own subordination.[201] This competition for status, power, and identity moved beyond individuals to cities and was played out in the arena of imperial cult, which was widespread in the provinces of Greece and Asia Minor.[202] A comprehensive exaltation of the emperor as the *saviour* and bringer of *peace* is found in the inscription of the decree of the Provincial Assembly of Asia dated to ca. 9 BCE.

---

197 Horace, *Epistles* 2.1.15–17 (Fairclough, LCL) Cited from Crossan, "Roman Imperial Theology," 60.

198 Ethelbert Stauffer, *Christ and Caesars: Historical Sketches*, trans. K. and R. Gregor Smith (Philadelphia: Westminster, 1955), 96–97 writes, "In the framework of an ancient liturgy he was invoked like one of the ancient national gods of Rome, he was given the title of Augustus (which means worthy of reverence or worship), and he was surrounded with such an abundance of religious honour that many people thought there was nothing left for the worship of the heavenly gods."

199 Carter, *Matthew and Empire*, 32.

200 Christopher Kelly, *Roman Empire: A Very Short Introduction* (Oxford: Oxford University Press, 2006), 47–48.

201 S. R. F. Price, *Rituals and Power: The Roman Imperial Cult in Asia Minor* (Cambridge: Cambridge University Press, 1984), 62.

202 Phil Perkins and Lisa Nevett, "Urbanism and Urbanisation in the Roman World," in *Experiencing Rome: Culture, Identity and Power in the Roman Empire*, ed. Janet Huskinson (Milton Keyes: Open University, 2009), 215.

> The most divine Caesar … we should consider equal to the Beginning of all things …; for when everything was falling [into disorder] and tending toward dissolution, he restored it once more and gave to the whole world a new aura; Caesar … the common good Fortune of all … the beginning of life and vitality …. All the cities unanimously adopt the birthday of the divine Caesar as the new beginning of the year …. Whereas Providence, which has regulated our whole existence … has brought our life to the climax of perfection in giving to us [the emperor] Augustus, whom it [Providence] filled with strength for the welfare of men, and who being sent to us and our descendent as Savior, has put an end to war and has set all things in order; and [whereas,] having become [god] manifest (*phaneis*), Caesar has fulfilled all the hopes of earlier times … in surpassing all the benefactors who preceded him…, and whereas, finally, the birthday of the god [Augustus] has been for the whole world the beginning of good news (*euangelion*) concerning him [therefore let a new era begin from his birth].[203]

However, underneath this elite rhetoric of the celebrated *pax Romana*, things were more complicated than supposed. Social hierarchy and status negotiation coloured everyday life of people under the Roman rule from the lowest peasant right up to the emperor.[204] It is into this world Luke takes his message of a new saviour and Lord who inaugurates a new world order. The resistant adaptation of the imperial theology is quite visible beginning from the birth annunciation of Lukan Jesus.

> But the angel said to them, "Do not be afraid; for see—I am bringing you *good news* of great joy for all the people: to you is born this day in the city of David a *savior* who is messiah, the *Lord*…. And suddenly there was with the angel a multitude of the heavenly host, praising God saying, "Glory to God in the highest heaven, and on earth *peace* among those whom he favors!" (emphasis added, 2:10–11, 13–14).

What is striking here is that the themes such as "good news," "saviour," "Lord," and "peace" that permeates the birth of Jesus are major motifs of the imperial theology ascribed to Caesar and advertised via the media of imperial religion.[205] In fact, at the beginning of the twentieth century, Adolf Deissmann had already noted that "there arises a polemical parallelism between the cult of the emperor and the cult of Christ, which makes itself felt where ancient words derived by Christianity from the treasury of the Septuagint and the Gospels happen to

203 *Orientis Graeci Inscriptiones Selectae*, ed. Wilhelm Dittenberger, 2 vols. Leipzig: Hirzel, 1903–1905.

204 Valerie Hope, "Status and Identity in the Roman World," in Huskinson, *Experiencing Rome*, 127, 150.

205 Crossan, "Roman Imperial Theology," 73.

coincide with solemn concepts of the imperial cult which sounded the same and similar."[206] But for the most part of the twentieth century, New Testament scholars failed to appreciate the "polemic parallelism" that the early Christians produced for counter social formation under the shadow of the empire. Bultmann thinks that, the "Kyrios-title" of Jesus is not used as a counterpart of the ruler cult, at least not primarily.[207] However, there is a burgeoning acknowledgement in the recent times that the New Testament writers subversively mimic imperial languages. With regard to Luke 2:10–14, Richard Horsley claims, "Regardless of what Luke or a conceivable pre-Lucan story had in mind, any reader or hearer of this story in the Hellenistic-Roman world, particularly in Palestine, would have understood here a direct opposition between Caesar, the savior who had supposedly brought peace, and the child proclaimed as the savior, whose birth means peace."[208] In short, the Gospel presents Jesus as "an alternative to the imperial ideology."[209]

There is an obvious reminiscence of imperial theology in Lukan portrayal of Jesus. Jesus is the υἱὸς τοῦ θεοῦ (Son of God, 1:35; 4:3, 41), σωτὴρ (saviour, 2:11), κύριος (Lord, 2:11) whose birth is εὐαγγέλιον (good news, cf. 2:10) and εἰρήνη (peace, 2:14). The implication is that by attributing Jesus as Lord, saviour and the peace bringer, Luke is "presenting an alternative to the dominant imperial ideology."[210] The Gospel stresses that Jesus is Lord, starting from the birth narratives (2:11). Caesar's claim to be lord is not mentioned in Luke, but to use κύριος so prominently for Jesus could not but signal the readers who are accustomed to Caesar's claim to be lord in the empire that "Luke was making a counter-claim for Jesus over against Caesar."[211] Luke employs the language of "salvation" more frequently than the other evangelists.[212] In 2:11, Jesus is specifically called σωτὴρ (Acts 5:31; 13:23). This title and the language of salvation used in Luke is an imitation of the language used of Caesar.[213]

206 Adolf Deissmann, *Light From the Ancient East,* trans. Lionel R. M. Strachan, 2nd ed. (London: Hoder & Stoughton, 1909), 346.

207 Rudolf Bultmann, *Theology of the New Testament,* trans. Kendrik Grobel (New York: Charles Scribner's Sons, 1954), 124.

208 Horsley, *The Liberation of Christmas,* 33.

209 Andrew T. Lincoln, "'Born of the Virgin Mary': Creedal Affirmation and Critical Reading," in *Christology and Scripture: Interdisciplinary Perspective,* ed. Andrew T. Lincoln and Angus Paddison (London: T&T Clark, 2008), 90.

210 Yamazaki–Ransom, *The Roman Empire in Luke's Narrative,* 83.

211 Walton, "Luke's View of the Roman Empire," 26.

212 Walton, "Luke's View of the Roman Empire," 27, puts the statistics thus: twenty five times in Luke; twenty two times in Acts; fifteen times in Matthew; sixteen times in Mark; and eight times in John. For Luke, salvation is a present reality (cf. 4:21). The content of salvation is the saving activity of God in Jesus. "Jesus has already intervened, the era of salvation has already begun." François Bovon, *Luke The Theologian: Thirty-Three Years of Research (1950–1983),* trans. Ken McKinney (Allison Park, PN: Pickwick, 1987), 263.

213 Walton, "Luke's View of the Roman Empire," 27.

Luke's Gospel also used the title king to refer to Jesus more frequently than the other Gospels.[214] This entitlement begins in the birth narratives itself where Jesus' reign is said to last forever (1:33). When Jesus enters Jerusalem, he was again acclaimed king (Luke 19:38). Commenting on Luke 1:32–3; 19:38, Walaskay argues that Conzelmann is wrong in arguing that Luke's use of βασιλεύς is a non-political view of kingship.[215] Luke heightens the sense of Jesus' kingship in his account of the triumphal entry into Jerusalem.[216] Brent Kinman opines that Jesus' statement in 19:30–31 may suggest an accentuation of royal tone of Jesus' entry, as E. Stauffer has indicated that ὁ κύριος αὐτοῦ χρείαν ἔχει (vv. 31, 34) "is to be understood as an official requisition formula."[217] In 22:29–30, Jesus spoke of his kingdom and promised to his disciples, who stood by him in his trials, that they will be judges over the twelve tribes of Israel. In the passion account, Jesus was accused of claiming to be king, which he does not deny (Luke 23:2; cf. 23:37–8). Steve Walton argues that behind this claim surely stands Caesar's claim of kingship (cf. "another king" Acts 17:7).[218] As noted above, Caesar is claimed in inscriptions and literature as the saviour of the world who has put an end to war. According to Steve Walton, the disruptive mimesis of Caesar's title in Luke for Jesus such as Lord, king, and saviour suggest that

> Luke presents the early Christians as subversively using Caesar's titles for Jesus. When we add to this the strong statements in the face of the Jewish authorities that obeying God is more important than obeying mere human beings (Acts 4:19; 5:29), the reading of Jesus' 'render to Caesar' saying … Luke's view that the kingdoms of the world are in the hands of the devil (Luke 4:5–6), we have a picture of a movement that, to a Roman loyalist, could not but be seen as subversive and anti-emperor.[219]

The discourse that emanates from the subjugated hybridises the dominant discourse and shifts the foundation of authority. Writing a story that counters the claims of Roman Empire, Luke appropriates imperial languages and proclaims a

214 Walton noted that βασιλεύς and βασιλεύω are used seven times of Jesus by Luke while Matthew and Mark uses only six times that too mainly in the passion narrative: 1:32–33; 19:38; 22:29–30; 23:2, 37–38; Acts 17:7. See Walton, "Luke's View of the Roman Empire," 26.

215 Paul W. Walaskay, *"And So We Came to Rome": The Political Perspective of St. Luke*, SNTSMS 49 (Cambridge: Cambridge University Press, 1983), 17 Cf. Conzelmann, *Theology of St Luke*, 139.

216 Brent Kinman, *Jesus' Entry into Jerusalem: In the Context of Lukan Theology and the Politics of His Day* (Leiden: Brill, 1995), 91–103.

217 Kinman, *Jesus' Entry into Jerusalem*, 93 cf. E. Stauffer, "Messias oder Menschensohn," *NovT* 1 (1956): 85.

218 Walton, "Luke's View of the Roman Empire," 26.

219 Walton, "Luke's View of the Roman Empire," 27.

counter empire with a named saviour, Lord, and Son of God (cf. 1:35), who is Jesus, the bringer of peace.

3.4.2.2. Census, Tributes, and Legion

The most visible marks of colonial imprints in Luke's Gospel are, the explicit mention of census, taxation and legion. There is no denying that census and tributes were the reasons that generated Jewish resistance against the Roman rule. Thus, when the Gospel narrates that Jesus was born at a time when Augustus Caesar decreed a worldwide census, when Quirinius was the governor of Syria (2:1–2), Luke is deliberately signalling that Jesus' Palestine was under the colonial rule of Rome. Lukan scholars have detected Luke's anachronism in the forceful convergence of Jesus' birth and the census taken by Quirinius with lengthy notes and appendices.[220] However, obsession with historical (in)accuracy deviates the main issue that the Gospel underlines—Roman census for tribute.[221] Census in Luke is an imprint of the colonial rule, not a "purely literary device," so that Jesus birth will take place according to the scripture as some have suggested.[222] While Lukan literary artistry can be conceded, in that, census provided the christologically necessary shift of scene from Nazareth to the "city of David," the Augustan census decree that demands each person to return to their native land for tax enrolment reveals the system of domination and exploitation.[223]

Since the dawn of Augustan period, the census registered males and females, children and slaves. And although census during the Roman Republic was more to do with recruiting for military service and voting right, under the Roman Empire, census was carried out primarily to levy tax, at the same time it had its interest in keeping "a record of people liable to compulsory services such as the *corvee* works on the canals, and to extract other capital taxes."[224] Thus, Brook W. R. Pearson observes that the Roman census had a dual purpose, that is, for taxation and social control.[225] Writing about taxation process with specific reference to Egypt, Roger Bagnall and Bruce Frier state, "It is entirely possible that both taxation and control of the population were among the government's motives from the beginning of the periodic census.... It is also possible that the symbolic value of the poll tax, representing subjection to Roman power, extended to the census

220 Fitzmyer, *Luke I–IX*, 400–405.

221 Horsley have argues that, what is significant here is not the historical accuracy but the Roman census. This point is supported by the elaborate setting in 2:1–5 for the description of the census whereas, Jesus birth is given shorter description in vv. 6–7. Horsley, *The Liberation of Christmas*, 34.

222 Fitzmyer, *Luke I–IX*, 393.

223 Horsley, *The Liberation of Christmas*, 36.

224 Livia Caponi, *Augustan Egypt: The Creation of a Roman Province* (New York: Routledge, 2016), 84.

225 Brook W. R. Pearson, "The Lukan Censuses, Revisited," *CBQ* 61 (1999): 276.

itself—that the census itself was a means of demonstrating Roman control of the world."[226] Census was taken periodically, and it is likely that Joseph and Mary going to their original village had some truism with the Roman census procedure. In this regard, Brook Pearson quotes W. M. Ramsay: "The Romans tried to cope in another way the difficulty of numbering people who might be far from home, viz., by allowing them at some time during the enrolment-year to their proper and original home; and they permitted them to come for enrolment at anytime during the year."[227] The main purpose of imperial census was to tax, to exercise social control, and to make the colonial subject internalise the Roman power.

Pyung Soo Seo observes, "[C]ensus was an exercise of Roman power, and that taxation was rooted in census."[228] However, the empire justifies taxation in terms of good governance. In Tacitus' writing, a Roman general says to the Gauls: "We ourselves, despite many provocations, imposed upon you by right of conquest only such additional burdens as were necessary for preserving peace. Stability between nations cannot be maintained without armies, nor armies without pay, nor pay without taxation" (*Hist.* 4.74). There were direct taxes and indirect taxes,[229] however, it is noted that, the details and levy of the taxes varies from region to region.

Like any other provinces, Palestine paid tribute to Rome. According to both Oakman and Freyne, the *tributum soli* imposed by Pompey, Herod (*Ant.* 14.202–203), and Tiberius (cf. Tacitus, Ann. 2.42) in Palestine was heavier than the other provinces of the empire.[230] In Roman Palestine, apart from the direct *tributum*, indirect taxes such as market taxes (cities), transit tolls, port tax, access rents—city controlled resources, labour for state projects such as building of aqueducts and roads were imposed upon the people.[231] On top of that, the Jerusalem temple had its own exaction of resources from the people in the form of tithe (for support of priest), head tax (half-shekel per year), agricultural products and animal offerings as well as material goods vowed to the temple. The burden of heavy taxation naturally provided the elite the opportunity to gain power over peasant through

226 Roger Bagnall and Bruce Frier, *The Demography of Roman Egypt* (Cambridge: Cambridge University Press, 1994), 29–30.

227 Brook W. R. Pearson, "Lucan Censuses, Revisited," *CBQ* 61 (1999): 275 citing W. M. Ramsay, Luke's Narrative of the Birth of Christ," *ExpTim* (1912): 483.

228 Seo, *Luke's Jesus in the Roman Empire*, 55.

229 As a general rule two kinds of direct taxes were levied on the people such as *tributum agri* or *tributum soli*, which is a tax on landed property estimated on the basis of annual yield of crops and cattle, and *tributum capitis*, which is a head tax.

230 Douglas E. Oakman, *Jesus and the Economic Questions of His Day* (Lewiston: Mellen, 1986) 68–69; Freyne, *Galilee*, 188–192.

231 Cassidy, *Jesus, Politics, and Society*, 96; Hanson and Oakman, *Palestine in the Time of Jesus*, 114.

loan and to take over or control peasant land in the case of debt defaults.[232] On the other hand, rising indebtedness and loss of land led to the breakdown of the traditional village based social structure as well as economic structure.[233] Direct evidences of debt crisis come from Josephus' description of the burning of the debts archives by the rebels at the beginning of the Jewish revolt (66–73 CE; see *J. W.* 2.426–427) and the *prosbul* measure attributed to Hillel. The burden of taxes caused economic impoverishment and often precipitated both non-violent and violent resistance.

Roman legion was a symbol of might and terror. Roman emperors hung on to a large force of army to deter rivals.[234] "The crucial thing was that they validated an expectation among allies and enemies that sooner or later they would be there to deal with dissent and revolt."[235] Martin Goodman writes, "It was only necessary that the enemies of Rome should know that Rome would always retaliate—in time."[236] Luke's mentioning of the names of the emperors and Roman provincial governors itself call to mind the Roman military formation—legion—the military might of the Roman Empire. Luke provides cues to show how the Roman military operates. The soldiers apparently extort by means of threat or false accusation (3:14); the imperial soldiers "go" and "come" as commanded by the commander (7:8). Luke's narration of "Jerusalem surrounded by armies" (21:20) indicates that he probably knew that it was the Roman legion under the command of Vespasian's son Titus that razed down the city and the temple in 70 CE.

The most significant mention of legion is in the pericopae of the exorcism of the Gerasene demoniac (8:26–39 par Mark 8:28–9:1; Matt 5:1–20). Legion is both the name and symbol of Roman military might that enforced census and taxation. The possessed Gerasene demoniac was a symbolic expression of the Decapolis being under the control of the Roman legion.[237] When Jesus asked the Gerasene demoniac "What is your name?" he replied "Legion" (8:30). Wink observes, "Mythological language and bizarre pathology act as a screen to mask political unrest that cannot be safely expressed."[238] Thus, the demoniac was able to name the demons as legion; however, he does it so only through madness, since he could not express his hostility to the Romans in sanity. Paul Hollenbach

232 Hanson and Oakman, *Palestine in the Time of Jesus*, 152.

233 Horsley, "The Imperial Situation of Palestinian Jewish Society," 401.

234 Martin Goodman, "Opponents of Rome: Jews and Others," in *Images of Empire*, ed. Loveday Alexander, 235, observes that Octavian's own early career had demonstrated the ease with which legions could be raised on private initiative by the ambitious, and it was characteristic of Augustus that he viewed Roman politics in the light of his own success.

235 Paula James, "The Language of Dissent," in Huskinson, *Experiencing Rome*, 296.

236 Martin Goodman, "Opponents of Rome: Jews and Others," in *Images of Empire*, ed. Loveday Alexander, 233.

237 Cf. Wink, *Unmasking the Powers*, 46.

238 Wink, *Unmasking the Powers*, 47.

writes that demoniac possession was "at once both the result of oppression and an expression of resistance to it."[239] The possession of the Gerasene by the legion is a pointer that other demoniacs in the Gospel would be possessed by similar demons—the Roman military occupation of the indigenous land. In short, the Roman military presence in Luke's story world of Palestine informs the readers the reality of empire.

3.4.2.3. Rome and Its Political Collaborators

Virginia Burrus rightly noted that, throughout Luke-Acts, "events are informed by the complex dynamics of power circulating between various mediating 'brokers' of imperial dominion."[240] In Luke's Gospel, there are the governor Pontius Pilate, the centurion, and the soldiers representing direct Roman presence; the Herodian client king who was dependent on Roman support; and the chief priests who control the temple, the political and economic powerhouse and thus exert enormous influence over the land of Israel. Though the chief priests exercised certain autonomy in matters of local politics they collaborated with the Herodian client king and the Roman governor, who had the authority to appoint the high priest on their terms. There was also the Sanhedrin, which was not only a judicial and cultic body, but also had the financial responsibility to pay taxes directly into the imperial treasury. In Luke's narrative, the emperors do not come to the open scene but are "purely off-stage presences … as in the lives of most subjects of empire."[241]

The implication of colonial collaboration is vividly portrayed in passion account (22:47–23:25) beginning with the tension set up by Jesus' temple act (cf. 19:45–47). Since, Jesus' strategic presence in the temple threatens the authority and privilege of the chief priests, they begin to catch Jesus by setting up traps. When they failed in their initial attempts, they directly arrested Jesus and brought before the governor Pilate (who represented the direct face of Rome) with accusations that Jesus was perverting the nations and forbidding tribute to Caesar with claims of being a king (23:2). When they saw that Pilate was not quite convinced of the accusation, they added, "he stirs up the people, teaching throughout all, from Galilee even to this place" (23:5). On learning that Jesus was a Galilean, the governor sends the accused Jesus to the Roman client king Herod. The client king Herod adopted a cautious strategy and deferred to the Roman governor for final decision but "clothed in an ambiguous message" (23:11).[242] This deference worked. Luke reports, "that same day Herod and Pilate became friends with each other; before this they had been enemies" (23:12). When Pilate gave his verdict to release Jesus, there was an outcry of protest on the part of chief

239 Hollenbach, "Jesus, Demoniacs, and Public Authorities," 581.

240 Burrus, "The Gospel of Luke and Acts of the Apostles," 134.

241 Burrus, "The Gospel of Luke and Acts of the Apostles," 135.

242 Burrus, "The Gospel of Luke and Acts of the Apostles," 135.

priests and rulers since they stood to gain by eliminating Jesus who destabilised their power and privilege. The court proceeding ended. Pilate yielded "to their will" (23:25). It is often argued that Luke categorically blames the Jewish leaders, especially the Jerusalem rulers, for the death of Jesus.[243] But such argument can only be maintained by ignoring the power relation operative in the politics of the empire. Colonial collaborators were all part of the injustice meted out to Jesus because Rome would not tolerate any dissenters.

3.4.2.4. Jesus' Conflict with Authorities and Rulers

Jesus' conflict with authorities began at the very outset of his public activity. Luke reports that after the temptation in the wilderness, Jesus returned to Galilee "filled with the power of the Spirit" (4:14). Luke sets Nazareth, a Galilean town not far from the military stronghold of Sepphoris, as the launching pad of Jesus' career. The eventful preaching delineates Jesus' policies and ideology. He proclaimed the good news to the poor, release of prisoners, sight to the blind and the acceptable year of the Lord juxtaposing Isa 61:1–2a and 58:5d–6. In its original context, Isa 61 is a text that gives hope to the Jews in exile and those who remained in Judah under the colonial rule of Babylon. Thus, the people who heard this in the first century would expect liberation from Roman domination.[244] Jubilee Year was indeed an acceptable year to all types of oppressed persons.[245] However, for Jesus the good news was not exclusively for the Jews, but was universally extended to the Gentiles. His retelling of Gentiles as the recipients of divine healing enraged the synagogal authority and he was rejected from his own town Nazareth. The rejection at Nazareth anticipated the Jewish public response to Jesus that was worked out in the Gospel. Notable Jesus was rejected for his favourable treatment of the Gentiles.[246]

One of the main conflicts between Jesus and the cultural authorities was on the question of holiness. Though in antiquity, commensality with others generally signify fellowship and acceptance, within Judaism commensality acquired a heightened significance of symbolising a "cultural dynamic of holiness," of which

---

243 Cf. E. Jane Via, "According to Luke, Who Put Jesus to Death?" in *Political Issues in Luke-Acts*, ed. Richard J. Cassidy and Philip J. Scharper (Maryknoll, NY: Orbis Books, 1983), 133, 140. Jon A. Weatherly, *Jewish Responsibility for the Death of Jesus in Luke-Acts*, JSNTSup 106 (Sheffield: Sheffiled Academic Press, 1994), 271–272.

244 J. Massyngbaerde Ford, *My Enemy is My Guest: Jesus and Violence in Luke* (Maryknoll, NY: Orbis Books, 1984), 55. Historically it is not known how far Jubilee year was put into practice. Robert North finds five instances in Josephus and one in 1 Maccabees, reference to the Sabbath years. See, Robert North, "Maccabean Sabbatical Years," *Bib* 34 (1953): 503–506.

245 Ford, *My Enemy is My Guest*, 55.

246 Joseph B. Tyson, "The Jewish Public in Luke-Acts," *NTS* 30 (1984): 578.

the Pharisees were the chief advocates.[247] This has a deeper meaning, in that for the Judaism of the Pharisees, table fellowship exemplified both the shape of the community loyal to God and its teleological consequences of being a kingdom of priests. However, Jesus had open commensality with tax collectors and sinners—"the Son of Man has come eating and drinking, and you say, 'Look a glutton and a drunkard, a friend of tax collectors and sinners" (7:34 cf. 19:1–10).[248] This open commensality resists both the Pharisaic quest for an exclusive holy community of Israel[249] and the patron sponsored Mediterranean meals designed to show the social hierarchy at the dinner table.[250] S. Scott Bartchy observes that Jesus' lifestyle and open commensality was a radical breakaway from both Jewish dietary laws and Hellenistic culture of meal fellowship. He writes,

> One distinctive feature of the historical Jesus' public life was his practice of a radically inclusive, status leveling, and honor-sharing fellowship at the table as a central strategy in his announcement and redefinition of the in-breaking ruling of Israel's God. In so doing, Jesus of Nazareth ... profoundly challenged the inherent exclusivism and status consciousness sustained by the prevailing cultural values and social codes.[251]

Jesus' unconventional open commensality certainly provoked angry resistance from his host and those who sought mealtime honour (ch. 14). However, Jesus' radical style of table fellowship became a possibility across status lines and eventually across ethnic barriers as well. Philip Esler observes, "It is surely through no inadvertence on Luke's part that the types of people specified in Lk 14:21 as replacement guests are virtually identical to the groups promised the good news in Lk 4:18 and extolled as blessed in the beatitudes in Lk 6:20–21."[252] The forging of a new community of equals, which Jesus initiated, was conflictual with the boundary markers and status quo maintenance of their world. Luke reinterprets the subversive social practice of Jesus and his followers to forge an alternative

---

247 Marcus Borg, *Conflict, Holiness and Politics in the Teachings of Jesus* (New York: Edwin Mellen, 1984), 80.

248 In first century Palestine, sinners are referred to an identifiable group of social outcasts: tax collectors, adulterers, prostitutes, murderers, idolaters, and all who fail to observe the law according to the interpretation of the religious authorities (which includes Samaritans and Gentiles).

249 Borg, *Conflict, Holiness and Politics in the Teachings of Jesus*, 120.

250 Cf. Hope, "Status and Identity in the Roman World," 128.

251 S. Scott Bartchy, "The Historical Jesus and Honor Reversal at the Table," *The Social Setting of Jesus and the Gospels*, ed. Wolfgang Stegemann, Bruce J. Malina and Gerd Theissen (Minneapolis: Fortress, 2002), 175.

252 Philip F. Esler, *Community and Gospel in Luke-Acts: The Social and Political Motivations of Lucan Theology* (Cambridge: Cambridge University Press, 1987), 186.

ekklesia over against the dominant cultural values typical of the Mediterranean world under the Roman Empire.

Jesus' healing activities especially exorcism was another factor which brought Jesus in conflict with the authorities. Hollenbach reasoned that, while demon possession and exorcism had their place in the social system, Jesus exorcism was countercultural and disrupted the social stability in that he countered the social structure with his own dominant value of "social healing,"[253] which inevitably earned him conflicts with the authorities and the rulers of the society. He observes that

> it was all right for professional exorcists to ply their art; but it was not all right for an unauthorized exorcist to make so much over demon possession and demoniacs that he identified their healing with God's saving presence and led a widespread exorcising mission that attracted a large following, thereby challenging the prevailing social system and its underlying value system.[254]

Though Luke did not name the opponents of Jesus in the Beelzebul controversy (11:14–16),[255] there was apparently a popular opposition to Jesus' exorcism. Luke seems to suggest that Herod was alarmed at the activity of Jesus probably because Jesus not only exorcises but also associates his exorcising activity directly with the coming of the kingdom of God (11:20). Such claim was a threat to the governing elite of Galilee, and concurrently to the Judean elite. Luke is ambiguous whether Herod is really hostile to Jesus' popularity or had ordinary curiosity about Jesus (9:9b; 23:8). However, when certain Pharisees warned Jesus that Herod intends to kill him, Lukan Jesus unequivocally replied: "Go and tell that fox for me, 'Listen, I am casting out demons and performing cures today and tomorrow, and on the third day I finish my work'" (13:32). This suggests exorcism as both the central activity of Jesus and the cause of his conflicts with the authorities. Crossan considers Jesus' activities as an art of resistance. "It was not, of course, as open as the acts of protestors, prophets, bandits, or messiahs. But it was more open than playing dumb, imagining revenge, or simply recalling Mosaic or Davidic ideals. His eating and healing were, in theory and practice, the precise borderline between private and public, covert and overt, secret and open resistance."[256]

The most sustained Jesus' conflict with the rulers and authorities is vividly narrated in Jesus' temple act and the consequent forceful criminalisation of Jesus on the ground of sedition. In order to appreciate the gravity of Jesus' temple act

---

253 Hollenbach, "Jesus, Demoniacs, and Public Authorities," 584.

254 Hollenbach, "Jesus, Demoniacs, and Public Authorities," 583.

255 In Mark the opponents of Jesus are the scribes who came down from Jerusalem (Mark 3: 220 in Matthew it was the Pharisees (Matt 12:24).

256 J. D. Crossan, *Jesus: A Revolutionary Biography* (San Francisco: Harper Collins, 1994), 105.

that aggravated the rulers' collusion to execute Jesus, it is pertinent to note the significance of the Jerusalem temple for the Jews. It was the religious nucleus of Judaism and the cultural nucleus of Israel.[257] Furthermore, the temple is considered as the locus of divine presence, God's own abode.[258] Thus, the popular view was that the temple is the proper place to offer sacrifice to God and these sacrifices were not only appropriate but also necessary. Josephus gave a vivid expression to the strategic importance of fortified places in the city.

> Whoever was master of these [fortified places] had the whole nation in his power, for sacrifices could not be made without (controlling) these places, and it was impossible for any of the Jews to forgo offering these, for they would rather give up their lives than the worship which they are accustomed to offer God. (*Ant.* 15.248 [Ralp Marcus and Allen Wikgren, LCL]).

In this sacred place, Jesus acted out contrary to the normal expectation surprising the custodian of the temple. Luke's account of the temple act was very restrained and short, but the criticism against the establishment was sharp: "'My house shall be called a house of prayer'; but you have made it a den of robbers" (19:46). Earlier scholarship had predominantly viewed Jesus' action in the temple as *cleansing* the temple. Thus, Alfred Edersheim writes, "The whole of this traffic—money-changing, selling doves and market for sheep and oxen—was in itself, and from its attendant circumstances, a terrible desecration."[259] Gustaf Aulén also argues that Jesus' act was an attack against the priestly class who irresponsibly transformed the temple into a profit making trade centre in a violation of the law of holiness of the temple.[260] Etiene Trócme also thinks that Jesus' action was in defence of God's honour that the temple market had profaned.[261] In the words of Joachim Jeremias, the temple priesthood "misuse their calling ... by carrying on business to make profit."[262]

However, E. P. Sanders in his *Jesus and Judaism* comprehensively argues that since trading is indispensible for sacrifice, the idea of cleansing the supposed profit making economic exchange from the temple does not fairly explain Jesus'

257 Gregory R. Lanier, "Luke's Distinctive Use of the Temple: Portraying the Divine Visitation," *JTS* 65 (2014): 437, notes that religiously the temple was the sole locus of sacrificial cultus, authoritative teaching, worship and prayer, and the destination for Jewish pilgrimage. Culturally it was the centre for the administration of justice as well as commerce and banking.

258 Gottlob Schrenk, "ἱερός," *TDNT* 3:243.

259 Alfred Edersheim, *The Life and Times of Jesus the Messiah* (Grand Rapids: Eerdmans, 1956), 370.

260 Gustaf Aulén, *Jesus in Contemporary Historical Research*, trans. Ingalill H. Hjelm (Philadelphia: Fortress, 1976), 77.

261 Etienne Trocmé, *Jesus as Seen by His Contemporaries* (Philadelphia: Westminster, 1973), 118.

262 Joachim Jeremias, *New Testament Theology: The Proclamation of Jesus*, trans. John Bowden (New York: Charles Scribner's Sons, 1971), 145.

action.[263] He studies the sayings about the destruction of the temple in conjunction with Jesus' temple act and claims that, in the eschatological context, Jesus' action symbolises the destruction of the temple.[264] Horsley pushes Sanders position further and claims that insofar as the temple is the super-sacred institution in antiquity, the central institution of the political economy of Judea (and the Jews), and also the instrument of Roman rule in Judea, Jesus' action in the temple was an anti-imperial protest. He writes, "The action in the Temple, however, was far more than a forcible disruption of Temple operations; it was a profanation of the most sacrosanct institution and a challenge to imperial rule. It was a prophetic action symbolising God's judgment."[265] There was no retreat from such an action. The empire soon struck back.

Luke narrates that owing to Jesus' strategic presence in the temple, "the chief priest, the scribes, and the leaders of the people" began to plot to destroy Jesus (19:47b–48a).[266] J. D. Kingsbury identifies "religious authorities," the antagonists of Luke's story, as a monolithic group comprising of "the Pharisees, Scribes (lawyers, teachers of the law), chief priests, captains (officers) of the temple, elders, rulers, and Sadducees."[267] However, this seems over generalisation since the Pharisees' acrimony with Jesus cannot be placed in the same plane with those of the vindictive "chief priest, scribes, and the leaders of the people" (19:47), based in Jerusalem who were all out to kill Jesus. Probably, the naming of the three groups indicates that it is an official delegation of the Sanhedrin.[268] The vindictive plot of the rulers in Jerusalem against Jesus led to its obvious end. Having failed to trap Jesus with various strategies, they charged him of sedition and brought to the Roman procurator Pontius Pilate, who eventually sentenced him.

3.4.2.5. Rome and Luke's Gospel

The marks of domination and resistance in the following discussions show that Luke's Gospel is a resistance discourse produced by a community in tension with the world of its composition. But it may be noted that the hermeneutical question of Luke's view of the Roman Empire has attracted a protracted debate. Beginning with the work of C. A. Heumann in 1721, Lukan scholars have regularly viewed Luke-Acts as a defense of the church before Roman officials who considered Christianity a threat to the empire.[269] This *apologia pro ecclesia* was furthered by

263 E. P. Sanders, *Jesus and Judaism* (London: SCM, 1985), 62–70.

264 Sanders, *Jesus and Judaism*, 70–71.

265 Richard A. Horsley, *Jesus and the Powers: Conflict, Covenant, and the Hope of the Poor* (Minneapolis: Fortress, 2011), 172.

266 Luke associates Jesus death only with Jerusalem (13:33; cf. 9:31; 18:31–34).

267 J. D. Kingsbury, *Conflict in Luke: Jesus, Authorities, Disciples* (Minneapolis: Fortress, 1991), 21, 97.

268 James M. Dawsey, "Confrontation in the Temple: Luke 19:45–20:47," *PRSt* 11 (1984): 159.

269 Walaskay, *And So We Came to Rome*, 5–14.

Henry Cadbury in 1927 arguing that Luke-Acts is an apology to Rome defending the innocence of Jesus and Paul as well as for Christianity as a *religio licita* like Judaism.[270] However, it is pointed out that, *religio licita* is a modern construction since no such concepts exist in antiquity.[271] Conzelmann argues that, in the context of tension created by the delay of parousia, the evangelist sought to forge a workable relationship between the church and the Roman Empire by emphasising the Jewish role in the various Christian trials while minimising the Roman one.[272]

However, in 1983, Paul Walaskay reversed this approach by arguing that Luke's Gospel is an apology to Rome as it presented the Roman Empire in a positive light to convince the church to live peaceably with the empire.[273] Robert Maddox also thinks that the purpose of Luke is an *apologia pro imperio* to ward off any possible Christians provocative attitudes to the authorities.[274] Philip Esler rejects both the apologetic arguments and identifies Luke's general strategy as legitimation of Christianity to those who needed "strong assurance that their decision to convert and to adopt a different life-style had been the correct one."[275] The legitimation discourse sought to assure the community members that one can still be faithful Christians even while employed in the Roman military or administrative services. However, "Luke-Acts present Jesus, rather than Caesar as Lord and king,"[276] and this uninhibited counter claim suggests that Luke is not done with for some conciliatory position. Richard J. Cassidy's work *Jesus, Politics, and Society: A Study of Luke's Gospel* is one that argues that Jesus did not advocate armed revolt but he was directly critical of Roman officers and client rulers, and their violence and exploitation.[277] In the light of this debate, Virginia Burrus observes that Luke is provocatively ambiguous in its political stance that it naturally provides the possibility to interpret Luke-Acts as both radically subversive and skillfully accomodationist with the Roman powers.[278] However, Luke's ideological critique of Roman Empire has been on the offing in the recent studies. In 2007, in an article, Steve Walton has weighed the positive and negative

---

270 Henry J. Cadbury, *The Making of Luke-Acts*, 2nd ed. (Peabody, MA: Hendrickson, 1999), 308–316.

271 Koester, *History, Culture and Religion in the Hellenistic Age*, 226.

272 Conzelmann, *Theology of St. Luke*, 138–40.

273 Walaskay, *"And So We Came to Rome,"* 16–22. Luke-Acts is a narrative designed to persuade members of the church that "the positive benefits of the empire far outweigh the occasional intrusiveness of an errant emperor" (64).

274 Robert Maddox, *The Purpose of Luke-Acts* (Edinburgh: T&T Clark, 1982), 96–97.

275 Esler, *Community and Gospel in Luke-Acts*, 16–17.

276 Walton, "Luke's View of the Roman Empire," 9.

277 Cassidy, *Jesus, Politics, and Society*, 61–62. For review of Cassidy's work on Luke's view of Rome in relation to the purpose of the Gospel see, Walton, "Luke's View of the Roman Empire," 7–9.

278 Burrus, "The Gospel of Luke and Acts of the Apostles," 153.

pictures of Roman Empire in Luke's writing and concluded that Luke "offers his readers a strategy of critical distance from the empire."[279] This study holds the position that Luke's Gospel is a document of a resistant community that is critical about the values and status quo of the empire. Jesus' resistance to the values of empire reflects Lukan community's faithful resistance to the hierarchical and exploitative status quo of the empire that coloured their daily life. But who is the author? Who is Theophilus? Who are the audience and what is their social location?

3.4.3. Luke and His Reading Communities

It is generally agreed that Luke's Gospel betrays an urban Hellenistic setting, but beyond that to identify the precise social location of the author and his reading communities is a difficult task. Given the difficulty, Joseph Fitzmyer concludes, "the place of composition of the Lucan Gospel ... is really anyone's guess. The only thing that is certain is that it was not written in Palestine.... In the long run, it is a matter of little concern, because the interpretation of the Lucan Gospel and Acts does not depend on it."[280] Obviously there are limits to this search, but even a meagre insight into the character of the author and the audience would provide a great potential to appreciate the text. Like any other literary text, Luke's Gospel itself is a cultural product. It is "a representation of the values and contexts within which it was generated,"[281] which both reflects and is in conflict with the dominant cultural ethos of the world in its composition.

3.4.3.1. The Setting and the Date of Composition of the Gospel

H. J. Cadbury has demonstrated that Luke must have written the work in an urban context.[282] Luke's own contextual assumptions provide textual clues in the Gospel that he adapted rural Palestinian situations into Hellenistic ears. For example, the thatch roof of Mark 2:4 is adapted to a tile one in Luke 5:19; house foundations substitute rock and sand in the parable of the wise and foolish builders (Luke 6:48–49 cf. Matt 7:24–27). So also Luke adapts Semitic titles to Greco-Roman counterparts. For example, ραββουνι in Mark 10:51 is changed to κύριος in Luke 18:41, and γραμματεύς in Mark 12:28 is changed to νομικός in Luke 10:25. This suggests Luke's Hellenistic setting though it is not necessary to posit that a

279 Walton, "Luke's View of the Roman Empire," 35.

280 Fitzmyer, *Luke I–IX*, 57.

281 Green, *Gospel of Luke*, 11.

282 To justify this point Cadbury points to several Lukan traits: editorial insertions of the word 'city' to proper place names; the locus of Jesus and early Christian missionaries almost exclusively in cities, introduction of named cities into unlikely places in the source materials (Luke 8:27, 39; 9:10); the frequent mention of a city as the scene of an episode even when he does not named the place (Luke 18:2, 3; 19:17; 23:19). Cadbury, *Making of Luke-Acts*, 245–249.

solely Gentile audience.[283] Luke's affinity with city setting is also evident in the important place given to Jerusalem and also the urban focus of mission in Acts.[284]

In an ancient prologue dated to third century or earlier Luke was identified as "a Syrian of Antioch," who wrote the Gospel "in the regions of Achaea."[285] Scholars have also proposed several Lukan connections with the city such as Ephesus,[286] Philippi,[287] and other Macedonian locales.[288] There are certainly limits to press for a specific city for the place of composition of the Gospel is difficult to determine, but Lukan associations with the cities of Greece and Asia Minor attested in Acts suggest that it is most likely that the Gospel was produced in an urban setting in the Roman controlled Greece or Asia Minor. Luke's Gospel significantly betrays "'typical' aspects of urban life in a Greco-Roman city" such as a mixed demography, patronage system, the culture of honour, commensality, tension between the rich and the poor.[289]

With regards to the date of composition, some scholars opine that the Luke-Acts was written in the sixties before Paul's trial and death, while others date the Gospel some time in the first half of the second century.[290] The main reason for the early dating of Luke's writing in the sixties is that Acts comes to an abrupt end with Paul's house arrest sometimes in 62–63 CE, but without mentioning Paul's trial and death. Based on the reason, J. A. T. Robinson has made a strong case for an early dating of the Gospel in the early sixties.[291] But Luke's own acknowledgement that "many" have undertaken to write Jesus-story before him (1:1) do not square with a very early date. On the other hand, J. C. O'Neil's proposal of a date between 115–130 CE is considered far fetched.[292] Among scholars, Joseph Fitzmyer and Philip Esler have clearly shown that on the

---

283 Fitzmyer, *Luke I–IX*, 58–59.

284 It is noted that one half of the reference to the word πόλις (city) in the New Testament is found in Luke-Acts, which shows that Luke used the term more than any of the New Testament writers. See Richard L. Rohrbaugh, "The Pre-Industrial City in Luke-Acts: Urban Social Relations," in *The Social World of Luke-Acts: Models for Interpretation*, ed. Jerome H. Neyrey (Peabody, MA: Hendrickson, 1991), 125.

285 R. Alan Culpepper, "The Gospel of Luke: Introduction, Commentary, and Reflections," in *NIB*, ed. Leander E. Keck, vol. 9 (Nashville: Abingdon, 1995), 67; Fitzmyer, *Luke I–IX*, 38–39.

286 Culpepper, "Gospel of Luke," 9.

287 John Nolland, *Luke 1–9:20*, xxxix.

288 François Bovon, *Luke 1: A Critical Commentary on Luke 1:1–9:50*, Hermeia, trans. Christine M. Thomas (Minneapolis: Fortress, 2000), *Luke 1*, 8–9.

289 Halvor Moxnes, "The Social Context of Luke's Community," *Int* 48 (1994): 381–387; Vernon K. Robbins, "The Social Location of the Implied Author of Luke-Acts," in Neyrey, *Social World of Luke-Acts*, 316–318.

290 For a detail discussion of these two extreme views see Fitzmyer, *Luke I–IX*, 54–57.

291 J. A. T. Robinson, *Redating the New Testament* (London: SCM, 1976), 92.

292 Cf. J. C. O'Neill, *The Theology of Acts in Its Historical Setting* (London: SPCK, 1961), 21.

one hand Luke's Gospel clearly shows that it was written after the destruction of the Jerusalem temple,[293] and on the other hand, it betrays no acquaintance with the Pauline corpus, which appear to have gained currency in collected forms by *c.* 95 CE.[294] Thus, the most likely date is around 80–90 CE.

3.4.3.2. The Author and the Dedicatee

The ancient ascription εὐανγέλιον κατὰ Λουκᾶν is found at the end of the Gospel in the oldest extant ms. P^{75}, which is dated from 175–225 CE.[295] According to church tradition, the author is Luke, the "beloved physician" and the companion of Paul, who is mentioned in the Pauline and deutero-Pauline epistles (Phlm 24; Col 4:14; 2 Tim 4:11).[296] This position is mostly based on the "we" sections found in Luke (especially Irenaeus),[297] where the narrator used the first person plural. However, it is possible that such a use of the first person in the narration may be a literary style as sometimes pointed out.[298]

Scholars sought to identify whether the author was a Jewish Christian or a Gentile Christian since the author has a good command of Koine Greek, who is able to write in the style of Hellenistic historiography and has a profound knowledge of the Jewish Bible exegesis.[299] A majority of scholars opine that Luke

---

293 Luke's reference to Jerusalem temple in some texts strongly signals that Luke is writing after its destruction. In Luke 13:35a Lukan Jesus addressed Jerusalem stating "Behold, your house is forsaken" (RSV). Luke also preserves a unique tradition that laments over the impending destruction of Jerusalem (19:43–44) that is considered an allusion to the siege of the city. And most importantly, the "desolating sacrilege" in Mark 13:14 becomes in Lukan version "Jerusalem surrounded by armies" (cf. 21:20). It is most likely that Luke has altered Markan apocalyptic prophecy into the description of the siege of the city itself by Titus. Fitzmyer, *Luke I–IX*, 54; Esler, *Community and Gospel in Luke-Acts*, 27.

294 Fitzmyer, *Luke I–IX*, 57; Esler, *Community and Gospel in Luke-Acts*, 28.

295 Nolland, *Luke 1–9:20*, xxxiv–xxxv.

296 According to Irenaeus (*Against Heresies* 3.1.1): "Luke, too, the companion of Paul, set forth in a book the gospel as preached by him." The Muratorian Canon (ca 170–180 CE, but suspected by some as a fourth century document) also attests that Luke the physician who travelled with Paul wrote the Third Gospel. The date of anti-Marcionite Prologues and Monarchian Prologues is not certain. They provide information that Luke was from Antioch, a physician and a disciple of Paul. Cf. Fitzmyer, *Luke*, 37–39; Bovon, *Luke 1*, 9.

297 Fitzmyer, *Luke I–IX*, 38.

298 Many suspect that the church tradition is simply an intelligent deduction from New Testament evidence that a companion of Paul penned Acts. There are some scholars who regard the church tradition as the best answer to the issue of authorship. Cf. Marshall, *Gospel of Luke,* 33–34; Fitzmyer, *Luke I–IX*, 41. But going by the prologue, the author was not an eyewitness of the life of Jesus. παρηκολουθηκότι in v. 3 does not mean literal following but "to have followed in thought," or "pursued" intellectually. Luke also names the apostles, the eyewitnesses as transmitters of the gospel tradition to "us" (v. 2), distinguishing for himself a direct link with "them" which he did not admit for many (cf. *Life* 357). Bovon, *Luke 1*, 8–9, 21–23.

299 Bovon, *Luke 1*, 8.

was a Gentile Christian. This is evident in Luke's high quality Greek, his rare use of Aramaic or Hebrew, the Hellenistic colouring of Palestinian local details and so on.[300] Bovon thinks that Luke may have been a Macedonian himself who was converted to Christianity.[301] On the other hand, Fiztmyer thinks that, Luke is a Gentile Christian, however at least not a Greek, but a non-Jewish Semite, a native of Antioch, who had a good education in the environment of Hellenistic culture.[302]

But baring the larger narrative from which one sifts out important information about the author and the audience, the prologue of Luke and Acts provides a starting point to identify at least two members of the community.[303] Loveday Alexander argues that Luke's literary convention is compatible with the social and educational level of most early Christians and finds its closest parallels in Greco-Roman scientific and technical writing, not classical historiography or biography, which are usually compared. She surmises that the writing style is "literate but not literary." In other words, "Luke is writing from within a Christian social context which is in significant respects like that of the hellenistic schools themselves."[304] He is educated and has a command over written Greek of official and technical document,[305] and had financial security to afford time to write. However, Milton Moreland argues that, Luke cannot be compared to Roman professional writers of the dominant culture, for unlike them, Luke's socio-political situation is far messier as he is deeply entrenched in the community formation of a new religious movement that is socially and politically a questionable group in the empire.[306] He writes about Jesus the carpenter's son and the leather worker Paul "without a trace of irony" who were not in any standard elite or would interest elite readers.[307] This suggests that Luke's perspective is apparently from the social location of artisan class,[308] though his audience may be from varied

300 Fitzmyer, *Luke I–IX*, 41–42.

301 Bovon opines that, Luke's precise knowledge of Macedonia, in particular Roman institutions, as is related in Acts 16:9 (–13) makes this region (Philippi?) a probable native place. Cf. Bovon, *Luke 1*, 8–9.

302 Fitzmyer, *Luke I–IX*, 42.

303 Miller, *Rumors of Resistance*, 78.

304 Loveday Alexander, *The Preface of Luke's Gospel: Literary Conventions and Social Context in Luke 1.1–4 and Acts 1.1*, SNTSMS 78 (Cambridge: Cambridge University Press, 1993), 210–211.

305 Alexander, *The Preface of Luke's Gospel*, 170–171.

306 Milton Moreland, "The Jerusalem Community in Acts: Mythmaking and the Sociorhetorical Function of a Lukan Setting," in *Contextualizing Acts: Lukan Narrative and Greco-Roman Discourse*, ed. Todd Penner and Caroline Vander Stichele, SBLSymS (Atlanta: SBL, 2003), 294–295, 305.

307 Alexander, *The Preface of Luke's Gospel*, 177.

308 Green, *Gospel of Luke*, 35. Studies in early Christianity show the presence of such persons as free artisans and persons who have small businesses in early Christianity. Cf. Wayne A.

socio-economic background. Thus, one can plausibly posit that Luke was a non-elite with some means, education, and social connection, who is an esteemed community member among the non-elite audience of Jesus-followers.[309]

Theophilus, to whom the Gospel was dedicated, is equally an enigmatic figure. Since Luke addressed his Gospel to the "most excellent Theophilus" (Luke 1:4), it is generally assumed that Theophilus may have been Luke's patron and "a leading figure in whichever group Luke had in mind as his first readers."[310] The name is commonplace in antiquity. But it is also suggested that the meaning of the name "Lover of God," could symbolically "represent a wider Gentile-Christian readership."[311] However, in all probability, he is perhaps a real person acquainted with Luke, otherwise the appellation κράτιστος (most excellent) would have no point.[312] Of course κράτιστος (most excellent), the title given to Theophilus is generally used to address Roman and local elites, but it is also used as an honorary address, especially in the case of work like dedication to a son, a peer, a colleague, a courtier or even to the emperor.[313] In this case Luke's dedication points to at least the importance of Theophilus in the production of his work. Here it is important to note that literary works were mostly published in the first century through social networks like elite circles, patron-client relationships, technical schools, family and friends and business associates.[314] Theophilus is most probably an important person with a higher socio-economic profile than Luke and who has the advantage of promoting Luke's work to the wider audience for public readership.[315]

3.4.3.3. The Reading Communities

In Lukan studies, when it comes to the question of audience, quite a good energy is invested to construct the community's situation in terms of its religious background, that is whether Luke was addressing a Gentile Christian, Jewish Christian, or a mixed of both.[316] But it is equally important to inquire the social dimension of Luke's community. Virginia Burrus observes, not without consideration of internal evidence that the Gospel reflects imperial debris and

---

Meeks, *The First Urban Christians* (New Haven: Yale University Press, 1983), 51–73.

309 Green, *Gospel of Luke*, 34–35; Miller, *Rumors of Resistance*, 79.

310 Maddox, *The Purpose of Luke-Acts*, 12; Paul S. Minear, "Dear Theo: The Kerygmatic Intention and Claim of the Book of Acts," *Int* 27 (1973): 132.

311 Johnson, *Gospel of Luke*, 28.

312 Green, *Gospel of Luke*, 44.

313 Alexander, *Preface*, 188–90; Green, *Gospel of Luke*, 44–45.

314 Loveday Alexander, "Ancient Book Production and the Circulation of the Gospels," in *The Gospels for all Christians: Rethinking the Gospel Audience*, ed. Richard Bauckham (Grand Rapids: Eerdmans, 1998), 99–100.

315 Green, *Gospel of Luke*, 44–45.

316 For reviews and discussion see Esler, *Community and Gospel in Luke–Acts*, 24–33.

conflicts between the "rich and poor, urban and rural, Jew and Gentile, the Jerusalem temple and the land of Israel, Rome and those subjugated under imperial rule."[317] This suggests the diversity of socio-economic and socio-cultural background of Lukan audience. A broad approach is taken here to inquire whether the audience belonged to any particular socio-economic framework and cultural framework.

The Socio-economic Framework

Joel B. Green writes, "Luke's social world was defined around power and privileges ... and is measured by a complex of phenomena—religious purity, family heritage, land ownership (for nonpriests), vocation, ethnicity, gender, education and age."[318] In this regard, Gerhard Lenski's model of social stratification in an agrarian society provides a good model to look for implications of socio-economic stratification in Luke's Gospel.[319] Lenski's analysis of agrarian empires classified nine significant classes.[320] The first two classes such are the *ruler* (a class in himself) and the *governing class* are the ruling elites with power and privilege. The following three classes such as the *retainer class*, *merchant class*, and *priestly class* were (generally speaking) retainers who served the ruling elites. The remaining four classes such as the *peasants*, *artisans*, the *unclean class* and the *expendables* constituted the lower strata.[321]

Both Caesar Augustus (2:1) and Tiberias Caesar (3:1) were the emperors, though they are offstage character in the Gospel. The governing/aristocratic class in Roman Empire are those who belonged to the *ordines*—the senators,

317 Burrus, "The Gospel of Luke and Acts of the Apostles," 133.

318 Green, *Gospel of Luke*, 60.

319 Green, *Gospel of Luke*, 60; Millers, *Rumors of Resistance*, 32–38. Examples of New Testament scholars who makes use of Lenski's model in the study of Gospel are Crossan, *Historical Jesus*; Stegemann and Stegemann, *Jesus Movement*; Philip F. Esler, *The First Christian World* (New York: Routledge, 2000), 11–12; Marcus Borg, *Jesus: Uncovering the Life, Teachings, and Relevance of a Religious Revolutionary* (San Francisco: Harper San Francisco, 2006), 77–108.

320 For a detail reading on social classes of "agrarian societies" refer to Gerhard E. Lenski, *Power and Privilege*, 210-284. According to Lenski's scheme, only about 2% of agrarian population belongs to the ruling class, and about 8% comprises of the service class or retainers in the cities who caters to the need of the ruling class. The remaining 90% of the population belong to the lower underprivileged class.

321 It is noted that Lenski's model does not account for gender in any adequate manner. Married woman's status can be clubbed together with their husband's status. But there were also independent single women with independent status and resource (cf. Luke 8:1–2). Women could have power and influence through their property (Stegemann and Stegemann, *Jesus Movement*, 65–66). For instance, Claudia Capitolina, from a Roman senatorial social background is recorded to have been a patron to a synagogue in Asia Minor (Maraget Williams, "Jews and Jewish Communities in the Roman Empire," in Huskinson, *Experiencing Rome*, 312).

equestrians, and decurians.[322] In Luke the powerful people such as Herod the Great (1:5), Pontius Pilate, Herod Antipas, Philip, Lysanias, Annas, Caiaphas (3:1–2), the unnamed landlord in 12:16, the rich man with an estate in 16:1 can be identified as the ruling class. These belonged to the upper stratum with wealth, power and privilege.[323] The retainer class in Luke such as the centurion (7:1), the soldiers (3:14) the tax collectors (19:1–10), household manager (16:1) the scribes (9:22) and the Pharisees (14:1) are embedded in the status quo of the empire. Especially the centurion, the soldiers, and the tax collectors are dependent on the ruling class. In Luke, the priestly class, who function as the religious leaders are shown to collaborate with Rome instead ancestral traditions of justice and mercy, which Jesus preached with the vision of a new society.[324]

Apart from the above noted upper socio-economic strata, Luke's Gospel indicates that the experience of poverty for a majority of audience who belonged to the lower socio-economic strata was real.[325] Notably, the Lukan Jesus addresses the πτωχος (poor) both in the Nazareth proclamation (4:18–19) and in the Sermon on the Plain (6:20). Philip Esler maintains that the word πτωχοί in a Greco-Roman city in the first century did mean "beggars" although "it would be incorrect to translate *'anāwīm* at Isa 61.1 as 'beggars.'"[326] Lukan Jesus began his public activities by specifying the πτωχοί or the urban dregs of the Hellenistic cities and others who were in the margins of the social register of the society as recipients of the good news. Luke's accentuation of the realities of the poor pitted against the rich in the context of economic imperialism (1:52–53; 6:24–25) is also indicative of the composition of Lukan audience. The protest character of the audience is also revealed in the parables of Jesus (cf. 19:11–27; 20:9–16).

322 Senators and equestrian constitute the upper and lower strata of the Roman nobility respectively, while the decurians are local gentry in the provincial cities whose privileges were comparable with the senators at Rome. Esler, *Community and Gospel*, 171–172.

323 Douglas E. Oakman, "The Countryside in Luke-Acts," in Neyrey, *Social World of Luke-Acts*, 162.

324 Miller, *Rumors of Resistance*, 36.

325 The reference to those who lack proper clothing and sufficient food (3:11; 6:20), the hungry and sorrowing (6:20–25), those anxious for material needs (12:22) and daily bread (11:3), the hungry crowd (9:10–17), the powerless and have–nots (8:18), debtors (12:58–59) suggests that Lukan audience includes these group of people whose situation is typical of peasantry in an agrarian empire. Jesus' addressed to the crowd who are poor (cf. 6:20) with the language of hope and reversal of fortunes suggests that most of Luke's audience would be from the class who maintain simply subsistence level. At the same time Lukan reference to the unclean and the expendables (Cf. Lenski, *Power and Privilege*, 280–282) such as the prostitute (sinful woman, 7:37), lepers (5:12; 17:11–19), the man with unclean spirit (4:33–36), the paralytic (5:18), the man with a withered hand (6:6), demon possessed (8:26–39; 9:37–43), crippled women (13:10–17), man with dropsy (14:1–60), the blind beggar (18:35), the crippled, the blind, and the lame (14:21) also suggests that Lukan audience includes these groups of people.

326 Esler, *Community and Gospel in Luke-Acts*, 180.

William Herzog argues that parables contain subversive speech that exposes the exploitation of the impoverished peasants by the aristocratic elites. He rightly attaches the community aspects of the parables and points out that, parables are not monologue to be heard and accepted but an invitation to conversation and communal reflection.[327] Thus, it is presumed that the socio-economic dimension of the audience will direct the hearers to the Roman imperial system as the context of Luke's Gospel.

However, there are apparently wider socio-economic diversities in the reading communities of Luke's Gospel. The preceding discussion shows that the author and the dedicatee Theophilus belong to two different status and social groups, but both belonging to non-elite group, though Theophilus was perhaps a person of some means. It is possible that Luke's audience includes a few well to do members who could provide place for worship, food, money, and assist the materially poor in the community. Luke has several reflections on proper use of wealth (Luke 12:13–21; 14:7–24; 16:1–31; 18:18–30) and several traditions on Jesus' and the disciples' relationship with the wealthy and powerful (Luke 7:1–10; 8:1–3; 40–56; 19:1–10).[328] Luke's portrayal of women in the Gospel is also significant. They are frequently associated with food, meals and hospitality (4:38–39; 7:36–50; 8:1–3). In the case of Luke 8:1–3, the women actually provided hospitality, acting as patrons of Jesus. Though in the Greco-Roman society women's role is usually limited to the household but not in the public spheres, non-elite women were more independent and could pursue career on their own like vendors of merchandise. Paul Tribelco has shown that there were women in the western parts of Asia Minor who held prominent social political positions.[329] This provides an interesting background to see independent women in Luke's narrative. Picturing a dinner setting for the reading of Luke-Acts, F. Gerald Downing imagines a mixed audience coming from varying status, profession and life experiences along with Theophilus including men, women, children, slaves, free and freedman.[330] Nonetheless, socio-economically, Luke's community is composed of non-elite; the community is at best a subordinate group in the context of Roman Empire.

327 William R. Herzog II, *Parables as Subversive Speech: Jesus as Pedagogue of the Oppressed* (Louisville, Kentucky: Westminster/John Knox Press, 1994), 265.

328 Miller, *Rumors of Resistance*, 82.

329 Paul R. Tribelco, *Jewish Communities in Asia Minor* (Cambridge: Cambridge University Press, 1991), 104–126.

330 F. G. Downing, "Theophilus's First Reading of Luke-Acts," in *Luke's Literary Achievement: Collected Essays*, ed. C. M. Tuckett, JSNTSup (Sheffield: Sheffield Academic Press, 1995), 94–95.

Socio-cultural Framework

Luke's Gospel also betrays a forging relationship with the social "other." The Lukan Jesus deliberately breaks the socio-cultural barriers of clean vis-à-vis unclean culturally, insider vis-à-vis an outsider ethnically. Probably the social formation of Lukan Christian group in the late first century in the Roman world demanded a vision of inclusiveness that can accommodate disparate identities and also break away from the carryover of colonial culture. Luke's own evaluation of the dominant city culture, patronage system, benefactions, and the quest for honour that characterise socio-cultural relationship in the Hellenistic cities would provide an ingress to the salient features of Luke's community.

Meals and hospitality scenes that occupy a major part of the Gospel will illustrate how social interaction plays out and can be taken as the first instance. Table fellowship was not just one of eating together; it was a "miniature models for the rules of association and socialization ... a map of economic discrimination, social hierarchy, and political differentiation."[331] It served as a means of social interaction as well as competition and patronage.[332] And thus, hospitality demanded a reciprocal action from the other as well. At the same time, in the Greco-Roman and Jewish worlds of the first century, table-fellowship was a hospitality in which the stranger/guest was welcomed into the most affective space of sharing. It indicates that the invited person was being accepted into a relationship.[333] For the Diaspora Jews, "commensality served as an expression of their identity, circumscribed by strong rules concerning boundaries and purity."[334] It is significant that Luke portrays Jesus at meals sometimes as guest and sometimes as host (5:29–32; 7:36–50; 14:1–24; 19:5–10). The meal scenes both reflect the conflicts within the community and the challenge to cultivate a vision of free social relationship irrespective of social status in contrast to the hierarchical and reciprocal culture of the empire (5:29–32; 14:1–24). The parable in Luke 14 indicates a social challenge to the imperial culture of reciprocal social relationship. Probably, like any other groups in the Greco-Roman world, meals must have played an important part in the life of Luke's community.[335] But to base hospitality on the basis of generalised reciprocity (free gifting without expectation of return) not only breaks the colonial culture and its values but it also invites being exposed to social sanctions.[336] The countercultural dimension of Lukan

331 Crossan, *Jesus: A Revolutionary Biography*, 68.

332 Moxnes, "The Social Context of Luke's Community," 383.

333 Graham Stanton, "Message and Miracles," in *The Cambridge Companion to Jesus*," (Cambridge: Cambridge University Press, 2001), 69.

334 Moxnes, "The Social Context of Luke's Community," 383.

335 Moxnes, "The Social Context of Luke's Community," 383.

336 Moxnes, "The Social Context of Luke's Community," 387.

Jesus' open commensality suggests that Lukan community is a mixed group socio-economically and socio-culturally.

But the diversity of Lukan community can be noted further. According to Milton Moreland, social and community formation in the first century Roman context was propelled by "social and religious dislocation" and "Roman political and social control impacted all new groups."[337] This dislocation was caused by the relative ease in travel to the new place, trading ventures into new cities, military resettlement, slavery system and so on. Each of these forces separated the individuals from their ties with their *patris*.[338] There was much socio-cultural change in the Roman context that, "Being ruled by Rome was a complex experience that created ambiguity in the articulation of that experience."[339] In Luke's narrative, there was the tax collector seeking Jesus; the Roman centurion, a patron to Jewish synagogue lauded by Jesus (7:1–10); the prodigal son who was lost in foreign land but finds a home with celebration (15:11–32); the Samaritan merchant on the road (10:29–37); and women who provided for Jesus and his disciples (8:1–3). It is noted that in the Greek east, many rural villages and areas were connected to the cities and were considered to be part of the economic, political and religious life. Jim Grimshaw has shown that there was probably much exchange between the rural providers and urban consumers in Luke's food market district.[340] This suggests that even though Luke's community is perhaps dominantly urban, one should not rule out the rural presence both from the displacement noted above and the regular city and country interaction.

Thus, given the notable diversity of Luke's communities, in terms of socio-economic situation, ethnic cultural roots, and urban-rural composition, one has to nuance the description of Lukan audience. One can plausibly posit that Lukan audience is a mixed group from diverse ethnic roots, occupations, and religious background with different levels of wealth, status, and citizenship.

3.4.3.4. Forging New a Community in the Midst of Conflict and Resistance

Luke's Gospel suggests the forging of a marginal community in the context of conflict and resistance engendered by Roman imperialism. This is clear in the countercultural discourse of the Gospel and the social formation of a marginal community in tension with the rulers and powers. It is noted that Roman rule was characterised by census collection for social control, tributes, imperial military presence, and native collaboration especially those who controlled the temple. But right under the nose of Roman rule, Luke begins his Gospel by introducing the birth of John the Baptist and Jesus who led resistance movements critical of

337 Moreland, "Jerusalem Community," 299.

338 Moreland, "Jerusalem Community," 300.

339 Jerry Toner, *Popular Culture in Ancient Rome* (Cambridge: Polity Press, 2009), 187.

340 Jim Grimshaw, "Luke's Market Exchange District: Decentering Luke's Rich Urban Center," *Semeia* 86 (1999): 40.

the rulers and powers. In the opening chapter itself, Luke introduces an image of a world turned upside down—the reversal of fortune of the rich and poor, powerful and downtrodden, social insider and outsider through the voice of a virgin yet pregnant and unmarried girl Mary (cf. 1:51–53). This theme of reversal is reiterated in Jesus' Nazareth speech (4:16–30 cf. 6:20–26; 7:18–23; 17:7–24). Such a reversal of fortune runs counter to the metanarratives of the hierarchy and domination system of the empire. Luke's Gospel thus reflects that Lukan community is a resistant community.

3.5. Conclusion

In the first part, this chapter underlined the various Jewish group formations and resistance movements both in the Hellenistic-Hasmonean and Roman-Herodian period as the background and foreground of Jesus' movement. Each movement despite their peculiarity was a response to the predicament of colonialism and imperialism. Each movement was anchored on the group's understanding of Israelite traditions. It is noted that Jesus' movement was one of the movements that responded to the Roman Empire. The second part of the chapter noted how Luke's Gospel makes use of Jesus traditions to inform and transform the social formation of an early Christian community that is struggling to assert its identity in the context of late first century Roman Empire. It is noted that the colonial imprints of domination and resistance to domination that filled the Gospel reflects both the conflictual context and the resistant character of the Gospel community. The discussions on the setting of the Gospel, the author and the social composition of the Gospel's audience based on the internal evidence have highlighted the marginal character of the Gospel community. The following chapter will take up the role of the Spirit in the social formation of the resistant community.

Chapter 4

The Spirit and Prophetic Protest in Luke's Gospel

4.1. Introduction

The preceding chapter highlighted the socio-political milieu of the convoluted Jewish response to the changing empires behind Luke and Lukan community's social formation in the midst of conflict and resistance. This chapter explores the role of the Spirit in the Lukan canticles with a special focus on the Magnificat (1:46–55), the Benedictus (1:67–79), and Jesus' Nazareth proclamation (4:16–30). This study argues that the Spirit-inspired Lukan canticles and the Nazareth proclamation demonstrate the activity of the Spirit in engendering a community of resistance that challenges and subverts the claims of the Roman Empire with a vision of liberation and counter social formation for survival and self-representation. It is anticipated that, reading these texts from the vantage point of the dominated from within the context of first century Palestine under the Roman hegemony will proffer a resistance paradigm of Lukan pneumatology.

4.2. The Spirit and the Lukan Canticles

There are four Lukan canticles such as the Magnificat (1:46–55), the Benedictus (1:67–79), the Gloria in Excelsis (2:13–14), and the Nunc Dimittis (2:28–32). There is a divine agency involved in the singing of all these canticles.[1] Especially, the role of the Spirit of God is explicit in the singing of the Benedictus and the Nunc Dimittis, and implicit in the singing of the Magnificat and the Gloria in

1 Though Luke did not explicitly mention that Mary sang the Magnificat under the inspiration of the Holy Spirit, it is implicit in the promise of the Holy Spirit in the annunciation of Jesus birth (cf. 1:35). The angelic army sung the Gloria in Excelsis (2:13–14). There is an explicit mention that Zechariah sang the Benedictus "filled with the Holy Spirit" (1:67). Similarly, Simeon sang the Nunc Dimittis under the influence of the Holy Spirit (2:25–32).

Excelsis. Since, the canticles are not merely songs of praises but contain political overtones with subtle colonial mimicry, it is important to explore the role of the Spirit in the canticles by attending to the characters and experience of the singers in their socio-political context. The Magnificat and the Benedictus are chosen for a detailed study, since they contains radical voices of resistance from the margins of the society. To foreground a postcolonial reading of the chosen canticles, a brief discussion on the Spirit in Lukan infancy narratives, the literary aspects of the canticles and traditional interpretations are in order.

4.2.1. The Spirit in the Infancy Narrative

Lukan infancy narrative 1:5–2:52 is recognised as the first major section of Luke's Gospel. It is separated from the fine literary Greek prologue (1:1–4), by a shift to heavily Semitic Greek, and is distinguished from the fresh narrative setting of ch. 3 that shows a different geopolitical setting.[2] It is striking to note that two significant temporal markers (1:5; 2:1–3) informed the Lukan infancy narrative that underline the colonial situation of the birth of the messiah. The birth of John and Jesus took place in the days of King Herod (1:5). More emphatically, the birth of Jesus took place at a time of Augustan imperial census. Luke adumbrates this political landscape and narrates the birth of the messiah with images of the temple, priesthood, and the deliverance of the people of God, which are Israelite identity markers, saturated by references to the Spirit.[3]

Given the sudden outburst of the prophetic Spirit in the infancy narratives, it is often noted that Lukan Holy Spirit is rooted in the heritage of Jewish Spirit of prophecy.[4] However, Lukan infancy narrative shows that, in the socio-cultural milieu of Roman-Herodian rule, the Spirit was breathing powerfully among the people giving vitality and passion in fomenting resistant discourse for counter social formation. The Spirit filled John the Baptist is said to walk in the spirit of Elijah[5] "to make ready a people prepared for the Lord." Mary will bear a son through the Holy Spirit and he will be called Son of God (like any of the Roman emperors) and he will inherit the Davidic throne, which is a dangerous political claim under Herod's rule. Filled with the Spirit, Elisabeth recognised Mary as the

---

2 Nolland, *Luke 1–9:20*, 76.

3 Cf. Kuecker, *Spirit and the 'Other,'* 51.

4 Schweizer, "πνεῦμα πνεύματος," *TDNT*, 6:407–413; Menzies, *Empowered for Witness*, 115, 227. Also see G. W. H. Lampe, "The Holy Spirit in the Writings of St. Luke," in *Studies in the Gospels: Essays in Memory of R. H. Lightfoot*, ed. D. E. Nineham (Oxford: Blackwell, 1957), 165ff.

5 Lampe "The Holy Spirit in the Writings of St. Luke," 166–167, maintains that certain characteristic features of the Old Testament figures such as Elijah, Samson, Samuel, and even Jeremiah are coded in the description of the person of John the Baptist. The Baptist is clearly presented as the prototype of Elijah whose movement represents a social movement from the underside of the society against the establishment. Cf. Gottwald, *The Hebrew Bible*, 352. Horsley and Hanson, *Bandits, Prophets, and Messiahs*, 140.

mother of "my Lord" (1:43). Mary (1:46–55), and Zechariah (1:68–79), sang the liberating vision of God with subjecthood for re-presentation. The Spirit also came upon Simeon who was looking for the "consolation" of Israel. The saturated political overtones with languages of national salvation shows that Lukan understanding of the Holy Spirit is not simply a Spirit of prophecy. It is more. It is a Spirit of resistance that is at work among the marginalised, empowering them to resist their oppressor and to transform their identity with new visions of world order.

4.2.2. The Magnificat and the Benedictus

The Magnificat and the Benedictus are transmitted in the form of poems recited by Mary and Zechariah respectively. However, they are not generally regarded as being composed by Mary, Zechariah, and Luke. The languages in these hymns are highly Semitised, and thus many scholars debate over the original language of composition.[6] Douglas Jones claims that many terms and phrases of the hymns are from the Hebrew Bible particularly from Psalms and other hymnic texts, "never directly quoting, but nevertheless revealing a direct dependence."[7] He argues that the canticles are better understood as composed originally in Hebrew, as they betray no "clever imitation of a Greek writer," but "the product of highly developed tradition of psalmody."[8] But R. E. Brown in his magisterial treatment of Lukan infancy narratives concludes, "The linguistic opponents have fought them to a draw."[9] Though the original language of composition is not the immediate concern of this study, it is important to note that the hymns are modelled after Hebrew psalms of praise.

6 Scholars are divided over the difference of opinion between Adolf von Harnack, who argued for Lukan composition of the canticles in Greek (and thus had no pre-history), and Herman Gunkel who opines that the Magnificat (without 1:48) and Benedictus (without 1:76–79) were Jewish hymns and that v. 48 and 76–79 were Christian additions. For a detailed discussion of the original language of the hymns see Douglas R. Jones, "The Background and Character of Lukan Psalms," *JTS* 19 (1968): 19; Stephen Farris, *The Hymns of Luke's Infancy Narrative: Their Origin, Meaning and Significance,* JSNTSup 9 (Sheffield: JSOT Press, 1985), 31–50.

7 Jones, "The Background and Character of Lukan Psalms," 43.

8 Jones, "The Background and Character of Lukan Psalms," 19, 21, 44.

9 Raymond E. Brown, *The Birth of the Messiah: A Commentary on the Infancy Narratives in Matthew and Luke* (Garden City, NY: Doubleday, 1977), 246. Brown's statement seems to stand. Stephen Farris has tried to prove wrong Brown's statement by revisiting previous debate with a fresh analysis of Luke 1–2 and concludes, "It does appear that these hymns may depend upon Semitic, probably Hebrew, originals." Farris, *Hymns*, 62. However, Michael D. Goulder has countered Farris and argues in favour of a Greek original since the "Magnificat and the Benedictus seem to belong together both in thought and in method of composition." Michael D. Goulder, *Luke: A New Paradigm*, vol 1. JSNTSup 20 (Sheffield: Sheffield Academic Press, 1989), 231, 243.

The form of the canticles have close parallel with Old Testament psalmody especially the declarative hymn of praise[10] and passages from Second Temple literature. The Magnificat in particular, now embedded in the Lukan birth narrative stands in the same tradition of the Hebrew songs of liberation such as the song of Miriam (Exod 15), Deborah (Judg 5), and Judith (Jdt 16).[11] Raymond Brown summed the opinion of scholarly consensus that, the styles and religious outlook of the Lukan canticles have their closest parallel in the Jewish hymns and psalms found in 1 Maccabees, Judith, 2 Baruch, 4 Ezra and the Qumran Scrolls.[12] What is notable is that most of these literary repertoires were a product-of and resistance against the empire. Probably, Luke found these hymns liberative as they enact the status reversals and provide visions of an alternative order that allows his community to counter the hierarchical and status quo maintained by the empire system of domination.

There are various proposals to the community of origin. Paul Winter has suggested that the canticles are Maccabean war songs.[13] J. Massyngberde Ford also argues that Lukan canticles echo many of the aspiration of the Zealots' anticipation of the deliverance of God from the oppressor.[14] On the other hand some opine that the canticles come from non-militant groups, for example, the group of John the Baptist.[15] Especially, R. E. Brown assumes that it originated in the worship of the earliest Jewish Christians[16] or more particularly (a hypothetical) Jewish Christian *anawim*.[17]

---

10 Old Testament hymn of praise consists of three parts: an introduction of praising God, the body of hymn (listing the reasons of praise) and a conclusion (which often repeats the elements of the body). The commonly agreed upon Old Testament hymn of praise are Pss 8, 19, 29, 33, 47, 48, 100, 103, 117, 135, 136 and so on. Cf. Fitzmyer, *Luke I–IX*, 359–360; Brown, *Birth of the Messiah*, 355.

11 Horsley, *Liberation of Christmas*, 108. Horsley points to the general observation that, although the hymns fit generally into the category of psalms of praise they do not fall into a particular *Gattungen*. The Second Temple psalms such as Sirach, the Qumran *Hodayot* and Judith 16 still have considerable traditional pattern of Hebrew psalms and especially Ben Sira and Qumran authors come from the educated class of scribes and sages, but Lukan canticles seem to come from less educated popular folks as its literary feature shows. He argues that art is forgotten in the over emphasis on the mighty acts of God and there is lack of self-conscious art revealing the purpose of the psalm; didactic or reflective elements in contrast to the learned contemporary psalmody (108–109).

12 Brown, *Birth of the Messiah*, 349 cf. Ford, *My Enemy is My Guest*, 20.

13 Cf. Paul Winter, "Magnificat and Benedictus: Maccabean Psalms?" *BJRL* 37 (1954): 328–47. The untenability to embrace this theory is explained by Farris, *Hymns*, 86–88.

14 J. Massyngberde Ford, "Zealotism and the Lukan Infancy Narratives," *NovT* 18 (1976): 280–292.

15 Cf. David Flusser, *Judaism and the Origins of Christianity* (Jerusalem: Magnes, 1988), 148.

16 Cf. Jones, "The Background and Character of Lukan Psalms," 47–48.

17 Brown, *Birth of the Messiah*, 352–353.

However, Horsley argues that greater openness to the diversity of events and movements, for instance the popular Palestinian messianic movements might proffer "possible milieu from and in which they should be heard rather than to place too much emphasis on the question of origin itself" rather than trying to locate the hymns based on the Christian and Jewish canons of historical events.[18] Nevertheless, the ascription to the Jewish Christian origin of these hymns seems probable though hypothetical. Stephen Farris writes "it does seem very likely that they were composed in the Palestinian church."[19] Though the community of origin cannot be located with certitude, the canticles probably originated in the Palestinian Jewish milieu.[20] The date of composition is also very conjectural. However, it is reasonable to assume that it was composed before the terrible event of 70 CE since one might not expect the canticles with all the aspiration for national redemption after that year.[21] Amanda C. Miller writes, "Luke's evident admiration of the early Jerusalem gathering of Jesus-followers (see, for example, Acts 2:41–47; 4:32-35) might explain how their hymnic compositions made their way into the worship and writings of Christians in the hellenized cities of Greece and Asia Minor."[22] These hymns express the aspirations and longings of the people who were crushed by the rich and the mighty.

4.3. The Magnificat (Luke 1:46–55)

4.3.1. Analysis of the Text (Luke 1:46–55)

The Magnificat celebrates the imminent birth of the messiah. In its narrative context, the Magnificat is placed in the meeting of two mother-to-be Mary and Elisabeth following the annunciation of Jesus' birth. In the textual tradition it is disputed whether the song is to be attributed to Mary or Elisabeth.[23] However, it is more likely that the song is originally attributed to Mary as attested by the best textual traditions.[24] The hymn resonates strongly with the social status of Mary

---

18 Horsley, *Liberation of Christmas*, 109.

19 Farris, *Hymns*, 97.

20 Brown, *Birth of the Messiah*, 354; D. Gerhard Delling, *Worship in the New Testament*, trans. Percy Scott (London: Darton, Longman & Todd, 1962), 90–91.

21 Farris, *Hymns*, 98.

22 Miller, *Rumors of Resistance*, 109.

23 A majority of witnesses attribute the speaker of the Magnificat to Mary. However, three Latin manuscripts such as ms. a of the fourth century (*Elisabeth*), ms. b of the fifth century (*Elisabel*) and ms. 1* of the seventh and eighth century (*Elisabeth*) as well as some patristic writers preserve Elisabeth as the subject of εἶπεν in Luke 1:46. See Bruce M. Metzger, *A Textual Commentary on the Greek New Testament,* 2nd ed. (Stuttgart: Deutche Bibelgesellschaft, 2002), 109. It is most likely that "Elisabeth" is not the "harder reading" (*lectio difficilior*) but "the result of change introduced by some copyists who sought to relate the canticle to 1:41 and the 'her' (autē) of v. 56, which presently has a very remote antecedent, to Elizabeth." Fitzmyer, *Luke I–IX*, 366 cf. Farris, *Hymns* 112.

24 Cf. Marshall, *Gospel of Luke*, 78; Farris, *Hymns*, 110–112.

as will be discussed below. Mary sings praises to God after being received by the Spirit-filled Elisabeth, who honours the former as the mother of her Lord (1:43) and called her εὐλογημένη (blessed, 1:42) and μακαρία (blessed, 1:45). Aaron Kuecker argues that Mary's song is devoid of the Spirit's inspiration.[25] However, a majority of scholars opine that there is a clear connection between the promise of the Spirit to Mary in Luke 1:35 and the prophetic utterance in 1:46–55.[26] But studies that focus on Lukan pneumatology do not adequately engage the text of Mary's song apart from noting that the song was uttered under the inspiration of the Holy Spirit. Nonetheless, since the inspired Mary sang this hymn of protest, the political function of the Spirit must be paid attention.

The structure of the Magnificat begins by focusing on the individual Mary and ends by focusing on the corporate Israel.[27] Going with the structural pattern of Hebrew hymns of praise, it is pointed out that, the Magnificat has an introduction (vv. 46b–47), the body of the hymns in two major strophes (vv. 48–50, 51–53) and a conclusion (vv. 54–55).[28] However, it can be suitably studied in two-halves (vv. 46–50 and 51–55). The first half (vv. 46–50) is the reaction of an individual (Mary) and the second half (vv. 51–53) expresses the reaction of oppressed communities. Mary's song exhibits features of both an individual psalm and a communal psalm.[29]

In the first half, Mary exalts God as her σωτήρ, which means "saviour" (a title frequently ascribed to Augustus and later Roman emperors) and ὁ δυνατός, which means the "mighty one" (a title ascribed to God as the divine warrior-champion of Israel who accomplishes deliverance, e.g., Zeph 3:17).[30] God's great act has specifically executed the reversal of Mary's status from her lowliness to a blessed status, which all generations will acknowledge. In the Greek text the verbs

25 Kuecker cites four factors to argue the absence of Spirit's inspiration in Mary's song. Each of his points can be countered otherwise. Firstly, the promise of the Spirit in 1:35 cannot be limited to conception alone. The movement and action of the lowly Mary has to be understood in terms of Spirit empowerment. This is also the case with Jesus. The coming of the Spirit upon Jesus set a new stage of his life and work. Secondly, the temporal distance of 1:35 and the Magnificat does not really count for the lack of Spirit inspiration. Rather one can argue that Mary's visit to Elisabeth is the result of the working of the Spirit in Mary. Thirdly, most of the authoritative ancient texts place the Magnificat in the mouth of Mary. Fourthly, Luke does not employ a specific formula to mark out Spirit's presence and absence in the characters of his Gospel. For instance, after the Nazareth preaching, Luke did not say again that Jesus was filled with the Spirit as he preached and healed, but the presence of the Spirit in his life and work is reiterated in Acts 10:38. Cf. Kuecker, *Spirit and the 'Other,'* 61.

26 Robert P. Menzies, *Empowered for Witness*, 115, 227 cf. Lampe, "The Holy Spirit in the Writings of St. Luke," 165ff.

27 Green, *Gospel of Luke*, 101.

28 Fitzmyer, *Luke I–IX*, 360.

29 Brown, *Birth of the Messiah*, 357.

30 Jones, "The Background and Character of Lukan Psalms," 23; Horsley, *Liberation of Christmas*, 111; Ford, *My Enemy is My Guest*, 20–23.

usually stood first in their respective lines, and both conjunctions and articles were eliminated so that the action verbs become prominent.[31] In the second strophe, the poetic lines change from synonymous and synthetic parallelism to antithetic parallelism showing sharp contrast and conflict, especially in vv. 51–53. Amanda Miller observed that if Mary's song ended with the first strophe, it would pose no problem for the empire or its supporter, but it did not end there; the song "not only expresses her joy at the gracious love of God, but also expresses that love's implication for liberation and politics."[32] Mary exalts a God, who has strong preference for the hungry and the humble, and a bias against the powerful and the rich (vv. 51–55).

What would this strong anti-powerful and anti-rich strain mean for a first century Palestinian audience who lived under the domination of foreign empire and its client rulers? Is there any significance for the hymn sung by Mary? How would one understand Luke's inclusion of a vision of God overthrowing the powerful from their thrones in a work that is dedicated to Theophilus who probably was a beneficiary of the Roman Empire?

4.3.2 Traditional Interpretations

Traditional interpretations have sidelined the protest voices and hidden transcripts of the hymn owing to insufficient sensitivities to the Roman colonialism of first century Palestine. Many commentators have provided theological interpretations and neglected the concrete experiences and aspirations of the victims of the empire embedded in the hymns. Some have regarded the Magnificat as an eschatological hymn,[33] whereby, God's favour for Mary is praised as "the sign of God's eschatological act for the world" and the gift of the child as an image of "God's eternal purpose."[34] Notably, God's deeds of bringing down the powerful and lifting up the lowly that the poem inscribes are not explicated in specific terms. In *The Birth of the Messiah*, Raymond Brown made a magisterial study of the Lukan canticles. His interpretation is representative of spiritualising interpretations. He concluded that "the canticles embodied the piety of the Anawim"— that is, the canticle exhibits the *anawim's* spiritual humility.[35] Though he asserts that one should not forget the physical realities of the early Christians, "The poverty and hunger of the oppressed in the Magnificat are primarily spiritual."[36] Similarly, John

31 Robert C. Tannehill, "Magnificat as Poem," *JBL* 93 (1974): 273.

32 Miller, *Rumors of Resistance*, 90.

33 Tannehill notes that the classifying of the Magnificat as "an eschatological hymn" goes back to Herman Gunkel. Tannehill, "Magnificat as Poem," 265 cf. Herman Gunkel, "Die Lieder in der Kindheitsgeschichte Jesu bei Lukas," *Festgabe A. von Harnack zum 70. Geburgstag dargebracht* (Tübingen: Mohr, 1921), 43–60.

34 Tannehill, "Magnificat as Poem," 274.

35 Brown, *Birth of the Messiah*, 353.

36 Brown, *Birth of the Messiah*, 363.

Nolland maintains, "It is not that Mary has some personal or individual affliction; her affliction is simply that of God's people awaiting his saving intervention on their behalf."[37]

François Bovon certainly recognises the contribution of the sociological reading of the Third World interpreters, however, his reading could not move out from theological moorings. Commenting on vv. 52–53 Bovon states, "The song is not about the dangers of power and possessions; no more does it demonize the political and economic world.... When God inaugurates his reign, he necessarily shakes the mighty from their thrones and demands the money of the rich.... The child's birth signifies the end of many privileges and oppression."[38] But this is at best very vague. Mary's song is definitely critical of the political and economic world of the day and certainly to say that the "child's birth signifies the end of many privileges and oppression" is not persuasive at all. To avoid the socio-economic and political aspects of the hymn would miss the discontent and protest voice of the vulnerable and the victims of the empire.

Perhaps, it is important to quote here the most politically subversive tone of status reversal in the Magnificat (Luke1:51–53) to problematise the traditional interpretations.

> He has shown strength with his arm
> He has scattered the proud in the thought of their hearts
> He has brought down the powerful from their thrones, and lifted up the lowly
> He has filled the hungry with good things, and sent the rich away empty.

Scholars are puzzled with how to interpret the aorist tense of all the finite verbs in these verses, as they are open to several options of interpretations. François Bovon succinctly puts these options thus:

> Are they ordinary observations of past history, or gnomic attestation of God's usual conduct? Are they ingressive aorists, signalling the beginning of eschatological events? Or are they influenced by the prophetic perfect in Hebrew, and thus pictures of the future? In sum, is this hymn a genuine praise to God for help granted, or a hidden prophecy of hoped-for salvation?[39]

According to Raymond Brown, "The aorists refer to a definite action in the past namely, the salvation brought about through the death and resurrection of Jesus."[40] For Farris, the aorists express an eschatological tension—it points back to

37 Nolland, *Luke 1–9:20*, 75.

38 Bovon, *Luke 1*, 63.

39 Bovon, *Luke 1*, 57.

40 Brown, *Birth of the Messiah*, 363.

the Christ event, but that also points to the future.[41] However, it can legitimately be asked, where have the powerful been pulled down from their thrones and the lowly being lifted up? Interpretations that view the Magnificat through the eyes of post-Easter community seem far fetched because there is nothing in the hymn that points to the death and resurrection of Jesus.[42] Preoccupation with one of the possible aorist options does not help elucidate the voice of the Spirit crying out through the voice of the colonised, rather it obscures the resistance voice into an empty triumphalism of God's mighty deeds. The hymn should be interpreted in the light of the experience of those who were exploited and oppressed by the rich and the powerful to the extent that they are literally humiliated and go hungry for want of food. This perspectival reading would naturally ask who are the proud, rich and the powerful vis-à-vis the lowly and hungry?

It can be conceded that some of the recent commentators give importance to the socio-political tone of the hymn. Joel B. Green argues if one places the hymn in the context of colonial rule, the socio-political message cannot be ruled out. Moreover, since Luke is concerned about salvation "today" (cf. 4:21; 23:43) "the revolution embodied in Mary's Song is a vision for the present."[43] But Green cautions that the hymn is not a call to revolutionary human action since the hymn primarily celebrates God's action against those who would take power into their own hands. On the other hand God seeks out faithful partners like Anna and Mary, from its audience outside the narrative, to participate in God's redemptive work.[44] In a similar manner, noting the fresh sociological reading of the Third World theologians in his analysis of the history of interpretation, François Bovon states that the Magnificat is "one of the New Testament text with the most strongly political and liberating content. It calls us on to take the word concretely, and to fight against oppression in order to take the Lord of history seriously."[45]

4.3.3. Postcolonial Reading

There are leading interpreters from the socio-political viewpoints who have invariably emphasised the resistance strain and the discursive engagement of the community with the empire. Gustavo Gutierrez sees in the Magnificat thanksgiving and joy closely linked to God's action of liberation by humbling the proud. His hopeful conclusion is, "The future of history belongs to the poor and exploited. True liberation is the work of the oppressed themselves; in them the Lord saves history."[46] The Sabbath conversation of the Solentiname congregation

---

41 Farris, *Hymns*, 116.

42 Horsley, *Liberation of Christmas*, 113.

43 Green, *Gospel of Luke*, 100.

44 Green, *Gospel of Luke*, 100.

45 Bovon, *Luke 1*, 65.

46 Gustavo Gutiérrez, *A Theology of Liberation: History, Politics and Salvation*, trans. Caridad Inda and John Eagleson (Maryknoll, NY: Orbis Books, 1973), 208.

in Nicaragua accounted in Ernesto Cardinal's *The Gospel in Solentiname* also provides an intriguing interpretation of how the *campesinos* understand the Magnificat. The *campesinos* think that if Herod had heard Mary's song, Herod would brand Mary a communist (or a revolutionary). They understood the phrase "filling the hungry with good things" mean that "the hungry is going to eat."[47] The *campesinos* of Solentiname understood Mary's song as a song of protest and liberation. According to Elsa Tamez, Mary's song does not speak "of individual undergoing moral change but of the restructuring of the order in which there are rich and poor, mighty and lowly."[48] The liberating implications of Magnificat is brought out more clearly by third world postcolonial readers whose engagement with their current situations of economic, political ethnic injustices under neocolonialism have recognised the revolutionary strain that has inspired their vision. According to Leonardo Boff, the Third World readers find "privileged hermeneutical lens for the reading of Mary's Magnificat and for becoming hearers of its message."[49] However, Ghanaian scholar Paul Bemile maintains that, Latin American liberation theologians take the message of Magnificat too far, into the realm of violence, revolution and class warfare.[50] At any rate, these interpretations from the perspectives of the Third World clearly recognises the hymn as a hymn of resistance.

Richard Horsley calls Lukan canticles as "songs of liberation" as it resonates with Hebrew victory hymns and Jewish hymns from the period of intense conflict and resistance to the Hellenistic and Roman imperialism. For him, the hymn "focuses on praise of God as the champion of the people and evokes a long and deep memory of God's great acts of deliverance such as the exodus from Egypt and of prophetic promises of renewed redemption."[51] He writes,

> In the very structure of the imperial situation, imperial regime ruled through local aristocracies and client kings, ... liberation of the people from arrogant rulers would have meant toppling of both local and alien rulers from their thrones.... But the liberation described in the Magnificat is not simply "political." It is social as well; for the poor, marginal peasantry, heretofore exploited to the point that they went hungry themselves in order to render up the tribute and taxation

---

47 Cardenal, *Gospel in Solentiname*, 31.

48 Elsa Tamez, *Bible of the Oppressed*, trans. Matthew O'Connell (Maryknoll, New York: Orbis Books, 1982), 68.

49 Leonardo Boff, *The Maternal Face of God: The Feminine and its Religious Expressions*, trans. Robert R. Barr and John W. Diercksmeier (San Francisco: Harper & Row, 1987), 190.

50 Paul Bemile, *The Magnificat within the Context and Framework of Lukan Theology: An Exegetical Theological Study of Lk 1:46–55*, Regensburger Studien zur Theologie 34 (Frankfurt am Main: Lang, 1986), 239–240.

51 Horsley, *Liberation of Christmas*, 111.

> demanded by their local and imperial rulers, are being "filled with good things."[52]

The Magnificat begins by praising God for lifting up the lowly. The question is who are the ταπείνωσις (the lowly, vv. 48 and 52) and the hungry who are lifted up and filled with good things? In the LXX the word family ταπεινούν/ταπεινός/ταπείνωσις (make low) and πτωχός/πτωχεία (poor, poverty) are often the preferred equivalent of the Hebrew word ענה, which describes the experience of affliction or people in oppressed, constrained, fatal situations.[53] The Septuagint uses the word ταπεινός to refer to those who are "bowed down" and "oppressed," often used in the context of foreign political and military oppression.[54] It also means oppression of the rich and the mighty (Amos 2:7; Isa 58:4). There is also a direct relation between poverty and lowliness because poverty is one of the factors that makes a person susceptible to oppression (Amos 8:6).[55] In this case ταπείνωσις in the Magnificat could refer to the everyday experience of those living in conditions of poverty, powerlessness, and low status (cf. Prov 16:18–19; Sir 11:12–14).[56] The desire for food reflects the situation of those who pray for their daily bread (cf. 11:3). Therefore, the Magnificat is a song of the oppressed, who take their oppression as a site of resistance against their oppressor. One may ask if there is anything beneath Mary's self-description as ταπείνωσις that might proffer significance to this hymn of protest.

Mary rejoices in God her saviour because God has regarded the ταπείνωσις of his servant (v. 48). Plummer suggests that Mary's ταπείνωσις (lowliness) refers to Mary's position of a carpenter's bride.[57] And Brown opines that Mary's lowliness refers to childlessness.[58] Still Fitzmyer suggests that humble status refers to "her unworthiness to be the mother of Davidic Messiah and the Son of God."[59] But Jane Schaberg opines that Mary's ταπείνωσις as humiliation refers to Mary's sexually compromised status as pregnant but unwed woman.[60] If the ταπείνωσις

---

52 Horsley, *Liberation of Christmas*, 113.

53 E. Gerstenberger, "הנע," *TDOT* 11:234, 236 cf. Walter Grundmann, "ταπεινός, ταπείνοω, ταπείνωσις," *TDNT* 8:6.

54 Deut 26:7; 1 Sam 9:16; 2 Kgs 14:26; Ps 136 (LXX 135): 23; Jdt 6:11; 1 Macc 3:51; 14:14; 3 Macc 2:12).

55 Grundmann, *TDNT* 8:9. Also see Sir 13:23 in which πτωχὸς and πλούσιος are used in opposition.

56 Miller, *Rumors of Resistance*, 115.

57 Alfred Plummer, *The Gospel According to S. Luke*, ICC, 5th ed. (Edinburgh: T&T Clark, 1922; repr., 1960), 32. However, Plummer thinks that, the ταπεινούς in v. 52 primarily means the oppressed poor as opposed to the tyrannical rulers (33).

58 Brown, *Birth of the Messiah*, 361.

59 Fitzmyer, *Luke I–IX*, 367.

60 Jane Schaberg, *The Illegitimacy of Jesus: A Feminist Theological Interpretation of the Infancy Narratives* (New York: Crossroad, 1990), 96 cf. Miller, *Rumors of Resitance*, 115.

in v. 48 is read together with the ταπείνωσις of v. 52, in which the hymn celebrates the lifting up of the lowly over against the pulling down of the powerful their thrones, it obviously refers to those who are oppressed socially and economically.[61] But what is Mary's plight that reduced her to lowly estate?

Jane Schaberg and Marianne Sawicki suspect that behind Mary's virginal conception might lie a real story of Mary being a victim of colonial (sexual) violence. Jane Schaberg argues, "Luke alludes to Deut 22:23–27 as the law that applies to Mary's story."[62] Basing on literary evidence from both Christian and Jewish sources she argues that Jesus' birth was scandalous.[63] Marianne Sawicki also argues that Mary's lowly estate is probably attached to colonial violence that ravaged Sepphoris and the surrounding area when the city was sieged to suppress the popular insurrection in 4 BCE, in which time many young people were sexually abused by the Roman soldiers. From a socio-cultural standpoint, whether or not Mary succumbs to sexual abuse, if she was hiding in Sepphoris when it fell to the siege of 4 BCE, her life as a prospective bride was lost.[64] In this case, Sawicki asserts that, the news that Mary's life would not be the same would have been delivered not by an angel but by a soldier. But Mary's "yes" to go on living is "the word of trust that God would find a way to provide a future for her and for Israel, the involuntarily occupied land."[65]

Therefore, it is significant that Mary sang the Magnificat, addressing God as σωτήρ (1:47) who has looked upon her favourably despite her lowly estate. In Luke's scheme the self-effacing Mary becoming a prophet singing song of protest is clearly the work of divine empowerment. Mary voices God's favour to the humiliated and downtrodden. Her story is about a young pregnant woman in an occupied land "struggling against victimization and for survival and dignity."[66] Mary's calling on God as σωτήρ (saviour) implies that though there was no human saviour for Mary God acted as her saviour. The title σωτήρ (saviour) is also given to epic heroes, military commanders, and local benefactors in the Greco-

61 Horsley, *Liberation of Christmas*, 111–112.

62 Jane Schaberg, *The Illegitimacy of Jesus,* 96. She argues that "Luke saw the appropriateness of the Jewish Christian hymn for use as Mary's canticle, and inserted it as hers in order to communicate the tradition he received: that she had been violated and made pregnant, but that God vindicated her, protecting her and her child, even recognizing and causing to be recognized this child as God's Son and Messiah" (95).

63 Cf. Schaberg, *The Illegitimacy of Jesus.*

64 Marianne Sawicki points to a provision later recorded in the Mishnah that every girl in a besieged city lost her high-caste marriageability regardless of whether a soldier had laid a hand on her or even an eye upon her or not. See, Marianne Sawicki, *Crossing Galilee: Architecture of Contact in the Occupied Land of Jesus,* (London: Continuum, 2000), 192.

65 Sawicki, *Crossing Galilee*, 192.

66 Fiorenza, *Miriam's Child Sophia's Prophet*, 187.

Roman world. Augustus Caesar then appropriated this title,[67] during whose reign according to Luke's Gospel the Magnificat was sung (Luke 2:1). As noted above, a decree from the Koinon of Asia declared Augustus to be the divinely given saviour who would bring peace to the people.[68] Since, "Recognizing the *princeps* as savior became a personal sign of loyalty to him and to the imperial system he represented" as Gary Gilbert observes,[69] calling on God of Israel as σωτήρ (saviour) within the Roman Empire was a subversion of the emperor's claim as saviour. But Luke allowed Mary's song to function exactly this way. The first readers of the Gospel in the Hellenistic cities who were accustomed to the claims of Caesar, as saviour in prayers, inscriptions, and monuments would not miss the counter claim of the hymn. This indicates that Luke made use of the Spirit-inspired countercultural song of the early Christians which was attributed to Mary to find self-expression for the Christian community of his time. The "resistant adaptation" of the dominant discourse shows a community negotiating its identity while inhabiting the world of Roman Empire.

In vv. 51–53, what is called the text of great reversal celebrates the pulling down of the mighty from their thrones and sending away the rich empty. As noted above, there are aorist options that will have implications for the interpretation of this text. But the ambivalence of the aorist verbs should be seen as a hidden transcript of subjugated communities that veil open criticism of the imperial hierarchy and status quo, which could be dangerous for a subjugated community. However, one should not miss the resistant voices of the victims of the empire in the Magnificat. The hymn expresses the voice of the oppressed community protesting against the hierarchical structure of the empire in which the powerful and the wealthy oppressed the vulnerable. George M. Soares-Prabhu who studied the biblical poor as a social class points out that the poor are (1) a *sociological* group from certain social situations, (2) a *dialectic* group in opposition against their oppressor, and (3) a *dynamic* group through whom God's saving action is enacted in history. And given that the rich are contrasted with the poor in the status reversal in Luke (1:52–53; 6:20–26), he maintains, the rich are exploiters of the poor.[70] The rich are mainly recognised by their greed and wholehearted devotion to mammon (Matt 6:24; Luke 16:10–14) that makes them indifferent to God and/or neighbour.[71] In the context of the first century Roman occupied Palestine, the powerful and the rich are not spooks but real people with power

---

67 Ceslas Spicq, "σωτήρ," *TLNT* 3:351–353; Gary Gilbert, "Roman Propaganda and Christian Identity in the Worldview of Luke-Acts," in *Contextualizing Acts: Lukan Narrative and Greco-Roman Discourse*, ed. Todd Penner and Caroline Vander Stichele (Atlanta: SBL, 2003), 238.

68 Brent, "Luke-Acts and Imperial Cult in Asia Minor," 411–438

69 Gilbert, "Roman Propaganda," 239.

70 George M. Soares-Prabhu, "Class in the Bible: The Biblical Poor as a Social Class?" in *Voices from the Margins*, ed. R. S. Sugirtharajah (Maryknoll: Orbis Books, 1991), 160.

71 Soares-Prabhu, "Class in the Bible: The Biblical Poor as a Social Class?" 161.

and wealth. The rich and powerful are the rulers; from minor officials to the emperor who runs the empire. The proud are the enemies of Israel, primarily the Romans and the ruling elites.[72] The proud, the mighty, and the rich, include foreign oppressors, Caesar and his armies as well as local rulers such as Herod and his court.[73] They appropriate tributes and taxes to maintain their privileged status.

Richard Horsley asserts that the liberation of the people from the arrogant rulers would mean overthrowing both the foreign and local rulers from their power position.[74] In similar strain, Robert McAfee Brown opines that the political implication of the hymn is obviously "a call to revolutionary action."[75] Since waiting around the rich to feed the poor is not the way to go about; the poor will have to take matters into their hand and "challenge the political and economic systems that help the rich get richer and the poor gets poorer."[76] However, it should be noted that the Magnificat does not envisage a violent revolutionary action that involves an armed resistance against the empire. But the hymn does offer active resistance to the imperial order by subverting the logic of imperial hierarchy. The hymn refused to accept the colonial gaze that sees the colonised bodïes as sites of hunger, need, and dependence and envisions an alternate order in which the lowly will be lifted up and the hungry will have food. This prophetic vision inspired by the Spirit of God challenges the socio-economic inequality and political domination that characterise the foundation of the empire.

The Spirit-inspired prophetic vision of status reversal in favour of the poor and the lowly deliberately counters the imperial propaganda of status reversal that the empire offers that can be seen in such text a as Virgil's *Aeneid* and Horace's *Carmen saecularae*. Virgil's *Aeneid* for example inscribes the god-ordained destiny of Rome (in the person of Augustus) "to rule Earth's peoples … to pacify, to impose the rule of law, to spare the conquered, to battle down the proud." Horace's *Carmen saecularae* also presents Augustus as both mighty and compassionate: "May he be victorious in battle over his foes yet merciful once they are down" (lines 49–52).[77] These texts celebrate the Roman order that is maintained by military might. But

72 Burton Scott Easton, *The Gospel According to St. Luke: A Critical and Exegetical Commentary* (Edinburgh: T&T Clark, 1926), 15.

73 F. Godet, *A Commentary on St. Luke's Gospel*, vol. 1 (London: T&T Clark, 1870), 104 includes Pharisees and Sadducees among others, but they themselves were reform groups who practice Judaism. It is not tenable to argue that the Magnificat refers to them as rich, mighty, and proud.

74 Horsley, *Liberation of Christmas*, 113.

75 Robert McAfee Brown, *Unexpected News: Reading the Bible with Third World Eyes* (Philadelphia: Westminster, 1984), 81

76 Brown, *Unexpected News*, 80.

77 Michael Putnam, *Horace's Carmen Saeculare: Ritual Magic and Poet's Art* (New Haven: Yale University Press, 2001). 98 maintains that this hymn is recognised to be unusual in that, it is not apotropaic (that is, designed to ward of evil), but a hymn to confirm by incantation the glory of the Roman status quo. Cf. Frances Hickson Hahn, "Performing the Sacred: Prayers

the Spirit-inspired voice of the nondescript peasant girl Mary transgresses the imperial propaganda by celebrating a different status reversal that overturns the table of imperial hierarchy. By means of colonial mimicry, Mary's song offers a "counter melody" to the imperial status quo with "an alternative vision of a world not subject to Rome's will or power … where social norms are challenged rather than accepted, and where eternal peace and blessing are offered to people of any race and status, not only those born into certain situation."[78]

This radical alternative vision emerges from the marginal space—the space where "vitality, tenacity, promise, and hope" are birthed; the space where the divine is made manifest.[79] The constitution of a new subjecthood from this privileged space of marginality indicates the activity of the Spirit working amidst the margins enabling them to claim their dignity and humanhood. Like the voice of the prophets, Mary's song gives expression to the voice of the margins. The prophetic voice and vision of the Magnificat demonstrate the activity of the Spirit in engendering a community of resistance that challenges and subverts the claims of the imperial propaganda that privileges a few and victimises the majority.

Many have observed that the Magnificat is modeled upon Hebrew hymns of praise especially with Hannah's song as its principal model.[80] However, since the Magnificat is more like a "virtual collage of biblical texts"[81] some have argued that except in Luke 1:48 where a direct quotation of 1 Sam 1:11 is clear, in every verse in the Magnificat there are closer verbal links to other parts of the Old Testament than to Hannah's song.[82] But the intertextual connection between Hannah's song and the Magnificat is hard to miss. Not only the striking similarities in opening lines and the theme of reversal of fortune, but the quotation of Hannah's word in Luke 1:48 (cf. 1 Sam 1:11) seems deliberate.[83] Joan E. Cook claims that, Hannah's

---

and Hymns," in *A Companion to Roman Religion*, Blackwell Companion to the Ancient World, ed. Jörg Rüpke (Malden, MA: Blackwell, 2007), 245.

78 Miller, *Rumors of Resistance*, 108, cf. Brent, "Luke-Acts and Imperial Cult in Asia Minor," 427–33; Warren Carter, "Singing in the Reign: Performing Luke's Song and Negotiating the Roman Empire (Luke 1–2)," in *Luke-Acts and Empire: Essays in Honor of Robert L. Brawley*, PTMS 151, eds. David Rhoads, David Esterline, and Jae Won Lee (Eugene, OR: Pickwick, 2011), 41–43.

79 Mary Philip (Joy), "Majestic at the Margins," in *Still at the Margins: Biblical Scholarship Fifteen Years after the Voices from the Margins*, ed. R. S. Sugirtharajah (London: T&T Clark, 2008), 104, 110.

80 Plummer, *Luke*, 30; Fitzmyer, *Luke I–IX*, 359.

81 Green, *Gospel of Luke*, 101. Cf. Plummer, *Luke*, 30–31; Brown *Birth of the Messiah*, 358–60.

82 J. M. Creed, *The Gospel According to St. Luke: The Greek Text with Introduction, Notes, and Indices* (London: MacMillan, 1930), 303–304; Farris, *Hymns*, 116.

83 The opening line of praise is strikingly similar, except Hannah's song uses "heart" and the Magnificat uses "soul and spirit" as the agency of giving praise to God (ἡ καρδία μου in 1 Sam [LXX 1 Kgs] 2:1 cf. ἡ ψυχή μου (Luke 1:46); τὸ πνεῦμά μου (1:47). The three reversals of fortunes mighty/feeble (1 Sam 2:4) rich/poor (vv. 7–9) and hungry/full (v. 5) in Hannah's

song in its canonical position articulates the program for the kingdom of Israel and that the Magnificat articulates a "program of new era in the spirit of Hannah's song."[84] Though the socio-political context of Hannah's song and Mary's song are quite different, both the speakers are situated within the wider history of their people.[85] However, there is already a shift in the focus of the Magnificat as it is related to the kingdom of God and not to the kingdom of Israel.[86] The Magnificat does not celebrate a total inversion of reversal where the oppressed will become the oppressor, rather, it envisions a "radical social redefinition and reversal between the arrogant and those who fear God, the rulers and the lowly, the rich and the hungry."[87] The *rich* in v. 53 is contrasted with the hungry and not the *spiritualised poor*. This is clear in the way Jesus "tends to act out reversal principles very literally by healing the sick (as in Luke 4:38–41; 5:12–26; 6:6–11; 8:40–56; 18:35–43) helping the poor and exhorting his listeners to do the same (as in 4:11–17; 6:20–49; 16:19–31; 18:18–30), and incorporating those of low status back into the community (as in 7:36–50; 8:26–39; 13:10–17; 14:7–24; 19:1–10)."[88]

In sum, the Magnificat is modelled upon Hebrew victory songs with Hannah's song as its principal model. But it is not so much a song of victory as a song of protest of an oppressed community. The Spirit-inspired song of Mary calls on Israel's God as saviour by evoking God's great acts of salvation and destabilises the claim of Caesar as Saviour. The Spirit gives voice to the resistant community to resists the empire system of domination and exploitation that renders the vulnerable in miserable conditions and calls for a restructuring of socio-economic and political relationship, unsettling the imperial status quo. The Spirit-inspired

---

Song are repeated with some modification in the Magnificat. The proud and the mighty are held in opposition to the lowly (Luke 1:51–52), and the rich are held in opposition to the hungry. More specifically, the Magnificat includes the linguistic quotation from Hannah's words ἐπιβλέψῃς (ἐπὶ τὴν ταπείνωσιν τῆς δούλης) "he has looked with favour on the lowly condition of his/your servant" (1 Sam [LXX 1 Kgs] 1:11, Luke 1:48). See Niall McKay, "A Political Reading of Luke 1:51–52 and 3:8–9 in the Light of Ezekiel 17—Inspired by John Howard Yoder and a Poststructural Intertextuality," *Neotestamentica* 47 (2013): 40.

84 Joan E. Cook, "The Magnificat: Program for a New Era in the Spirit of the Song of Hannah," *Proceedings EGL & MWBS* 15 (1995): 35–43.

85 The Lukan births are noted in relation to the Roman Empire. In the case of Hannah's song, the time can be adduced in relation to the Philistines' capture of the Ark at Ebenezer and Aphek and the subsequent events till it was kept in Kiriath-jearim for twenty years. But both the songs are fully anchored in the political and socio-economic circumstances within which they took place. Cook, "The Magnificat: Program for a New Era in the Spirit of the Song of Hannah," 39.

86 Cf. Cook, "The Magnificat: Program for a New Era in the Spirit of the Song of Hannah," 43.

87 Miller, *Rumors of Resistance*, 111–112.

88 Miller, *Rumors of Resistance*, 91–92.

Mary's song demonstrates that it is the Spirit of God that empowers resistance and the social formation of the oppressed community.

4.4. The Benedictus (Luke 1:67–79)

4.4.1. Analysis of the Text (Luke 1:67–79)

In its narrative context, the Benedictus comes as a climax to the birth and naming of John the Baptist. The song does not in itself refer to Jesus or John by name. However, from the context of Lukan infancy narratives it is understandable that "the horn of salvation in the house of David" point to the child Mary conceived but yet to be born.[89] As noted above, form critically it is a declarative psalm of praise in the Hebrew Bible tradition that begins with a blessing (v. 68a).[90] With regards to the structure of the hymn, some scholars think that the Benedictus is composed of two distinct sections (vv. 68–75 and vv. 76–79)[91] because the phrase "in all the days of our lives" in v. 75 indicates a clear break, a phrase that is often found at the end of the psalm (cf. 23:6; 30:13). Moreover, till v. 75, the finite verbs are aorist in the third person, but in v. 76 a new sentence starts with a change in the person (from third to second) and tense (from aorist to future).[92] Form critically some have remarked that the second-half is no longer a song of praise to God but a *genethliakon* or a "birth ode."[93] However, scholars like R. E. Brown and Joseph Fitzmyer have argued that the hymn is a unified composition though Lukan redaction or insertion is clearly noticeable especially in vv. 76–77.[94]

89 Horsley, *Liberation of Christmas*, 115.

90 "Blessed be the Lord, the God of Israel" (v. 68a) is found at the end of the psalter in four of the five books of Psalms (cf. 41:13; 72:18; 88:53; 105:48). It is also found in 1 Kgs 1:48, spoken by David at the enthronement of Solomon. The blessing also resembles the opening formula of the Hymn of Return in the Qumran War Scroll, a hymn which like Benedictus speaks of God's covenant mercy and salvation (1QM 14.4, cf. 13.2).

91 Heinz Schürmann, *Das Lukasevangelium*, part 1, *Kommentar zu Kap. 1,1–9,50* 3rd ed., (Frieburg: Herder, 1984), 84–94 argues that vv. 76–79 constitute the Lukan canticle which originally answered the question raised in v. 66b, and it was attached to v 67, while vv. 68–75 were secondary insertion. Bovon, *Luke 1*, 68–69 assumes that verses 76–79 come from a Baptist source. Brown, *Birth of the Messiah*, 380 opines vv. 76–77 as Lukan insertion into an otherwise hymn Luke inherited from a Jewish Christian circle.

92 Bovon, *Luke 1*, 67.

93 Bovon, *Luke 1*, 67; Hendrickx, *Third Gospel for the Third World: Preface and Infancy Narrative (Luke 1:1–2:52)* (Collegeville, MN: Liturgical), 146.

94 In the pattern of Hebrew hymn of praise, the Benedictus can be divided into three parts: an introduction praising God (68a), followed by the main body listing the reasons of praise beginning with "because" clause in 68b (68b–77b) and a conclusion which recapitulates some of the motifs of the hymn. In the original the main body of the hymn probably consisted of two balanced strophes (68b–71b; 72a–75), but a third strophe has been added that describes the future of John the Baptist (76a–77b). Brown, *Birth of the Messiah*, 380–381; Fitzmyer, *Luke I–IX*, 378.

Zechariah's song begins praising God for raising a horn of salvation in the house of David, his child, (οἴκῳ Δαυὶδ παιδὸς αὐτοῦ, v. 69). It evokes God's covenantal promise "to our fathers" (πατέρων ἡμῶν, v. 72), particularly the Abrahamic covenant (v. 73).[95] In verse 76–77, the song shifts attention to John the Baptist underlining his work profile as "prophet of the Most High" who will go "before the Lord and prepare his ways." It is noted that vv. 76–77 answers the question posed in v. 66, "what then will this child be?"[96] The last part of the hymn recapitulates what was expressed in vv. 68–75. God's visitation of the desperate and demoralised people is expressed in terms of God's intense compassion (σπλάγχνα ἐλέους) or "tender mercy" through the dawning of light from on high.[97] Apart from vv. 76–77, which is about John the Baptist, the Benedictus speaks of the coming of salvation through the yet unborn Jesus.

4.4.2. Traditional Interpretations

The significance of the Benedictus for this study is the explicit role of the Spirit in enabling the dumb Zechariah to sing the hymn "filled with the Holy Spirit" (1:67). Some scholars have noted that the hymn is concerned with political liberation.[98] But more important is to note that the Benedictus is a song of the oppressed. Zechariah is representative of the community who sung the song with a longing to be delivered from the "enemies" and "all who hate us." The numerous references to the enemies of the community such as ἐχθρῶν (enemies); ἐκ χειρὸς πάντων τῶν μισούντων ἡμᾶς (from the hand of those who hate us); χειρὸς ἐχθρῶν (hand of the enemies) as found in vv. 71, 74, and the explicit reference to "those who sit in darkness and in the shadow of death" indicates the hymn comes from those in the margins of oppression. But all hope is not lost; the Spirit breathes among the subjugated people empowering them to resist their oppressors and enabling them to construct counter community for survival and self-representation. Notably, some have noted the militaristic (Paul Winter)[99] and political (Richard Horsley; J. M. Ford)[100] tone of the hymn that proffers a liberative reading. But, a political reading of the hymn do not concern a majority of commentators, and thus, albeit

---

95 Kuecker, *Spirit and the 'Other,'* 61.

96 Shürmann, *Lukasevangelium*, 90; Brown, *Birth of the Messiah*, 389.

97 In the Septuagint ἀνατολή translates צמח, the "sprout" or "scion" of David (Jer 23:5; Zech 3:8; 6:12). The scion of David also appears significantly in the Qumran scrolls (4QPBless 3; 4QFlor 1:11).

98 Ford, *My Enemy is My Guest*, 27; Horsley, *Liberation of Christmas*, 114–119.

99 Paul Winter, "Magnificat and Benedictus: Maccabean Psalms?" *BJRL* 37 (1954) 328 opines that Magnificat and Benedictus are Maccabean war songs, which found way into the Gospel via Jewish-Christian (Nazarene) adaptation of the Baptist's birth story.

100 Horsley, *Liberation of Christmas*; Ford, *My Enemy is My Guest*, 27 opines, "it expresses a messianic and salvific hope that is consonant with the Old Testament and the Judaism of the first century B.C.E and C.E. The deliverance expected comprises social and political freedom, which was closely integrated with religious independence for the Jews throughout

traditional interpretations has brought out many important aspects of the hymn, it has not paid adequate attention to the ideological discourse of the hymn and the role of the Spirit in engendering a community of resistance for liberation.

Traditional interpretation is predominantly occupied with the christological and the pneumatological aspects of the hymn. Firstly, the strong covenantal language embedded in the hymn has influenced a majority of scholars to view the hymn as an eschatological or prophetic fulfilment of God's promises to David (cf. 2 Sam 7:8–14) and to Abraham (cf. Gen 12:1–3) in the births of John and Jesus.[101] According to R. E. Brown, the hymn is christological, in that the hymn stresses "the fulfillment of the promise to David and his house, which was spoken by the prophets, and of an oath to Abraham and his descendants."[102] Fitzmyer also opines "the main thrust of the canticle is an affirmation of the messianic role of Jesus."[103] Certainly, the Benedictus celebrates the imminent birth of Jesus and as a fulfillment of promise (v. 72) and reference to "a horn of salvation in the house of David" clearly cast Jesus as a Davidic messiah. However, christological interpretations (cf. Brown and Fitzmyer) do not elucidate the political implications of Luke's Christology.

Obviously, "a horn of salvation" or "a mighty savior" (v. 68) is surely an oblique critique to the powers that be and that God "visited and redeemed his people" (v. 68) cannot simply mean a spiritual (or apolitical) visitation or redemption.[104] However, many commentators believe that rescue from the "enemies" and "all who hate us" in v. 71 and v. 74 cannot refer to the rescue of the Jewish nation from the Roman imperial rule. Fitzmyer writes, "On the lips of Zechariah, it [enemies] scarcely refers to the Roman occupiers of Palestine, but rather to all forms that hostility to the chosen people took over the ages. In the Lukan setting of the canticle the 'enemies' would include all those who resist or refuse to accept the new form of God's salvation-history."[105] However, this is to remove the texts from their socio-political context.[106] Deliverance from the enemies "who hate us"

---

history but especially reflects the spirit of the Maccabees and the later revolutionaries who emulated them in the first century C.E.

101 R. Alan Culpepper, "The Gospel of Luke," *NIB* vol. 9, ed. Leander E. Keck (Nashville: Abingdon, 1995), 59. Cf. Bovon, *Luke 1*, 73; Robert Tannehill, *Luke*, Abingdon New Testament Commentaries (Nashville: Abingdon, 1996), 59; L. T. Johnson, *The Gospel of Luke*, Sacra Pagina, vol. 3 (Collegeville, Minnesota: Liturgical, 1991), 47. Charles Talbert, *Reading Luke: A Literary and Theology Commentary on the Third Gospel* (New York: Crossroad, 1982), 27.

102 Brown, *Birth of the Messiah*, 383.

103 Fitzmyer, *Luke I–IX*, 379.

104 Cf. Fitzmyer, *Luke I–IX*, 383; Johnson, *Gospel of Luke*, 46, 48.

105 Fitzmyer, *Luke I–IX*, 384.

106 Tannehill, *Luke*, 60.

(v. 71) is not simply a stereotyped language of the psalter.[107] Even if one considers the correspondence between the Benedictus and Psalms such as 18:17 par 2 Sam 22:18 and 106:10, one would find that the enemies in Psalms refer to concrete domestic or foreign political enemies. In the case of Zechariah's song which was sung in the historical context of oppressive Roman-Herodian rule, the enemies would have meant the Romans, the Herodians, the temple rulers, rich landlords and so on.[108]

Secondly, the Benedictus also provides scholars to study (the role of) the Holy Spirit in Luke's Gospel. A majority emphasise that the Holy Spirit mentioned in 1:76 refers to the Spirit of prophecy.[109] Roger Stronstad, J. B. Shelton, and Robert P. Menzies offer the major thrust of this reading. Stronstad argues that for Luke, "filled with the spirit" (cf. 1:67) always describes prophetic inspiration.[110] However, as Aaron Kuecker rightly pointed out, those who connect the Spirit with inspired speech fail to examine the content of what the Spirit inspires.[111] Obviously, the Spirit here inspires Zechariah but the voice of the Spirit points to the liberative work of God. Kuecker asserts that, in Luke, the transformative effect of the Spirit that "results in the formation of an allocentric identity"[112] first evidenced in Zechariah's song. Kuecker picks up 1:79 and argues that the reference "to those who sit in darkness and in the shadow of death, to guide our feet in the way of peace" refers not only to Israelites but extends to the non-Israelites.[113] Kuecker rightly recognises the theological outlook of Luke that presents Jesus as forming an inclusive transcultural community over against the fixed cultural boundaries maintained by dominant Judaism of the day.

However, the work of the Spirit in the Benedictus is more than effecting allocentric identity. The voice of the Spirit is strongly tied to forming of political consciousness of those who are pushed to the margins. The themes of deliverance such as λύτρωσις (v. 68), σωτηρία (v. 71) and ῥυσθέντας (v. 74) express the deep longing for liberation from political domination. It proclaims that God has raised "a horn of salvation" (Luke 1:69) that will deliver the people from the enemies.[114]

---

107 Cf. Brown, *Birth of the Messiah*, 385. Bovon, *Luke 1*, 73.

108 Tannehill, *Luke* 60, Horsley, *Liberation of Christmas*, 117.

109 Menzies, *Empowered for Witness*, 108–109; Youngmo Cho, *The Spirit and the Kingdom in the Writings of Luke and Paul: An Attempt to Reconcile these Concepts* (Milton Keynes: Paternoster, 2005), 137–139; Turner, *Power From on High*, 143.

110 Roger Stronstad, *The Charismatic Theology of St. Luke* (Peabody: Hendrickson, 1984), 55.

111 Kuecker, *Spirit and the 'Other,'* 59 n. 40.

112 Kuecker, *Spirit and the 'Other,'* 59.

113 Kuecker, *Spirit and the 'Other,'* 62–67.

114 For instance, the "horn of salvation" evokes a political Messiah who rescue the people of God. In 2 Sam 22:3, it refers to God but in Psalm 132:17 the horn of salvation refers to an anointed one from Davidic lineage whom God will raise up. See Ford, *My Enemy is My Guest*, 26.

In the first century Palestinian milieu, which was politically volatile due to the multiple Jewish political groups' overt or covert resistance against colonial rulers and the native collaborators, the deep-seated revolutionary hope expressed in the Benedictus would surely be heard as a song of protest. But for Luke, it is precisely the Spirit that is actively present in the counter social formation of the colonised victims. In other words, for Luke, the Spirit resists oppression and liberates the victims of oppression.

4.4.3. Postcolonial Reading

Postcolonial readers would pose a set of questions to the hymn. Who is the saviour and who are the enemies the hymn refers to? What kind of deliverance or salvation the hymn talks about? What kind of freedom and peace the song envisions? And most importantly who is singing the hymn or whose voice is it anyway? Joel B. Green observes that, setting the Benedictus against the background of a "grossly oppressive militaristic, economic, and political foreign presence will lead us to read in Zechariah's song the expression of deep-seated revolutionary hopes held by a people thrust violently to the margins of society."[115] This deep-seated hope is expressed by those who found in Jesus the Spirit-incarnated messiah as the saviour vis-à-vis the claim of Roman emperors as saviour and bringer of salvation and peace.

It is true that the hymn is concerned with political liberation/salvation. This is supported by the Old Testament imageries that filled the hymn. Benedictus praises God for having "visited his people and redeemed them" (v. 68) by raising a "horn of salvation in the house of David" (v. 69). In the Septuagint, ἐπίσκεπτεσθαι is used for concrete deliverance from political and economic predicaments (cf. Exod 4:31; Ruth 1:6).[116] Similarly, λύτρωσις is not used in the Gospel with sin or in the cultic sense (Heb 9:12). Luke employs the term again in 2:38 and 24:21 with clear reference to political and economic redemption of the people, namely, of Jerusalem or of Israel, from concrete enemies.[117] Horsley noted that v. 69 is a "bold political statement," in that the explicit mention of the "horn of salvation" raised in the house of David recalls memories of David's role in establishing the independence of Israel and thus evokes whatever hopes it might engender on a new Davidic leadership.[118]

Themes such as saviour who brings victory, peace, and salvation run through the Benedictus.[119] It is noted that by the end of the first century, Roman religious discourse inextricably glued together the idea of saviour and peace with Rome and

115 Green, *Gospel of Luke*, 114.

116 Cf. Horsley, *Liberation of Christmas*, 115.

117 Cf. Horsley, *Liberation of Christmas*, 115.

118 Horsley, *Liberation of Christmas*, 115–116.

119 Pyung Soo Seo, *Luke's Jesus in the Roman Empire and the Emperor in Luke's Gospel* (Eugene, Oregon: Pickwick Publishers, 2015), 164–165.

the emperor.[120] Luke's Gospel is unique among the Synoptic Gospels in referring to Jesus as saviour (Luke 2:11; Acts 5:31; 13:23) and also associating him as the peace bringer (Luke 1:79; 2:14; Acts 10:36).[121] Allen Brent claims that Luke "wished to parallel the birth of Jesus with that of Augustus not simply as emperor but as founder of the Imperial Cult, and thus to compare the religious claims made by the latter with his claim for the former."[122] The Benedictus appropriates imperial ideologies to project Jesus as Saviour, Lord and the bringer of peace and thereby displaces the claim of Augustus and his successors who were hailed with those titles. The Benedictus portrays Jesus' coming as a rising horn of salvation to rescue people from the enemies so as to establish freedom to serve God and as a dawning light to the dark world to pave the way of peace.[123] This is a clear manipulation and hybridisation of imperial discourse. Allen Brent claims that the projection that Augustus and his successors "made war to cease and adorned peace is indicated in Luke 1:55, 71, 79; 2:11, 14, 29."[124] As Augustus saved his people from the enemies, "a mighty savior" (v. 68) in Luke will save people from the enemies.[125] Thus here is a community shifting the authority of Caesar as the saviour of the world to Jesus. This shows the hybrid and resistant character of the singing community which blurs the authority of the legitimising discourse of Roman peace and salvation. In the first century context of Roman hegemony, the claim of another saviour is a mimesis of Roman political propaganda and a subversion of Roman political foundation. Whoever claims another saviour is forming a counter allegiance to that saviour in opposition to the Roman emperors. However, Luke is precisely pointing to the formation of an alternative community around another Saviour (Jesus) in opposition to the empire of Caesar.

There is also an implicit critique to Roman salvation and peace in the song. As noted in the previous chapter on imperial theology, Roman peace "spares the conquered and crushed the proud" (Virgil's *Aeneid* 6.850–53). Roman peace was imposed by military might. Tacitus has the Caledonian chieftain say to his fellow Britons in a famous passage: "To robbery, slaughter, plunder, they give the lying name of empire; they make a solitude and call it peace" (*Agricola* 30). The Jewish Palestinian experience of Roman peace was probably no different from what the Caledonian chieftain said. The Benedictus counters the Roman imperial ideology by appropriating imperial language but subverting their meaning. The hymn

120 Gary Gilbert, "Luke-Acts and Negotiation of Authority and Identity in the Roman World," in *The Multivalence of Biblical Texts and Theological Meanings*, SBLSym. Series 37, Christine Helmer and Charlene T. Higbe eds. (Atlanta: SBL, 2006), 100.

121 Gilbert, "Luke-Acts and Negotiation of Authority and Identity in the Roman World," 100.

122 Brent, "Luke-Acts and the Imperial Cult in Asia Minor," 431.

123 Jesus as bringer of peace is reiterated at his birth where the angelic armies proclaim "peace on earth among whom he favours" (2:14 cf. 19:38).

124 Allen Brent, *Imperial Cult and the Development of Church Order* (Brill: Leiden, 1999), 105.

125 In the Benedictus σωτηρία occurs three times (1:69, 71, 77).

proclaims Jesus as the peace bringer not Caesar. This claim is made even more explicit at the birth of Jesus (2:14).

The transformative power of the Spirit in raising the consciousness of the people in forming their identity in opposition to their oppressor (enemies) is evident in the Benedictus. Here the singing community re-inscribes covenantal promise using language of national salvation (1:68–75). In the context of first century Roman rule of Palestine through the Herodian client kings, such a remembering (politics of memory) is both a protest against the (indirect) colonial rule and a forging of (renewed) Israelite identity. The Spirit gives voice to the voiceless and political stance to the subjugated people to resist their oppressors, which in turn engenders the formation of the people (cf. 1:17). The use of "we" and "us" vis-à-vis "our enemies" and "those who hate us" are expressive of social formation for re-presentation in the context of colonial domination. For the Lukan Jesus-followers of the late first century, the Spirit-inspired Zechariah's song would function as a song of liberation that mobilises the oppressed from the margins of the empire for counter social formation.

4.5. The Nazareth Proclamation (Luke 4:16–30)

The Nazareth proclamation is regarded as programmatic[126] in Luke's Gospel. However, given the prominence of Lukan universalism in the Gospel, a major emphasis is expended on the issue of Jewish and Gentile relationship both in Jesus' time and Luke's time in reading this pericope. One of the early twentieth-century commentators on Luke J. M. Creed noted that, "the rejection by Nazareth foreshadows the rejection by Jewish people and the subsequent universal mission of the Church," particularly noting that Elijah-Elisha pericope "provide good precedent for a mission to Gentiles."[127] Albeit Gentiles mission continues to be emphasised,[128] many scholars find this pericope more to do with ecclesiological issues of the Jews and Gentiles believers.[129] But there are radical voices of socio-

126 Marshall, *Gospel of Luke*, 183–84; Nolland, *Luke 1–9:20*, 195.

127 Creed, *Gospel According to St. Luke*, 66. E. Earle Ellis, *The Gospel of Luke* (London: Thomas Nelson, 1966), 96 also holds the same position. In the face of Nazarenes rejection, Jesus sounds a warning of their rejection by God. Also see, Hugh Anderson, "Broadening Horizons: The Rejection of Nazareth Pericope of Luke 4:16–30 in the Light of Recent Critical Trends," *Int* 18 (1964): 259–275.

128 Tannehill, *Luke*, 94.

129 Bovon, *Luke 1*, 156. Larrimore C. Crockett, "Luke 4:25–27 and Jewish-Gentile Relations in Luke Acts," *JBL* 88 (1969): 183, opines that the Elijah-Elisha allusion "must be seen as a prolepsis not simply of the gentile mission, and certainly not of God's rejection of Israel and turning to the gentiles, but rather of Jewish-gentile *reconciliation*, the *cleansing* of the gentiles which makes it possible for Jews and gentiles to live and eat together in the new age" (emphasis original). David R. Catchpole, "The Anointed One in Nazareth," *From Jesus to John* ed. Martinus C. de Boer, JSNTSup 84 (Sheffield: JSOT Press, 1993), 249, interprets Nazareth episode as a warning against the false confidence of privileged Israelite identity. Jeffrey S. Siker, "'First to the Gentile': A Literary Analysis of Luke 4:16–30," *JBL* 111 (1992):

political discontent in the Nazareth proclamations that challenge the system of injustice and domination with Jubilee theology. How would the first century audience of Jesus and Luke understand such proclamation in the context of Roman imperium? What would the favourable year of the Lord mean to the original audience? Could it be that the Spirit-anointed Jesus' Nazareth proclamation of good news to the poor and Jubilee Year (4:18–19) leverage potential threat to the Roman backed political establishment of Jewish Palestine? Before proceeding to a postcolonial cultural exegesis of this pericope, a few important points of discussion such as Jesus and the Spirit in the preceding chapters, literary analysis of the Nazareth proclamation, traditional interpretations of the text are in order.

4.5.1. Jesus and the Spirit

Luke associates Jesus with the Spirit of God more than any other Gospels. In the infancy story, Luke presents Jesus as the Spirit-incarnate Son of God (1:35). The conception of Jesus is attributed to the work of the Holy Spirit. As Jesus begin to appear in public scene, the Gospel accounts three episodes that link Jesus to the Spirit. Firstly, Luke declares that at the baptism in river Jordan, the Holy Spirit descended upon Jesus in a bodily form like a dove (3:21–22). Secondly, Lukan temptation narrative emphasises that Jesus was "full of the Spirit" as he was led into the wilderness to resist the devil (4:1) and emerges "filled with the power of the Spirit" and returned to Galilee (4:14). The phrase "filled with the power of the Spirit" is a leitmotiv in Luke that drives home the point that Jesus acts in the power of the Spirit.[130] Thirdly, Luke makes a final point that Jesus is the Spirit-incarnate messiah in the Nazareth proclamation: "The Spirit of the Lord is upon me" (4:18).[131] What is notable in Luke's depiction of the Spirit in relation to Jesus is that, the Spirit of God incarnated in Jesus and became the driving force that empowers and authorises Jesus in all his activities (4:18; cf. Acts 10:38). The theological implication of this assertion is that, the unsettling resistant strain for justice and liberation in the Nazareth proclamation is voiced out in the power and authority of the Spirit of God.[132]

83, sees this pericope as a challenge issued to the Jews to accept the gentiles if they want to be accepted in the reign of God.

130 Cf. Fitzmyer, *Luke I–IX*, 522.

131 In Luke's (and Matthew's) infancy account, Jesus did not have a biological father, but is conceived through the creative agency of the Holy Spirit. At his baptism, once again the Holy Spirit descended upon him and a heavenly voice declared "you are my beloved son, in you I am well pleased," which is a citation from the Old Testament (Ps 2:7; Isa 42:1), and thus legitimating Jesus as the awaited Spirit-messiah son of God.

132 This also explains the relative absence of the mention of the Spirit of God after the Nazareth proclamation, since the words and deeds of Jesus is carried out in the power of the Spirit of God.

4.5.2. Analysis of the Text (Luke 4:16–30)

Luke 4:14–44 forms a narrative block within the Galilean section of the Gospel[133] in which Jesus proclaims the good news in Jewish synagogues by words and deeds with 4:14–15 and 4:42–43 forming an *inclusio* around 4:16–41.[134] Source critically, the Nazareth episode where Jesus receives a poor welcome from his townsfolk as he returned and taught in the synagogue is also found in Mark 6:1–6 (cf. Matt 13:53–58). Mark and Matthew too report the question about Jesus' parentage and the saying, "Prophets are not without honor except in their home town" (Mark 6:4 cf. Matt 13:57). But there are significant differences between Lukan and Markan (followed by Matthew) narration of event. In Mark and Matthew, Jesus visited his hometown in the middle of his ministry, but Luke made Nazareth proclamation the starting of Jesus public life. In Mark and Matthew, there is no mention of what Jesus taught in the synagogue, but Luke has Jesus reading from Isa 61:1–2 clustered with Isa 56:8. Furthermore, Luke is unique in alluding to Elijah-Elisha traditions in Jesus' inaugural speech. The historicity of the Nazareth event is an open question in scholarly debate. Probably changes and additions come from Luke's hand. But beyond this educated guess, a consensual opinion has not been derived using source criticism.[135] Nevertheless, Luke's presentation of the starting point of Jesus public life has a pneumatological significance. Mark and Matthew did not associate Jesus with the Spirit when Jesus began to proclaim "the kingdom of God/heaven" (Mark 1:14–15; Matt 4:12–17). But for Luke, Jesus inaugurates his public life in the Nazareth synagogue with the anointing of the Spirit of God (4:18).

The form of Luke 4:16–30 is variously described. From a form-critical perspective, Bultmann and Bovon think that it is an expanded apophthegm or pronouncement story.[136] Fitzmyer thinks that the narrative is a conflation of two stories. It is "on the one hand, it is a fulfillment ending on the note of Jesus' success; on the other there is the rejection story."[137] It can also be noted that, some

---

133 The structural division of the Third Gospel vary among scholars. However, 4:16–9:50 (or 4:14–9:50) is generally considered by almost all as the Galilean section of the Gospel as Jesus life and work in this section is concentrated in Galilee. Cf. Marshall, *Gospel of Luke*, 178.

134 Green, *Gospel of Luke*, 203.

135 In earlier scholarship, the Nazareth sermon is viewed as a free composition by the evangelist like any of the speeches in Acts cf. e.g., Cadbury, *The Making of Luke-Acts*, 188–189. However, in recent scholarship some have suggested a historical basis for Luke's version in written or oral document not available to Mark or Matthew. See Nolland, *Luke 1–9:20*, 193; Michael Prior, *Jesus the Liberator: Nazareth Liberation Theology (Luke 4:16–30)* (Sheffield: Sheffield Academic Press, 1995), 38, 78, 87–88; Sharon H. Ringe, *Jesus, Liberation and the Biblical Jubilee: Images for Ethics and Christology*, OBT (Philadelphia: Fortress, 1985), 41.

136 Bultmann, *History of Synoptic Tradition*, 31–32; Bovon, *Luke 1*, 151.

137 Fitzmyer, *Luke I–IX*, 528.

finds a chiastic structure within the account.[138] However, Darrell Bock maintains that the narrative structure has more of a two cycles presentation and rejection: in the first cycle, one finds Jesus' address and the crowd's doubt (vv. 18–22); in the second cycle, Jesus quotes a proverb with its following warning and this provokes the anger of the crowd (vv. 23–29). The introduction (vv. 16–17) and the conclusion (v. 30) of the account bracket these two cycles.[139] It would seem Lukan Jesus' challenge against the status quo of the empire has caused conflict and resistance at the Nazareth episode.

4.5.3. Traditional Interpretations

Many have studied the Nazareth proclamation from multifarious angles. A majority of traditional interpretations and standard commentaries give importance to the theological and eschatological significance of Jubilee concept.[140] This line of interpretation clearly underrates the concrete socio-political dimension of the Jubilee theology. Many have also studied this text from the vantage point of socio-political concerns, focusing on the jubilary motif of the text.[141] Furthermore, major pneumatological enquiries of Luke-Acts have also highlighted the Spirit-inspired character of the Nazareth proclamation. An appraisal of previous interpretations of Nazareth proclamation can be roughly grouped into three: historical-literary interpretation,[142] jubilary interpretation,[143] and pneumatological interpretation.[144]

---

138 Nolland, *Luke 1–9:20*, 191; Talbert, *Reading Luke*, 54–55. Cf. Darrel L. Bock, *Luke 1–9:50*, BECNT 3A (Grand Rapids: Baker Books, 1994), 399.

139 Bock, *Luke 1–9:50*, 399.

140 Marshall, *The Gospel of Luke*, 183–84; Nolland, *Luke 1–9:20*, 197; Robert H. Stein, *Luke*, NAC 24 (Nashville: Broadman, 1992), 156; Johnson, *Gospel of Luke*, 81. Also see, David Hill, "The Rejection of Jesus at Nazareth (Luke iv: 16–30)," *NovT* 13 (1971): 161–180; James A. Sanders, "From Isaiah 61 to Luke 4," in *Luke and Scripture: The Function of Sacred Tradition in Luke-Acts*, ed. Craig A. Evans and James A. Sanders (Minneapolis: Fortress, 1993), 46–69; Bruce D. Chilton, "Announcement in Nazara: An Analysis of Luke 4:16–21," in *Gospel Perspectives*, vol. 2, ed. R. T. France and D. Wenham (Sheffield: JSOT Press, 1981), 147–172.

141 André Trocmé, *Jesus and the Nonviolent Revolution*, trans. Michael H. Shank and Marlin E. Miller (Scottdale, PA: Herald Press, 1973), 19–76; John Howard Yoder, *The Politics of Jesus* (Grand Rapids: Eerdmans, 1972), 28–33, 64–77. P. D. Miller, "Luke 4:16–21," *Int* 29 (1975): 417–421; R. B. Sloan, *The Favorable Year of the Lord: A Study of Jubilary Theology in the Gospel of Luke* (Austin: Schola, 1977); Ford, *My Enemy is My Guest*; Ringe, *Jesus, Liberation and the Biblical Jubilee*; Robert Willoughby, "The Concept of Jubilee and Luke 4:18–30," in *Mission and Meaning: Essays Presented to Peter Cotterell*, ed. Antony Billington, Tony Lane and Max Turner (Carlisle: Paternoster, 1995).

142 Marshall, *The Gospel of Luke*, 183–84; Nolland, *Luke 1–9:20*, 197; Green, *Gospel of Luke*.

143 Trocmé, *Jesus and the Nonviolent Revolution*; John Howard Yoder, *The Politics of Jesus*; Sloan, *Favorable Year of the Lord*; Ringe, *Jesus, Liberation and the Biblical Jubilee*.

144 Stronstad, *Charismatic Theology of Luke*; Menzies, *Empowered For Witness*; Wenk, *Community Forming Power*; Kuecker, *Spirit and the 'Other.'*

To begin with, the historical-literary approaches acknowledged that the Jubilee motif lies at the background of the Nazareth proclamation, but their emphasis on eschatological and spiritual reading limited these approaches to adequately bring out the jubilary motif of the text. For instance, Marshall maintains that Nazareth proclamation is eschatological, in that the Scripture has come to be fulfilled "this day" and the last days have begun in the life and work of Jesus, the Spirit endowed eschatological prophet.[145] He argues that 4:19 contains an allusion to the Jubilee Year but opines that this is now "made symbolic of his own [Jesus'] saving acts."[146] Similarly, Joel B. Green maintains that, the eschatological interpretive trends of the Jubilee motif in the Second Temple literatures, encourages one to see Luke 4:18–19 as "the announcement of the eschatological epoch of salvation, the time of God's gracious visitation, with Jesus himself presented as its anointed herald."[147] However, Jesus' emphatic statement that the Scripture is fulfilled "today" (4:21), rules out any ambiguity about the time of salvation/liberation. An eschatological interpretation does not bring out the demand for justice in the here and now which constitute the thrust of the Nazareth proclamation.

Notably, the disinterest in the Jubilee concerns of Jesus' preaching is clear in a number of commentators. Fitzmyer underlines the intertextuality of Nazareth proclamation with 11QMelchizedek, Isa 62:1–2, Lev 25:10–13 and Deut 12:5 but evaded elucidating the theme of Jubilee.[148] Robert H. Stein clearly distances the Jubilee motif from the Nazareth proclamation noting, "Although Isa 61:1–2 develops certain themes from the concept of the Jubilee Year (cf. Lev 25:8–55), Luke did not seem to have been thinking of this here."[149] Luke Timothy Johnson dissociates Jesus' proclamation of release from the concrete socio-political liberation. He writes, "Rather than picturing Jesus' work in terms of political or economic reform, Luke portrays his liberating work in terms of personal exorcisms, healings, and the teaching of the people."[150] John Nolland is more emphatic in blunting the concrete liberative message of Jesus:

> It is not finally an analysis of the language of Isa 61:1–2, but rather the perceived nature of men's bondage in the Lukan frame that must determine the force of the words as used here.... The Lukan Jesus is no social reformer and does not address himself in any fundamental way to the political structure of his world, but he is deeply concerned with

145 Marshall, *Gospel of Luke*, 178.

146 Marshall, *Gospel of Luke*, 184.

147 Green, *Gospel of Luke*, 212.

148 Fitzmyer, *Luke I–IX*, 532–533.

149 Stein, *Luke*, 157.

150 Johnson, *Gospel of Luke*, 81.

the literal, physical needs of men (Acts 10:38), as with their directly spiritual needs.[151]

Given the scholarly disinterest in the social and political dimension of the Nazareth proclamation, it is not surprising that, many interpreters view ἄφεσις (release, cf. 4:18), one of the most notable jubilary terminologies as forgiveness of sin. Howard Marshall viewed Luke's use of ἄφεσις here as forgiveness whereas αἰχμαλώτος (captives) clearly refers to concrete prisoners (cf. Rom 16:7; Col 4:10). He goes further to assert that "to set free the oppressed" (4:18c cf. Isa 58:6) adds nothing to the meaning of preceding proclamation "unless we are to stress the idea of forgiveness in ἄφεσις." Similarly, Robert Stein also argues that freedom/release (ἄφεσις) in 4:18 is to be understood as forgiveness of sin for the obvious reason that Luke uses the term always to refer to forgiveness of sin elsewhere.[152] Thus, the primary emphasis on socio-political dimension of liberation is neglected.

The *poor* represented by the Greek word πτωκός in 4:18 is also rendered a metaphorical meaning in some readings. Several scholars tend to read the poor in a metaphorical language whereas reference to the blind is considered more literal. The "acceptable year" is mainly described in terms of liberation from satanic bondage, and Jesus' healings.[153] Others emphasise the term as encompassing the poor people in all aspects of their neediness and being oppressed.[154] Only those scholars who are sensitive to the socio-political concerns of Luke's Gospel have emphasised the socio-economic dimension of the term and assume that the poor represent the economically oppressed, the underprivileged.[155] Lukan juxtaposition of Isa 61:1 and 58:6 in Luke 4:18 and Lukan overall concern for the poor in his writing shows that the poor refers to the economically oppressed and the underprivileged.[156]

Some leading socio-political reading that seriously takes into account the Jubilee motif have provided a this-worldly interpretation of Jesus Nazareth proclamation. Notable here is André Trocmé and John Howard Yoder. Trocmé argues that Isa 61 from which Jesus quotes is about social liberation. Trocmé

---

151 Nolland, *Luke 1–9:20,* 197.

152 Cf. Luke 1:77; 3:3; 24:47; Acts 2:38; 5:31; 10:43; 13:38; 26:18. See Stein, *Luke*, 156.

153 Marshall, *Luke*, 183; Max Turner, *Power*, 231; Ellis, *The Gospel of Luke*, 97; Stein, *Luke* 153–154; Robert J. Karris, "Poor and Rich: The Lukan Sitz im Leben," in *Perspectives in Luke-Acts*, ed. C. H. Talbert (Edinburgh: T&T Clark, 1978), 116–125.

154 Robert Tannehill, *The Narrative Unity of Luke-Acts: A Literary Interpretation,* vol. (Philadelphia: Fortress, 1986), 65–66; Walter E. Pilgrim, *Good News to the Poor: Wealth and Poverty in Luke-Acts* (Minneapolis: Augsburg Publishing House, 1981), 65–84; Joel B. Green, *The Theology of the Gospel of Luke* (Cambridge: Cambridge University Press, 1995), 82; Johnson, *Gospel of Luke*, 79.

155 Sloan, *The Favorable Year*, 39–42; Ringe, *Jesus, Liberation*, 163–169; Esler, *Community and Gospel in Luke-Acts*, 164–200; Prior, *Jesus the Liberator*, 163–182.

156 Wenk, *Community Forming Power*, 214.

argues "Jesus was indeed proclaiming a Jubilee, consistent with Moses's sabbatical instructions in AD 26, a Jubilee capable of solving the social problems of Israel at that time."[157] Jesus took upon himself the role of the messiah that the prophet announced and "demanded that the law be put into practice immediately."[158] He underlined four major imperatives of the Jubilee such as letting the land lie fallow, remitting of all debts, liberation of slaves, and the return to one's patrimony and insists that the Jubilee motif is found throughout Luke's Gospel. While the historical veracity of this thesis is questionable, John Howard Yoder concurs with Trocmé and reproduces the latter's thesis that Jesus indeed proclaim the Jubilee Year in 26 CE.[159] For Yoder, the Nazareth proclamation is clearly socio-political; it is about "economic restructuring of relations."[160]

In opposition to a strictly socio-political reading, R. B. Sloan's *The Favorable Year of the Lord*, which studies the jubilary theology of Luke provides an eschatological interpretation arguing that the Jubilee trajectory had already been rendered eschatological.[161] For Sloan, the Nazareth proclamation is both cultic and social. Concurring with Sloan, Willoughby maintains that Yoder is uncomfortable to accept that Luke's employment of Jubilee motif through Isaiah is anything but metaphorical, but "Jesus used the Isaiah text in an established eschatological and messianic way similar, though not identical, to the usage found in 11QMelchizedek."[162] Notably, Jubilee concept was reinterpreted in different historical contexts some of which has rendered an eschatological and spiritualised interpretation (cf. 11QMelchizedek), but Luke's reinterpretation does not betray such eschatological tendency.

There are some notable works that read the Nazareth proclamation from the vantage point of liberation. Sharon H. Ringe's *Jesus, Liberation, and the Biblical Jubilee: Images for Ethics and Christology* is one that focuses on the power of Jubilee "images" and its implication for contemporary society and world. For her, the work of Christ in the Jubilee images "point toward God's liberating and healing intent wherever institutions, customs or physical conditions are seen to limit human life."[163]

> The one who meets us as herald of the Jubilee of God's reign does so in particular historical, social and economic circumstances of his time,

---

157 André Trocmé, *Jesus and the Nonviolent Revolution*, trans. Michael H. Shank and Marlin E. Miller (Scottdale, PA: Herald Press, 1973), 47–48.

158 Trocmé, *Jesus and the Nonviolent Revolution*, 30.

159 John Howard Yoder, *The Politics of Jesus* (Grand Rapids: Eerdmans, 1972), 64–77.

160 Yoder, *The Politics of Jesus*, 39.

161 Willoughby, "The Concept of Jubilee and Luke 4:18–30," in 50–51 cf. Sloan, *Favorable Year of the Lord.*

162 Willoughby, "The Concept of Jubilee and Luke 4:18–30," 51.

163 Ringe, *Jesus, Liberation*, 92.

> just as we are responsible for recognizing and responding to the same message in the midst of our own historical and cultural particularity. The message is no safe one, confined to an otherworldly or religious sphere of life, but rather strikes us now, as it did those who first heard it, in the midst of the institutions and assumptions by which our lives are recognized.[164]

Sharon Ringe avoids discussion of an actual Jubilee. However, to speak of Nazareth proclamation simply as mirroring Jubilee images is inadequate to hear the voice of the margins. While the historicity of an actual Nazareth event is an open question, Lukan presentation of Jesus as the Spirit-messiah, which builds up a constellation of Old Testament hope, in an official congregation of Nazareth synagogue is a concrete socio-political act of resistance. The resistance paradigm deeply implanted in Jesus Nazareth proclamation is important to hear the voice of the margins.

Micahel Prior's *Jesus the Liberator: Nazareth Liberation Theology (Luke 4:16–30)* is one of the most comprehensive study of Luke 4:16–30. Prior objected to the position of Trocmé and Yoder and raises the question whether one can read the Nazareth text against the background of an actual Jubilee Year. For Prior, Christology is the hermeneutical key to understand the Hebrew Scriptures.[165] Lukan direct quotation from Isaiah 61 and indirect presentation of Jesus as a counterpart of Elijah suggest that for Luke, Jesus is the fulfillment of the Old Testament passages.[166] For Prior, as his work title suggests, Jesus is the liberator and his conclusion on Nazareth proclamation is noteworthy.

> The core of Jesus' message is that the good news of Isaiah 61, originally directed at the consolation of the returned exiles from Babylon, is transposed into good news for all who are oppressed.... The Isaiah text as recorded by Luke is free of any reference to that exclusiveness which is a feature of many religious traditions. Ethnicity and 'nationalism' is being challenged. The introduction of Isaiah 58:6 into Isaiah 61 text intensifies the social implications of Jesus' message of freedom. Moreover, Jesus declares the moment of liberation to be today. The Lukan Jesus' radical reinterpretation of the concept of election, challenging the notion of God's choice of one specific people,

---

164 Ringe, *Jesus, Liberation*, 93. She argues that, an attempt to draw a simple direct/literal connection between the Jubilee tradition of the Bible and contemporary situation of human struggle will not only violate historical particularity of Jubilee texts but distorts the way in which "these traditions meet us as images" (91).

165 Prior, *Jesus the Liberator*, 129.

166 Prior, *Jesus the Liberator*, 89.

is intensified by his appeal to the example of two of the great Hebrew prophets, Elijah and Elisha.[167]

The problematic aspect of Prior's argument is that he does not think that the Isa 61:1 or Nazareth proclamation is grounded in the Jubilee Year though the link word ἄφεσις (liberation) is present since "Luke does not use the terminology peculiar to Jubilee nor does he develop peculiar Jubilee concepts in the course of his writing."[168] He claims that the word ἄφεσις (release) should mean liberation from sin, since forgiveness of sin is an important theme in Luke-Acts.[169] But it cannot be denied that the word ἄφεσις (release) points strongly to the Jubilee motif in the Nazareth text.[170] Nonetheless, Prior's comprehensive view of the Nazareth proclamation as addressing not only the socio-economic issues but also ethnicities and nationalism is significant and opens up avenues for further postcolonial analysis of the text. Since postcolonialism goes beyond the preoccupation of liberation theologies with economic poverty and address the issues of culture, race, gender, and religion, Nazareth proclamation can be fruitfully exploited as a postcolonial discourse.

Many works on the study of Lukan pneumatology have neglected the potential resistive voice of the Spirit-messiah embedded in this text.[171] Several scholars concur that the reference to the Spirit in Luke 4:18 is the Spirit of prophecy in varying degree of explanation. Roger Stronstad sees the anointing of Jesus by the Spirit as a vocational gift for prophetic ministry. Jesus being conscious of the Spirit's anointing on him, deliberately models his public ministry after the three Old Testament prophets: Isaiah, Elijah, and Moses.[172] But Stronstad did not attend to the ancient prophets activities of resistance to "the powers that be" and the concomitant counter social formation at the margins. A few scholars dispute Luke's redaction of the Isaiah passages in Luke 4:18–19 to determine whether Luke's Spirit does more than empower speech. According to Robert Menzies, "The passage as it stands undeniably emphasizes preaching as the most important dimension of Jesus' mission."[173]

---

167 Prior, *Jesus the Liberator*, 141.

168 Michael Prior, "Isaiah, Jesus and the Liberation of the Poor (Luke 4.16–30)," *Scripture Bulletin* 24 (1994): 41 cf. *Jesus the Liberator*, 139.

169 Prior, "Isaiah, Jesus and the Liberation of the Poor (Luke 4.16–30)," 42.

170 A. Destro and M. Pesce, "Forgiveness of Sins without a Victim: Jesus and the Levitical Jubilee," in *Sacrifice in Religious Experience*, ed. Albert I. Baumgarten (Leiden: Brill, 2002), 167 n. 35.

171 For instance Stronstad, *Charismatic Theology of Luke*; Menzies, *Empowered For Witness*; Wenk, *Community Forming Power*.

172 Stronstad, *Charismatic Theology of Luke*, 44–45.

173 Menzies, *Empowered For Witness*, 150. Similarly Youngmo Cho *Spirit and Kingdom*, 176, also argues that Lukan replacement of the word καλέσαι (to announce) in LXX Isa 61:2

There are two notable works that focus on the Spirit and community formation in Luke. Matthias Wenk's *Community-Forming Power* deals with the socio-ethical dimension of the Spirit that effects community formation. But he does not treat the entire passage of the Nazareth proclamation, but links prophetic speech in 4:18–19 with perlocutionary effect: "The Spirit serve to authorize the prophet in proclaiming a message, guarantees the God-spoken character of it, and is the agent by which the salvation is accomplished."[174] In *The Spirit and the 'Other,'* Aaron Kuecker attempts a cultural exegesis of Luke 4:16–30 and points out that Jesus resists the narrow circumscribed privileged identity of his townsfolk and emphasises the role of the Spirit in effecting allocentric identity.[175] Kuecker's emphasis on the transformative role of the Spirit in effecting allocentric identity is limited to the ecclesiological issues within the Lukan church. Thus, the expected interpretation of the Spirit-inspired resistant discourse that engenders counter social formation at the margins of the empire is not brought out. It is expected that a postcolonial socio-cultural exegesis of the text would proffer a holistic appreciation of the Spirit-inspired Nazareth proclamation of Jesus.

4.5.4. Postcolonial Socio-cultural Exegesis of the Nazareth Proclamation

The Nazareth town in southern Galilee, which was under the Roman client ruler Herod Antipas, was not far away from the military stronghold of Sepphoris, which shifted between Roman and Jewish control.[176] Galilee was more than a geographical location in the cultural map of Palestine. It was the heart of agricultural production marked by peasant culture reflected in the Galilean section (4:14–9:50).[177] Galilee also stands out as the heart of Jewish resistance to Roman Empire rife with revolutionaries and resistance movements though Sean Freyne challenged this in his work on Galilee.[178] Jesus' teachings apparently found some resonance with the experience of the Galilean people enough to make rumours about his popularity to spread across the region (4:14–15).[179] As Lukan Jesus returned to Galilee filled with the power of the Spirit, he went to the Nazareth synagogue[180] and announces, with the empowering of the Spirit, an anti-imperial propaganda by quoting Isa 61:1–2 and 58:6 in the periphery of Roman occupied Palestine.

---

with κηρύξαι (to proclaim) in v. 19 is "Luke's deliberate intention to highlight the powerful proclamation inspired by the Spirit."

174 Wenk, *Community Forming Power,* 220.

175 Kuecker, *Spirit and the 'Other,'* 217.

176 Freyne, *Galilee*, 122–128.

177 Green, *Gospel of Luke*, 200.

178 Freyne, *Galilee*, 245–247.

179 Cf. Miller, *Rumors of Resistance*, 160.

180 Synagogue is an official and authorised space, which serves social, political, and religious functions. See Prior, *Jesus the Liberator*, 109–113.

> The Spirit of the Lord is upon me,
> because he has anointed me
> to bring good news to the poor.
> He has sent me to proclaim release to the captives
> and recovery of sight to the blind
> to set the oppressed go free,
> to proclaim the year of the Lord's favor. (Luke 4:18–19).

Luke 4:18–19 is composite of Isaiah 61:1–2 and 58:6. Trito-Isaiah is a document of postexilic community in Jerusalem who were struggling to rebuild the city, the temple, and the identity of the people.[181] If one follows Norman Gottwald's chiastic structure of Trito-Isaiah (56–66), Isa 61:1–2 from which Luke 4:18–19 is taken, stand as the literary and thematic centrepiece of Trito-Isaiah.[182] The transformation of the Jubilee Year legislation (Lev 25) in the contexts of Persian hegemony by Trito-Isaiah and by Luke in the context of Roman hegemony is undoubtedly a response to the reality of the empire.

It can be noted that according to Leviticus 25, Jubilee Year completes the cycle of the seventh sabbatical years. It has two main thrusts such as release/liberty and return/restoration of land, property and human. However, it is debated whether it was ever observed since the Old Testament is silent about a national Jubilee (cf. Jer 32; Ruth 4). Some scholars think that Jubilee code is late, idealistic, and comes from the same time as Holiness code. But others regard Jubilee as a constituent part of Israel's earliest pre-monarchic law, which became irrelevant and fell into disuse.[183] Nonetheless, the Jubilee tradition is used and reused in various historical contexts and the concept underwent significant changes as each interpreter reinvented the potential of Jubilee year.[184] But there is a radical newness

181 Joseph Blenkinsopp, *Isaiah 56–66: A New Translation with Introduction and Commentary*, AYB 19B (New Haven: Yale University Press, 2011), 63–64, writes that in Trito-Isaiah one finds a "picture of a ... community in which there are rich and poor, those close to the sources of power and those deprived of it—a community in which the poor are exploited by the wealthy as always, a community going about its civic and religious business, and especially a community under severe stress."

182 Gottwald, *The Hebrew Bible*, 508.

183 Cf. Christopher J. H. Wright, "Jubilee, Year of" *ABD* 3:1028.

184 The Jubilee legislation (Lev 25), especially the freeing of debt slave is also issued in Deut 15:12 (cf. Exod 21:2–6) and is referenced in Jer 34:14 and in Isa 58:6. Trito-Isaiah dismantles the fixity of fifty years calendar and "calls for and impels a social praxis at all times ... a prophetic 'time' that is not measured by calendar days or years but by reality." José Saverino Craoto, "From the Leviticus Jubilee Year to the Prophetic Liberation Time: Exegetical Reflections on Isaiah 61 and 68 in Relation to the Jubilee," in *God's Economy: Biblical Studies from Latin America*, ed. Rose Kinsler and Gloria Kinsler (Maryknoll, NY: Orbis, 2005), 91. The prophet also took a small step to include the nations in God's favour in Isa 61:11. Qumran's reuse of the Jubilee tradition in 11Q Melchizedek (11Q13) is somewhat opposite to Isaiah. Isaiah 61:1–2 seems to provide the eschatological context for

in Lukan Jesus citation of Isaianic text as Luke introduced notable changes, which can be highlighted below in a parallel column.

Luke 4:18	Isaiah 61:1 (LXX)
Πνεῦμα κυρίου ἐπ' ἐμὲ	Πνεῦμα κυρίου ἐπ' ἐμέ,
οὗ εἵνεκεν ἔχρισέν με	οὗ εἵνεκεν ἔχρισέν με·
εὐαγγελίσασθαι πτωχοῖς,	εὐαγγελίσασθαι πτωχοῖς
ἀπέσταλκέν με,	ἀπέσταλκέν με,
	ἰάσασθαι τοὺς συντετριμμένους τῇ καρδίᾳ,
κηρύξαι αἰχμαλώτοις ἄφεσιν	κηρύξαι αἰχμαλώτοις ἄφεσιν
καὶ τυφλοῖς ἀνάβλεψιν,	καὶ τυφλοῖς ἀνάβλεψιν,
	Isaiah 58:6
ἀποστεῖλαι τεθραυσμένους	ἀπόστελλε τεθραυσμένους ἐν ἀφέσει
ἐν ἀφέσει,	καὶ πᾶσαν συγγραφὴν ἄδικον διάσπα·
Luke 4:19	Isaiah 61:2
κηρύξαι ἐνιαυτὸν κυρίου δεκτόν.	καλέσαι ἐνιαυτὸν κυρίου δεκτὸν
	καὶ ἡμέραν ἀνταποδόσεως,
	παρακαλέσαι πάντας τοὺς πενθοῦντας.

Firstly, Luke included the phrase "to set free the oppressed" from Isaiah 58:6 in the citation of Isa 61:1–2 so that the good news of Isa 61, which is originally directed at consoling the postexilic community is transformed into good news for all who are oppressed, and thus intensified Jesus' message of liberation.[185] Secondly, the infinitive καλέσαι (to announce) in Isa 61:2 (LXX) is changed to κηρύξαι (to proclaim) in Luke 4:18, which was effected probably to emphasise the proclamation of the kingdom of God. Thirdly, Luke excluded "the day of vengeance" of Isa 61:2. This suggests that Nazareth proclamation placed a major emphasis on the liberation of the poor and the oppressed. And finally, it can be noted that Jesus explicitly claimed that the Isaianic status reversals are fulfilled "today" (v. 21). This means, the coming of God's reign is "no longer strictly one year in seven or one year in fifty but a new age of perpetual liberty for all God's

---

the pesher of the Jubilee Year though 11Q13 focuses on Lev 25 with only implicit reference to Isaiah 61. F. Merrill P. Miller, "The Function of Isa 61:1–2 in 11Q Melchizedek," *JBL* 88 (1969): 467; George J. Brooke, "Shared Intertextual Interpretations in the Dead Sea Scrolls and the New Testament," in *Biblical Perspectives: Early Use and Interpretation of the Bible in the Light of the Dead Sea Scrolls*, ed. Michael E. Stone and Esther G. Chazon (Leiden: Brill, 1998), 37. Typical of the Qumran community orientation towards the last days, the Jubilee pesher in 11Q13 is future oriented. So also the beneficiaries of Jubilee is circumscribe to the "sons of light" and vengeance will be upon Belial and the sons of darkness. Moreover, there is a spiritualising of liberty, in that "liberty is defined specifically as release from the debt of all their iniquities." Miller, *Rumors of Resistance*, 157–158.

185 Wilfrid J. Harrington, review of *Jesus the Liberator: Nazareth Liberation Theology, Luke 4:16–30,* by Michael Prior, *CBQ* 59 (1997): 170 (169–171).

people from every kind of oppression."[186] The beneficiary of the good news is not circumscribed to a privileged group but is universal (cf. 4:20–27). This inclusion of the "other" as beneficiary of the good news is the unique feature of the Nazareth proclamation. Thus, one can see the nuancing of resistance, in that, the Nazareth proclamation not only challenges the prevailing order of things but also offers a pedagogy to the oppressed (the Nazareth congregation) about there own limited understanding of liberation. But before turning to the question of the *social other* that spurs negative response from the Nazareth congregation, the question of the poor and the oppressed and their resistive discourse against the prevailing system can be highlighted.

The Hebrew word ענוים (poor) translated as πτωχοῖς in the LXX Isa 61:1 from which Luke quotes in 4:18 are literally the bowed down, the poorest of the poor, afflicted, the weak, and the humble.[187] George Soares-Prabhu who explored the poor in the Bible argues that the poor is basically a sociological category. They are those who are deprived not just economically but of human dignity, "the 'wretched of the earth', the marginalized, the exploited, all those who are actually or potentially oppressed."[188] But the biblical poor are not the romantic poor that entreats charity, but the site of critical reflection and dynamic engagement with the order of things.[189] The Spirit-inspired Nazareth proclamation gives expression to the protest voices of the oppressed against the colonial situation of poverty, inequality, sickness, suffering, and exclusion that calls for reversal of the status quo with a vision of a new order. It challenges the imperial logic of concentration of wealth in the hand of a few and the victimisation of the many and issues out a restructuring of socio-economic relationship that will give human dignity to all.

The good news to the poor is elaborated by three infinitival clauses such as to proclaim release to the captives and recovery of sight to the blind; to set the oppressed go free; and to proclaim the acceptable year of the Lord. Lukan Jesus has deleted the phrase "to bind the broken-hearted" as he quote Isa 61:1 and replaced it with "to set the oppressed go free" from Isa 58:6 (Luke 4:18c). Michael Prior argues that ἄφεσις in Luke is solely forgiveness of sins, because outside Isaiah 61 quotation, the concept of release has no connection with the Jubilee emphasis on liberation from debt and slavery.[190] The problem with this argument is that Jesus connects ἄφεσις with Jubilee emphases, that too in a prominent

186 Ross Kinsler and Gloria Kinsler, *The Biblical Jubilee and the Struggle for Life* (Maryknoll, NY: Orbis, 2000), 105.

187 Francis Brown ed., *The New Brown, Driver and Briggs Hebrew and English Lexicon of the Old Testament* (Lafayette, Indiana: Associated Publishers and Authors, 1981), 776.

188 George M. Soares-Prabhu, "Class in the Bible: The Biblical Poor as a Social Class?" in *Voices from the Margins: Interpreting Bible from the Third World*, ed. R. S. Sugirtharajah (Maryknoll, NY: Orbis Books, 1991), 157.

189 Soares-Prabhu, "Class in the Bible: The Biblical Poor as a Social Class?" 161–166.

190 Prior, *Jesus the Liberator*, 139–140.

place where Jesus lays out the heart of his mission.[191] On the one hand, one who is αἰχμαλώτος (captive) is a socio-political prisoner (cf. Luke 21:24) and in the Septuagint, the term is used explicitly for political prisoners (cf. Tob 1:10; 1 Macc 10:33). On the other hand, the LXX used the term ἄφεσις to render יובל and דרור in the Jubilee legislation (Lev 25:10),[192] so that, לקרא דרור (LXX Isa 61:1, κηρύξαι … ἄφεσιν cf. Luke 4:18), would mean, "to proclaim liberty," which echoes the Jubilee legislation of Lev 25:10 with its main act of releasing all debt slaves.[193] In fact first century Jewish inscriptions (41 and 81 CE) attest that liberation of slaves was carried out in synagogue.[194] Thus, "to proclaim release to the captives" could refer to political prisoners as well as those who were imprisoned for debt default with no means to pay their debt.[195] It is significant to note that the Nazareth discourse of release from colonial situation shifts to postcolonial reflection and emancipatory ideology that accounts for the issue of ethnicity, gender, class and so on (cf. vv. 22–30).

One who is τυφλός might be the literally blind (Luke 7:21–22; 18:35). "Recovery of sight to the blind" is the one phrase that can be rendered metaphorically. However, primarily it refers to Jesus ministry of healing the literally blind. Only secondarily, one may find a metaphorical interpretation. Strikingly, the Vulgate renders it as opening up the prisons.[196] In a Dalit Commentary to the Gospel of Luke, James Massey writes that the captives also mean "those people who were captives to ideologies and of various kinds and structures. Such structural captivity included the captives of various systems pertaining to religious, cultural, economic, social and political spheres.... Likewise … the 'blind' consisted not only in those afflicted with physical blindness, but also those whose mind and heart are closed to truth and values."[197]

"To proclaim the acceptable year of the Lord" clearly points to the proclamation of the Jubilee Year (Lev 25). It is not certain whether Jubilee was ever practiced.[198] Considering the fact the Roman Empire was an agrarian empire with high level of control maintained by the elite ruling groups in matters of economics, Jubilee enactment would have been difficult to implement since the powerful elite stood to lose. However, the first century Galilean peasant's congregation as well as Lukan congregation who were caught in economic crises

191 Miller, *Rumors of Resistance*, 150.

192 Bultmann, "ἀφίημι, ἄφεσις," *TDNT*, 1: 510.

193 Miller, *Rumors of Resistance*, 144.

194 Cf. Prior, *Jesus the Liberator*, 113.

195 Cf. Kinsler and Kinsler, *Biblical Jubilee*, 104.

196 Sanders, "From Isaiah 61 to Luke 4," 50.

197 James Massey, *The Gospel According to Luke*, Dalit Bible Commentary, vol. 3 (New Delhi: Centre for Dalit/Subaltern Studies, 2007), 72.

198 1 Maccabees 6:49–54 describes a sabbatical year practice of leaving the land fallow, but there is no mention comparable to the year of Jubilee.

or debt slavery would eagerly like to experience the ramifications of Jubilee year. John Dominic Crossan expresses the power of such legislation even though real practice may be a distant reality. The inclusion of Jubilee legislation in the canon indicates that it is "*something that could be done in this world even if it never were*" (emphasis original), and the concern for the non-elite is mandated as an important value.[199]

Miller argues that the Nazareth proclamation stands as a stark contrast to the mission of Rome envisioned in Virgil's *Aeneid*:

> Romans, remember by your strength to rule
> Earth's peoples—for your arts are to be these:
> To pacify, to impose the rule of law,
> to spare the conquered, battle down the proud.

In both the passages a list of infinitives elaborate the goal of the mission. However, Miller observes, "the content of Rome's mission is in many ways antithetical to that of Jesus; rather than pacifying and conquering foreigners, Jesus proclaims release for prisoners of war, relief from oppression by the rule of (Roman dictated) law, and in later part of the chapter, an acceptance of foreigners as equally worthy of God's grace and favor."[200] The Nazareth proclamation, which set the tone of Jesus' mission of liberation, is important against the foreground of the oppressed status of Israel vis-à-vis Rome and the Herodian dynasty.[201] Isaiah 61 anticipates the restoration of Israel in which there will be an inversion of status where foreign nations will serve the Hebrews who were captive then (Isa 61:5–7). Quoting from Isaiah 61 would raise the same aura of expectation in the first century Palestine safe that Jesus gave a new twist that challenges not only the empire system of oppression but the Nazareth folks' own narrow universe of identity politics.

With the anointing of the Spirit, Jesus expounds that the good news to the poor and the favourable year of the Lord is for all people irrespective of race, status and gender by alluding to Elijah-Elisha traditions (vv. 24–27). The Gospel narrates that, the response of the audience was at first positive (4:22), but when Jesus speaks about Elijah-Elisha traditions, the Nazareth congregation was filled with rage (4:28). From socio-cultural standpoint, Jesus problematised his townsfolk's assumption that the privileged entitlement of good news is only for the in-group by extending it beyond ethnic boundaries. James A. Sanders also thinks that Jesus' insistence on the extension of God's favour to the Gentiles is a "challenge to in-group meanings of election."[202] But Lukan Jesus' vision includes

---

199 J. D. Crossan, *The Birth of Christianity: Discovering What Happened in the Years Immediately After the Execution of Jesus* (New York: HarperCollins, 1998), 195–197.

200 Miller, *Rumors of Resistance*, 165.

201 Ford, *My Enemy is My Guest*, 54.

202 Sanders, "From Isaiah 61 to Luke 4," 69.

the convergence of different social classes in mutual relationship as it is seen in the story of Elijah and the Sidonian widow, and the story of Elisha and the Aramean warrior. The envisaging of such countercultural inclusive community is an act of protest not least against the cultural-religious norms but against the very fixity of social order, which ensures ostensible social stability. Thus, as much as the Nazareth proclamation challenges the colonial oppression and injustice perpetuated by the rulers and powers, it also challenges the non-elite groups characterised by the Nazareth congregation who leverage privileges identity to a circumscribe cultural group, and thus open up space for the formation of an inclusive transcultural community.

4.6. Conclusion

This chapter has explored the connection between the Spirit and the prophetic voices in Luke's Gospel by taking the Magnificat, the Benedictus and the Nazareth proclamation as key texts. The prophetic nature of these texts are evident not least in that the speakers are associated with the Spirit but also that these texts are bold proclamations from the margins of the society about God's new world over against the world order of Roman Empire. A postcolonial cultural exegesis has highlighted that these texts are resistant voices from the colonised world, which appropriate imperial language with "resistant adaptation"[203] of the dominant discourse for re-presentation. In Luke's scheme, the Spirit is the driving force behind the formation of such new subjecthood and the formation of a resistant community.

The Magnificat sung by a nondescript young pregnant woman in an occupied territory calls on the God of Israel as the mighty one and her saviour who has looked upon with favour the lowly and the humiliated. Such calling on God of Israel as saviour and the mighty one in the context of Roman hegemony subverts the imperial discourse that proclaims Caesar as saviour. The reversal of fortune of the rich and poor, powerful and downtrodden embedded in the Magnificat overturns the imperial hierarchical logic of lording over others with a vision of socio-economic and political restructuring of relationship in which people will be free from exploitation and domination. Similarly the Benedictus also offers a counter discourse to the Roman hegemony by claiming that God has raised a "horn of salvation" to deliver his people from the enemies. It re-inscribes covenantal promises to the fathers using language of national salvation but also with a subtle appropriation of the language of imperial hegemony such as salvation, peace and claims it for Jesus. And thus, the oppositional voice in the Benedictus subverts Caesar's claim as saviour and the bringer of peace and expresses that it is Jesus who is the saviour and the bringer of peace and not

203 This phrase is borrowed from John M. G. Barclay, "The Empire Writes Back: Josephan Rhetoric in Flavian Rome," in *Flavius Josephus and Flavian Rome*, ed. Jonathan Edmondson, Steve Mason and James Rives (Oxford: Oxford University Press, 2005), 318.

Caesar. One can see how Luke's Gospel employs the oppositional voice of the early Christians to find self-expression for the Christian community of his time through the "resistant adaptation" of the dominant discourse.

The theme of reversal is reiterated in the Nazareth proclamation (Luke 4:16:30). The Nazareth proclamation heralds an anti-imperial socio-political protest against the victimisation of the vulnerable with the Jubilee theology of liberation. The good news to the poor and the favourable year of the Lord proclaimed by Jesus stands in sharp contrast to the Roman rule that battles down the opponents of the imperial order and oppressed the conquered with "registration taxation, policing identities."[204] With the anointing of the Spirit, the Lukan Jesus challenges the Roman Empire with the good news of the Kingdom of God that liberates and set free the oppressed from their socio-political bondage. The Nazareth proclamation also strips away all ethnic or nationalistic exclusiveness and challenges the notion of divine election of a specific race (Romans or Jews) and envisions an inclusive community. This creative resistance to the culture of cultivating privilege (colonial) identity hybridises the Us-and-Them binary of social relationship by challenging the alterity of colonial representation. Perhaps the issue involving the contestations and negotiations of the second or third generation Christian identity involving multi-ethnicities demanded a new vision of Jesus who with the anointing of the Spirit transcends cultural boundaries to form an inclusive community. Luke apparently sees the formation of this countercultural resistant community as the work of the Spirit.

204 Cf. Yoder, *Politics of Jesus*, 23.

Chapter 5

The Spirit and Healing Miracles in Luke's Gospel

5.1. Introduction

In the previous chapter, the Spirit in Luke's Gospel was discussed as a Spirit of protest, which manifests in the protest voices of the oppressed, that was embodied fully in the Spirit-messiah Jesus. This chapter elucidates further the resistance aspects of the Spirit in Luke's Gospel by arguing that the Spirit-anointed Jesus' exorcism and healing activities are modes of socio-political resistance against the colonial domination and cultural authorities of the day. It is noted that Jesus returned to Galilee filled with the power of the Spirit. In his inaugural preaching at Nazareth, Luke claimed that Jesus was anointed by the Spirit of the Lord in order to drive home the point that hereto for the entire Jesus' activities were carried out in the power of the Spirit (cf. Acts 10:38). But Luke did not explicitly state that Jesus heals or exorcises by the Spirit; rather, Luke claims that Jesus heals and exorcises with δύναμις (power) and ἐξουσία (authority). These two terms are closely rooted in the Spirit's anointing of Jesus. Thus, it is pertinent to underline the relationship of πνεῦμα (spirit) with δύναμις (power) and ἐξουσία (authority) in order to elucidate the activity of the Spirit at the deeper level of Jesus' exorcism and healing. Noting that Jesus was an exorcist/healer in his milieu, and that Luke account for δύναμις (power) and ἐξουσία (authority) as the media by which the Spirit-anointed Jesus performed healing miracles, this chapter explores the exorcism at Capernaum synagogue (Luke 4:31–37) and the healing of the paralytic (Luke 5:17–26) from the vantage point of postcolonial socio-cultural exegesis.

5.2. Exorcism and Healing Miracles of Jesus in Luke's Gospel

John P. Meier struck an important note when he said, "Nothing is more certain about Jesus than that he was viewed by his contemporaries as an exorcist and a healer."[1] It is difficult to catalogue the miracles of Jesus since scholars do not always agree on which pericope has to be taken as a separate story and which has to be treated as a variant or parallel found in another Gospel. At any rate, David Aune's tally[2] provides a good perspective according to which there are six accounts of exorcisms,[3] seventeen healings,[4] and eight so-called nature miracles.[5] One or more variant traditions of several of the stories are found in other Gospels. Furthermore, the Synoptics also provide summary reports of Jesus' healings and exorcisms,[6] which give the impression that Jesus did miracles

1 John P. Meier, "Jesus," in *NJBC*, (Bangalore: TPI, 1991), 1321.

2 David E. Aune, *Apocalypticism, Prophecy, and Magic in Early Christianity* (Grand Rapids: Baker Academic, 2008), 385.

3 Six exorcisms: (1) the Capernaum demoniac (Mark 1:21–28 // Luke 4:33–37); (2) the Gerasene/ Gadarene demoniac (Mark 5:1–20 // Matt 8:28–34 // Luke 8:26–39); (3) the daughter of Syrophoenician (or Canaanite) woman (7:24–30 // Matt 15:21–28); (4) the boy suffering from fits (Mark 9:14–29 // Matt 17:14–21 // Luke 9:37–43); (5) the dumb demoniac (Matt 9:32–33); and (6) the blind and dumb demoniac (Matt 12:22–23 // Luke 11:14–15). Matthew 9:32–33 appears to be a variant of Matt 12:22–23, and thus some might count only five exorcisms.

4 Seventeen healings: (1) Peter's mother-in-law (Mark 1:29–31 // Matt 8:14–15 // Luke 4:38–39); (2) the leper (Mark 1:40–45 // Matt 8:1–4 // Luke 5:12–16); (3) the paralytic (Mark 2:1–12 // Matt 9:1–8 // Luke 5:17–26); (4) The man with the withered hand (Mark 3:1–6 // Matt 12:9–14 // Luke 6:6–11; (5) the daughter of Jairus (Mark 5:21–34, 35–43 // Matt 9:18–19, 23–26 // Luke 8:40–42, 49–56); (6) the women with the haemorrhage (Mark 5:25–34 // Matt 9:20–22 // Luke 8:43–48; (7) the deaf mute (Mark 7:31–36); (8) the blind man near Bethsaida (Mark 8:22–26); (9) blind Bartimaeus (Mark 10:46–52 // Matt 20:29–34 (cf. the doublet in Matt 9: 27–31) // Luke 18:35–43; (10) the young man at Nain (Luke 7:11–17); (11) the woman bent over (Luke 13:10–17); (12) the ten lepers (Luke 17:11–19); (13) the man with dropsy (Luke 14:1–6); (14) the paralytic by the pool (John 5:1–9); (15) the raising of Lazarus (John 11); (16) the man born blind (John 9); and (17) centurion's servant (Matt 8:5–13 // Luke 7:1–10 // John 4:46–54).

5 Eight nature miracles: (1) stilling of the storm (Mark 4:35–41 // Matt 8:23–27 // Luke 8:22–25); (2) feeding of the five thousand (Mark 6:30–44 // Matt 14:13–21 // Luke 9:10–17 // John 6:1–15); (3) feeding of the four thousand (Mark 8:1–10 // Matt 15:32–39); (4) walking on the water (Mark 6:45–52 // Matt 14:22–33 // John 6:16–21); (5) cursing of the fig tree (Mark 11:12–14, 20–26 // Matt 21:18–22); (6) coin in the fish's mouth (Matt 17:24–27); (7) miraculous catch of fish (Luke 5:1–11 cf. John 21:1–11); and (8) change of water into wine (John 2:1–11).

6 Aune lists four summaries: (1) Mark 1:32–34 // Matt 8:16 // Luke 4:40–41; (2) Mark 1:39 // Matt 4:23–24 (cf. the parallel statement in 9:35); (3) Mark 3:10–12 // Luke 6:17–19 (cf. Matt 12:15–16); and (4) Mark 6:55–66 // Matt 14:35–36). There are also brief references to the exorcistic activities of Jesus and others in the Synoptics. They are exorcism of some women including Mary Magdalene from whom seven demons were cast out (Luke 8:2 cf. Mark 9:16); Jesus empowering the disciples to exorcise and/or heal in the mission command

far more than recorded. This data shows that Luke has preserved the exorcism and healing accounts as much as Matthew and Mark.

The long list of Jesus' deeds is not in itself a proof that all the incidents happened in the life of Jesus.[7] However, the multiple attestations, the frequency and quantity of tradition about Jesus' miracles in the Synoptic Gospels suggest that, whatever historical credibility one ascribes to the actual details of the story, there is no reason to doubt the historical fact of Jesus' extraordinary deeds which are called healing miracles.[8] However, since the Enlightenment philosopher David Hume, who claimed that miracles are contrary to human experience, "much of modern academia has a priori ruled out claims of direct supernatural activity in the natural world."[9] David Friedrich Strauss' *Leben Jesu* (1835-36),[10] called for a mythical interpretation of Jesus' miracles since rational or supernatural interpretation is not tenable to the modern mind. After Strauss, the teachings of Jesus became the centre of interest in the study of the historical Jesus, while the miracles became of little value. For instance, the form critic Rudolf Bultmann writes, "we can know almost nothing concerning the life and personality of Jesus, since the early Christian sources show no interest in either, are moreover fragmentary and often legendary."[11] Thus the quest for the historical Jesus carried out by Bultmann's students was mainly to focus on the words of Jesus with theological and hermeneutical interests.[12]

However, since the 1970s, there has been more openness to the miracle tradition and to view Jesus as a healer in his historical context. This has resulted in many scholars acknowledging that Jesus was known as a healer and an exorcist in the earliest traditions, and that these activities constituted one of his main

(Mark 3:15; Matt 10:1 // Luke 9:1); "another" exorcist practicing exorcism in Jesus' name (Mark 9:38–41 // Luke 9:49–50); disciples failure and success in performing exorcism (Mark 9:18; Luke 10:17–20).

7 It is generally recognised that most of nature miracles seem to stem from the early church. John P. Meier, *A Marginal Jew: Rethinking the Historical Jesus,* vol. 2, *Mentor Message and Miracles* (New York: Doubleday, 1994), 13.

8 Meier, *A Marginal Jew*, 2:630; Gerd Theissen and Annette Merz, *The Historical Jesus: A Comprehensive Guide*, trans. John Bowden (London: SCM, 1998), 292–293; Christian Strecker, "Jesus and the Demoniacs," in *The Social Setting of Jesus and the Gospels*, ed. Wolfgang Stegemann, Bruce Malina and Gerd Theissen (Minneapolis: Fortress, 2002), 118.

9 Craig S. Keener, *Miracles: The Credibility of the New Testament Accounts,* vol. 1 (Grand Rapids: Baker Academics, 2011), 83.

10 David Friedrich Strauss, *The Life of Jesus Critically Examined*, trans. G. Eliot, Life of Jesus Series (Philadelphia: Fortress, 1972).

11 Rudolf Bultmann, *Jesus and the Word* (New York: Charles Schribner's Sons, 1934), 4. Bultmann thinks that the miracles are ascribed to Jesus very early on and the Hellenistic origin of the miracles is overwhelmingly probable. Bultmann, *History of Synoptic Tradition*, 238–240.

12 Halvor Moxnes, "Ethnography and Historical Imagination in Reading Jesus as an Exorcist," *Neotestmantica* 44 (2010): 329.

activities.[13] Jesus' healing activities perhaps provided umpteen opportunities for teaching. Ben Meyer writes, "Jesus thus epitomized his public career not as words but as exorcisms and cures."[14] In fact the Synoptic traditions present Jesus as a healer and an exorcist, whose exorcism is inextricably tied to the coming kingdom of God (Matt 12:28 // Luke 11:20). It is also to be noted that Jesus' healing and exorcism attracted opposition from the rulers and powers of Judea and Galilee (Mark 3:20–23; Matt 12:25–28; Luke 11:1–20; 13:31–33). Jesus' contemporaries understood his healing activities to be political. The political significance of Jesus' healing miracles in its historical context is of burgeoning interest among recent scholars.[15] It will be seen that Luke however, invested much energy in reporting the activities of Jesus as an exorcist and a healer, who attracted both acclamation from the crowd and opposition from the elite quarter.

5.2.1. Exorcism in Luke's Gospel

Luke's Gospel not only reproduces most of the exorcism traditions found in Mark and Q but also preserves some unique materials. Luke's shortening the summary statement of Jesus' ministry found in Mark is obvious, but Luke preserves or adds another summary statement of Jesus that includes Jesus curing those with evil spirits (Luke 7:21). As for the passing references about Jesus' exorcism, only Luke records the exorcistic ministry of the seventy(two) (Luke 10:17–20) and the exorcism of some women found in Luke 8:2.[16] Except for the exorcism of the daughter of Syrophoenician women (Mark 7:24–30), Luke's Gospel reproduces the other three exorcism narratives found in Mark such as the exorcism of the demon possessed at Capernaum synagogue (4:33–37 // Mark 1:21–28); Gerasene demoniac (8:26–39 // Mark 5:1–20); and the boy suffering from fits (9:37–43 // Mark 9:14–29). Luke also preserved the Q exorcism narrative found in Luke 11:14. Apart from the narratives, Luke also preserves prominent sayings concerning Jesus' exorcism in the pericope of Beelzebul controversy such as the accusation against Jesus that "he casts out demons by Beelzebul, the ruler of the demons" (Luke 11:15 cf. Matt 9:34;

13 Geza Vermes, *Jesus the Jew: A Historian's Reading of the Gospels* (Philadelphia: Fortress, 1973), 22; J. D. G. Dunn, *Christ and the Spirit* (Grand Rapids: Eerdmans, 1998), 174–176; Morton Smith, *Jesus the Magician* (New York: Harper & Row, 1978); E. P. Sanders, *Jesus and Judaism* (Philadelphia: Fortress, 1985); J. D. Crossan, *The Historical Jesus: The Life of A Mediterranean Jewish Peasant* (San Francisco: HaperSanFrancisco, 1991), 303–353.

14 Ben Meyer, *The Aims of Jesus* (Eugene, OR: Pickwick, 2002), 154.

15 J. D. Crossan, *Jesus: A Revolutionary Biography* (San Francisco: HaperSanFrancisco, 1994), 76–93; Eric Eve, *The Healer from Nazareth: Jesus' Miracles in Historical Context* (London: SPCK, 2009); Santiago Guijarro, "The Politics of Exorcism," 159–174; Amanda Witmer, *Jesus, the Galilean Exorcist: His Exorcism in Social and Political Context* (London: Bloomsbury, 2012).

16 If the original ending of Mark's Gospel at 16:8 is asserted, the influence of Luke 8:2 upon Mark 16:9 is highly possible.

12:24), and Jesus' response which says, "But if it is by the spirit/finger of God that I cast out the demons, then the kingdom of God has come to you" (Luke 11:20 // Matt 12:28). The parable of the strong one (Luke 11:21-22 // Matt 12:29) is also probably connected to Jesus' exorcism. A further hint of Jesus' exorcism recorded only by Luke is found in Jesus' message to Herod: "Go and tell that fox for me, 'Listen I am casting out demons and performing cures today and tomorrow... and the next day I must be on my way because it is impossible for a prophet to be killed outside of Jerusalem'" (Luke 13:32).

The exorcism of the Gerasene demoniac can be noted here to substantiate the politically subversive nature of Jesus' exorcism. When Jesus asks the Gerasene demoniac, "'What is your name?' He said, 'Legion, for we are many'" (Mark 5:9 // Luke 8:30). Legion refers to the Roman military occupation that tormented the indigenous population. But if demon possession is caused by the Legions, Jesus' exorcism is by default a challenge against the Roman imperial presence. The people's response to the success of exorcism is not simply amazement and wonder (cf. Luke 4:36). The Gerasene's townsfolk were worried about the potential political implication of exorcism and urge Jesus to leave their town (Luke 8:37). Of course, how far this story reflects an actual event in the life of Jesus is difficult to sustain. Meier argues that, too many layers of literary activity and theological imagination makes it difficult to attribute this story as a single event going back to the historical Jesus.[17] Nevertheless, it represents the view that Jesus' exorcism was a mode of resistance against the political hegemony of the Roman Empire that had colonised and tormented the indigenous people.

Some have noted that the accusation levelled against Jesus for his exorcistic activities, in instance like the Beelzebub controversy, corresponds to the sociological and anthropological studies on deviance that have noted that those in power use deviance labelling as a weapon of social control.[18] The reasons for the opposition to Jesus' exorcistic activities are probably that Jesus drew on large crowds and continued his activities in a way that challenged the status quo of the establishment.[19] Jesus' exorcisms are reported to have occurred in public spaces (in the synagogue or in the open place), where the people gathered. And Jesus associates exorcism with the inbreaking of the kingdom of God which naturally constitutes an open challenge to the established political order. If one considers Q's subtle use of Satan's kingdom (Luke 11:18 // Matt 12:26 cf. Luke 4:5–7 // Matt 4:8–10) against which Jesus inaugurates the kingdom of God by casting out demons, the clash of Roman backed political establishment and Jesus' kingdom of God is clearly in view.[20]

17 Meier, *A Marginal Jew*, 2:652–653.

18 Guijarro, "The Politics of Exorcism," 165.

19 Cf. Witmer, *Jesus, the Galilean Exorcist*, 19.

20 Cf. Seo, *Luke's Jesus in Roman Empire and the Emperor in Luke's Gospel*, 133–134.

While the political subversiveness of associating exorcism with the inbreaking of the kingdom of God is already noted, it is also significant to note the pneumatological significance of Jesus' exorcism. Jesus claimed the divine origin of his power and authority. Matthew is explicit in claiming exorcism as the work of the Spirit of God (Matt 12:28). It is notable that Luke preferred the "finger of God" to the "Spirit of God" in this particular context. Nevertheless, both the phrases mean the "power of God."[21] Plausibly, Luke's use of the "finger of God" is influenced by Moses' feat against Pharaoh (cf. 8:19), as it provides the meaning of God's intervention to liberate people from domination. But for Luke, the acts of the Spirit-anointed Jesus are acts of the Spirit of God. There is a close connection between Jesus' power and authority to perform exorcism and his Spirit's anointing. The emphasis on Jesus power and authority can also be seen in Jesus' healing activities.

5.2.2. Healing in Luke's Gospel

Of the seventeen healings stories narrated in the four Gospels (noted above), Luke preserves twelve.[22] Four of these healings are unique to Luke's Gospel.[23] In Luke's Gospel, some healings are blurred between exorcism and healing. For instance, Lukan Jesus rebukes the fever of Simon's mother-in-law as though it is an exorcism (4:39). The crippled woman's sickness was attributed to a spirit (13:11). Most of Lukan Jesus' healing occurred among the poor, the social outcasts and the impure. Religious authorities saw most of Lukan Jesus' healings as either breaking the sanctity of the Sabbath or contravening the purity laws. This is because a number of Jesus' healing events occurred on the Sabbath.

Jesus' healings involves two things—physical contact with the impure and Jesus' pronouncement of the forgiveness of sin. Since purity issues cut across the Second Temple Israelite society, Jesus' healing in the public arena which involves touching the impure have potential political implications for Jesus as a healer.[24] The acts of touching the impure are cultural issues for leaders of political religion.

---

21 The Spirit and "hand of the Lord" (finger of God cf. Exo 3:20; 8:19) are used as synonymous concepts to the Hebrew manner of speech (Ezek 3:14; 8:1–3; 37:1 cf. Ps 8:3 with 33:6; 1 Kgs 18:12 with 2 Kgs 2:16) both of which describe the powerful action of God. Cf. Robert G. Hamerton-Kelly, "A Note on Matthew 12:28 Par. Luke 11:20," *NTS* 11 (1965): 169; Dunn, *Jesus and the Spirit*, 46.

22 The five healing stories not found in Luke's Gospel are, the healing of the deaf mute (Mark 7:31–36); the blind man near Bethsaida (Mark 8:22–26); the paralytic by the pool (John 5:1–9); the raising of Lazarus (John 11); and the healing of the man born blind (John 9).

23 They are: the resuscitation of the young man at Nain (Luke 7:11–17); the healing of the woman bent over for eighteen years (Luke 13:10–17); the man with dropsy (Luke 14:1–6); and cleansing of the ten lepers which included a Samaritan (Luke 17:11–19).

24 Stuart L. Love, "Jesus Heals the Hemorrhaging Woman," in *The Social Setting of Jesus and the Gospels*, ed. Wolfgang Stegemann, Bruce J. Malina and Gerd Theissen (Minneapolis: Fortress, 2002), 93.

And thus the cultural authorities branded Jesus as deviant or unclean for coming into physical contact with the impure.[25] At the same time they question the legitimacy of Jesus to forgive sins (5:21). But Jesus' constituency acknowledges his authority to heal (7:16; 9:8, 19; 14:19). In the first century cultic context of Judaism in which the temple is the venue of healing, Jesus' healing activities acted like "the mobile embodiment of the temple"[26] healing many sick persons away from the physical location of the temple. Thus Jesus' healings function as a mode of socio-political resistance against the Jerusalem temple's map of purity and its monopoly in dispensing forgiveness of sin. Jesus' healing naturally attracted opposition from the religious authorities, since Jesus' power and authority was not derived from the established relgious institution. But Luke claims that Jesus performed the healings with δύναμις (power) and ἐξουσία (authority). Lukan usage of δύναμις (power) and ἐξουσία (authority) in relation with πνεῦμα (Spirit) will probably shed light on Luke's claim of Jesus' power and authority, since it is the Spirit's anointing that set in motion Jesus' powerful and auhtoritative words and deeds.

5.2.3. πνεῦμα, δύναμις, and ἐξουσία in Lukan Jesus' Healing Activities

The terms δύναμις and ἐξουσία are closely related and they generally mean "power"—an ability to perform an action.[27] The term ἐξουσία approximates δύναμις, but the distinction remains, in that δύναμις denotes external power whereas ἐξουσία has a more inward reference, in that ἐξουσία is essentially the "right to do something or the right over something," which is best rendered by the word "authority."[28] In *Naming the Powers*, Walter Wink helpfully brings out the dual aspects of power by arguing that every power tends to have a visible pole which is the outer form (political systems, appointed officials, chair of an organisation, laws) and an invisible pole, an inner spirituality or the driving force that sanctions, legitimises, and regulates the manifestation of power.[29] In other words, the institution of earthly political powers and structures of authorities one finds in Luke such as ἀρχιερεῖς and ἄρχοντες (chief priests and rulers, 24:20); ἀρχας and ἐξουσίας (rulers and authorities, 12:11); ἀρχῇ (authority), ἐξουσία (jurisdiction) and ἡγεμόνος (governor, 20:20); ἄρχοντας (rulers, 23:13) and so

25 Cf. Jerome H. Neyrey, "Clean/Unclean, Pure/Polluted, and Holy/Profane: The Idea and the System of Purity," in *The Social Science and the New Testament Interpretations*, ed. Richard L. Rohrbaugh (Peabody, MA: Hendrickson, 1996), 92–95.

26 Nicholas Perrin, *Jesus the Temple* (London: SPCK), 154.

27 Walter Grundmann, "δύναμαι/δύναμις," *TDNT* 2:284–286; Werner Foester, "ἐξουσία," *TDNT* 2:562–563.

28 See Foester, *TDNT* 2:562–563.

29 Wink, *Naming the Powers*, 4–12, 104–107.

on,[30] have a dual aspect, "possessing both an outer, visible form (constitutions, judges, police, leaders, office complexes), and an inner, invisible spirit that provides its legitimacy, compliance, credibility and clout."[31] Especially, the main use of the term ἐξουσία in the New Testament is "in reference to the legitimations, sanctions, and permissions that undergird the everyday exercise of power."[32] Thus the question, "With what authority are you doing these things?" (20:2), was a pressing question put to Jesus from the elite quarters, since Jesus was clearly an outsider of the established institutions of power and authority.

There is no doubt that Luke speaks of the authority (ἐξουσία) of the devil (4:6), power of the adversary (12:5) and the power (ἐξουσία) of darkness (22:53). But Luke is very categorical that the power of darkness is given only for a time.[33] But Luke claims for Jesus divine power and authority, an authority that surpasses the claims of earthly rulers and powers instituted in the office of emperor, governor, rulers, chief priests and so on. Luke collocates ἐξουσία and δύναμις relation to Jesus' words and deeds (4:36; 9:1 cf. 10:19) to drive home the point that Jesus possesses not only power but also the divine authority. And this claim is rooted in the Spirit's anointing of Jesus at Jordan (3:22). Luke avoided explicit mention of πνεῦμα (as the Spirit of God), and preferred to employ δύναμις (power) and ἐξουσία (authority) as the means by which Jesus performed healings and exorcisms.[34] But it is presumed that Jesus' power and authority are not the delegated authority of the political institutions; they are derived from God. A brief analysis of the relationship of ἐξουσία (authority) and δύναμις (power),

30 Luke also uses ἐξουσία in reference to the "power" of Satan (12:5) and to human "authorities" (12:11).

31 Wink, *Unmasking the Powers*, 4.

32 Wink, *Naming the Powers*, 17.

33 Conzelmann, *Theology of St Luke*, 182.

34 This has provided the ground for some scholars to argue that the Spirit of God is not associated with miracles in Luke. For instance, Eduard Schweizer, "πνεῦμα," *TDNT* 6:407–413, maintains that Luke shares with Judaism the view that the spirit is "essentially the Spirit of prophecy." Thus, healing and exorcism belongs to the domain of δύναμις, and that Lukan downplaying of miraculous signs in 4:23–27 that the Spirit anointed announced in 4:18 shows a clear disconnect of the Spirit and miracles. He writes, "Though the miracles are important for Luke, they are never ascribed to the Spirit" (407). Menzies, *Empowered for Witness*, 227 also writes, "Luke retained the Jewish understanding of the Spirit as the source of special insights and inspired speech" but shows reluctance to associate the Spirit with the miraculous and thus used δύναμις for the miraculous. Menzies opines that Lukan prophetic pneumatology can be differentiated from the more charismatic pneumatology of Mark and Q and the soteriological pneumatology of Paul (226–227). However, Graham Twelftree has noted that in the Judaism of Luke's world the Spirit was not entirely devoid of the miraculous function. He noted that when the Septuagint uses the "spirit of the Lord" (πνεῦμα κύριου), the miraculous elements are present without doubt as in the case of Samson (Judg 14:6; 15:14) and also Ezekiel (Ezek 3:14). See Graham H. Twelftree, *Jesus the Miracle Worker* (Downers Grove, Illinois: Intervarsity Press, 1999), 168.

with πνεῦμα (spirit) will clarify the point that Jesus' δύναμις (power) and ἐξουσία (authority) are rooted in his Spirit's anointing.

Luke categorically describes δύναμις (power) as the power of the Spirit (πνεῦμα) in 4:14. Here, Luke unambiguously states that, after his baptism and the temptations, Jesus returned ἐν τῇ δυνάμει τοῦ πνεύματος (in the power of the Spirit, 4:14) into Galilee to begin his public career. The source of Jesus' power was his anointing with the Spirit at his baptism.[35] This can be substantiated with several instances where the connection between δύναμις and πνεῦμα is vivid. Luke 1:17 and 1:35 clearly present δύναμις and πνεῦμα as synonymous parallels. Similarly, there is a clear substitution of πνεῦμα with δύναμις in 24:49. Here the resurrected Jesus promised the disciples that they will be clothed (ἐνδυω) with "power from on high," (cf. 1:35) which undoubtedly refers to the Holy Spirit as Acts 1:8 suggests. There is still another reference to δύναμις that can be seen in the light of Jesus' Spirit anointing. In the narrative of the healing of the paralytic, Luke 5:17 states, "the power of the Lord was with him to heal." Here, δύναμις apparently refers to the power of the Spirit to heal. In fact, given the close connection between δύναμις and πνεῦμα, some have noted that the Spirit and power are indissolubly related and are used as synonyms in Luke's Gospel.[36]

Since, Luke has collocated ἐξουσία and δύναμις in several places such as 4:36; 9:1 cf. 10:19, it raises the question whether they are used synonymously or not. Barrett thinks that there is no obvious reason that they are different.[37] But Conzelmann opines that Luke kept the formal distinction between the two words in that, δύναμις stands for actual power and ἐξουσία for potential power.[38] Probably, Lukan collocation of the two terms is intended to emphasise that Jesus possesses not only the power to act but also the divine authority to act as the Spirit-messiah. Thus the use of the term ἐξουσία in Mark 1:27 // Luke 4:36 and Mark 6:7 // Luke 9:1 apparently points to the divine authority of Jesus. Jesus clearly makes a distinction between the authority that originates from God and the authority that originates from human institution (cf. Luke 20:2–7), and implicitly claims for himself the authority of a prophet like John the Baptist. There is one instance where ἐξουσία denotes divine authority (Luke 5:24). For Luke, the ἐξουσία of Jesus is rooted in his baptism with the Spirit.

---

35 Barrett, *Holy Spirit and the Gospel Tradition*, 76. Barrett differentiates the connotation of δύναμις between Mark and Luke noting, "[T]he third Evangelists seems to have regarded 'power' as the energy of the Spirit, while the characteristic connotation of δύναμις in Mk. is eschatological, that is to say, it is used (9.1; 13.26) in prophecies about the last days" (77). In other words, Luke takes a detour from Mark's eschatological connotation and linked the δύναμις with the Spirit (cf. 4:14) in association with the activities of Jesus without the eschatological tone. See Conzelmann, *Theology of St Luke*, 183.

36 Walter Grundmann, "δύναμαι/δύναμις," *TDNT* 2:301; Schweizer, "πνεῦμα," *TDNT*, 407; Brown, *Birth of the Messiah*, 290.

37 Barrett, *Holy Spirit and Gospel Tradition*, 78.

38 Conzelmann, *Theology of St Luke*, 181.

Thus, it is apparent that for Luke the Spirit of God that anointed Jesus is the source of Jesus' ἐξουσία and δύναμις. And so, when Luke's Gospel uses ἐξουσία and δύναμις in relation to Jesus it is referring to the authority and power of the Spirit of God. In other words, when Luke notes, "the power of the Lord was with him to heal" (5: 17c), he means that the power of the Spirit of the Lord was with Jesus to perform healing. Therefore, although Luke did not explicitly mention the Spirit (of God) in any of Jesus' healing activities, Luke understood healings as the work of the Spirit because they are the works of the Spirit-messiah Jesus who was endowed with divine power and authority. But this power is a transforming power that heals more than the physical body; it is also an integrated healing that creates a new community. A postcolonial cultural reading of 4:31–37 and 5:17–26 will elucidate this subversive community forming dimension of Jesus' healing.

5.3. Capernaum Synagogue Exorcism (Luke 4:31–37)

The exorcism of the man who had "a spirit of unclean demon"[39] at the Capernaum synagogue is the first liberative act of the Spirit-messiah Jesus whose mission is announced in Luke 4:16–30. Lukan initial reference to the power of the Spirit in 4:14 and the anointing of the Spirit in 4:18 began to manifest in the powerful and authoritative teaching and exorcism of Jesus in Capernaum (4:32, 36).[40] This narrative is significant to underline the pneumatological significance of Jesus' exorcism because Luke is emphatic that Jesus expelled the demon with ἐξουσία

39 Luke's first reference to the evil spirit occur in 4:33. πνεῦμα δαιμονίου ἀκαθάρτου literally means "a spirit of an unclean demon." Luke could have simply used the usual Palestinian Jewish expression πνεῦμα πονηρόν (7:20; 8:2) or πνεῦμα ἀκαθάρτον (6:18). However, Lukan clumsy construction is apparently deliberate. Firstly, by designation the spirit as unclean Luke is clarifying that the spirit here is not the Holy Spirit. Secondly, "demon" is a neutral or positive entity of divinities in the Greco-Roman world although the Second Temple Judaism considers demon as diabolical. In short, Luke to is specifying his audience his own vocabulary for evil spirits. Cf. Green, *Gospel of Luke*, 222; Fitzmyer, *Luke I–IX*, 544.

In almost all the narratives about possession, an unclean spirit (πνεῦμα ἀκαθάρτον) is said to possess the possessed (4:33, 36; 8:29; 9:42 cf. 6:18; 8:2; 11:24, 26). Apart from using the taxonomy of spirit in relation to posession, Luke also indicates certain sickness as caused by (evil) spirits, which is notably predominant among the women. For instance, Jesus freed some of his women followers from evil spirits and informities (8:1–2); there is also a woman who had a spirit that had crippled her for eighteen years (13:11). It can also be noted that Lukan Jesus stood over Peter's mother-in-law and rebuked a "fever" as though it were an exorcism of a spirit called fever (4:38–39). In the raising of the daughter of Jairus, Luke reports: "Her spirit returned, and she got up at once" (8:55). See John J. Pilch, "Sickness and Healing in Luke-Acts," in Neyrey, *Social World of Luke-Acts*, 202. Thus, it is noted that as much as Luke uses πνεῦμα to designate the Holy Spirit or the divine Spirit, Luke also uses πνεῦμα many times to designate malevolent spirit that caused possession or sickness. However, it is obvious in Luke's Gospel that the healer and exorcist Jesus is able to address and overcome the predicament of spirits by the powerful healing Spirit of God. Pilch, "Sickness and Healing in Luke-Acts," 202.

40 Green, *The Gospel of Luke*, 203.

(authority) and δύναμις (power) which are rooted in the Spirit-anointing of Jesus (3:22; 4:18).[41]

5.3.1. Analysis of the Text (Luke 4:31–37)

Analysing source critically Luke 4:31–44 one notes that it is taken from Mark 1:21–39. Form critically Rudolf Bultmann maintains that the exorcism of the unclean demoniac (Mark 1:21–28 // Luke 4:31–37) exhibits all the typical features of a miracle story, especially that of an exorcism: the demons recognise the exorcist and put up a challenge; the exorcist offers a command or threat; the demon departs, making a scene; and the bystanders response.[42] The major Lukan redactions can be pointed out. (1) The use of the singular verb κατῆλθεν (he went down, v. 31), instead of the Markan εἰσπορεύονται (they entered, Mark 1:21); (2) the addition of "a city in Galilee" (v. 31); (3) the omission of comparing Jesus' authority to that of the scribes (v. 32 cf. Mark 1:22); (4) the description of the demoniac as a man who had a "spirit of an unclean demon" (v. 33 cf. Mark 1:23); (5) the addition of the interjection "Ha" (NRSV translate this as "Let us alone" v. 34); (6) the addition that the demon threw the man down without harming him (v. 35); (7) the substitution of "words" for the Markan "new teaching" (v. 36 cf. Mark 1:27);[43] (8) and the additional emphasis on Jesus' "power" (v. 36 cf. Mark 1:27).

John P. Meier opines that the multiple attestations of Capernaum as a pivotal place of Jesus' Galilean ministry suggest that Jesus performed miracles including exorcisms in Capernaum. However, for him the story of the demoniac in the Capernaum synagogue on Sabbath is a "paradigmatic scene" and "it would be unwise to press for details" of this exorcism. "In particular, the themes of the demon's knowledge of Jesus true identity, his crying out of a christological title, and Jesus commands to be silent may all be expressions of Mark's theology of the messianic secret."[44] The Fellows of the Jesus Seminar came to the same conclusion, though they "allowed for the possibility that it reflected a particular event."[45] Graham H. Twelftree argues that this story is "a faithful reflection of an event in the life of historical Jesus,"[46] in that this story contains traces of

41 Cf. Fitzmyer, *Luke I–IX*, 543.

42 Bultmann, *History of Synoptic Tradition*, 210.

43 Cf. Fitzmyer, *Luke I–IX*, 542.

44 Meier, *A Marginal Jew*, 2:648, 649.

45 Robert W. Funk and the Jesus Seminar, *The Acts of Jesus: The Search for the Authentic Deeds of Jesus* (New York; San Francisco: HarperCollins Publishers, 1998), 58.

46 Twelftree, *Jesus the Miracle Worker*, 286. (1) Mark does not conform to 1 Kings 17:18 that best explains the background of the Semitic expression "why are you bothering us" (Mark 1:24 // Luke 4:34) or use this expression consistently (cf. Mark: 5:7). (2) If the evangelists or the early church wanted to introduce a title for Jesus, one could expect such a title as the Son of God (cf. Mark 3:11). But the demon calling Jesus of Nazareth points to the earliest memories of Jesus. (3) The crude use of the word ἀπολέσαι, "to destroy" (a word which is

authenticity of Jesus performing exorcism at Capernaum, though, one cannot deny that there are already theological and narrative embellishments in Mark and then in Luke.

The setting given in Capernaum could well have been part of the original story, since all the evangelists attest Capernaum as the mainstay of Jesus activities. According to Luke's story, Jesus escapes a mob rage from Nazareth and went down to Capernaum "a city in Galilee," and was teaching the people on the Sabbath.[47] There are clues that indicate the power of the Spirit of God at work in Jesus. The most significant point is that Luke emphatically notes that the people were amazed because ἐν ἐξουσίᾳ καὶ δυνάμει ἐπιτάσσει τοῖς ἀκαθάρτοις πνεύμασιν καὶ ἐξέρχονται (with authority and power he rebukes the unclean spirits and they come out, v. 36). There is an obvious connection between Jesus' Spirit-anointed preaching at Nazareth and Jesus' (teaching[48] and) exorcism with authority and power at Capernaum. The use of "power" in v. 36 is reminiscent of Luke's report that Jesus came back from the wilderness with "the power of the Spirit" (4:14). Luke is apparently signalling here that the authority and power of Jesus is rooted in his Spirit-anointing. The words ἐξουσίᾳ and δυνάμει "recalls that Jesus is the Spirit-guided agent vested with the power of God."[49]

5.3.2. Traditional Interpretations

Traditional interpretations have not paid sufficient attention to the socio-cultural dimension of possession and "the politics of exorcism"[50] since they are strange and alien to scientific mode of thinking. Christian Strecker argues that there is an inclination to psychologise, rationalise and pathologise the phenomena of possession described in the New Testament owing to three fatal mechanisms of reduction that characterise Western scientific discourse such as egocentrism, logocentrism, and ethnocentrism.[51] However, many cultural anthropologists have

---

not used in New Testament in relation to Jesus' ministry) and φιμώθητι, "be silent" (instead of the verb σιωπάω cf. Mark 10:48) to silence the demon, a word which is well known in the magical papyri to have the connotation of binding or restricting suggest that these words most probably belong to the primary strata of the tradition. (4) Jesus' command, "Come out of him" is a commonplace expression in ancient literature, and since there is no discernible reason why this command should have been added to the tradition of the early church, it belongs to the historical data of this story (285).

47 It is not very clear whether τοῖς σάββασιν refers to several Sabbaths or to one. Luke can use the plural phrase ἡ ἡμέρα τῶν σαββάτων (4:16) for a single day. Luke is not very consistent on this. Possibly singular meaning is intended here. Cf. Marshall, *Gospel of Luke*, 191.

48 Luke also reports here that the people at Capernaum synagogue were astounded because ἐν ἐξουσίᾳ ἦν ὁ λόγος αὐτοῦ (his words were with authority, v. 32b).

49 Fitzmyer, *Luke I–IX*, 547.

50 The phrase is borrowed from Santiago Guijarro's essay title "The Politics of Exorcism," in *The Social Setting of Jesus and the Gospels*, 159.

51 Strecker, "Jesus and the Demoniacs," 119.

highlighted that possession is trans-temporal and trans-cultural and that it is not exclusively an ancient Mediterranean phenomenon but is found in many of the Third World even today, especially among dissatisfied social groups. But in the Gospel studies, the influence of form and redaction criticism have led most of the commentators to look for how the traditions of Jesus' exorcism function among the early Christians rather than how Jesus' exorcisms functioned in the life and work of Jesus. For clarity, traditional interpretations can be classed into three: theological interpretations of Jesus' exorcism, typological analysis of Jesus as an exorcist, and sociological and anthropological investigation of Jesus' exorcism. The last interpretive trend will provide entrée to postcolonial cultural exegesis of the Lukan Capernaum exorcism.

Most of the interpretations of exorcism that are premised on historical criticism emphasise the theological significance owing to the influence of form and redaction criticism's emphasis on the function of the Jesus' exorcism among the early church.[52] E. Earle Ellis opines that the theme of Jesus' activities in Capernaum in this pericope is the "authoritative word" of Jesus, both in teaching and exorcism.[53] Likewise, Herman Hendrickx argues that, Lukan redaction "consciously emphasizes Jesus' teaching as well as the characterization of his word as spoken with authority (Luke 4:31–32). The whole pericope is ultimately conceived as a text which by means of the word proclaimed sheds light on Jesus himself and his powerful word."[54] Similarly, several scholars maintain that the pericope emphasises the effective word of Jesus and therefore it produces a corresponding event.[55] This reading places undue emphasis on Jesus' word with the preponderance that Jesus was a teacher and less a healer.

There are some scholars who emphasise on the christological function of Jesus' exorcism following Rudolf Bultmann who argues, "the exorcisms of demons are in the first place the chief demonstrations of the Messiahship of Jesus."[56] Thus, Allan Richardson writes, "[T]he power of Jesus over the daemons would be regarded as a singular authentication of His divine mission and of His

52 Martin Dibelius thinks that the miracle narratives emerge from a literary genre of the popular story, the "novella," which found its way into the Gospel from Hellenistic environment. Martin Dibelius, *From Tradition to Gospel* (London: Ivor Nicholson and Ivor, 1934), 70–103. Similarly, Rudolf Bultmann did not think the miracles of Jesus go back to the life of Jesus but were the creation of the early church imported from the Hellenistic atmosphere. Bultmann, *History of Synoptic Tradition*, 238–239.

53 Ellis, *Gospel of Luke*, 99.

54 Herman Hendrickx, *The Miracle Stories of the Synoptic Gospels* (London: Geoffrey Chapman: 1987), 61.

55 Eduard Schweizer, *The Good News According to Luke*, trans. David E. Green (Atlanta: John Knox, 1984), 99; Nolland, *Luke 1–9:20*, 205; Tannehill, *Luke*, 97.

56 Bultmann, *History of Synoptic Tradition*, 219.

teaching."[57] For Robert Stein, the devil recognised Jesus as the Holy one of God that is essentially synonymous with the title Christ, Lord, Son, and Son of Man in Luke. And this account omits "anything that might detract from a christological emphasis."[58] Similarly David Tiede maintains that this exorcism demonstrates Jesus as "the true prophet with God's word in his mouth (Deut. 18:18)."[59] More recently, Todd Klutz's *The Exorcism Stories in Luke-Acts: A Sociostylistic Reading* argues argues that the most prominent emphasis of the episode is foregrounding Jesus' authority—an emphasis that "divine authority essential for exorcistic activity is present in Jesus' own person," which constitute a deviation from biblical intertexts.[60] Though Klutz's interpretation suggests that the exorcism heals not only the individual person but cleanse potential source of pollution from the community,[61] he did not consider the symbiotic nature of demonic possession, pollution of the land, and imperialism, and thus, his reading does not offer the socio-political significance of exorcism for a postcolonial situation.

Beginning in the 1970s, some Jewish scholars began to study the life of Jesus in the typology of ancient miracle-worker from a sociohistorical perspective. For instance, Geza Vermes places Jesus in the milieu of charismatic Judaism, and compared Jesus as a miracle-worker with Honi (the Palestinian rainmaker) and Hanani ben Dosa (the Galilean miracle worker).[62] There are obvious differences when one compares Jesus with Honi and Hanani ben Dosa, [63] but the value of Vermes work lies in emphasising the importance of placing Jesus in his own milieu. Morton Smith claims, "'Jesus the magician' was the figure seen by most ancient opponents of Jesus" but the Gospels suppressed this truth by making Jesus

57 Allan Richardson, *The Miracle Stories of the Gospels* (London: SCM, 1941, reprinted 1963), 68–70.

58 Stein, *Luke*, 162–163.

59 David L. Tiede, *Luke*, ACNT (Minneapolis: Augsburg Publishing House, 1988), 113.

60 Todd Klutz, *The Exorcism Stories in Luke-Acts: A Sociostylistic Reading* (Cambridge: Cambridge University Press, 2004), 80.

61 Klutz, *Exorcism Stories in Luke-Acts*, 79.

62 Vermes, *Jesus the Jew*, 69–78.

63 Cf. Meier, *A Marginal Jew* 2:586–588, Meier noted at least three important differences between Jesus on the one hand and Honi and Hanani on the other hand. Firstly, he noted that, source critically, the traditions of Honi and Hanani miracles were reported a century after the events narrated. On the other hand written sources about Jesus existed a little over one generation after Jesus' death. Secondly, Jesus performed miracles directly by giving a command or giving a gesture. But it is not so for Honi and Hanani. Thirdly, neither of them are characterised as Galilean charismatic in the earliest sources.

the Son of God.[64] Many have critically reviewed Smith's work.[65] But he makes an important note that emphasises the significance of Jesus' miracles. He states,

> [T]he rest of the tradition about Jesus can be understood if we begin with the miracles, but the miracles cannot be understood if we begin with a purely didactic tradition.... Teachers of the law were not in this period, made over into miracle workers. Neither were the authors of apocalyptic prophecies.... But a miracle worker could easily come to be thought a prophet and an authority on the Law.[66]

E. P. Sanders worded Smith's point in this manner: "One can move from *miracles* to *crowds* to *teaching* to *tumult* to *death* much more easily than from a *teacher* of law to a *miracle worker* to a *prophet* whose passion for sanctity irritated the authorities in Jerusalem" (emphasis original).[67] Morton Smith thinks that Jesus attracted a large crowd because of miracles something that was considered dangerous by the authorities.[68] He writes that, "unless he had a large following, he would not have been crucified."[69] Though Vermes and Smith argue forcefully that historical study of Jesus must place Jesus' activities in the sociohistorical context of first century Palestine, they did not particularly focus on exorcism.

Graham Twelftree juxtaposes Jesus as a charismatic and ritual miracle workers.[70] In his work *Jesus the Exorcist*, Twelftree argues that if one compares Jesus' exorcisms against the varied background of contemporary exorcisms, in most "technical" aspects Jesus is to be described as a very ordinary exorcist.[71] Twelftree's most important conclusion is that "*Jesus was the first to make the connection between exorcism and eschatology*" (emphasis original).[72] He considers Luke 11:20 // Matt 12:28 as a crucial text to understand this point, but avoided how the struggle between God and demonic forces is played out among the

---

64 Morton Smith, *Jesus the Magician* (New York: Harpers and Row, 1978), vii. According to him, the real Jesus was a magician who grew up in the environment of a strong strain of native, Galilean, Palestinian, Semitic paganism (68). Smith finds his arguments in the parallelism of Jesus' miracles and those of pagan miracles especially Apollonius of Tyana (84–93). He also cites the many parallels between the Gospel accounts and the Greek Magical Papyri, which includes whole stories, types of miracles and formulae (96–139).

65 Barry Crawford, review of *Jesus the Magician*, by Morton Smith, *JAAR* 47 (1979): 321–322; Sean Freyne, review of *Jesus the Magician*, by Morton Smith, *JBL* 41 (1979): 658–661; Sanders, *Jesus and Judaism*, 164–173.

66 Smith, *Jesus the Magician*, 16.

67 Sanders, *Jesus and Judaism*, 164.

68 Smith, *Jesus the Magician*, 16–17.

69 Smith, *Jesus the Magician*, 24.

70 Graham H. Twelftree, *Jesus the Exorcist: A Contribution to the Study of Historical Jesus* (Eugene, OR: Wipf and Stock, 2010) cf. Theissen and Merz, *Historical Jesus*, 289.

71 Twelftree, *Jesus the Exorcist*, 172–173.

72 Twelftree, *Jesus the Exorcist*, 224.

common people in Jewish society. In the case of Capernaum exorcism, Twelftree thinks that Lukan redaction stresses the demons obedience to Jesus' authority, and it is in this connection a report went out (cf. Luke 4:35b; 37). However, despite his claim of the authenticity of Jesus exorcisms, he simply spiritualised Jesus' exorcism as though it cannot have any connection with the turbulent social, political, and religious conflicts in which Jesus audience were caught. He argues, "[L]iberation came not through political freedom but on a personal level through exorcism."[73] However, Jesus' exorcisms were public phenomenon involving the social body that approve or repudiate the act in the public arena.

Any meaningful interpretation of possession by demons/evil spirits and exorcism found in the Gospel must account the context of Greco-Roman Empire and its cultural imperialism that have besieged the Jewish political and cultural life. It is noted that the political and cultural force of Greco-Roman Empire threatened not only the Jewish political life but also the Jewish cultural identity that it sparked Jewish nationalism from various quarters since the Maccabean time.[74] The development of demonology and evil spirits in the Second Temple period is associated with the experience of marginality in the context of Greco-Roman Empire. In the late Hellenistic (167–37 BCE) and early Roman Empire (37 BCE–70 CE), the Mediterranean cosmology is many layered populated by supernatural beings and among these were demons.[75] In the Greco-Roman writings, the demons (δαιμόνια) are described as both helpful and harmful to human and they play a crucial role in the supernatural activities.[76] However, the Second Temple Jewish source and Christian texts viewed demons negatively.[77] The notion that evil spirits might take possession of a person develops in the Second Temple period with the corresponding shift from monism to dualism.[78]

Marginal and dualistic perspective can be seen in the Second Temple Jewish texts especially in Jubilees, 1 Enoch, and the documents found at Qumran. One of the way in which Qumran define its identity is to ascribe the community as sons of light and outsiders as sons of darkness.[79] And the sons of darkness are typically associated with foreigners and apostate Jews.[80] First Enoch and Jubilees, which were produced in Palestine within two centuries of the time of Jesus, though

73 Twelftree, *In the Name of Jesus*, 111.

74 Cf. Hengel, *Judaism and Hellenism.*

75 Naomi Janowitz, *Magic in the Roman World: Pagans, Jews and Christians* (London: Routledge, 2001), 28–31.

76 Janowitz, *Magic in the Roman World*, 27–28; Witmer, *Jesus, the Galilean Exorcist*, 33.

77 Eric Sorensen, *Possession and Exorcism in the New Testament and Early Christianity*, WUNT 2/157 (Tübingen: Mohr Siebeck, 2002), 80; Janowitz, *Magic in the Roman World*, 35.

78 Witmer, *Jesus, the Galilean Exorcist*, 34.

79 1QS III–IV; IQM.

80 1QS I, 16–II, 8; III, 13–IV, 26; 1QM I, 1–7, 13–16.

describes spiritual realities, they are not devoid of concomitant political events of the time.[81] Eric Eve writes,

> The author's [of Jubilees] polemic against mixing with Gentiles and insistence on maintaining ancestral customs, especially ritual ones, is perfectly understandable against the background of the attempted Hellenization of the Antiochan period. But it can also be understood, not simply as a desire to maintain racial and cultural identity in the face of threat of assimilation, but as an attempt to maintain order in the face of the chaotic forces represented by the Gentiles. This is further suggested by the way in which the text tends to associate Gentiles with demonic forces.[82]

This dualistic perspective is reflective of the social boundary the marginal community is charting for themselves in the face of cultural threats from outside. Dualistic perspective is also found in other Second Temple literatures that express the destruction of evil spirits with the coming reign of God. For instance, in Dan 10:13 and 21, the angel Michael fights with angelic evil princes associated with the rule of the nations; the T. Dan. described the *one* who will arise from the tribes of Judah and Levi to fight against Beliar; and in 1 En. 53–55, Satan and evil human kings are depicted in an analogous manner in the judgement scene.[83] These texts associate the coming messiah with restoration of justice especially for the marginalised.[84] However, it is telling, that these texts do not say that the demons actually possess humans, except that they bring suffering on them in some form. Although works like Jubilees, 1 Enoch, and Qumran scrolls cannot provide much evidence of exorcism, "they do suggest that a belief in the

---

81 First Enoch and Jubilees attributes the coming of the evil into the world to the actions of the Watchers described in Gen 6 as the giants or *Nephilim*. Both the texts claim that the Watchers came down from the heavenly abode and mated with mortal women, resulting in the race of giants. While the giants were killed, their spirits lived on and brought troubles to humans. The divine accusation against the Watchers is implicitly that they cross the forbidden spirit-flesh boundary by mating with mortal women and thus bringing oppression, war, and moral problems to the human world (1 En. 15:7–11). See Witmer, *Jesus, the Galilean Exorcist*, 38.

82 Eric Eve, *The Jewish Context of Jesus' Miracles*, JSNTSup 231 (Sheffield: Sheffield Academic Press, 2002), 156 cited by Witmer, *Jesus, the Galilean Exorcist*, 38–39.

83 George Nickelsburg interprets the mythical languages of the *Book of Similitudes* in 1 En. 37–71 a document which he dates "around the turn of the era" into the political relations of the time. He writes that in 1 En. 37–71 one finds "[o]n the one side are God, God's heavenly entourage, the agent of divine judgment … and God's people.… On the other are the chief of demon Azazel, his angels and the kings and the mighty … [who] would have their counterparts among the Roman generals, governors, triumvirs, and monarchs whose activities in Judea are well documented in the sources. The author might also have in mind the late Hasmoneans and Herods." See George W. E. Nickelsburg, *Jewish Literature between the Bible and the Mishnah*, 2nd ed. (Mineapolis: Fortress, 2005), 249, 255.

84 Witmer, *Jesus, the Galilean Exorcist*, 40.

malevolent spirits and spirit affliction was present within the Jewish community and that it was connected in the texts with political oppression on the ground."[85] One can assume demon possession and exorcism found in the Gospel to have socio-political counterparts in Jewish resistance to Roman imperial rule. Of course the trajectory of Jewish nationalism is multifaceted involving militant resistance, cultural nationalism, and non-violent resistance. But, in the least even non-violent resistance resorts to a kind of cleansing the people from the pollution of the cultural imperialism of the empire as evidenced by the Baptist's movement.

Cultural anthropologists who underlined that the social phenomenon of possession is closely tied to a situation of oppression and social tension pave a significant direction in the study of possession and exorcism. Especially, the works of cultural anthropologists like I. M. Lewis, Erika Bourguignon, Vincent Crapanzano provide useful exegetical insights to biblical scholars to interpret possession and exorcism found in the Gospels as a social one. For instance, I. M. Lewis' *Ecstatic Religion* (1971)[86] has drawn a close connection between possession and oppression, whether the case is patriarchal oppression of women or imperial oppression of the native by an alien people. He calls possession that emerges from the weaker section of the society as peripheral possession because the possessed are in the periphery of the society and the spirits which possessed them are thought to come from outside. From a wide range of anthropological study, Lewis argues that in most societies, "possession is treated not by permanently expelling possessing agency, but by reaching a viable accommodation with it. The spirit is tamed, domesticated rather than exorcised" by inducting the possessed into a cult group so that possession loses "its malign significance."[87] According to Lewis, peripheral possessions serve a social function as an oblique aggressive strategy and call group-possession as a protest cult or ritualised rebellion,[88] whereby the subordinates or the powerless deal with their oppressors in a manner that does not destabilse socio-political status quo. However, Lewis also noted that this protest cult or ritualised rebellion does not exhaust the angst of the oppressed; there always remains potential dissent and subversion of the whole system and thus they are held in check by means of witchcraft accusations.[89] In other words, possession is often associated with marginality or the status of being the "other" whether they are geographical, ethnic, or religious, and that countervailing witchcraft accusation is

85 Witmer, *Jesus, the Galilean Exorcist*, 41.

86 Iaon Lewis, *Ecstatic Religion, A Study on Shamanism and Spirit Possession*, 2nd ed. (London: Routledge, 1989).

87 Lewis, *Ecstatic Religion*, 26.

88 Lewis, *Ecstatic Religion*, 27–28, 100.

89 Lewis, *Ecstatic Religion*, 109. For a condensed summary of cultural anthropological theories to study possession and exorcism see Hollenbach, "Jesus, Demoniacs, and Public Authorities," 573.

employed to mark boundaries between cultural and religious identities, especially within a context of oppression and social distress.

A careful use of sociological and anthropological theories provides the most fruitful interpretation to understand Jesus' exorcism as it locates possession and exorcism in the specific socio-cultural and political background of the Roman imperial rule and underlines how Jesus' exorcism both challenge and impact the universe of demon possession and its accommodation. Drawing insights from the cultural anthropological theories of possession (especially that of I. M. Lewis), Paul Hollenbach argues that Jesus' exorcism might have disrupted the dominant pattern of accommodation of possession in the society. He sees the episode of the Gerasene demoniac (Mark 5:1–20 // Luke 8: 26–39) as an "oblique aggressive strategy" (via Lewis) of an oppressed native against an invading colonial power.[90] He argues that by exorcising, Jesus had brought in the open the neighbourhood's hatred for the Romans, and this explains why the community urges Jesus to go away from the place.[91] Hollenbach argues that this politically subversive aspect of Jesus' exorcism invited not only Beelzebub (or witchcraft) accusation against Jesus but also led to his execution. Hollenbach is criticised for being uncritical and unhistorical in his treatment of the Gerasene demoniac's story,[92] but his political reading opens up windows to appreciate the subversive nature of Jesus' exorcism.

J. D. Crossan too sees the usefulness of Iaon Lewis' idea that there is a close connection between possession and oppression, and like Hollenbach picks up the story of the Gerasene demoniac to explain Jesus' exorcism.[93] In the exorcism of the Gerasene, Crossan argues that the demon is one and many as it is named "Legion" which designates Roman power, but this Legion is forced into the swine and cast into the sea, which would be a dream of every Jewish patriot. Crossan concurs with Mary Douglas' concept of the physical body as the microcosm of the social body, and thus sees a political dialectic between possessed individual and the possessed society.[94] Therefore, "colonial exorcisms are at once less and more

90 Hollenbach, "Jesus, Demoniacs, and Public Authorities," 581, reasoned that the Gerasene demoniac's "tension between his hatred for his oppressors and the necessity to repress this hatred in order to avoid dire recrimination drove him mad. But this very madness permitted him to do in a socially acceptable manner what he could not do as sane, namely express his total hostility to the Romans; he did this by identifying the Roman legion with demons."

91 Hollenbach, "Jesus, Demoniacs and Public Authorities," 581.

92 According to Meier, Hollenbach gullibly took the Gerasene demoniac's story as a "videotape replay of a historical event in the life of Jesus" while the physical location and the textual questions would resist any historical probability. Moreover, given that, except for Jesus and his disciples, all other actors are pagans in the story, the exorcism of the Gerasene demoniac, which is located in the Decapolis, cannot be a Palestinian Jewish phenomenon. See Meier, *A Marginal Jew* 2:666–667.

93 Crossan, *Historical Jesus*, 314–318; ibid, *Jesus: A Revolutionary Biography*, 89–90.

94 Crossan, *Historical Jesus*, 313, 315.

than revolution"[95]—a protest against foreign domination. He argues that there are modern equivalents of possession that are linked to political domination.[96] On the other hand, Stevan L. Davies asserts that it is neither Roman occupation nor indebtedness that germinates demon possession in Galilee.[97] He interprets demon-possession in the Gospels as intra-family coping mechanism and stresses the significance of the exorcisms of Jesus in the kinship sphere. Davies argues that, "it is almost certain that the majority of the 'demon-possessed' individuals whom Jesus exorcised found themselves to be in intolerable circumstances of social subordination *within their family groups* and it is likely that many and perhaps most of these were women (as Luke indicates in 8:1–3)" (emphasis original).[98] However, Jesus' exorcism is not a private kinship affair; it was public and demonstrative.[99]

Santiago Guijarro explicates the politics of exorcism with deviant theory taking Beelzebub controversy as the key text. He writes, "By interpreting the casting out of demons as a sign of the coming kingdom of God, and by making his exorcism part of his strategy for restoring Israelite integrity, Jesus threatened the stability of the social order."[100] And thus, he argues, that the demonic interpretation of Jesus' exorcism by his opponents "belongs to a broader strategy, whose purpose was to discredit Jesus, to declare him an outsider in his society and to assign him a new identity."[101] Jesus' repudiation against Beelzebub accusation and redefinition of his exorcism is a "characteristic feature of behaviour that seek political change."[102] Guijarro's argument resembles what Hollenbach and Crossan had already noted, in that it emphasises the politically subversive nature of Jesus' exorcism.

Christian Strecker is wary of the functional approach that sidelines the whole complex of possession by limiting the possessed person as *reactors* to a social system rather than *real* actors in the social arena. In an essay entitled, "Jesus and the Demoniacs" he proposed "possession as performance" and Jesus' exorcism as transformance.[103] Christian Strecker argues that possession is an interactive process that blurs the boundaries between performance and reality

---

95 Crossan, *Historical Jesus*, 318.

96 For further reading see Crossan, *Historical Jesus*, 315–317.

97 Stevan L. Davies, *Jesus the Healer*, (London: SCM Press, 1975), 80–81.

98 Stevan L. Davies, *Jesus the Healer*, 85.

99 Strecker, "Jesus and the Demoniacs," 119f. ; Guijarro, "The Politics of Exorcism," 162f.

100 Guijarro, "The Politics of Exorcism," 166.

101 Guijarro, "The Politics of Exorcism," 172.

102 Guijarro, "The Politics of Exorcism," 171.

103 Christian Strecker draws on Vincent Crapanzano's description of "possession idiom" of the society as a cultural construct that defines both the queer patterns of behavior of the possessed and also the meaning that the society makes of possession, thus making possession an interactive process within a culture. Crapanzano also already noted that exorcism also

for both the actors and the audience.[104] Thus, "possession may be understood as a performance that creates a demonic reality in the sense of *effet de reel* [the effect of reality], physically putting into action the possession idiom of a society that itself is constituted and formed by the performances."[105] He argues that in the case of Jesus' exorcism the demonic identity of the possessed is performatively destroyed in the direct encounter with Jesus, who embodied a higher divine order as a medium. The result is a transformance, a tangible change of reality that can be grasped by others. The exorcistic transformance also effects the social integration of the formerly possessed person into the mainstream society.[106] While Strecker's interpretation of exorcism as transformance is well taken, it needs to be qualified that this performative transformance is socio-politically unsettling to the status quo, and that it is this unsettling factor that attracted both a community of followers and opponents to Jesus.

5.3.3. Postcolonial Cultural Exegesis

Cross-cultural and anthropological studies have noted that "[s]ituations of social tension such as the following are often indicated as the causal context of possession: class antagonisms rooted in economic exploitation, conflicts between traditions where revered traditions are eroded, colonial domination and revolution."[107] It is also noted that the political domination of Rome fractured the socio-cultural and socio-economic life of Palestine that made the region a political volatile with resistance to the empire from various quarters. At the same time, as noted above the experience of marginality in colonial context prompted the development of demonology in the Jewish Second Temple literatures that demystified the harsh experience of foreign domination with the populating of demons in the land that harassed the people. Most probably, the situation of domination and oppression of the colonised by the Roman imperial rule in the first century Palestine provided a fertile ground for possessions as the Gospels narrate about demon possession and Jesus' exorcism.

There are voices in the scholarly guild that oppose political reading of the exorcisms of Jesus on the ground that there is no indication that Jesus' exorcism was opposed to an earthly political institution, much less against non-existent Roman occupation of the land.[108] However, leading socio-political interpreters as noted above, have illustrated the political significance/implications of Jesus'

---

constitutes transformance. Cf. Vincent Crapanzano, "Spirit Possession," in *Encyclopedia of Religion*, ed. Mircea Eliade et al., vol. 13 (New York: MacMillan, 1987), 12–19.

104 Strecker, "Jesus and the Demoniacs," 123.

105 Strecker, "Jesus and the Demoniacs," 124.

106 Strecker, "Jesus and the Demoniacs," 127–128.

107 For a concise discussion on cross-cultural and anthropological theories concerning possession see Hollenbach, "Jesus, Demoniacs, and Public Authorities," 573.

108 Cf. Twelftree, *In the Name of Jesus*, 111; Davies, *Jesus the Healer*, 80–81.

exorcism. While the emphases of their interpretation vary, all have noted the subversive action of Jesus' exorcism—it destabilises the socio-political order of status quo. Perhaps owing to the absence of overt political overtones in the text the exorcism at Capernaum synagogue (4:31–37) has not attracted an interested political reading. But this study argues that Jesus' exorcism at the Capernaum synagogue is a mode of resistance against the colonial domination and a cleansing of space from the occupation of alien rule represented by the demon. The text in consideration can be cited as thus:

> He went down to Capernaum, a city in Galilee, and was teaching them on the sabbath. They were astounded at his teaching, because he spoke with authority. In the synagogue there was a man who had the spirit of an unclean demon, and he cried out with a loud voice, "Let us alone! What have you to do with us, Jesus of Nazareth? Have you come to destroy us? I know who you are, the Holy One of God." But Jesus rebuked him, saying, "Be silent, and come out of him!" When the demon had thrown him down before them, he came out of him without having done him any harm. They were all amazed and kept saying to one another, "What kind of utterance is this? For with authority and power he commands the unclean spirits, and out they come!" And a report about him began to reach every place in the region (Luke 4:31–37).

This is a text of hope. It inaugurates the expulsion of demonic domination from the land and the people and signals the future of God's domination-free order. One can claim that this text does not have any explicit reference to colonialism nor does this exorcism provide anything explicit about a political phenomenon. But Luke has subtly described Capernaum as "a city in Galilee" (absent in Mark), which is not a mere penchant style of the evangelist who is interested in an orderly account, but underscores the colonial cartography of Galilee in the political map of the Roman Empire (3:1). At the same time, this incident points to issues of power and authority (4:36), which though cast in the contest between Jesus and the demon, would have a corresponding contest for power over the place and the people in earthly reality. As already noted above, historically during the time of Jesus, Galilee was under the rule of the Roman client king Antipas (3:1). Here, it is notable how Luke details the movement of Jesus from a peripheral Nazareth town (4:29) to Capernaum city (4:31), that too, as an authoritative figure (4:32) but whose authority does not stem from the established institution. This suggests that, Jesus' coming down from Nazareth town and entering Capernaum "a city in Galilee" represents a power from the fringes of the society stepping into an established power centre of provincial Jewish social order, and into the synagogue, which is the sacred space.

The sacral setting and the public arena of the possession demonstration of the Capernaum demoniac are significant. Given that Palestine was colonised by the Roman Empire, it is most likely that, demon possession of the Capernaum demoniac was caused by Roman domination of the land. One is inclined to suppose that the Capernaum demoniac event functions as a peripheral possession. The Capernaum community probably accommodated the demoniac in their synagogue because his possession provided them both to ritualised their protest against imperial domination and as an escape valve to their sheeting discontent of alien rule.[109] The boundary line of social accommodation of the Capernaum demoniac is clear in his resistance to Jesus' presence in the synagogue. The Capernaum demoniac, who is both one and many (4:34),[110] like the Gerasene demoniac who was possessed by the Legion (cf. 8:30), resisted Jesus to leave without disturbing them in the synagogue. To state again the obvious, the oppressed demoniac cried out, but the polyvalent overtone of the *collective voice* cannot be missed: "What have you to do with us ... have you come to destroy us" (4:34). Amanda Witmer's work *Jesus, the Galilean Exorcist* which studied spirit possession and exorcism "as part of broader Judean Galilean response to the politically charged and socially oppressed context of first-century Roman Palestine,"[111] has argued that the Capernaum encounter of Jesus and the demoniac "displays evidence of the social role that exorcisms played."[112] She writes,

> [I]n the case of the exorcism in the Capernaum synagogue, social reality is expressed by and reflected in both possession of the man by the unclean spirit and the public event of his exorcism. Through the encounter between Jesus and the man, both healing and change occur, but only after a struggle, and only as part of the larger social context, the Jewish community at Capernaum, to which the man belongs. Once the man's status has changed, the community must also change in response.[113]

Witmer continues that Jesus' exorcism would not have been popular with everyone and this explains the two forms of responses to Jesus' exorcism: amazement and devotion to Jesus on the one hand, and countervailing witchcraft accusation on the other hand, especially from the social elite who do not want social change to happen.[114] This is because the transformation effected by the exorcism threatens the socio-political order. Thus, Jesus' exorcism of the Capernaum demoniac can be seen as a disruption of the socially

109 Cf. Hollenbach, "Jesus, Demoniacs and Public Authorities," 581.

110 Cf. Witmer, *Jesus, the Galilean Exorcist*, 159.

111 Witmer, *Jesus, the Galilean Exorcist*, 3.

112 Witmer, *Jesus, the Galilean Exorcist*, 164.

113 Witmer, *Jesus, the Galilean Exorcist*, 165.

114 Witmer, *Jesus, the Galilean Exorcist*, 65–166.

acceptable "oblique aggressive strategy" or "protest rituals," which both resists and accommodate domination. Such disruption would bring into the open the Capernaum hatred against colonial domination. The closure of the exorcism is intriguing in that "a report about him began to reach every place in the region" (4:37). The rumour may not be so much about Jesus' popularity than the revolutionary excitement created by his exorcism.

Here, Halvor Moxnes[115] claims of Jesus' exorcism as "liberation of place" in the reading of Q 11:14–24 provides a cue to read the exorcism at Capernaum synagogue. Moxnes points out that Taussig's study of shamanism among the colonised Indians in Columbia shows how "exorcism could be a part of a language of opposition, of exercising power from below in protest against colonial control over land and livelihood."[116]

> Taussig's study shows that in this colonized society, sorcery and healings by Indian shamans must be understood in the context of a colonial history, its complex relationships are part the politics of the control over space. To colonize meant to take control of the land of the Indians, and therefore all conflicts were related to this control of land. Although, the white colonizers and their dependents had the political control, the Indian sorcerers had a more subtle power, that of the deeper meaning of the land governed by spiritual powers.

This would mean that exorcism of the demoniac at Capernaum synagogue is the first emancipatory act of Jesus; it is the beginning of a counter movement, the inauguration of the kingdom of God that challenges and defeats the demonic power that possessed the land and the people. The broader context of Luke's story of Jesus shows that the preaching of the kingdom of God and exorcisms are combined with reports of potential tension with the earthly powers (Luke 9:9; 13:31–33). This shows that, as Halvor Moxnes noted, Jesus' exorcism represented a form of power from below that challenges the established authorities.

Clearly, Jesus' authority does not stem from the political establishment, and this is the reason why the people said, "What kind of utterance is this? For with authority and power he rebukes the unclean spirits, and they come out!" (v. 36). Exorcism at Capernaum synagogue is like a cleansing of the demonic powers from the place. The exorcism signals that Capernaum synagogue is under God's rule and control and not under the demonic control. Thus, the meaning of the

---

115 Moxnes, "Ethnography and Historical Imagination," 327–341. Based on John and Jean Camaroff's *Ethnography and the Historical Imagination* (1992) which shows the close linkage between modern medicine and colonisation, and Michael Taussig's *Shamanism, Colonialism, and the Wild Man: A Study in Terror and Healing* which illustrate how shamanism function as an expression of native power against the effects of colonisation, Moxnes argues that Jesus' exorcism represented a form of "power from below" (339) that was a challenge to the established authorities.

116 Moxnes, "Ethnography and Historical Imagination," 335.

exorcism of the demoniac from the synagogue goes beyond the individual person and his health. It is an assertion of God's sovereignty over the people and the place.[117]

The pneumatological significance of exorcism at Capernaum lies in that Jesus' exorcises the unclean spirit with divine authority and power. Though Luke did not explicitly state that Jesus performed exorcism by the Spirit of God in Luke 4:31–37, as noted above the authority and power of Jesus (4:32; 36) is grounded in the power of the Spirit (3:22; 4:14; 18).[118] As Fitzmyer observed, the joining of authority and power in v. 36, "echo those of 4:32 and 4:14.... The *dynamis* with which he has worked the miracle is that of the Spirit."[119]

Thus, on a socio-cultural and political plane, exorcism is a resistance and repudiation of colonial authority over the land and the people. It destabilises the socially acceptable form of possession and brings the native hatred against the coloniser into the open. It marks the liberation of the place and the people from demonic control of the coloniser, and the beginning of a revolution. Theologically, exorcism is a manifestation of God's power and sovereignty over the place and the people. It is by the power of God that Jesus casts out demons and inaugurates the kingdom of God (cf. 11:20). It is by the authority and power of the Spirit of God, the Spirit-messiah Jesus casts out demons and claims the sovereignty of God at Capernaum synagogue. The spread of rumours about the incident all over the region hints at the potential political implications of Jesus' exorcism. But the politics of exorcism that fixes God's coming reign as inevitable engenders a community of resistance around Jesus that continues to challenge not only "demonic imperialism"[120] but also the Jewish cultural, religious, and social boundaries, which sees the margins as unclean and dangerous.

5.4. Healing of the Paralytic in Luke's Gospel (Luke 5:17–26)

Jesus' conflict with the cultural and religious figures from Galilee, Judea, and Jerusalem first appeared in the healing of the paralytic (5:17–26). It is telling that Luke explicitly mentions that scribes and Pharisees also came from Judea and Jerusalem. Geopolitically there was urban-rural tension in Galilee since colonialism creates economic centres in urban places while the villages were isolated politically and culturally[121] though connected geographically.[122] Particularly, the *Galileans* as designating the country people were opposed to

117 Cf. Moxnes, "Ethnography and Historical Imagination," 339.

118 Green, *Luke*, 224; Fitzmyer, *Luke I–IX*, 543; Twelftree, *Jesus the Miracle Worker*, 147.

119 Fitzmyer, *Luke I–IX*, 547.

120 This phrase is borrowed from Crossan, *Historical Jesus*, 313.

121 Joy, *Mark and its Subaltern*, 65.

122 Stambaugh and Balch, *Social World of First Christians*, 93, note that despite the city-country divide, the locales of Jesus' career were located in the busy trade routes connected to the imperial administration.

townspeople of Tiberias, Sepphoris, and Gabbara.[123] It is often noted that the Galilean geopolitical structure, its culture, and its ideological opposition to Jerusalem were products of prolonged trajectory of colonialism.[124] Apparently, country Galileans became the force of resistance against Roman colonialism to the extent that it opposes the religious authorities in Jerusalem who collaborated with the Romans. Horsley argues that the first century Galileans were Ephraimite descent, and they would have shared with the Judeans such as exodus tradition, mosaic covenant, Sabbath, circumcism and so on, but would find the laws of the Judean different from their version of Judaism as they have undergone eight centuries of separate development.[125] And thus the Judean temple, its taxes, and the role of the high priest were superimposed on the Galileans that were otherwise foreign to them. He claims that there is little evidence to show that the Judean temple-state was of defining importance for the Galileans during the Jerusalem rule.[126]

However, Jonathan Reed and Mark A. Chancey think that it is difficult to sustain Horsley's argument that Israelite culture spanned from the Assyrian conquest to the Roman times in Galilee.[127] They argue that the numismatic evidence shows Galilee was economically and politically connected to Judea and the repopulation of Galilee was associated with the Hasmonean rule.[128] Similarly, Sean Freyne writes,[129]

> By the first century CE the successors of these Hasmonean settlers constituted the bulk of Galilean Jews, even if other elements, Jewish and non-Jewish, had entered the mix as a result of the conquests and rule of Herod the Great and his son, Antipas. It is important to acknowledge, therefore, contrary to several modern claims about Galilean opposition to Jerusalem, that there was a strong attachment to

123 Sean Freyne, "The Galileans in the Light of Josephus' VITA," *NTS* 26 (1980): 400, 412. It is notable that the Synoptic tradition did not mention the two most important cities in Galilee i.e., Sepphoris and Tiberias, while it associates the towns and villages as the locale of Jesus' career. See Theissen and Merz, *Historical Jesus*, 171.

124 Joy, *Mark and its Subaltern*, 64–70.

125 Richard Horsley, *Galilee: Politics, History, People*, 50–51. Horsley's argument is based on the likelihood that there was a continuity of the settlement of the Northern Israelite tribes even after the Assyrian conquest, though the Israelites were largely deported. Horsley does not think that the Hasmonean rule did anything substantial to have integrated the Galileans to the pan Israelite national ideology.

126 Richard Horsley, *Galilee: Politics, History, People*, 156.

127 Jonathan Reed, *Archaeology and the Galilean Jesus: A Re-examination of the Evidence* (Harrisburg: Trinity Press International, 2000), 34; Mark A. Chancey, *The Myth of a Gentile Galilee* (Cambridge: Cambridge University Press, 2002), 34.

128 Reed, *Archaeology and the Galilean Jesus*, 41–43; Chancey, *The Myth of a Gentile Galilee*, 46.

129 Sean Freyne, *Jesus, a Jewish Galilean: A New Reading of the Jesus Story* (London: T&T Clark, 2004), 81–82.

the mother-city, its temple and customs, among Galilean Jews of Jesus' day. The archaeological investigation of Roman-period Sepphoris, as well as other sites in Galilee, has produced compelling evidence of Jewish observance in domestic settings at these centres, based on the frequency of similar evidence from Judea and Jerusalem. This would explain the continued interest in Galilee by the Jerusalem religious authorities.

In all probability Galilean Jews of Jesus' day had strong contact with Jerusalem and the temple remained the locus of their faith as evidenced by the frequent pilgrimage and protest against pollution of the temple.[130] Nonetheless, apparently "the Galileans showed no genuine inclination towards Jerusalem-centred Judaism"[131] and the priestly aristocracy who were from wealthy families and collaborators of Rome. Josephus has noted the Galilean love for freedom (*J. W.* 3.41) that was rooted in the traditional faith that God is the sole owner of the land that it should not be polluted by foreign rule. Jesus himself lashes out that the Jerusalem priesthood has made the temple a den of robbers (Mark 11:17 // Luke 19:46). It appears that the Pharisaic interpretation of the Torah, especially on matters of purity was hardly predominant in Galilee at the time of Jesus. Josephus accuses John of Giscala, the leader of Zealots, for eating unclean food proscribed by the law and thus violating the rules of uncleanness (*J. W.* 7.264). The rabbis also considered the Galileans, even their sages, as ignorant of ritual purity.[132] This possibly explains the tension between the Galilean healer Jesus who was least concerned about ritual purity that excludes people and the cultural entrepreneurs from Jerusalem who imposed a strong boundary maintaining purity system of Judaism. The healing of the paralytic would reveal this aspect of conflict.

5.4.1. Analysis of the Text (Luke 5:17–26)

The healing of the paralytic is connected to the scheme of the programmatic Nazareth proclamation scene of Luke 4:16–30. It is the first of the five controversy stories Luke has introduced in his Gospel (5:17–6:11) drawn from Mark (2:1–3:6),[133] which involves Jesus' boundary breaking activities for the outcasts and the opposition from Pharisees and scribes.[134] From a form-critical perspective, the pericope as it stands in Luke (as in Mark) exhibits a complex structure that

130 Freyne, *Galilee*, 287–295; Theissen and Merz, *Historical Jesus*, 176–177.

131 Joy, *Mark and its Subaltern*, 66.

132 Vermes, *Jesus the Jew*, 54–54.

133 Luke 5:17–26 is solely drawn from Mark 2:1–12; Matthew too has a version in Matt 9:2–8.

134 There is a gradual heightening of Jesus' liberating action in Luke's Gospel. In the Capernaum section (4:31–44), Jesus is depicted as an exorcist and a healer. From ch. 5 onwards Jesus is presented as restoring social outcasts into the community (5:12–16), forgiving sins (5:17–26), and then even associating the so-called sinners (5:29–32).

does not correspond to the form-critical categories.[135] From a form critical point of view, scholars find it difficult to establish how far the story goes back to Jesus and whether the story is originally a simple miracle story, or were there two stories—a miracle story and controversy dialogue?[136] However, since Luke and even Matthew (who has shortened the story, Matt 9:2–8) preserve the miracle of healing and the dispute over the authority to forgive sin, the original unity of the story is probable.[137] Meier maintains that, alongside the many other motifs, when one considers the unparalleled action taken by the four men for the paralytic, the account suggests "some event in the public ministry stuck on the corporate memory precisely because of its strange circumstances."[138] David Daube suggests that the story fits a tripartite form: Jesus performs a revolutionary action; the Pharisees and the Scribes remonstrate or protest against the action; and Jesus silences the remonstrants.[139]

There are significant Lukan redactions: (1) Luke begins "one of those days" with no reference to place or time omitting Marcan reference to Capernaum and Jesus' home in the introductory verse (Luke 5:17 cf. Mark 2:1); (2) Luke portrayed the Pharisees and the teachers of law as "seated" from the beginning of the story, and that they have come from all the villages of Galilee, Judea and Jerusalem (Luke 5:17bc cf. Mark 2:1, 6); (3) Luke adds the phrase, "the power of the Lord was with him to heal" (Luke 5:17d), which evokes Jesus' Spirit anointing (Luke 4:18); (4) Luke replaces the roof of branches and mud with a tile roof (Luke 5:19 cf. Mark 2:4); (5) Luke addresses the paralytic as "man" (ἄνθροπε, v. 20) instead of child (τέκνον, Mark 2:5); and (6) Luke also adds that God "alone" can forgive sins (Luke 5:21 cf. Mark 2:7).

Luke enlarges the Capernaum setting of Mark 2:1 to every village of Galilee and Judea and Jerusalem to introduced the Pharisees and the teachers of the law

---

135 Nolland, *Luke 1–9:20*, 231. The story is enmeshed with many unusual elements such as the unexpected initiatives of those who lowered the paralytic from torn-up roof; Jesus' surprising declaration that the paralytic's sin is forgiven; the reaction of the Pharisees and Scribes that Jesus blasphemes; Jesus' ability to read the thoughts and the christological import of the Son of Man.

136 Bultmann, *History of Synoptic Tradition*, 14, thinks that the story has two foci: the miracle and the saying about forgiveness, the latter somewhat extraneously inserted into the former. Taylor, *The Gospel According to St. Mark: The Greek Text with Introduction, Notes, and Indexes* (London: Macmillan, 1953), 191–192, concurs with Bultmann that the pericope has a composite character of miracle and forgiveness but (*contra* Bultmann), allows that "the account is historical and not *Gemiendetheologie*." René Latourelle, *The Miracles of Jesus and the Theology of Miracles*, trans. Matthew J. O'Connell (New York: Paulist Press, 1988), 93–95, argues that the story existed as a single miracle story.

137 Cf. Marshall, *Gospel of Luke*, 211.

138 Meier, *Marginal Jew*, 2:680.

139 David Daube, *The New Testament and Rabbinic Judaism* (London: Athlone Press, 1956), 170.

as spectators of Jesus' teaching and healing (v. 17).[140] Probably the Pharisees and the teachers of the law coming from every village of Galilee, Judea and Jerusalem (v. 17) had their grouse against Jesus for his contravention of Jewish purity laws—touching the leper and sending him cleansed to the priest (5:12–14).[141] It also hinted at the organised character of an official delegation from Jerusalem[142] that enforced its version of Judaism upon the Galileans. There is no doubt about the Galilean fidelity to the temple; their pilgrimage in the least demonstrates this fact.[143] However, it is noted that the religious character of Galilee was markedly different from the Jews of Jerusalem. As noted above, they did not subscribe to the Pharisaic halakah on clean*ness*. A third century rabbi tradition attributed to Johanan ben Zakkai (c. 70) says, "Galilee, Galilee, you hate the Torah" which reflects Galilean resistance to Pharisaic scruples.[144] And according to the Fourth Gospel the messiah does not come from Galilee (7:41), which may have had some truth about how the Jerusalem Jews demeaned the Galilean.

At the same time, the Roman rule through the priestly aristocracy in Judea, during the time of Jesus was economically exploitative. Jewish families connected to the Jerusalem temple were wealthy, as they owned estates, properties, and managed the treasury of the temple. However, the impoverished situation of Galilee did not concern the rulers of Jerusalem. The Jerusalem rulers did not lend a hand to address the Galilean socio-economic impoverishment brought about by the Roman colonialism.[145] Josephus reports about the arrogance of the high priestly family and the abuse of their office for economic gains: "But Ananias had servants who were utter rascals and who, combining operations with the most reckless men, would go to the threshing floors and take by force the tithes of the priests; nor did they refrain from beating those who refused to give. The high priests were guilty of the same practices" (*Ant.* 20.206–207 [Feldman, LCL]). J. D. Crossan has drawn a connection between sickness and economic impoverishment in Jesus' Palestine since physical malnourishment leads to sickness and sees Jesus' healing as a mode of resistance to the Jerusalem temple religiosity that blames sickness as a result of sin.[146] Therefore, Jesus' counter colonial ethic and countercultural healing of the paralytic must be seen in the light of the different religious character of Galilee and the unpopularity of the temple rulers.

140 Stein, *Luke*, 175.

141 Twelftree, *Jesus the Miracle Worker*, 150. Twelftree opines that the mention of Jerusalem (the place of Jesus' passion) in v. 17 is a hint that Jesus' miracles are part of the reasons for Jesus death.

142 Green, *Gospel of Luke*, 240.

143 Freyne, *Galilee*, 287–295; Theissen and Merz, *Historical Jesus*, 176–177; Chancey, *Myth of a Gentile Galilee*, 54–55.

144 Vermes, *Jesus the Jew*, 57; Theissen and Merz, *Historical Jesus*, 176.

145 Joy, *Mark and its Subaltern*, 70.

146 Crossan, *Historical Jesus*, 324.

5.4.2. Traditional Interpretations

There are two important culturally defiant yet liberative actions of Jesus in the episode of healing the paralytic—restoring the paralytic to his social station in the community and forgiving the paralytic of his sins. Both "forgiveness of sins" and healing (the paralytic) is a challenge against the religious monopoly of the priests and their powerhouse—the temple, which alone can mediate forgiveness of sins or pronounce an unclean person clean. If one consider that Luke's Gospel is one which negotiates socio-cultural space for the margins/outcasts, not only the healing of the paralytic but the whole of the five conflict stories should be seen as a socio-political protest against the fixed religiocultural systems of the official religion which maintain a binary opposition of the pure against the impure.[147] However, most of the traditional interpretations give importance to theological and christological significance of this text to the neglect of the cultural and political issues involved in it. For the purpose of clarity, previous interpretations of this pericope can be classed under two categories: the historical critical approach and the sociological approach.

The form critics investigate the setting in life of the church/evangelist that may have given shape to a particular saying or logion. Hence, for several scholars, the so-called interpretive comment at Mark 2:10a // Luke 5:24a forms the centre of discussion with a doctrinal emphasis on the authority of the Son of Man to forgive sins. For Martin Dibelius, the story is fictitious but the principal thing was the doctrinal ingression so that the healing took place "in order that you might know that the Son of man has power to forgive sins"[148] (cf. Mark 2:10a // Luke 5:24a). Bultmann thinks this story allows the church to trace back to Jesus its own right to forgive sins.[149] Similarly, George H. Boobyer posits that Mark 2:10a // Luke 5:24a is an interpretive comment of early Christian expositors addressed not to the scribes but to the believers, so that "those who came to believe in him as the Christ should have evidence of the divine authority which was his even in the days of his flesh."[150] Similarly, Richard T. Mead claims that Mark 2:10 // Luke 5:24 which forms the crux of the story is addressed not to the non-believers but to the believers on the authority of the Son of Man to forgive sins.[151] François Bovon

---

147 Jerome H. Neyrey, "The Symbolic Universe of Luke-Acts," in Neyrey, *Social World of Luke-Acts*, 274–285, provides the basic model of purity and order in Israel pertaining to persons, things, place, time and so on. And in this scheme, the lepers or paralytics do not belong to the healthy group and thus to the purity group (282).

148 Dibelius, *From Tradition to History*, 67.

149 Bultmann, *History of Synoptic Tradition*, 16, argues that the use of plural τοῖς ἀνθρώποις (human beings) in Matt 9:8 (parallel story) lends support to the understanding that the church was exercising Jesus' authority to forgive sins.

150 George H. Boobyer, "Mark II, 10a and the Interpretation of the Healing of the Paralytic," *HTR* 47 (1954): 120.

151 Richard T. Mead, "The Healing of the Paralytic—A Unit," *JBL* 80 (1961): 353.

also assumes that the functional setting of the controversy over forgiveness arose in the setting of early Christian polemic against the synagogues of the time. Thus, though the saying in v. 24a perhaps represents an authentic saying, in its present place it testifies to the "Christian authority to confer, and thereby to realize, the forgiveness of God in this age."[152]

This christological lens of the Son of Man paves the way for commentators to argue that this pericope primarily emphasises Jesus' power to heal and forgive as the Son of Man. For instance, Howard Marshall maintains that the healing miracle does more than prove the reality of the act of forgiveness—it validates Jesus' claim to be the Son of Man.[153] Similarly, Fitzmyer argues that hitherto Jesus is pictured as healing (4:38–39; 5:12–16), exorcising (4:31–37) and working nature miracles (5:4–9a), but with a new title Son of Man, who is the heaven-sent agent, Jesus' role is heightened to that of forgiving sins, which people normally ascribed to Yahweh *alone* (μόνος).[154] Joel B. Green also writes, "Jesus' power to heal and authority to forgive sins are manifest in the paralytic's return to his home, walking and carrying his bed, and confirmed by the responses of the people (vv. 25–26)."[155] Thus, a christological interpretation makes a simple point: Jesus' authority to forgive sin is confirmed by his power to heal the paralysed man. "Restoration to full health, an externally visible action, is testimony to Jesus' authority to perform the action of forgiveness of sins which is not visible to human eyes."[156]

The christological import emphasises the eschatological significance of the forgiveness of sins. Jonathan Knight argues, "The point of this story is that the forgiveness of sins is an eschatological function which Jesus discharges."[157] Nolland also considers Jesus' forgiveness of sins in terms of Jesus declaring "God's eschatological forgiveness,"[158] which is anticipated in the exilic prophecy such as Isa 44:22; Jer 31:34; Ezek 16:63. The emphasis on the eschatological significance of the forgiveness of sins fails to appreciate Jesus' countercultural ethic that challenges the dominant cultural universe of sin and sickness.

The preponderance of christological interpretation of the healings of Jesus fails to account for the social meaning of sickness and healing, sin and forgiveness. The concept of sickness and healing in the first century Palestinian/ Mediterranean world was not the same as the medically informed modern world. They are not merely biomedical but social. It is significant to note that the healing and forgiveness of the paralytic provokes opposition from the cultural elites.

152 Bovon, *Luke*, 183.

153 Marshall, *Gospel of Luke*, 211.

154 Fitzmyer, *Luke I–IX*, 580; Stein, *Luke*, 175.

155 Green, *Gospel of Luke*, 239.

156 Robert J. Karris, "The Gospel According to Luke," in *NJBC* (Bangalore: TPI, 1992), 693.

157 Jonathan Knight, *Luke's Gospel* (London; New York: Routlegde, 1998), 86.

158 Nolland, *Luke 1–9:20*, 235–236.

Therefore, it is equally important to attend to the socio-cultural dimension of healing and forgiveness of the paralytic.

Experts in socio-scientific interpretation of the Gospels assert that modern scientific perspective is inadequate to understand sickness and healing without cross-cultural anthropological understanding of the social world of the Gospels. This is because one cannot impose scientific knowledge of health and sickness and healing and curing to interpret the healings of Jesus without sensitivity to the cultural differences and the social meaning of what might constitute sickness and healing in the world of Jesus and Luke vis-à-vis the modern world. Cultural perspective of the concepts of sickness and healing, the health care system in antiquity, and taxonomy of illnesses are important categories for an informed reader to interpret the healings of Jesus.[159] One may establish a reading scenario by asking how sickness and healing were culturally constituted, what kind of a role a healer played in the kind of a society Jesus lived (health care system), and in which social domain (public or private) Jesus' healing operated. A branch of study in cultural anthropology that deals particularly with this kind of question is medical anthropology, which studies societies from the standpoint of healthcare.[160]

With regards to medical anthropology, the work of Arthur Kleinman's *Patients and Healers in the Context of Culture* has proved influential among New Testament scholars for providing terminological clarity and models applicable to first century Palestinian/Mediterranean health care system.[161] Kleinman makes a key distinction between sickness, disease and illness. Sickness is the generic term encompassing disease and illness.

> *Disease* refers to a malfunctioning of biological and/or psychological processes, while the term *illness* refers to the psychosocial experience and meaning of perceived disease. Illness includes secondary personal and social responses to primary malfunctioning (disease) in the individual's physiological or psychological status (or both). Illness ... is the shaping of disease into behaviour and experience. It is created by personal, social and cultural reactions to disease" (emphasis original).[162]

Here, it is important to note that, medical anthropology distinguishes between disease as biomedical malfunction and illness as a socially disvalued state

159 Pilch, "Sickness and Healing in Luke-Acts," 181–209.

160 Eve, *The Healer from Nazareth*, 52.

161 Crossan, *Birth of Christianity*, 295–296; Eve, *The Healer from Nazareth*, 51–63; Richard Horsley, *Jesus and the Powers: Conflict, Covenant, and the Hope of the Poor* (Minneapolis: Fortress, 2011), 113.

162 Arthur Kleinman, *Patients and Healers in the Context of Culture: An Exploration of Borderland Between Anthropology, Medicine, and Psychiatry* (Berkeley and Los Angeles: University of California Press, 1980), 72.

of being.[163] Illness not only affects the individual but also the sufferer's kinfolk, friends and the wider community. Thus, technically speaking a disease is cured by biomedical intervention, but an illness is healed when the sufferers together with their extended social network are satisfied that the problem is dealt with.[164] In other words, illness denotes a socio-cultural perspective and it is socially defined so that one cannot isolate the sick patient and the healer from the cultural system. Both the patient and the healer are embedded in a cultural system and it is the whole system that heals.[165] However, disease and illness are not mutually exclusive concepts or that disease is the modern concept while illness is the ancient concept. They are two different ways of viewing sickness, and represent ideal types in that "both ways of construing sickness may be present in any particular case."[166] It is also important to note that there is also the connection between socio-political and institutional forces in perpetuating sickness. Kleinman's definition of sickness in his work *Illness Narratives*: *Suffering, Healing and the Human Condition* makes this point. He define sickness,

> as the understanding of a disorder in its generic sense across a population in relation to macrosocial (economic, political, institution) forces. Thus, when we talk of the relationship of tuberculosis to poverty and malnutrition that places certain populations at higher risk for the disorder, we are invoking tuberculosis as sickness; similarly, when we discuss the contribution of the tobacco industry and their political supporters to the epidemiological burden of lung cancer in North America, we are describing the sickness cancer. Not just researchers but patients, families, and healers, too, may extrapolate from illness to sickness, adding another wrinkle to the experience of disorder, seeing it as a reflection of political oppression, economic deprivation, and other social sources of human misery.[167]

In other words, there is an inevitable interaction between sickness, illness and disease. Macrosocial forces can aggravate illness that follows from disease, but that is not all, "it can create the sickness that leads to disease."[168] Thus, Crossan comments, "It is possible to have unhealthy arising from any one, any two, or all three of those aspects—sickness, disease, illness—by whatever names they are

163 Pilch, "Sickness and Healing in Luke-Acts," 191 cf. Malina and Rohrbough, *Social-Science Commentary*, 315.

164 Eve, *The Healer from Nazareth*, 53; Pilch, "Sickness and Healing in Luke-Acts," 192.

165 Love, "Jesus Heals the Hemorrhaging Woman," 89.

166 Eve, *Healer from Nazareth*, 53.

167 Arthur Kleinman, *The Illness Narratives: Suffering, Healing and the Human Condition* (New York: Basic Books, 1988), 6.

168 Crossan, *Birth of Christianity*, 295.

called. Some health and unhealthy can be a case of mind over matter. But much more of it is a case of society over mind over matter."[169]

Malina and Rohrbaugh have noted that sickness described in the New Testament are not so much diseases as illnesses—humans conditions out of join with cultural normativity.[170] Particularly, the Gospels' reports about human health-related problems centres on illness and Jesus' dealings with the sick in Luke's Gospel are healings.[171] Having noted that Jesus' dealings with the sick in Luke's Gospel are healings, it is pertinent to consider what role Jesus played as a healer.

Once again, Kleinman's model, which divides health care systems into (1) professional sector (2) popular sector, and (3) folk sector proves useful for New Testament scholars.[172] The professional sector refers to those who practice medicine with official accreditation; the popular sector comprises of care-givers by the family, friends, and relatives; and the folk sector consists of those who practice healing to a greater extent than the popular sector but who are not accredited officially.[173] Jesus was not a "professional, trained and credentialed healer" but operated as a healer among those who experienced and treated illness at the popular and folk sector.[174] And though Jesus' healing is seldom portrayed as providing explanation to the sufferer's condition, and far less diagnosing the sickness, in the Synoptic context the forgiveness of sins that preceded the healing of the paralytic (Mark 2:1–12 // Luke 5:17–26) portrays Jesus "as sharing and explanatory model of illness with the wider culture and presumably with the sufferer."[175] In Luke's Gospel, the practical outcome of Jesus' healing is that the healed are restored to the community. His constituency affirms and accepts his authority (7:16; 9:8, 19; 14:19). However, there are oppositions to Jesus (11:5), which highlight the limitation of a folk healer's abilities (cf. 8:37).

Public opposition to Jesus' healing shows that Jesus' healings primarily belonged to the public and to the political Israelite domain.[176] Opposition to

169 Crossan, *Birth of Christianity*, 295–296.

170 Malina and Rohrbough, *Social-Science Commentary*, 315.

171 Pilch, "Sickness and Healing in Luke-Acts," 192.

172 Kleinman, *Patients and Healers in the Context of Culture* cf. Eric Eve, *Healer from Nazareth*, 55–58; Pilch, "Sickness and Healing in Luke-Acts," 192–200.

173 Eve, *Healer from Nazareth*, 55. There are some references to professional healers, physicians, in the New Testament (Mark 2:17 // Luke 5:26; Luke 4:23; 8:43; Col 4:14), mostly in proverbial sayings common in non-Christian literature.

174 Pilch, "Sickness and Healing in Luke-Acts," 192–200.

175 Eve, *Healer from Nazareth*, 57. One feature of folk healer that Kleinman emphasises was the explanatory models that folk healers employ to provide explanations to their patient in terms the latter can understand (55).

176 There are two social domains in the ancient Mediterranean world such as politics and kinship (family) and they are polar opposites. Religion and economics are embedded in politics and kinship. One may speak of political religion and domestic religion but not

Jesus' healings had to do with Jesus' contravention of what is clean/unclean, pure/impure as defined and guarded by the cultural authorities. Purity system[177] is "a cultural map which indicates 'a place for everything and everything in its place.'"[178] In the words of Malina and Rohrbaugh, "purity distinctions embody the core values of a society and thereby provides clarity of meaning, direction of activity, and consistency for social behavior. What accord with these values and their structural expression in a purity system is considered 'pure,' and what does not is viewed as 'polluted.'"[179] In Jewish tradition pure and impure may be predicated of time, things, place, and persons.[180] Pollution boundaries are thus maintained because what is impure is seen as dangerous and threatening to what is pure and holy. Jesus' contravention of the Jerusalem purity version probably reflects the general attitude of the Galilean stance towards the organised religion and the leaders of that religion based in Jerusalem.

Thus, from the vantage point of cultural anthropology, Jesus belonged to the folk sector who performed healing in the public domain with a Galilean ethic as opposed to Jerusalem based purity system which concomitantly attracted both a following and an opposition. This reading scenario proffers a better ingress to Jesus' healing of the paralytic.

From a sociological standpoint, many scholars have noted that, for the Jews, the crippled or paralytics were unwhole and thus impure or unclean.[181] Concomitantly, it is argued that Jesus' encounter with the paralytic violates the purity system of his day.[182] Thus, some suggest that this incident illustrates the game of challenge and riposte, which consists of a challenge (by word, gesture

purely of religion. Similarly, one may speak of political economy and domestic economy but not purely of economy. Bruce J. Malina, "Criteria for Assessing the Authentic Words of Jesus: Some Specifications," *Authenticating the Words of Jesus*, ed. Bruce Chilton and Craig A. Evans (Leiden: Brill, 2002), 30. Jewish religious functionaries are political personages and the Jerusalem temple is a political edifice where sacrifices are offered for the public good. In the same manner, domestic religion and economy centres on kinship. Love, "Jesus Heals the Hemorrhaging Woman," 90.

177 All culture has a sense of what is pure and what is impure, albeit what constitutes pure or impure is relative to cultures. Purity system provides a symbolic universe to a culture its sense of ordered relations in the social system. Many scholars follow Mary Douglas definition of purity as normality and wholeness, while pollution and taboo refer to things "out of place." See Love, "Jesus Heals the Hemorrhaging Woman," 91.

178 Neyrey, "The Symbolic Universe of Luke-Acts," 275.

179 Bruce J. Malina and Richard Rohrbough, *Social-Science Commentary on the Synoptic Gospels* (Minneapolis: Fortress, 1992), 319.

180 Neyrey, "The Symbolic Universe in Luke-Acts," 274–285 provides detail maps of purity in Israel.

181 Neyrey, "The Symbolic Universe of Luke-Acts," 287; Pilch, "Sickness and Healing in Luke-Acts," 205.

182 Elliott, "Temple Versus Household in Luke-Acts," 223, cf. Neyrey, "The Symbolic Universe of Luke-Acts," 291–292.

or action) that seek to undermine the honour of another person and a response that answers in equal measure or raise the bar of debate. Malina and Rohrbaugh observe that by successfully healing the paralytic, Jesus defends God's honour, his group's honour and his own honour.[183] In this case, Jesus has gained "acquired honour" through his successful conflict with the Pharisees and the Scribes.[184] However, apart from these sociological pointers, most importantly, a sociological reading rightly interprets the healing of the paralytic as restoration of the man's position in the community.

Malina and Rohrbaugh also note the sociological dimension of forgiveness of sins while commenting on Mark 2:9 // Luke 5:23. Sin is not so much a subjective guilt but an external ascription. Thus, accusation by outsiders (friends, neighbours or authorities) has the power to destroy, so also, forgiveness has the power to restore. They write,

> In the Gospels the closest analogy to the forgiveness of sins is the forgiveness of debts (Matt. 6:12; Luke 11:4), an analogy drawn from pervasive peasant experience. Debt threatened loss of land, livelihood, family. It made persons poor, that is, unable to defend their social position. Forgiveness would thus have the character of restoration, a return to both self-sufficiency and one's place in the community. Since the introspective, guilt oriented outlook of industrialized societies do not exist, forgiveness by God meant being divinely restored to one's position and therefore being from fear of loss at the hands of God.[185]

Without doubt, a sociological reading proffers a deeper appreciation of the pericope because it studies the text as a cultural script and not primarily as a theological text. However, since Jesus' healing of the paralytic violates the purity system of his day it is important to adequately point out the political implication of this pericope. Purity issues are deeply entrenched in Second Temple Israelite society, and thus cases of purity violation in public, which characterise Jesus' healing would have potential political ramifications as Neyrey observes there is a, "thorough correlation between socio-political strategy and bodily concerns."[186] Therefore, one must probe the vision of Jesus and the political implication of defying the cultural boundaries of what is clean/unclean, pure/impure. It is hoped that cross-cultural understanding of health/sickness and purity/pollution would provide a helpful reading scenario what socio-cultural implication Jesus' healing of the paralytic would entail.

183 Malina and Rohrbaugh, *Social Science Commentary*, 188.

184 Malina and Rohrbaugh, *Social Science Commentary*, 188, 315 cf. 204. Hendrickx, *The Third Gospel for the Third World*, vol. 2A, 204.

185 Malina and Rohrbaugh, *Social Science Commentary*, 188.

186 Neyrey, "Clean/Unclean, Pure/Polluted, and Holy/Profane," 93.

5.4.3. Postcolonial Socio-cultural Exegesis of Luke 5:17–26

The intensification of cultural nationalism was a hallmark of Jewish response to foreign rule since the time of Ezra, which was then heightened by the Hasidic movement and the Maccabean Revolt (167–160 BCE) during the Hellenistic Empires. The proliferation of groups within the Second Temple Judaism during the first century BCE, as noted above was a response to the colonial domination of the land and its people. One of the major loci of group formation within Judaism was defining the people of God and maintaining the boundary of the holy people of God with the idea of the system of purity.[187] But, though the purity system can be seen as a response to colonialism, it was nevertheless an oppressive system since it arbitrarily separated the pure and the impure.

The purity system during the Second Temple period was perhaps strongly tied to the temple though it probably went much beyond the temple.[188] Jacob Neusner argues that there was a close relationship between purity laws and the temple in early Judaism and that purity system was centralised in the temple cult.[189] He maintains, "Every important sect had to define its relationship to the temple, and one predominant question concerned actually keeping or not keeping the purity laws, making them into a metaphor for the ethical life, or otherwise reinterpreting them. The only thing no one could do was ignore them."[190] Pointing to the significance of the temple in the purity system Elliott claims "temple purity systems established and controlled the social identity, social classifications, and social boundaries of the Jewish people as the holy people of God."[191] Elliott writes,

> According to this system of economic and social stratification legitimated by purity classifications, the rich were ranked above the poor, the clergy above the laity, the urban dwellers (especially in Jerusalem) above the rural peasantry (especially in distant Galilee),

187 Several groups competed to define and control the purity system as it played an important role in defining the map of the holy people of God. The Qumran community receded to the Judean desert to form an exclusive holy people of God. The Pharisees popularised their rather liberal oral-Torah in order to provide leeway for the masses to follow the purity laws. The Sadducees who run the temple objected the oral-Torah as it threatened their socio-religious power over the purity system.

188 Especially, John C. Poirier, "Purity beyond the Temple in the Second Temple Era," *JBL* 122 (2003): 247, argues that purity laws goes much beyond the temple in the Second Temple period and that "there was no necessary connection between purity and the temple."

189 Jacob Neusner, *The Idea of Purity in Ancient Judaism* (Eugene, OR: Wipf & Stock, 1973), 29 cf. Susan Haber, *"They Shall Purify Themselves": Essays on Early Judaism* (Atlanta: SBL, 2008), 31–40.

190 Neusner, *The Idea of Purity in Ancient Judaism*, 33.

191 Elliott, "Temple Versus Household in Luke-Acts," 221.

> men above women, married above unmarried, healthy above the ill, and conformists above deviants.[192]

It can be stated further that, for the Jews, bodily holiness or wholeness was essential to be included into the community. Lack of bodily wholeness, lepers, the blind, the lame, eunuch and so on, were not whole or holy Israelites (Lev 21:16–20). Stuart Love noted that this Leviticus tradition continued in the writings of Philo, Josephus and Qumran community. Particularly, two Qumran passages relate to exclude the physically impaired and socially polluted from sacred location. In the first passage (4QMMT B. 49–54) the blind and the deaf are excluded from the community and in the second passage (11Q Temple 45:12–14) the blind are prohibited from entering the holy city where the temple is located.[193] Inasmuch as holiness was related to wholeness, anyone affected in the physical bodily zones (heart-eyes, mouth-ears, hands-feet) did not belong to the realm of the healthy.[194] Lepers were to dwell apart and cry "unclean" (Luke 5:12–16). In a similar manner, the crippled, the blind, the deaf and so on would be considered unclean.[195] It is this social construct of impurity or uncleanness that separates the unfortunate like the paralysed from the community. Since, Jesus' healing activities defied both the purity system of his time, it deserved a cultural exegesis and the politics involved in the conflict between Jesus on the one hand and the Pharisees and the Scribes on the other hand over the healing of the paralytic.

The healing of the paralytic (5:17–26) took place in public space in which the Pharisees and the legal experts who came from every village from Galilee, Judea, and Jerusalem were present. The Pharisees and the legal experts/scribes are described as "being seated" (καθήμενοι), a posture that goes with a teacher (4:20; 5:3) but also might suggest authority and judgement.[196] The Pharisees were known for their agenda of holiness for the land and people to preserve Jewish identity in the face of the Roman Empire.[197] The Scribes in Luke's Gospel are intimately linked with the chief priests of the Jerusalem temple especially in their opposition against Jesus (19:47; 20:19; 22:66). This suggests that the Scribes apparently represented the religious establishment of the Jerusalem temple that

192 Elliott, "Temple Versus Household in Luke-Acts," 222.

193 Love, "Jesus Heals the Hemorrhaging Woman," 92.

194 Pilch provides a model of taxonomy of illnesses in Luke-Acts in which he discussed taxonomy based on spirit aggression, taxonomy based on symbolic bodily zones affected and taxonomy based on impurity. Pilch delineates three symbolic body zones such as heart/eyes, mouth/ears, hands/feet in his discussion on taxonomy based on symbolic body zones affected, and argues that anyone affected in any of the zones are unhealthy. Pilch, "Sickness and Healing," 204–205.

195 Neyrey, "The Symbolic Universe of Luke-Acts," 282.

196 Green, *Gospel of Luke*, 240.

197 Saldarini, *Pharisees, Scribes and Sadducees in Palestinian Society*, 213; Neusner, *From Politics to Piety*, 153.

collaborated with the Romans. Jesus public healing provided a provocative site of conflict between Galilean healer and the Jerusalem base cultural elites.

The muddle of Galilee-Jerusalem relationship at the time of Jesus is a continuing debate. Horsley, who espoused that the Galileans' descent from the Northern Israelite tribes dating to the time of Assyrian conquest, thinks that the integration of Galilee with the Jerusalem temple-state during the Hasmonean period required an invasive and an oppressive action as the Galileans were "to live according to the laws of the Judeans" (*Ant.* 13. 318–319) including the observance of tithes and offerings in the manner the Judeans were expected. The ascendency of the Romans and the Herodian and Jerusalem aristocracy who collaborated with the Roman rule with the massive taxes imposed on the people would have intensified this feeling.[198] In short, Horsley claims the opposition between Galilee and Jerusalem. However, Sean Freyne espouses the position of a Jewish Galilee (*contra* Horsley) and nuanced the debate by pointing to two ideal types of the ideology of restoration, such as the lateral and vertical ethnicity ideologies, current in the Second Temple period; "one stressing the *extensive* dimension at the cost of an in-depth social bonding, and the other emphasising the *intensive* aspect by developing a tight-knit and circumscribed social culture" (emphasis original)[199] and how this would play out in the real life of the people.[200] Thus, the tension is not "a Galilee-Jerusalem opposition, but rather to different ways of envisaging an ideal Israel and the possibility for realizing that in the present."[201] The mitigating and alienating factors of these two ideologies probably explain Jesus' inclusive stance and the Jerusalem based clean and unclean separatist stance that become vivid in the healing of the paralytic.

From a socio-cultural standpoint, the Galilean healer Jesus' inclusive stance created a site of conflict with the guardians of Jerusalem based purity system. Luke chs. 1–4 presents Jesus to be observant of the Israelite holiness system, but from ch. 5 onwards Jesus is reported to be constantly breaching the lines of the holiness system.[202] Jesus has already intruded into the prerogative of the priest by cleansing and declaring the unclean leper clean (5:12–16 cf. Lev 14), for which he had to hide away in the deserted place for sometime (5:16). In the healing of the paralytic (5:17–26), Jesus claimed the prerogative of the divine action by

198 Horsley, *Jesus and the Powers*, 157–161.

199 Sean Freyne, "The Geography of Restoration: Galilee–Jerusalem Relations in Early Jewish and Christian Experience," *NTS* 47 (2001): 293.

200 Freyne, "The Geography of Restoration," 310, maintains that Jerusalem was the symbolic centre of both the ideology but playing a different role for each. For one, it is the temple of the great God that summons both Israel and other nations together, and for the other it is the ultimate centre of holiness that issues out rigid separation of clean and unclean, native and foreign.

201 Freyne, "The Geography of Restoration," 311.

202 Neyrey, "The Symbolic Universe of Luke-Acts," 292.

pronouncing forgiveness to the paralytic man, the prerogative, which only the priests, as God's agent, can exercise, that too in a public space where an organised and official delegation not only from every Jewish village but also from Jerusalem itself were present.[203] But Lukan ideological position is that, "the power of the Lord" was with Jesus to heal (v. 17c).

Luke narrates the event that some men carried a paralysed man on a bed and tried to bring him to Jesus (in the house), but finding no way to reach Jesus because of the crowd, "they went up on the roof, and through the tiles they lowered him with his bed into the middle, in front of Jesus" (v. 19).[204] On seeing "their faith," Jesus said, "Man your sins are forgiven you" (v. 20). It is this claim of divine prerogative of forgiving sins that provoked "Who is this who is speaking blasphemies? Who can forgive sins except God alone?" (v. 21). Jesus claimed the authority of the Son of Man to forgive sins and eventually healed the paralytic and sent him home.

In Jewish thought, there is apparently a connection between sin and sickness. Though only two healing stories of Jesus attest the connection of sin and sickness (Luke 5:17–26; John 9:1–12), this typifies Jewish thinking of the first century (cf. Jas 5:14–15; 2 Chro 7:14; Pss 41:3–4; 103:3; also the prayer of Nabonidas [4Q242, lines 3–4]). Thus, sickness often illustrates the problem of sin, which is a more basic problem than disease.[205] According to the rabbis, "A sick man does not recover from his sickness until all his sins are forgiven him" (Ned. 41a cf. Jas 5:15). Though there is no causal relationship between sickness and sin in the life of an individual (John 9:2–3), certain sicknesses are seen as the result of sin. This means, healing is not simply about physical restoration but requires removal of sins. In this pericope, the connection between sin and sickness is clearly specified.

Luke described the patient in the perfect passive form παραλελυμέωος (who was paralysed, v. 18 cf. παραλυπτικὸν, paralytic, Mark 2:3 // Matt 9:2) to describe the condition of the man. The story attributes the πίστις (faith) of the one who was paralysed and those who carried him,[206] as prompting Jesus to pronounce what was scandalous for the Pharisees and the Scribes: "Man, your sins are forgiven you" (v. 20). The perfect form ἀφέωνται (which is different

203 Green, *Gospel of Luke*, 240.

204 Whereas Mark speaks of unroofing (ἐξορύξαντες) specifying the mud and thatch construction of a Palestinian roof, Luke changed the description, introducing a tiled roof of a Hellenistic house to make intelligible the action to his Greek-speaking audience outside the Palestinian context (Mark 2:4 // Luke 5:19). See Robert A. Guelich, *Mark 1–8:26*, WBC 41A (Dallas: Word Books, 1989), 85; Fitzmyer, *Luke I–IX*, 582.

205 Robert H. Stein, *Mark*, Baker Exegetical Commentary on the New Testament (Grand Rapids: Baker Academic, 2008), 115.

206 Luke replaces Markan "four men" with "some men" as those who carried the man (Mark 2:3 // 5:18).

from the punctiliar present form ἀφίενται in Mark 2:5) "expresses the abiding force of the forgiveness."[207] In the context of his culture, Jesus transgresses both the Jewish theology that only God can forgive sins and the priestly duty of dispensing divine forgiveness at the temple. For the Scribes who represented the religious establishment that circumscribes God within the wall of Jerusalem temple cult practices, Jesus committed a blasphemous act. Their objection that none but God *alone* can forgive sins (v. 21) was a veiled assertion of their own social power.[208] Marcus Borg argues that, Jesus deliberately violates/challenges the purity/pollution system of the Pharisees and other groups in Judaism denying the equation of holiness with separation.[209] Jesus' healing of the paralytic not only defies the purity system of his day that excludes those with physical disability (crippled, lame, blind,) from the community on the ground of uncleanness but also redraws the map of a new community, in ways that are radically different from the map of organised religion based in Jerusalem.

But, the defiance towards the authority of organised religion in Jerusalem was probably connected to the apathy of Jerusalem temple-state towards the plight of the poverty stricken Galilee brought about by Roman colonialism. Crossan contends that the conjunction of sin and sickness is ironic since sickness is not so much the result of sin but economic impoverishment, especially in the case of first-century Palestine. Crossan writes,

> Excessive taxation could leave poor people physically malnourished and hysterically disabled. But since the religiopolitical ascendency could not blame excessive taxation, it blamed the sick people themselves by claiming that their sins had led to their illnesses. And the cure for sinful sickness was ultimately, in the Temple. And that meant more fees, in a perfect circle of victimization. When, therefore, John the Baptist ... or Jesus ... cured people of their sicknesses, they implicitly declared their sins forgiven and non-existent. They challenged not the medical monopoly of the doctors but the

207 Marshall, *Gospel of Luke*, 213. Several scholars argue that Lukan use of the perfect passive form ἀφέωνται (being forgiven) as "divine passive" meaning that Jesus only pronounced that God has forgiven the man's sin. See Joachim Jeremias, *Theology of New Testament: The Proclamation of Jesus*, trans. John Bowden (New York: Charles Scribner's Sons, 1971), 113–115; Fitzmyer, *Luke I–IX*, 583; Green, *Gospel of Luke*, 241; Guelich, *Mark 1–8:20*, 86. On the other hand some observes that, in both Mark and Luke, the context shows Jesus personally forgave the paralytic of his sins and thus perfect passive form ἀφέωνται could hardly be read as a divine passive. See Stein, *Mark*, 118; J. D. G. Dunn, *Jesus, Paul and the Law: Studies in Mark and Galatians* (London: 1990), 27; Marshall, *Gospel of Luke*, 215.

208 Cf. Ched Myers, *Binding the Strong Man: A Political Reading of Mark's Story of Jesus* Maryknoll, NY: Orbis Books, 1988), 155.

209 Borg, *Conflict, Holiness and Politics in the Teachings of Jesus*, 112–113.

> religious monopoly of the priests. All of this was religiopolitically subversive.[210]

One may not agree with Crossan, especially implicating the temple as perpetuating "a perfect circle of victimization," but it is important to recognise the macrosocial forces—political, socio-economic, religio-cultural institution—of the first century Palestine under the Roman rule that victimised the people. Roman rule was responsible for destroying the material base of the Palestinian peasants that caused a downward mobility even to the status of being outcasts for the less fortunate. However, the Jerusalem temple-state that brokered the Roman rule was indifferent to the socio-economic struggles of the people. On the other hand it controlled social identity and social boundaries based on the purity system that separates the clean from the unclean. In this system, the sick and the disabled are ostracised from the mainstream society because of their sickness, which was considered the result of sin. However, Jesus took an inclusive view of God's people and offered an explanatory model of illness and healed the paralytic by forgiving his sins. To concur with Crossan, Jesus implicitly declared the paralytic's "sins forgiven and non-existent."[211] Jesus thus offered an alternative understanding of God's rule vis-à-vis the Roman colonialism and Jerusalem authoritarianism by healing the paralytic.

It is important to underline the significance of Jesus' claim of the authority of the Son of Man on earth to forgive sins. It has puzzled interpretations whether Son of Man here simply mean "man" (בר אנשא) or that Jesus mean it to be a messianic title.[212] Norman Perrin studied Dan 7, 1 Enoch, 4 Ezra and concluded that in ancient Judaism and primitive Christianity "there is no 'Son of Man' concept but rather a variety of uses of 'Son of Man' imagery. Moreover, the use of this imagery is not restricted to Jewish apocalyptic and the New Testament but continues on into the midrashic traditions."[213] But while maintaining this basic meaning, Perrin conceded that "the Son of Man is a 'symbol of ancestral vitality' in Jewish apocalyptic and the New Testament and that it is given its different functions by associated with different myths."[214] Similarly, Geza Vermes claims that (א)בר נש in Jewish Aramaic there was a circumlocution for "I" used in idiomatic setting, which was native to the Palestinian-Galilean dialect attested in the earliest strata of Galilean-Aramaic,[215] and that "*bar nāsh(ā)* was ever

210 Crossan, *Historical Jesus*, 324.

211 Crossan, *Historical Jesus*, 324.

212 For a detail discussion on the question of Son of Man see Maurice Casey, *The Solution to the 'Son of Man' Problem* (London: T&T Clark, 2007), 1–55.

213 Norman Perrin, *A Modern Pilgrimage in New Testament Christology* (Philadelphia: Fortress, 1974), 26; idem, *Rediscovering the Teachings of Jesus* (London: SCM, 1967), 164–174.

214 Perrin, *A Modern Pilgrimage in New Testament Christology*, 39.

215 Geza Vermes, "Use of the בר נש/בר נשא in Jewish Aramaic," in *An Aramaic Approach to the Gospels and Acts*, ed. Matthew Black, 3rd ed. (Oxford: Clarendon, 1967), 326–327. The

employed as a messianic designation."[216] Nonetheless he conceded that Dan 7:13 had been "recognised in Judaism as a messianic text, and had served to create a new messianic name."[217] Recently, Maurice Casey iterates that the Aramaic term (א)(א) בר נשׁ (the Aramaic equivalent of the Greek ὁ υἱός τοῦ ἀνθρώπου) generally refers to human beings as a whole and at the same time in some instances it refers to "the speaker, or a group of people including the speaker, or someone else made obvious by the context."[218] Casey implicitly classes Jesus as belonging to a social subgroup who might have exercised the power to forgive sins, something that is not expected from everyone, but nonetheless the general level of meaning of the Son of Man imply that Jesus was a human being, not God.[219]

On the other hand, scholars like T. W. Manson opine that Jesus' use of Son of Man is a concept drawn from Dan 7, that stood for a corporate entity and that it "is embodied *par excellence* in Jesus himself in such away that his followers, who together with him constitute the Son of Man may be thought of as the extension of his personality."[220] And thus for Manson, the saying in Mark 2:10 // Luke 5:24 implies that the right to restore the paralytic to the community lies with the community who now acts through Jesus. From a postcolonial viewpoint, Simon Samuel also claims that the discourse on the Son of Humanity (or Man) found in Daniel 7:13; Similitudes of Enoch, 4 Ezra whose power and authority are set in oppositional terms with the kingdoms and empires of the nations originated in the Greco-Roman colonial contexts from among the subjugated Jews, which is "*an embodiment of native, anti-colonial nationalism and racial essentialism*" (emphasis original).[221] He claims that, Jesus reinvents this Jewish nationalistic political discourse by transforming the Son of Man's role as one of release/forgiveness that too here on earth.[222]

---

body of literature, which Vermes considers include the whole of Talmud Yerushalmi, the Aramaic portion of Genesis Rabba, 1Qap Gen, several materials from Palestinian Talmud including the Geniza fragments and Neofiti Codex.

216 Vermes, "Use of the נשא בר/נש בר in Jewish Aramaic," 327.

217 Vermes, "Use of the נשא בר/נש בר in Jewish Aramaic," 327–328.

218 Maurice Casey, *The Solution to the 'Son of Man' Problem*, 80.

219 Maurice Casey, *The Solution to the 'Son of Man' Problem*, 166–167.

220 T. W. Manson, *Studies in the Gospels and Epistles* (Philadelphia: Westminster, 1962), 143. He writes, "Jesus took the term Son of Man, and with its primary meaning from Dan. vii.... We have no good reason to suppose that he was aware of any other Son of Man than the Danielic" (143).

221 Simon Samuel, *A Postcolonial Reading of Mark's Story of Jesus* (London: T&T Clark, 2007), 118.

222 Jesus' claim that the Son of Man has authority to forgive sins on earth is nowhere attested in the postbiblical Jewish literature. Samuel, *Postcolonial Reading of Mark's Story of Jesus*, 124. Marshall, *Gospel of Luke*, 215, maintains that the function ascribed to the traditional Son of Man figure act as heavenly judge and ruler may implicitly include the authority to forgive.

The debate will continue whether the use of the Son of Man saying in Mark 2:10 // Luke 5:24 has the mundane meaning or the messianic meaning. However, in Luke, the claim of the authority of the Son of Man has a heightened significance in that the Spirit-messiah Jesus possesses the power of the Lord to heal. With the authority of the Son of Man, Jesus overturns the scribal view of God. And thus, Jesus outdoes the priestly monopoly of forgiving sins, and thus unsettles the exclusive categories of the sacred and the profane that the Pharisees, scribes, and the religious establishment sought to preserve.

Luke attaches pneumatological significance to this religio-political and counter cultural activity of Jesus healing. For Luke, it is the "power of the Lord" that provided the power to resist the dominant cultural script which equates holiness with separation. Many scholars have noted that Lukan emphasis on the "power of the Lord" in v. 17 is synonymous with the "Spirit of the Lord" (cf. 1:17, 35; 4:14; 24:49; Acts 1:8; 10:38).[223] Moreover, Luke has said about Jesus as one who "filled with the power of the spirit, returned to Galilee" (4:14). In Luke 4:18, Jesus himself declared, "The spirit of the Lord is upon me." Thus, from the outset Luke has already portrayed Jesus as one who is filled with the power of the spirit of the Lord. According to Green, "In a brief flashback, Luke reminds his audience that both Jesus' mission is carried out in the power of the Spirit and that this power, though now rarely mentioned in the narrative, is ongoing (cf. 3:21–22; 4:14–15, 18–19)."[224] This story thus, insists that Jesus' healing of the paralytic is the work of the power of the Spirit. This healing is an act of emancipating those who are oppressed by the religio-cultural system of purity, a mission which the Spirit-messiah Jesus had announced in the Nazareth proclamation.

5.5. Conclusion

Postcolonial cultural exegesis have highlighted that exorcisms and healings of Jesus are modes of socio-political resistance against the colonial hegemonic establishment and religious establishment of the day. With insights from cross-cultural study of possession that suggests the inextricable nexus between possession and a situation of oppression, this study has placed the Capernaum demoniac in a colonial situation in Galilee and argues that exorcism at the Capernaum synagogue is a mode of resistance against the colonial power, which had controlled and possessed the land and the people. The saying traditions (Luke 11:20 cf. 13:32–33) lend further support to the position that Jesus' exorcisms are politically disrptive actions that seek to replace the demonic/colonial rule with the rule of God. Other Lukan narratives on possession and exorcism (8:26–39; 9:37–43) can be explicated in a similar manner by placing the phenomenon in a situation of colonial domination.

223 Green, *Gospel of Luke*, 240; Stein, *Luke*, 176.

224 Green, *Gospel of Luke*, 240.

Postcolonial cultural exegesis of the healing of the paralytic has argued that Jesus' healing constitutes a challenge to the dominant discourse on sin/sickness, purity/pollution and the monopoly of healing and forgiveness of the religious establishment. If one considers that Luke's Gospel is one that negotiates socio-cultural space for the margins/outcasts, the healing of the paralytic is one case of the many other healing stories that attests the liberative acts of Jesus among the poor and the margins. The pneumatological significance of the exorcisms and healing of Jesus is that they are acts of the Spirit-messiah, who with the authority and power of God exorcises the demons from the possessed people, and healed the sick people of their illness. Lukan emphasis on ἐξουσία (authority) and δύναμις (power) of Jesus in narrating the exorcism of the Capernaum demoniac and the healing of the paralytic shows that, for Luke, it is by the authority and power of the spirit of God that Jesus, the Spirit-messiah performed exorcisms and healings that are politically subversive.

Chapter 6

The Spirit in Lukan Passion and Resurrection Narrative

6.1. Introduction

That the Spirit in Luke is a Spirit of resistance is being consistently discussed in this work. In the previous chapter, close attention was given to the subversive function of Jesus' exorcism that challenges the colonial authorities, and liberative healing which liberates the people from the pollution that sacerdotal gaze imposed upon the human body. This chapter turns to another element of Lukan pneumatology viz. the Spirit of God in the passion and resurrection of Jesus in Luke's Gospel. Recently, Martin William Mittelstadt has challenged the simple notion of Spirit-empowerment for witness and pointed out the neglected relationship between the Spirit and suffering within the context of Luke-Acts.[1] Though Mittelstadt himself did not treat the passion narrative and resurrection narrative, there are significant indications in Luke's narrative that the Spirit of God plays a key role in the passion and resurrection of Jesus. This chapter has three sections. First, the relationship between Spirit and suffering is offered. Second, it explores the role of the Spirit of God in Lukan passion narrative from the vantage point of postcolonial criticism. Similarly, the third section explores the role of the Spirit in the Lukan resurrection narrative and contends that the formation of a new discourse of witness and the witnessing community as the work of the Spirit of God.

---

1 Martin William Mittlestadt, *The Spirit and Suffering in Luke-Acts: Implications for a Pentecostal Pneumatology* (London: T&T Clark, 2004).

6.2. Spirit and Suffering in Luke's Gospel

The relationship between the Spirit and suffering has not received critical appreciation in Lukan studies in the past.[2] Mittelstadt points out that, in the studies on Lukan pneumatology, scholars have illuminated Luke's emphasis on Spirit-empowerment for witness, "yet neglects elements of the work of the Spirit in contexts of opposition."[3] In Luke's Gospel, although opposition to Jesus began right after his baptism at Jordan and the anointing of the Holy Spirit,[4] the main opposition comes from Jerusalem authorities.

It is often noted that historically Galilee and Jerusalem were two centres of early Christianity that entertained different messianic expectation. In this light Elisabeth Struthers Malbon has noted that scholars such as Lohmeyer, Lightfoot, Marxsen, and Kelber have posited that the "Son of Man" eschatology predominated in Galilee while "a nationalistic messianic" hope prevailed in Jerusalem.[5] It is debatable how far this is true, but Malbon analyses the structural opposition between Galilee and Jerusalem (via Levi Strauss) in Mark's Gospel and points out the spatial and the theological opposition of the movement of Jesus "going up" to Jerusalem and the Jerusalem scribes "coming down" to Galilee, which can be extended to Luke's Gospel.[6] In Luke's account, one first encounters the Pharisees and Scribes who come from every village in Galilee, Judea, and Jerusalem in the healing of the paralytic (5:17–26). The Pharisees and the Scribes, as representatives of the organised religion in Jerusalem, were very critical of Jesus' counter cultural activities such as forgiving sins—a priestly prerogative (6:24 cf. 7:48–49), open commensality (5:30–32), plucking grain on Sabbath (6:1–5) and healing on the Sabbath (6:6–11), that "they discussed with one another what they might do to him" (6:11).

This initial suspicion was heightened when Jesus' healing and exorcism became a major concern for the cultural and religious authorities. Jesus was accused of casting out demons with Beelzebub, the chief of the demons (11:15).[7] It is implicit that Jesus' accusers were the Scribes and Pharisees who were cultural

---

2 Keith Warrington, "Suffering and the Spirit in Luke-Acts," *JBPR* 1 (2009): 15, acknowledges the work of M. Hoek, "An Analysis of the Concepts of Suffering and Weakness in the context of the Spirit in Romans 8" (PhD. Diss., University of Manchester, 2006) as one that tackles the relationship of Spirit and suffering.

3 Mittelstadt, *Spirit and Suffering*, 27.

4 Soon after Jesus' Jordan experience, the Spirit led him into the wilderness and there he was tempted by the διαβόλος (4:2). As Jesus returned to Galilee filled with the power of the Spirit (4:14) and preached in Nazareth synagogue, his own townsfolk opposed him.

5 Elisabeth Struthers Malbon, "Galilee and Jerusalem: History and Literature in Marcan Interpretation," *CBQ* 42 (1982): 243.

6 Malbon, "Galilee and Jerusalem," 250.

7 Luke did not mention that it was the scribes from Jerusalem who accused Jesus (Cf. Mark 3:22).

and religious personages who employed countervailing strategies to brand those who were beyond the bounds of their control as deviant. It is also noteworthy that Herod the ruler was interested in Jesus too (9:7–9) who was apparently critical about Jesus' politics of exorcism (13:31–32). Though Jesus escaped direct conflict with Herod in Galilee, his entry into the Jerusalem set in motion conflict with the authorities that led to its logical end. Crossan observes that Jesus' egalitarian discourse exploded in indignation at the temple that was non-egalitarian, patronal, and even oppressive religiously and politically.[8] Horsley argues that the conflict portrayed in the Gospel(s) is political-economic-religious, in that the Jerusalem temple represents the face of the instrument of Roman rule, wherein the priestly rulers collect tributes for Caesar and also collects tithes and offerings for the temple which was burdensome for the village communities.[9] In Luke's Gospel, as the Spirit-anointed Jesus confronted the rulers; it is only consequential that the Jerusalem rulers handed Jesus over to the Romans as a threat to the imperial order.

Mittlestadt clearly expresses that Jesus' anointing with the Spirit necessarily involves opposition. He writes

> Jesus not only lives and ministers in the power of the Holy Spirit, but also experience opposition and persecution as a man of the Spirit. Further, the Lukan Jesus not only transfers the Spirit to his disciples, but also anticipates a similar fate for his followers, namely, opposition which leads to persecution (Lk.12.1–12). Finally Luke forecasts that this divine enablement of the Spirit also available for future witnesses brings with it a similar anticipation of the same rejection and opposition as experienced by Jesus. For Luke the experience of the Spirit, far from being a mere divine empowering, proves costly and results in suffering and persecution from opponents of Jesus and his message.[10]

Mittelstadt himself did not explore the motif of Spirit and suffering in relation with the passion of the Spirit-messiah Jesus. Nonetheless, his selective treatment of Simeon's Spirit-inspired prophecy (2:25–32), Jesus' rejection in Nazareth (4:16–30), and Jesus' preparation of his disciples (12:1–12),[11] provides a good entry into exploring the relationship between Spirit and suffering in Luke-Acts. Firstly, he argues that Simeon's Spirit inspired prophecy concerning the liberation the child would bring climaxes the jubilation of the initial stirring of lively sense of a great expectation for the fulfillment of the hopes of Israel and "introduces a clear tone of pathos."[12] Simeon prophesied, "Behold this one is

8 Crossan, *Historical Jesus*, 360.

9 Horsley, *Jesus and the Powers*, 7–8, 156–161.

10 Mittelstadt, *Spirit and Suffering*, 28.

11 Mittelstadt, *Spirit and Suffering*, 30–86.

12 Mittelstadt, *Spirit and Suffering*, 47.

set for the fall and rise of many in Israel, and to be a sign that is rejected—and a sword will pierce your own soul too—so that the inner thoughts of many will be revealed" (2:34b–35).

Secondly, Mittelstadt maintains that the the Nazareth pericope (4:16–30) provides a commentary on Simeon's second prophecy.[13] The paradox of Spirit's anointing and the rejection by the people constitute one of Luke's theological agenda: it is the will of God that the Son of Man must (δεῖ) suffer (9:22). Luke showed that the ministry of the Spirit is not free from opposition and suffering, but rather is a "pathway to conflict with those who oppose Jesus and his message."[14]

Thirdly, for Mittelstadt Luke 12:11–12 explicitly iterates the relationship between the Spirit and suffering, in which Jesus forewarns his followers of the coming persecution.[15] Mittelstadt maintains that pneumatological pronouncement in Luke 11:13 and 12:11–12 "form an *inclusio* connecting the materials between them"[16] in that the materials that follow 11:13 accentuate polarity of Jesus and his opponents.[17] Having exhorted the disciples about whom to fear (12:4–8), Luke speaks of a pardonable sin against the Son of Man and an unpardonable sin against the Holy Spirit (12:10), signaling that the disciple's Spirit-inspired witness itself will be vehemently opposed.[18] The emphasis on conflict and opposition continues right up to the exhortation, "When they bring you before the Synagogues, the rulers and the authorities, do not worry about how to defend yourselves or what to say; for the Holy Spirit will teach you at that same hour what is necessary to say" (Luke 12:11–12).[19] Here, Mittelstadt maintains, "Lukan Jesus promises the Spirit as support for

13 Mittelstadt, *Spirit and Suffering*, 48.

14 Mittelstadt, *Spirit and Suffering*, 65.

15 Luke 12:11–12 is part of the large section of Lukan travel narratives that focus on Jesus' journey to Jerusalem and his inevitable destiny suffering and death. Beginning with 9:51, Luke began to point out Jesus' destiny with explicit iteration that Jerusalem is the goal (9:53; 13:22, 33; 18:31; 19:28), interspersing with further references to the rejection, death and resurrection that will take place (12:49–50; 13:33–34; 18:31–34; 19:14). Cf. Mittelstadt, *Spirit and Suffering*, 67.

16 Mittelstadt, *Spirit and Suffering*, 67.

17 They are Beelzebub controversy (11:14–24), condemnation of the present generation (11:29–32) and the Pharisees (11:37–53).

18 Mittelstadt, *Spirit and Suffering*, 76 cf. Joseph Fitzmyer, *The Gospel According to Luke X–XXIV: Introduction, Translation, and Notes*, AB 28A (Garden City, NY: Double Day, 1985), 964. Also see Cunningham, *Through Many Tribulations*, 108–109 for a summary of four different interpretations offered to Luke 12:11–12.

19 Scott Cunningham, '*Through Many Tribulations*': *The Theology of Persecutions of Luke-Acts*, JSNTSup 142 (Sheffield: Sheffield Academic Press, 1997), 110, recognises that a similar statement occurs in a parallel pericope Luke 21:15: "I will give you eloquence and wisdom that none of your adversaries will be able to withstand or contradict." "Just as Jesus was filled with the Holy Spirit in his preaching the disciples will experience the Spirit's didactic ministry in their verbal response in the context of persecution."

persecuted disciples before the worldly authorities, whether Jewish or gentiles. Luke's readers are assured that human helplessness and inarticulateness will give way to the strength and eloquence that comes from God's Spirit."[20] In the following, this study extends the Spirit's empowering in enduring suffering and resistance to colonial violence.

6.3. Spirit and Lukan Passion Narrative

Lukan Jesus was a political convict, accused of allegedly claiming to be messiah, a king, and stirring the people throughout with his teaching beginning from Galilee, to Judea and to Jerusalem. The combined authorities of the Jerusalem religious establishment, the Roman client ruler Herod, and the Roman procurator annihilated him on the bloody cross. But Luke narrates that Jesus turns his passion and death into a site of resistance against the powers and authorities. Luke theologically insinuates the empowering role of the Spirit of God on Jesus to resist the silencing colonial violence till his last breath. However, before exploring the role of the Spirit in Lukan Jesus' passion and death, a brief digression into the source of Lukan passion narrative is pertinent.

6.3.1. Source of Lukan Passion Narrative

Martin Kähler has provocatively said that, "one could call the Gospel passion narratives with extended introductions."[21] Giving support to Kähler's statement form critics regarded the passion narrative as the first part of the Gospel traditions to have attained the form of a continuous or connected narrative whereas the rest of the Gospel traditions consisted of independent pericopae.[22] The four canonical Gospels have a passion narrative with striking similarity that is not the case elsewhere in Jesus' story; it "has the nature of a connected historical account more than any other part of the traditions" which suggests that, "the Evangelists had access to a relatively fixed complex of stories."[23] (This primitive nucleus of connected stories seems to have been the first expansion of such a proclamation as the kerygmatic passage found in 1 Cor 15:3–4. Paul has made repeated statement about the story of the cross [1 Cor 1:18], which suggests that he knew the passion, death, and resurrection of Jesus in a connected narrative. [24] Brown argues that

20 Mittelstadt, *Spirit and Suffering*, 80.

21 Martin Kähler, *The So-Called Historical Jesus and the Historic Biblical Christ*, trans. Carl E. Braaten (Philadelphia: Fortress, 1964), 80 n. 11.

22 See Dibelius, *From Tradition to Gospel*, 180; Bultmann, *History of Synoptic Tradition*, 279.

23 Vincent Taylor, *Formation of Gospel Traditions* (London: Macmillan, 1933), 44–45.

24 Such references are: Jesus' Last Supper and his betrayal (1Cor 11:23–25), his suffering (Phil 3:10), his cross (Phil 2:8), his crucifixion (Gal 2:20; 3:1; 1 Cor 1:23 etc.), his being hung on a tree (Gal 3:13), his death (1 Thess 5:10; 1 Cor 11:26) his burial (1 Cor 15:3), even to the "Jews who killed the Lord Jesus" (1 Thess 2:14–15), or to his being crucified by the "rulers of this age" (1 Cor 2:8). See, *Luke X–XXIV*, 1360. Also see Pheme Perkins, *Introduction to the Synoptic Gospel* (Grand Rapids: Eerdmans, 2007), 120.

1 Cor 15:11 offers an evidence that there was a common apostolic preaching about Jesus: "Whether then I or they, so do we preach [κηρύγσσειν] and so do you believe"). However, despite the striking similarities, there are also wide divergences in the narrative details and in the theology of the passion. This suggests that, the evangelists, as much as they are theologians themselves, were also influenced by the community traditions from which they had drawn.

An important issue in the study of Lukan passion narrative is whether Luke depended on Mark or had an independent special source?[25] This question arises because Luke has many non-Markan materials, which are self-contained and detachable from the larger narrative,[26] while at the same time Luke has omitted many Markan materials in his passion story;[27] whatever traces of Markan materials are found, they are transposed about four times more frequently than elsewhere.[28] Furthermore, Luke does not follow the narrative order of Mark.[29]

The attempts to determine the source of Lukan passion narrative revolve around two sources,[30] such as Mark and Special Lukan Source.[31] It was F. C. Burkitt who claimed that the third evangelist deserted Mark to "follow another story of the last scenes."[32] Apart from other scholars, A. M. Perry, B. H. Streeter,

---

25 It is instructive to use Brown's category to differentiate *source* to mean a sequential (most likely written) narrative of the whole passion or a good portion of it, and *tradition* to refer to isolated information and episodes many of which may have existed orally. Cf. R. E. Brown, *The Death of the Messiah: From Gethsemane to the Grave. A Commentary on the Passion Narratives in the Four Gospels,* vol. 1 (New York: Doubleday, 1994), 66.

26 See C. F. Evans, *Saint Luke* (London: SCM, 1990), 769. The major non-Markan materials are (1) Jesus' intense desire to have the Passover supper with the disciples (22:15–16); (2) dispute about greatness among disciples and Jesus' response (22:24–30); (3) the words of Jesus to Peter concerning the denial (22:31–34); (4) the tradition about the two swords (22:35–38); (5) the angelophany during Jesus' agony (22:43–44); (6) Herod's episode (23:39–43); (7) Pilate's defence of Jesus' innocence (Luke 23:13–16); (8) the women of Jerusalem (23:27–31); and (9) the episode of the two bandits (23:39–43).

27 For a detail reading of Lukan omission and redaction of Markan materials see Brown, *the Death of the Messiah*, 1:68–75.

28 Brown, *Death of the Messiah*, 67.

29 For the difference between Markan and Lukan order of passion narrative see, Matera, *Passion Narratives*, 153.

30 The proposal of Q as a possible source by F. C. Burkitt was dismissed very early, and so Q is a non-issue in the discussion of Lukan passion narrative.

31 The early proponents of the existence of typical Lukan special source (Proto-Luke) are P. Fiene, G. H. Müller, B. Weiss. J. Weiss and others whose critical opinions are neatly summarised in James Moffatt, *Introduction to the Literature of the New Testament*, 3rd ed. (Edinburgh: T&T Clark, 1918; repr., 1961), 276ff. These scholars argue for a theory of three sources in the composition of Luke (Q, Mark, and S [Luke's special source]) and ascribe Lukan passion narrative to come from a special source.

32 F. C. Burkitt, *The Gospel History and its Transmission* (Edinburgh: T&T Clark, 1906), 130. Burkitt finds an intrinsic merit in Lukan passion narrative and notes, "According to Mark, who is of course followed by Matthew, the chief priests try Jesus in the dead of night, and

and Vincent Taylor had attempted a thorough study in support of special Lukan source. A. M. Perry examined Lukan passion narrative in his work, *Sources of Luke's Passion Narrative*, and concluded that Luke uses a non-Markan source. Taylor summarises Perry's work thus:[33]

> After a detailed examination of the Passion narrative in Luke, Perry concludes that it has been taken from a non-Markan source, which he designates as J or the Jerusalem source, a Greek document, probably translated from Aramaic, which he conjectures, was produced in the community at Jerusalem about A.D. 45 by a disciple of Jesus.... Like Burkitt, Perry holds that in many of its peculiar features 'the narrative is inherently more probable than Mark, 'in its detail and narration.'

B. H. Streeter, who advanced the Proto-Luke hypothesis,[34] also assigns Lukan passion narrative to Proto-Luke as the probable source, except for the materials derived from Mark (which is problematic to discriminate).[35] Taylor also argues that Mark was for Luke a secondary source in the composition of passion account; it offers only supplementary materials.[36] Again in his *The Passion Narrative of St Luke*, Taylor makes a critical historical investigation and argues that, with an exception of the gaps at the beginning (in 22.14) and at the end (where reference to the burial was not supplied), which one may reasonably suppose that they were supplanted by Markan material, he writes, "It is remarkable that when we set aside the passages which have considerable agreement with Mark, we are left with a continuous and well articulated account."[37]

J. M. Creed is one of the early opponents of the plausibility of Proto-Luke hypothesis. Since the Lukan passion narrative retains complete sections which are taken from Mark (22:7–13; 54–61), and Markan phrases scattered in several sections, Creed maintains that, if Luke possessed a non-Markan independent source, "it seems unlikely that afterwards he would have interpolated occasional

---

the rough horseplay and buffeting appears to be done by some members of the Council themselves while they are waiting till it is time to go to Pilate, not by the Temple guards waiting till it is time for the Council to assemble. I venture to think that S. Luke's account is more probable" (137–138).

33 Taylor, *Passion Narrative*, 8.

34 In simple summary, according to Streeter's Proto-Luke hypothesis, Luke first combined L and Q about A.D. 60, and some twenty years later, expanded Q+L and produced his Gospel. See B. H. Streeter, *The Four Gospels: A Study of Origins* (London: Macmillan, 1930; repr., 1964), 208–214.

35 Streeter, *The Four Gospels*, 222. Streeter thinks the following verses are probably from Mark. 22:18, 22, 42, 46 f., 56–62 (though v. 62 is not genuine); 23:3, 22, 25f., 33–34b, 38, 44–46, 52f.; 24:6. He considers 22:69, 23.35, 49, 51; 24:1–3, 9f as assimilation to Mark.

36 Taylor, *Behind the Third Gospel*, 134.

37 Taylor, *Passion Narrative*, 137.

sentences and verses from Mark."[38] Several scholars who have paid close attention to the passion narratives such as Marion Soards, Frank Matera, and R. E. Brown posit that most of Luke's differences from Mark can be explained in terms of editorial works although additions are to be attributed to Luke possessing special traditions.[39] However, it should be noted that there are non-canonical witnesses (including Christian, Jewish, and Roman) that attest the execution of Jesus under Pontius Pilate and that perhaps will broaden the horizon that the tradition of Jesus' death is known in various circles. The non-canonical Gospel of Peter narrates the passion and resurrection of Jesus *much like but not quite* "with few verbatim agreements with the other Gospels."[40] J. D. Crossan has tried to establish the *Cross Gospel* out of the Gospel of Peter, which he thinks underlay the canonical Gospel.[41] However, the work is judged to post-date the canonical Gospel. But it is acknowledged that the Gospel of Peter preserves independent tradition about Jesus passion death and resurrection.[42]

The Jewish witness of Jesus' death is Josephus' description in *Jewish Antiquities* 18.63 and 20.200 from 93–94 CE. The following is John P. Meir's translation of the *Testimonium Flavianum* (*Ant.* 18.63) and the sentences in italics are often noted as Christian interpolation according to John P. Meir.[43]

> At this time there appeared Jesus, a wise man, *if indeed one should call him a man.* For he was a doer of startling deeds, a teacher of people who receive the truth with pleasure. And he gained a following both among many Jews and among many of Greek origin. *He was the Messiah.* And when Pilate, because of an accusation made by the leading men among us, condemned him to the cross, those who had loved him previously did not cease to do so. *For he appeared to them on the third day, living again, just as the divine prophets had spoken of these and countless other wondrous things about him.* And up until this

38 Creed, *The Gospel According to St. Luke*, lviii.

39 Marion L. Soards, *The Passion According to Luke: The Special Material of Luke 22*, JSNTSup 14 (Sheffield: Sheffield Academic Press, 1987); 119–123; Frank J. Matera, *Passion Narratives and Gospel Theologies: Interpreting the Synoptics through their Passion Stories* (New York: Paulist Press, 1986), 152–154; Brown, *Death of the Messiah*, 64–75. Brown explains that Lukan omissions are "deliberate excisions of items that do not fit with the Lukan picture of the disciples or of Jesus. The same motivations explain significant Lukan substitutions of what is not found in Mark. Luke's changing (transposing) the Markan order of events generally fits easily into Luke's stated preference for (logical) order and achieves greater narrative coherence" (emphasis original, 74).

40 Bart D. Ehrman and Zlato Pleše, *The Apocryphal Gospels: Texts and Translations* (Oxford: Oxford University Press, 2011), 375.

41 J. D. Crossan, *The Cross that Spoke: The Origins of the Passion Narrative* (San Francisco: Harper & Row, 1988).

42 Ehrman and Pleše, *The Apocryphal Gospels*, 375–376.

43 John P. Meir, "Jesus in Josephus: A Modest Proposal," *CBQ* 52 (1990): 84–87.

> very day the tribe of Christians, named after him, has not died out. (*Ant.* 18.63).

While the authenticity of this text is debated, Meir argues that "the simple extraction of the three obviously Christian statements within the *Testimonium* yields the original or 'core' text Josephus wrote, with no need to rewrite any words or phrases in the core."[44] Josephus' second text *Ant.* 20.200[45] clearly presumed the existence of the text just quoted above (Ant. 18.63).[46] The point here is that, the death of a marginal Jew Jesus was known to a prominent Jew Josephus, just as the latter also knew of another marginal Jew John the Baptist (*Ant.* 116–119).[47]

The Roman witness is from Tacitus who, in his *Annals* (120s CE) recorded how Nero blamed the Christians in the wake of the fire that swept Rome in 64 CE to exculpate himself from rumours against him.

> Consequently, to get rid of the report, Nero fastened the guilt and inflicted the most exquisite tortures on a class hated for their abominations, called Christians by the populace. Christus from whom the name had its origin, suffered the extreme penalty during the reign of Tiberius at the hands of one of our procurators, Pontius Pilatus, and most mischievous superstition, thus checked for the moment, again broke out not only in Judea, the first source of the evil, but even in Rome, where all things hideous and shameful from every part of the world find their centre and become popular. (Tacitus, *Ann.* 15.44).

These witnesses indicate that Jesus' execution under Pontius Pilate was well known in the wider circle. Obviously, these witnesses do not provide the step-by-step account of the passion like one find in the canonical Gospels. However, the fact that it was known in the wider circle cautions any simple conclusion that Luke solely depended on Mark. It is not possible to say with certainty what traditions were available to Luke, whether it is only Markan narrative plus some scattered traditions or Markan narrative plus some continuous passion narrative that is no longer extant. Nonetheless, a simple position that Luke depended on Mark does not satisfactorily explain the presence of so many special traditions not only in the passion account but the resurrection account that follows.

While it is strictly conjectural, the case for a Jerusalem source for the special traditions found in the Lukan passion seems probable. Firstly, Jerusalem played

44 John P. Meir, "Jesus in Josephus," 77.

45 Josephus, *Antiquities* 20:200 reads "And so he [Ananus, the high priest] convened the judges of the Sanhedrin [in 62 C.E. during the interregnum between the prefects Festus and Albinus] brought before them a man named James, the brother of Jesus, who is called the Christ, and certain others."

46 Crossan, *Historical Jesus*, 373.

47 Meir, "Jesus in Josephus," 99.

a significant role in Luke's thought and in the way he organised his Gospel.[48] Luke not only emphasises that Jerusalem is the ultimate destiny of Jesus, but structurally also Jerusalem dominates the Gospel.[49] Moreover, Luke supplies some local characters that are firmly tied to Jerusalem in Jesus' passion and resurrection narratives. For instance, the wailing daughters of Jerusalem while Jesus was led to the crucifixion; the people punching their breast at the sight of Jesus' death; and the story of Emmaus walk in the post resurrection. These are vivid narration of community traditions that remembered Jesus' passion, death, and resurrection. Some scholars maintain that the Old Testament plays a formative role in the development of the passion narrative and pushes their argument to the extent that no historical traces of Jesus' death are possible to reconstruct.[50] True, the scripture did play a role in the shaping since the followers of Jesus were interested not only in what happened but the meaning of what happened. But as Brown argues, the passion narratives were "not simply made out of Scripture; there was a core memory that governed the shaping of the tradition."[51] In this regard, the special traditions in Lukan passion and resurrection narratives that are linked to Jerusalem can be seen in the light of the social memory of the Jerusalem community.

Secondly, there is a strong similarity between the death of Jesus and Stephen. Whether the tradition of Jesus' death influences Stephen's or vice versa, what is clear is the shared pneumatological significance that the community remembered.

Thirdly, there are traditions common to Luke and John, especially with reference to Samaritan materials and the two Gospels' (structural) orientation to Jerusalem. J. A. Bailey argues that these common traditions betray their origin from Jerusalem.[52] Similarly, R. E. Brown posits that the best way to explain the parallel that exists between Lukan and Johannine passion narrative is to assume that they draw on similar traditions. For Brown this contact may be due to the

48 John Amedee Bailey, *The Traditions Common to the Gospels of Luke and John* (Leiden: Brill, 1963), 110.

49 Luke notified that Jesus turned his face in the direction of Jerusalem in Luke 9:51 and iterates this point in Luke 13:22 and 17:11 making the journey narrative oriented towards Jerusalem, though some materials in the journey section are of Galilean origin. The first two chapters are also located about Jerusalem and its temple and Judea (Bethlehem, 1:26–38). Luke's Gospel limits Galilee only to six chapters (4:14–9:50) whereas the preponderance on Jerusalem is evident in the rest of the chapters. Especially, Galilee is a matter of the past, and Jerusalem becomes the centre stage in the post resurrection (cf. 24:6, 47). In Mark's Gospel, the Galilean section (cf. Mark 1:14 to the end of ch. 9) makes up more than eight of the Gospel's sixteen chapters. So also Galilee still have priority even in the post-resurrection (Mark 16:8).

50 Crossan, *The Cross that Spoke*, 405 states, "[i]t seems to me most likely that those closest to Jesus knew nothing about the details of the event. They knew only that Jesus had been crucified, outside Jerusalem, at the time of Passover, and probably through some conjunction of imperial and sacerdotal authority."

51 Brown, *Death of the Messiah*, 51.

52 Bailey, *Traditions Common to the Gospels of Luke and John*, 108–110.

two evangelists' exposure to the Samaritan traditions.[53] This argument supports that Luke drew on the very early traditions of Jerusalem church.

6.3.2. Lukan Passion Narrative

Jesus' death has to be seen in the light of colonial violence that inflicted upon anyone who dares to challenge the empire. In Luke's passion story, Jesus' spectacular entry into the main political arena, Jerusalem, till his arrest was connected by a chain of events that were politically subversive. The Lukan Jesus entered Jerusalem like a king with the claim of peace that betrayed an anti-colonial import against the *pax Romana* (19:38 cf. 2:14; Ps 118:26). Jesus goes on to challenge the temple establishment by driving out the traders (19:45–46) and making the temple a strategic space of teaching that includes a veiled attack on the temple authorities (19:46; 20:9–19). Seeing the potential political implications of Jesus' nonconformist activities, the temple authorities began to devise plans "to hand him over to the jurisdiction and authority of the governor" (20:20) who represented the (off-stage) face of the emperor in Palestine. This is most vivid in the question they posed to the Lukan Jesus, "Is it lawful for us to pay tax to the emperor or not?" (Luke 20:22).

When the religious authorities could not trapped Jesus any longer, they directly arrested him and tried in the Sanhedrin. The Sanhedrin then manufactured false accusations against Jesus and brought before Pilate claiming that Jesus forbade payment of taxes to the emperor (23:2) and claiming himself as a king (23:2).[54] When their accusation could not persuade Pilate, they further added that Jesus incites rebellion throughout the land from Galilee to Jerusalem (23:5).[55] When Pilate came to know that Jesus was a Galilean, he sent Jesus to Herod Antipas, the tetrarch of Galilee, who was also in Jerusalem at that time. Probably there are good reasons why Pilate sent Jesus to Herod.[56] But, it is plausible that Luke is pointing to the whole constellation of colonial powers

53 Brown sees a connection between the evangelisation of Samaritans by the Samaritan women (not by Judean Jews) in John 4 and the evangelisation of the Samaritans by Philip in Acts 8, which was so successful that Peter and John went to Samaria to investigate the work of Philip. He thinks that Acts 8 is parallel to John 4, and in all likelihood the traditions from which John and Luke took had similarities and cross-fertilisation. Cf. Brown, *Death of the Messiah*, 91–92.

54 Johnson, *Gospel of Luke*, 368.

55 Kingsbury, *Conflict in Luke*, 64.

56 According to A. N. Sherwin-White, *Roman Law and Roman Society in the New Testament* (Oxford University Press, 1963; repr., Grand Rapids: Baker Books, 1992), 31, "Herod the Great, according to Josephus, had the abnormal privilege of extraditing offenders who fled from his kingdom to other parts of the Roman Empire. Possibly some remnant of this privilege underlay the sending of Christ to the second Herod; most of the activities of Christ had taken place in Galilee." Cf. *J.W.* 1.474. Another explanation is that Pilate was trying to placate Herod over the Galilean massacre (13:1). Cf. Ford, *My Enemy is My Guest*, 127.

converging in the trial of Jesus. Herod interrogated Jesus in vain, and sent him back to Pilate (23:11). Pilate "demonstrated his own power to grant or withhold political favors,"[57] conceded "magnanimously to the desires of the mob" and turned Jesus over to their will (23:25).

As Jesus was led to the place of crucifixion, Luke reports that a certain Simon of Cyrene who came from the countryside was made to carry the cross behind Jesus (23:26 cf. Mark 15:21; Matt 27:32). A great crowd (πόλυ πλῆθος) of people followed (ἐκολούθει) Jesus and among them were some women whom Jesus addresses as "daughters of Jerusalem" who were beating their breasts and wailing for Jesus. The action of the "daughters of Jerusalem" is a piece of tradition unique to Luke. It intensifies the mood of pathos as well as the voices of disapproval of the colonial cross being laid on Jesus. Two criminals were also led away to be crucified. While the procedure of crucifixion may have been lengthy, none of the evangelists dwell on the detailed event of the gruesome ordeal. Luke reported: "When they came to the place that is called The Skull, they crucified Jesus there with the criminals, one on his right and one on his left" (23:33).

It is commonly recognised that the Lukan passion narrative is significantly different from Mark. The major difference is in the characterisation of Jesus and the centurion's confession at the foot of the cross.[58] These differences probably stem from Lukan Christology and political pneumatology that have shaped the Gospel. Lukan Jesus' attitude towards the religious elites of Jerusalem, Herod and Pilate was substantially similar to that he adopted in his public life; he showed no deference or cooperation to the religious or political authorities even in his trial.[59] When Jesus was hanged on the cross, he spoke three times which subverted the silencing power and totality of the colonial cross. Firstly, he prayed to his Father God (not Caesar) to forgive his persecutors, which was a non-violent active engagement with the *powers that be*. Secondly, Jesus responded to the plea of one of the criminals by promising him a place in paradise "from today" (23:41). Thirdly, at the last moment, Jesus called unto his Father and committed his life in total trust to God (23:46). In not one moment, did Jesus yield to the colonial powers that executed him. In a similar manner, the centurion subversively declared Jesus

---

57 Burrus, "The Gospel of Luke and Acts of the Apostles,"136.

58 Luke clearly deviates from Mark in many instances. In Gethsemane, Mark 14:33–34 presents Jesus as deeply troubled or agonised (περίλυπός) unto death, and falling to the ground in prayer. However, in Luke 22:21, 45, Jesus reverently kneels to pray while the disciples sleep from grief (λύπης). The Markan Jesus cried out of dereliction at the cross "My God, my God, why have you forsaken me?" (Mark 15:3 cf. Ps 22:1). On the other hand, Lukan Jesus was composed and confidently pray, "Father, into your hands I commit my spirit" (23:46 cf. Ps 31:5 [LXX 31:6]). Furthermore, Markan centurion confesses Jesus as Son of God at Jesus death (Mark 15:39) while Lukan centurion glorified God declaring Jesus as innocent or just person.

59 Cf. Cassidy, *Jesus, Politics, and Society*, 75. This point will be discussed in detail below.

as a "just man." And the community stood behind (at a distance, 23:48) Jesus and observed his death.

What is notable in these politically subversive acts of Jesus (and also the centurion's statement) is that, Luke insinuates the activity of the Spirit in enabling and empowering Jesus to resist and remain resilient in the shameful and painful liturgy of crucifixion. The role of the Spirit in enabling and empowering Jesus can be seen in Jesus' calling God as Father which expresses his conscious intimacy with God even in the midst of suffering and pain. In the moment of excruciating pain and shame, Lukan Jesus remains composed and resilient till his last breath and died in peace, confident that God will vindicate him. The politically subversive function of the Spirit in empowering the colonial victim to resist the powers and rulers is often neglected in the study of Lukan passion narrative.

6.3.3. Traditional Interpretations

Given that Lukan passion narrative is rich literarily, theologically, and ideologically, it has attracted diverse interpretations from the vantage point of literary repertoire, theology, and Lukan political stance. However, as it will be seen, previous studies have not adequately attended to Lukan theology/pneumatology underpinning the ideological retelling of the passion story. An exhaustive review of previous interpretations is not possible here, but three lines of traditional interpretations are identified which are roughly representative of the different lines of interpretations. They are martyrological interpretation(s); theological/scriptural interpretation with the Old Testament as the lens; and an ideological interpretation, which is linked to Luke's purpose and his attitude towards the Roman Empire.

Firstly, Lukan Jesus' passion and death are seen in the line of early Jewish martyrs and Socratic noble death traditions. Martin Dibelius is the first to note that Lukan Jesus died as a martyr. He writes,

> [F]or Luke, the suffering Saviour is the Man of God who is attacked by evil powers and who, with His patience and forgiveness is a model of innocent suffering. Luke regards these events in the place where he consequently puts them not as the completion of salvation, but as the story of a saintly man closely united with God. The literary consequence of this view is that Luke presents the Passion as martyrdom. There were Jewish martyrdoms, as is proved by the literary record of them in the Martyrdom of Isaiah, and in II and IV Maccabees. Since these were read among the Christians the evangelist could expect that if he presented Jesus as a martyr he would be understood by Christian readers.[60]

60 Martin Dibelius, *From Tradition to Gospel*, 201.

Dibelius' martyrological interpretations do not emphasise that Jesus was a victim of colonial violence, though he has influenced many subsequent scholars to see Jesus' death as martyrdom or at least combine the martyrological motif with other emphases.[61] Charles Talbert writes, "On the one hand … Luke avoids any connection between Jesus' death and forgiveness of sins.… On the other hand, Luke portrays the death of Jesus as a martyrdom, the unjust murder of an innocent man by the established powers due to the pressure of the Jewish leaders."[62] For Talbert, martyrdom serves as a legitimating function for evangelistic profession.[63] However, the argument that Lukan Jesus' death does not have an atoning or a salvific significance has been refuted since Lukan Jesus himself speaks of his blood poured out "for you" (ὑπέρ ὑμῶν, 22:20).[64] Brian Beck concurs with Talbert and writes, "[a]s a martyr Jesus dies for the cause of his own teaching in obedience to the way of life that he has laid on his disciples. In this he is the pattern."[65] This line of reading is to a great extent informed by literary repertoire of some Jewish literature such as 2 and 4 Maccabees. R. E. Brown writes, "That the martyr image is intentional can be seen from the parallels that Luke has established between the death of Jesus and the death of Stephen."[66] But martyrological reading of Jesus' death almost exalts suffering but lacks critical understanding that martyrdom is not so much a virtue but a language of opposition to death-dealing imperial power.

It is noted that Jesus' death is also seen in the light of Socratic noble death traditions that view Jesus death as an *exemplum*.[67] In this regard, Greg Sterling

---

61 John Downing, "Jesus and Martyrdom," *JTS* 14 (1963): 279–93; Charles Talbert, "Martyrdom in Luke-Acts and the Lukan Social Ethics," in *Political Issues in Luke-Acts*, ed. Richard Cassidy and Phillip J. Scharper (Maryknoll, NY: Orbis Books, 1983), 99–110; Brian J. Tabb, "Is Lucan Jesus a 'Martyr'?: A Critical Assessment of a Scholarly Consensus," *CBQ* 77 (2015): 281.

62 Talbert, "Martyrdom in Luke-Acts," 99.

63 Talbert, "Martyrdom in Luke-Acts," 106.

64 Tabb, "Is Lucan Jesus a 'Martyr,'" 288 provides bibliography of those who affirms the atonement theology in Luke's writings.

65 Brian E. Beck, "Imitatio Christi and the Lucan Passion Narrative," in *Suffering and Martyrdom in the New Testament: Studies Presented to G. M. Styler*, eds. William Horbury and Brian McNeil (Cambridge: Cambridge University Press, 1981), 47.

66 Brown, *Death of the Messiah*, 32.

67 It is acknowledged that the Socratic death tradition has influenced not only Greco-Roman writers but Jewish writers as well. Socrates' trial and death, first recorded by Plato, inspired later Greco-Roman writers to cast noble death of the philosophers and famous people in the Socratic traditions, including Marcus Cato (Seneca, *Ep*. 24.6–8) and Seneca the Younger (Tacitus, *Ann*. 15.64). See Greg Sterling, "*Mors philosophi*": The Death of Jesus in Luke," *HTR* 94 (2001): 388–389; Tabb, "Is Lucan Jesus a 'Martyr'?" 291. So also in the Maccabees, Eleazar's death is seen in the light of Socrates. For instance, Jonathan A. Goldstein, *II Maccabees: A New Translation With Introduction and Commentary*, AB 41A (Garden City, NY: Doubleday, 1983), 285 observes, "[n]o educated Greek could miss the resemblance

claims that there are at least three major motifs that suggest that Socratic traditions have influenced Lukan Jesus' passion: calmness, innocence, and the paradigmatic nature of Jesus' death. Firstly, Sterling argues that Luke removes every hint of emotional anxiety in Jesus especially in the scene of Gethsemane and the crucifixion. Lukan Jesus was not presented like the Markan Jesus who was "deeply troubled" (περίλυπός, Mark 14:34).[68] Sterling also finds the parallel between Jesus' obedience to God's will (22:42) and Socrates words to Crito, "If this is the god's will, let it be" (Plato, *Crito* 43d).[69] The innocence of both Jesus and Socrates constitutes the second shared motif. Plato calls Socrates "the best and wisest of and most righteous man" (δικαιότατος) in *Phaedo* 118 (Fowler, LCL). Jesus is found to be innocent repeatedly (23:4, 14–15, 22). Sterling notes that Luke made this point by changing the confession of Markan centurion from "Truly this man was God's Son" (Mark 15:39b) to "Certainly this man was innocent (δίκαιος)" (Luke 23:47b). And finally, Sterling claims that like Socrates' death, Jesus' death is paradigmatic. This is evident in Simon the Cyrene who carries the cross "behind Jesus" (23:26). Stephen's trial and death demonstrate further numerous parallels with Jesus passion.[70]

As Sterling has shown, there are certain notable thematic similarities between the death of Socrates and Jesus, such as, their calmness, innocence, and the paradigmatic nature of their death.[71] However, there is a basic difference between the passion of Socrates and Jesus. Jesus was a victim of colonial violence while

of Eleazar to Socrates." Similarly, Marie-F. Baslez, "The Origin of the Martyrdom Images: From the Book of Maccabees to the First Christians," in *The Books of the Maccabees: History, Theology, Ideology: Papers of the Second International Conference on the Deuterocanonical Books, Pápa, Hungary, 9–11 June, 2005*, Géza G. Xeravits and József Zsengellér eds. JSJSup 118 (Leiden: Brill, 2007), 119, comments, "The author of the *4 Maccabees* considers Eleazar as a 'New Socrates,' the archetype of the semi-voluntary intellectual martyr."

68 Sterling opines that, the angelophany in 22:43–44, which shows Jesus' extreme distress runs counter to his otherwise placid composure described above, is a disputed text and is best understood as an insertion by a second-century scribe who tried to accentuate Jesus' humanity. Cf. Bart D. Ehrman and Mark A. Plunkett, "The Angel and the Agony: Textual Problem in Luke 22:43–44," *CBQ* 45 (1983): 401–416.

69 Sterling, "*Mors philosophi*," 397.

70 Sterling "*Mors philosophi*," 399–400.

71 The composure of Jesus in Luke's Gospel clearly shows his calmness. For further reading on Jesus calmness see Jerome H. Neyrey, "The Absence of Jesus' Emotions: The Lucan Redaction of Luke 22, 39–46," *Bib* 61 (1980): 153–171. So also, there are striking emphases on Jesus' innocence in the Roman trial (23:4, 14–15, 22) and in the centurion's confession. Furthermore, Stephen's trial and death demonstrate a pattern that follows Jesus' passion such as the appearance before the Sanhedrin (Acts 6:12; Luke 22:66), the Son of Man saying (Acts 7:56; Luke 22:69) and the last two prayers, committing his spirit to the Lord Jesus and praying for his persecutors (Acts 7:59–60 cf. Luke 23: 34, 46). For parallels between Jesus and Stephen see Ben Witherington III, *The Acts of the Apostles: A Socio-Rhetorical Commentary* (Grand Rapids: Eerdmans, 1998), 253.

Socrates was not. Obviously, "Socrates avoided all the indignity usually associated with death."[72] On the other hand, Jesus was beaten without honour (22:63), mocked (22:63; 23:11, 36, 39), and finally crucified (23:33) by colonial soldiers. At the same time, the preponderance on whether or not Jesus can be seen in the light of Jewish martyrs misses the point that the Jewish martyrs and Jesus were victims of imperial violence. They all bore the imperial brutality inflicted upon their physical body. It is this aspect of suffering imperial violence that the Jewish martyrs and Jesus' death are related.[73] And it is this aspect that distinguishes the death of Jesus (and Jewish martyrs) from Socratic noble death traditions, though some scholars contended that Jesus' death corresponds to Socratic tradition.

Secondly, another line of traditional interpretations have invested much energy on finding a scriptural precedent and identity of Luke's scriptural suffering messiah since Luke provides hermeneutical conundrum for interpreters by iterating the scriptural necessity of suffering and death of the messiah (9:22, 44; 13:33; 18:31–33; 24:26). Though Israel's scripture does not speak of a messiah figure that suffers,[74] scholars have sought to view Jesus' death in the light of the figure of the suffering servant of Deutero-Isaiah, the righteous sufferer in the Davidic Psalms, and the persecuted prophet. For instance, among others, E. Franklin and Joel B. Green noted that the suffering servant passages to which Luke obviously refer provides the common scriptural pattern of suffering and it is the suffering servant passages that most fully fit the passion of Jesus.[75]

However, another group of scholars think that it is the psalms of the anointed one's suffering that played a significant role in the Lukan passion narrative. David L. Tiede concedes that Lukan Jesus is an amalgamation of scriptural traditions but Luke did not develop Isaiah 53 explicitly to set it as the background for interpreting Jesus' death.[76] Peter Doble argues that the "consensual case for an

72 Emily Wilson, *Death of Socrates: Hero, Villain, Chatter Box, Saint* (London: Profile Books, 2007), 12. Brian Tabb cites Xenophon who writes that Socrates "escaped the hardest part of life and met the easiest sort of death" (*Apol.* 32) by drinking the poison calmly on his own terms (*Phaed.* 117b–c). Tabb, "Is Lucan Jesus a 'Martyr'?" 293. "Luke does *not* 'explain the "foolishness" of the cross' by presenting Jesus death in terms of evoking the *mors Socratis*.... The Lukan Jesus suffers according to the biblical pattern of the rejected prophets and the persecuted righteous" (emphasis original, 301).

73 But Tabb, "Is Lucan Jesus a 'Martyr'?" 284–290, also noted substantial differences between Jesus' death and Jewish martyrs in "(1) the narrative sequence, (2) the source and reason for persecution, and (3) theological emphases," such that the term "martyr" do not match Jesus death.

74 Gaston, *No Stone on Another*, 292. Green, *Gospel of Luke*, 484.

75 E. Franklin, *Christ the Lord: A Study in the Purpose and Theology of Luke-Acts* (Philadelphia: Westminster, 1975), 60–61; Green, *Gospel of Luke*, 827.

76 David L. Tiede, *Prophecy and History in Luke-Acts* (Philadelphia: Fortress, 1980), 101.

Isaianic Servant concept controlling Luke's passion narrative is flawed."[77] He asserts that a close reading of Lukan use of psalms especially in relation to David and messiah demonstrates that "distinctive elements in Luke's Passion Narrative are associated with the context-field of psalm allusions in his portrayal of Jesus' death and burial."[78] Joshua Jipp similarly argues that Luke's scriptural suffering messiah is "primarily indebted to the psalms and their depiction of King David's suffering."[79] Contrary to those who think that the concept of a suffering messiah as 'oxymoron,' Jipp argues

> Luke's 'suffering Messiah' is not an oxymoron and that his narrative gives readers all the clues necessary to identify the Scriptures to which Luke's Jesus is referring... fewer have noted the important role the psalms play in Luke's narrative in answering the question, Where is it written that the Messiah must suffer? Luke's use of psalms in his passion narrative is undoubtedly indebted to earlier tradition, but it is Luke who most interprets the death of Jesus in the light of psalms."[80]

According to Jipp, two Davidic themes are strongly embedded in the psalter such as the casting of David in relation to eschatology and messianism, and as the royal righteous sufferer. Notably, before the early Christians, there was already an outlook of eschatology and messianism in the way the editors of the psalter handled the psalms long after the demise of monarchy.[81] For instance, when one reads Ps 2, 132 in the context where Israelite monarchy is already a distant memory, it becomes obvious that the psalms are interpreted and invested with an eschatological meaning. There is also already a pre-Christian appropriation of messianic psalms in Psalms of Solomon. For instance, Pss. Sol. 17 and 18 appropriate Ps 2 in their depiction of Davidic messiah that iterates the eschatological and messianic character of Ps 2.[82] But more important for Luke's passion account is the portrayal of a Davidic figure under intense suffering and persecution by his enemies in the royal psalms. In the Davidic psalms, King David is portrayed as a royal righteous sufferer (Pss 7:1–4; 69:4; 109:3); his opponents surround him to make sport of him (Pss 22; 69; 89 cf. Luke 23:35–38).

---

77 Peter Doble, "Luke 24.26, 44—Songs of God's Servant: David and His Psalms in Luke-Acts," *JSNT* 28 (2006): 267.

78 Doble, "Luke 24.26, 44—Songs of God's Servant," 267.

79 Joshua W. Jipp, "Luke's Scriptural Suffering Messiah: A Search for Precedent, a Search for Identity," *CBQ* 72 (2010): 257.

80 Jipp, "Luke's Scriptural Suffering Messiah," 256.

81 Gerald H. Wilson, "The Use of Royal Psalms at the 'Seams' of the Hebrew Psalter," *JSOT* 35 (1986): 85–94.

82 Jipp, "Luke's Scriptural Suffering Messiah," 258.

But there are still some scholars who think that Jesus' death is best seen in the light of the violent death of prophets. Though the Old Testament does not have much information about the deaths of prophets, Lives of the Prophets records instances of violent deaths of prophets.[83] According to David A. deSilva, "the traditions about the violent deaths of prophets about which the Jewish Scriptures are silent have multiplied significantly by the time of Jesus, who is thus well poised to regard himself standing in line with this tradition."[84] In Luke's Gospel, Jesus is explicitly called a prophet (7:16, 39; 9:8, 19; 24:19), and Jesus himself interpreted his rejection in his hometown in the light of the rejection of a prophet (4:24). Brian J. Tabb particularly points to Luke 22:20 as presenting Jesus as a persecuted prophet. He argues that, Jesus' reference to his blood being poured out in Luke 22:20 parallels the shed blood of prophets (11:49–50), Stephen (Acts 22:20).[85] Tabb argues that the "blood poured out" here does not refer to sacrifice but to the violent death of God's representatives.[86] However, Tabb did not say clearly that the violent death of God's representatives were actually political murder. One may point to Luke's own reference to the violent death of prophets who were victims of political violence. The violent death of Zechariah who perished between the altar and the sanctuary (11:51 cf 2 Chro 24:20–22) is a case of political murder. Jesus' predecessor John the Baptist, who was (more than) a prophet (7:26) was assassinated for political reasons (9:7–9). Thus, it is not sufficient to view Jesus' death in the light of suffering figures in the biblical past; one must also account for the political machination of violence that the prophets who died in their lifetime opposes.

Thirdly, there are scholars who interpret Luke's political position in the light of Jesus death in the Gospel or vice versa. Many scholars see the Lukan passion narrative as an ideological narrative block that delineates both Luke's purpose

---

83 According to Lives of the Prophets, Isaiah was executed under Manasseh by being sawn in two (1:1); Jeremiah was stoned by his own people (2:1); Ezekiel and Micah were executed by the political leaders of Israel (3:1–2; 6:1–2); Amos was tortured and killed (7:1–3); Zechariah son of Jehoiada was killed near the altar (23:1). Cf. Tabb, Tabb, "Is Lucan Jesus a 'Martyr'?" 298.

84 David A. deSilva, "Jewish Martyrology and the Death of Jesus," in *Pseudepigrapha and Christian Origins: Essays from the Studiorum Novi Testamentis Societas*, ed. Gerbern S. Oegema and James H. Charlesworth (New York: T&T Clark, 2008), 57 cited by Tabb, "Is the Lucan Jesus 'Martyr'?" 298–299.

85 Luke 11:49–50 reads, "'I will send them prophets and apostles, some of whom they will kill and persecute,' so that *the blood* of all the prophets, *poured out* (τὸ ἅιμα ... τὸ ἐκκεχυμενον) from the foundation of the world may be charged against this generation." Jesus used the same terminology in Luke 22:20: "This cup is the new covenant *in my blood which is poured out for you*" (ἐν τῷ αἵματί μου τὸ ὑπὲρ ὑμῶν ἐκχυννόμενον) cf. Jer 31:31 (LXX Jer 38:31). So also in Acts 22:20 Paul speaks of "the blood of Stephen your witness being poured out" (ἐξεχύννετο τὸ ἅιμα).

86 Tabb, "Is the Lucan Jesus 'Martyr'?" 299.

and his attitude towards the empire. Steve Walton has provided five views of the previous scholarship on Luke's view of the Roman Empire:

> (1) Luke-Acts is a political apology on behalf of the church addressed to Roman officials; (2) Luke-Acts is an apology on behalf of the Roman state addressed to the church; (3) Luke-Acts is providing legitimation for the church's identity; (4) [Luke-]Acts is equipping the church to live with the Roman empire; and (5) Luke-Acts is not interested in politics at all.[87]

The first two positions, *apologia pro ecclesia*[88] and *apologia pro imperio*[89] did not critically account for the language of dissent that raises voices against the Roman justice system that criminalises the innocent. Luke hardly presents Jesus as politically neutral. Jesus had a disciple who was a Zealot (6:15), commanded his disciples to buy swords, (22:35–8), and acclaimed Jesus as savior, Lord and king (2:11; 23: 38).[90] Burrus has noted that Luke-Acts subtly repudiates the Roman order with the yardstick of the rule of law that Rome claims to hold high. The third position—that Luke-Acts is a legitimation of the Christian identity formation—is laudable, but Esler did not adequately engage how this social formation is played out in the context of the Roman Empire. In the fourth position, Richard Cassidy offers a bold reading that Jesus' social and political stance did not bend to the religious and political authorities in his trial. Cassidy thinks Luke-Acts intends to equip the readers by informing the nature of Roman trials so that they may be equipped for faithful imitation of Jesus and leading apostles.[91] And the fifth position that claims Luke's disinterest in politics is not tenable,[92] since Luke takes much care to place the story of Jesus in the wider ambience of the Roman Empire from the beginning of the Gospel. Moreover, Lukan Jesus is clearly criminalized as a political victim.

Traditional interpretations of Lukan passion story lack adequate attention to imperial violence and the language of opposition of the victims of empire. The martyrological reading makes Jesus' death an *exemplum*, but without paying attention to political violence that the martyrs opposes. The search for scriptural precedent of Jesus' suffering brings out much of the connection Lukan Jesus' passion with the righteous sufferer in the Old Testament. However, this interpretation focuses on how "God fulfilled promises made in scripture"[93] with a

---

87 Walton, "Luke's View of the Roman Empire," 2.

88 Cf. Cadbury, *Making of Luke-Acts*, 308–310, Conzelmann, *Theology of St Luke*, 87.

89 Cf. Walaskay, *And So We Came to Rome*, 64; Maddox, *The Purpose of Luke-Acts*, 94, 96–97.

90 Walton, "Luke's View of the Roman Empire," 5.

91 For a clear review of Cassidy's stance see Walton, "Luke's View of the Roman Empire," 11.

92 Eric Franklin, *Christ the Lord*, 134–139 cf. Jacob Jervell, *The Theology of the Acts of the Apostles*, 15–16, 86–88.

93 Cf. Doble, "Luke 24.26, 44," 276.

preponderance on God's salvific plan but fails to say clearly that Jesus' passion was an oppositional suffering that showcases the brutality of political violence. Even the approaches that tackle Luke's political position vis-à-vis the Roman Empire do not adequately bring out the aspect of resistance in Jesus' passion. A postcolonial viewpoint that attends to the language of opposition, hybridity, and mimicry of the subordinate groups will therefore proffer a better appreciation of how Lukan Jesus turns his passion as a site of resistance against the determinism of colonial violence, and Luke catches on to that narrative that explicitly portrays his intent.

6.3.4. Postcolonial Reading of Lukan Passion Narrative

A postcolonial reading of the passion and death of Jesus would however question the logic of crucifixion from the vantage point of victim's community. What is a crucifixion? Who imposes on whom and for what reason? Marcus Borg and J. D. Crossan observe that crucifixion was a form of "Roman imperial terrorism ... it was not just capital punishment, but a very definite type of capital punishment for those such as runaway slaves or rebel insurgents who subverted the Roman law and order and thereby disturbed the *Pax Romana*."[94] Crucifixion was designed to humiliate, torture, and show the crime of the condemned in the tortured and mutilated body of those who resisted imperial rule to serve as a deterrence for any who would dare challenge the empire. Joel Marcus writes,

> Crucifixion was intended to unmask, in a deliberately grotesque manner, the pretension and arrogance of those who had exalted themselves beyond their station; the authorities were bent on demonstrating through the graphic tableau of the cross what such self-promotion meant and whither it led. Crucifixion, then, is a prime illustration of Michel Foucault's thesis that the process of execution is a 'penal liturgy' designed to reveal the essence of the crime.[95]

Crucifixion was public, demeaning, and painful. According to ancient historians, crucifixion was the worst form of death (Cicero, *Verr.* 2.5.168; *J.W.* 7.203).[96] Crucifixion had the primary social and political purpose of deterring rebellion: "Whenever we crucify the condemned, the most crowded roads are chosen, where the most people can see and be moved by this terror. For penalties relates not so much to their punishment as to their exemplary effect"

---

94 Marcus J. Borg and J. D. Crossan, *The Last Week: The Day-by-Day Account of Jesus's Final Week in Jerusalem* (San Francisco: HarperSanFrancisco, 2006), 146.

95 Marcus Joel, "Crucifixion as Parodic Exaltation," *JBL* 125 (2006): 78–79 cf. Michel Foucault, *Discipline and Punish: The Birth of the Prison* (New York: Pantheon, 1977), 35, 43, 47 for "penal liturgy." It is in the chapter "The Spectacle of the Scaffold" that this reference occurs.

96 Craig A. Evans, "The Shout of Death," in *Jesus, the Final Days*, ed. Troy A. Miller (London: SPCK, 2008), 32.

(Ps.-Quintilian, Declamations 274; also in *J. W.* 5.450–51).[97] The evidence of the precise nature of Roman procedures of crucifixion is scarce and ambiguous.[98] To date, archaeology has unearthed only one victim of crucifixion—a man from Givat ha-Mivtar found in 1968 in an ossuary in northern Jerusalem.[99] Nonetheless, Martin Hengel suggests a summary sketch of how the Romans carried out a crucifixion: "it included a flogging beforehand, and the victim often carried the beam to the place of execution, where he was nailed to it with outstretched arms, raised up and seated on a small wooden peg."[100] The Gospels refuse to narrate the details of the grisly crucifixion. Luke's Gospel simply reports, "they crucified him" (23:33). Jesus died on a colonial cross as a political victim of the empire.

However, the Gospels narrate the story of Jesus' death as a story of resistance against the empire. Especially Luke's story of Jesus' unmasks the cruelty of the empire and its illegitimacy. It is a story that tells the empire that the colonised cannot be silenced by any imperial terrorism. In Luke's Gospel, Jesus subversively overturn crucifixion into a site of resistance and defies the colonial deterministic construction of the subjecthood of the colonised that presumes the colonised as requiring disciplining. Jesus did not keep silent (unlike the Isaianic suffering servant) in the face of the sacerdotal and colonial courtrooms. When he was questioned Jesus talked back. Jesus did not justify himself that he was no threat to the empire. In the following, a postcolonial reading of the oppositional language of Jesus on the cross and the centurion's declaration of Jesus' innocence at the foot of the cross is offered in order to bring out the politically subversive nature of Lukan passion narrative and the role of the Spirit in empowering resistance.

6.3.4.1. Invoking God the Father: Decentring Caesar's Fatherhood (Luke 23:34, 46)

In Lukan passion narrative, Jesus invokes God the Father three times. Firstly, in the Gethsemane garden, Jesus prays, "Father, if you will, remove this cup from me. Yet not my will, but let it be yours" (22:42). Secondly, when he was crucified, Jesus prays for his persecutors, "Father, forgive them; for they do not know what they are doing" (23:34).[101] And thirdly, his dying words were, "Father, into your

---

97 K. C. Hanson and Douglas E. Oakman, *Palestine in the Time of Jesus: Social Structure and Social Conflict*, 2nd ed. (Minneapolis: Fortress, 2008), 86; Evans, "The Shout of Death," 32; Green, "Crucifixion," 91.

98 There seem to be no standard technique of crucifixion. For instance, Josephus reports that in the siege of Jerusalem "the soldiers out of rage and hatred amused themselves by nailing their prisoners in different positions" (*J. W.* 5.449–51).

99 The remains suggest that a single nail was hammered on the heel bones of one foot, through the vertical beam. See Green, "Crucifixion," 90.

100 Martin Hengel, *Crucifixion* (Philadelphia: Fortress, 1977), 25 cf. Green "Crucifixion," 90.

101 The textual status of this verse is uncertain. Bruce M. Metzger opines that, in early and diverse witnesses as P^{75} B D* W Q, these words are absent and so it can scarcely be a deliberate excision by a copyists, though it betrays dominical origin and an unknown

hands I commit my spirit" (23:46). Jesus' calling on God as his Father expresses his deep intimacy with his Father God. This also harks back Jesus' identity as the Spirit anointed Son of God (3:22). In this way, Luke points to Jesus' consciousness of the Spirit's anointing in facing the trial and suffering. At the same time Jesus' calling on God as Father, in a tell-tale manner, subverts the fatherhood of Caesar whose imperial cross offers neither salvation nor peace.

Father is used as a metaphor to call on God to express one's trust. Joachim Jeremias popularised the notion that Jesus' use of *abba* reflects a familial language that carries the sense of warm intimacy and trust as that of children used to address, and that nowhere in Judaism is *abba* use in individual prayer.[102] Conzelmann points out that *abba* "need not have had a connotation of familiarity."[103] J. D. G. Dunn also argues that, despite the value of Jeremias's arguments, it is not possible to maintain that Jesus's use of *abba* was unprecedented since Sir 23:1, 4 already used πάτερ (father) like Jesus's prayer accenting a sense of intimate trust (cf. Sir 51:10).[104] Similarly, Mary Rose D'Angelo argues that, the texts from the Qumran have shown that in ancient Palestinian Judaism, "my father" was used as a personal address to God.[105] Nonetheless, Dunn insists, "Jesus' calling on God as 'Father' was *the language of experience rather than a formal address.* It was his experience of God which found expression in the *abba*-prayer" (emphasis original).[106] Thus, it

copyists incorporated it in its traditional place in the early transmission of the Gospel. See Metzer, *Textual Commentary* 2nd ed., 154. So also Creed, *Gospel According to St. Luke*, 286f; Burton Scott Easton, *The Gospel According to Luke: A Critical and Exegetical Commentary* (Edinburgh: T&T Clark, 1926), 348. However, scholars such as Martin Dibelius, P. Benoit, Earle Ellis accepted it as Lukan. See Dibelius, *From Tradition to Gospel*, 203 n 2; P. Benoit, *The Passion and Resurrection of Jesus Christ*, trans. Benet Weatherhead (London: Darton, Longman & Todd, 1969), 173; Ellis, *Gospel of Luke*, 267. Marshall, *Gospel of Luke*, 867–868, reasoned that excision is not impossible since anti-Judaic polemic is quite possible, and also scribes could have thought that the event of 66–70 CE showed Jesus' prayer was not answered. It is more likely that Jesus words influences Acts 7:60 instead of the other way round. The motif of forgiveness of the sins of ignorance is also in agreement with Lukan thought. And since in every block of the Lukan crucifixion narrative there is a saying of Jesus (23:28–34; 43; 46), it would skew the pattern if the saying were not Lukan. Lastly, Marshall claims that the language is Lukan.

102 Joachim Jeremias, *The Prayers of Jesus* (London: SCM, 1967), 57–62.

103 Hans Conzelmann, *An Outline of the Theology of New Testament* (New York: Harper & Row, 1969), 103.

104 Dunn, *Jesus and the Spirit*, 23.

105 Mary Rose D'Angelo, "*Abba* and "Father": Imperial Theology and the Jesus Traditions," *JBL* 111 (1992): 618.

106 Dunn, *Jesus and the Spirit*, 22. It can also be noted that in Luke, Jesus' calling God as Father indicates a deep sense of communion with God. For instance, Luke 11:21 relates that, at the success of the mission of the seventy, Jesus rejoiced in the Holy Spirit and said, "I thank you, Father, Lord of heaven and earth" (11:21). Lukan Jesus also instructs the disciples that if they pray so, "the heavenly father gives the Holy Spirit to those who ask him" (11:13). This text primarily teaches that, the heavenly father pours out the Holy Spirit in response to prayer

is important to note the role of the Spirit in enabling Lukan Jesus to call God as Father in the midst of extreme pathos.

The Lukan Jesus's first reaction on the cross was an intercession for his oppressor: "Father, forgive them; for they do not know what they are doing" (23:34). It would appear as though Jesus' is "putting into practice his own instruction regarding love for one's enemies: 'Pray for those who abuse you' (6:27–28)."[107] But praying for the oppressor is not a mere act of piety; it is a political praxis and a strategy of resistance. It is to tell the oppressor that their oppression is wrong. Jesus's intercession for his executioners exhibits what Walter Wink claims as Jesus's "third way" of engaging non-violently the system of domination. Commenting on Jesus' injunction not to repay evil for evil, Wink defines the third way as "a way that is neither submission nor assault neither flight nor fight, a way that can secure your human dignity and begin to change the power equation, even now, before the revolution.... They break the cycle of humiliation.... They recover for the poor a modicum of initiative that can force the oppressor to see them in a new light."[108] Jesus thus turns his suffering into a site of resistance challenging the legitimacy of colonial violence.

The mocking scene shows that the religious authorities scoffed at Jesus saying, "He saved others; let him save himself if he is the Messiah of God, his chosen one!" (23:35). The soldiers mocked him, "If you are the King of the Jews, save yourself!" (23:37). Even one of the criminals crucified alongside derided him saying, "Are you not the Messiah? Save yourself and us" (23:39). What is noticeable in the mocking scene is that the verb "to save" is repeated four times with respect to Jesus' incapacity to save himself.[109] But for Jesus, salvation does not lie in retaliation, it only spirals violence. What is required is resistance to imperial violence with an alternative praxis that will expose the limit of imperial violence. Jesus promised one of the criminals the assurance of hope in Paradise by saying, "Truly I tell you, today you will be with me in Paradise" (23:43),[110] thereby hybridising the usual expectation of crucifixion, which ends the life of the victim. Ideologically speaking, Lukan passion narrative privileges the power of the colonial victim to dislocate the colonial discourse of crucifixion in the power of the Spirit of God.

For the third time Jesus calls on God as Father before his death: "Father, into your hands I commit my spirit" (23:46). In all the three Synoptic Gospels,

---

(cf. Acts 2). But this also suggests that there is proximity of the father and the Holy Spirit in Lukan language.

107 Green, *Gospel of Luke*, 820.

108 Wink, *Engaging the Powers*, 185.

109 Green, *Gospel of Luke* 818.

110 Paradise refers to the king's royal garden. A word of Persian origin, it was used in the LXX for the garden of Eden (Gen 2:8), and thus a future paradise as identified with the garden of Eden. Marshall, *Gospel of Luke*, 872–873.

the dying words of Jesus are taken from the psalms, but Luke's use of Ps 31:5 is significantly different from the cry of forsakenness in Mark and Matthew who quotes Ps 22:1: "My God, my God, why have you forsaken me?" The *Gospel of Peter* also has Jesus dying words as "My power, O power, thou have forsaken me."[111] It is unmistakeable that Jesus' dying words were taken from Ps 31:5. In Psalm 31, the king was scorned by his opponents, plotted against by many, while his companions stood at a distance. Lukan Jesus had a similar fate. His enemies scoffed at him, while his companions stood at a distance (23:49a).[112] And like the righteous sufferer, Jesus expresses his hope in God at the point of his death. But Lukan Jesus significantly reinvents the righteous sufferer's prayer by adding *Father* in his dying words. The prefixing of Father to the psalm has theological/pneumatological and ideological implications.

J. D. G. Dunn writes, "the only occasion we know of where Jesus did not use *abba* in prayer to God was in his cry of dereliction on the cross (Mark15.34)—in his awful abandonment by God he could not cry 'Abba.'"[113] However, for Lukan Jesus, it is not so! Even on the cross, Lukan Jesus experiences the divine-Father's presence and he is conscious of that. In that shameful and painful moment of nakedness, Jesus found in God a Father who he believes is with him in his suffering. The prayer to the Father was not a cry of hopelessness; it was a prayer of one who was filled with the Spirit to the God of justice.[114]

The ideological implication of calling God as Father is that, it disrupts and challenges the colonial symbol of the father. The term πάτερ (father) is a wide concept and is used with a variety of meanings.[115] Invocation of Zeus in prayer is found in all the ages in the Greek world.[116] For example, Homer pictures the Greeks and Trojans joining in prayer: "Father Zeus, that rulest from Ida, most glorious, most great, whichsoever of the twain it be that brought these troubles upon both peoples, grant that he may die and enter the house of Hades, whereas

---

111 The text is cited from *New Testament Apocrypha*, vol. 1, ed. Wilhelm Schneemelcher, English trans. ed. R. McL. Wilson (Philadelphia: Westminster, 1963), 184.

112 Jipp, "Luke's Scriptural Suffering Messiah," 262–263.

113 Dunn, *Jesus and the Spirit*, 23.

114 There is a striking parallel between the death of Jesus and Stephen. It is most probable that Stephen's death was modelled after Jesus' death. Luke emphasises that Stephen was a man full of the Spirit 6:5, 10. Luke once again iterates that before his death Stephen was filled with the Holy Spirit (7:55), and while his persecutors were stoning him, he prayed, "Lord Jesus receive my spirit" (7:59).

115 It is firstly genealogical and then legal and sociological. It is also used in the secular office in the Greco-Roman world to refer to an officer incharge of certain position. It also has the religious usage to refer to Zeus as Father. For a detailed reading refer to Gottlob Schrenk, "πατήρ," *TDNT*, 5:952–953.

116 Schrenk, *TDNT* 5:952–953.

to us there may come friendship and oaths of faith" (*Illiad* 3.320-23).[117] But most significantly, Father (πατήρ) is also attributed to the emperor (*pater patriae*; father of the fatherland) and it functioned to explain his relation to the empire as a whole.[118] When Octavius Caesar ascended the throne, both Augustus and *pater patraie* functioned as imperial titles throughout the first and second century CE and were disseminated on coins and inscriptions.[119] D'Angelo argues that the images such as "father" emerged in (anti-)imperial context and as a challenge to the imperial order.[120] In the context of the Roman Empire, Lukan audience will not miss that Jesus was counterpoising Caesar's title with God. Hence, Jesus' calling of God as Father is a disruptive mimesis of the imperial title. Jesus' invocation of God as Father problematises Caesar's title and decentres Caesar's authority to save.

6.3.4.2. This is a Just Man: Overturning the Imperial Justice System (Luke 23:47)

The radical change in the Lukan centurion's confession from that of Mark has to do with Lukan theological and ideological purposes. Scholars have debated the connotation of δίκαιος in the centurion's confession whether it should be rendered as *innocent* or *righteous*.[121] G. D. Kilpatrick maintains that, δίκαιος should be translated as innocent as it fits well with the general theme of the chapter which emphatically declares Jesus' innocence (23:4, 14–15, 22, 41).[122] He claims that the emphasis on Jesus' innocence is important to allay the danger of Christians being seen by outsiders as a politically subversive group who resisted Rome.[123] Many popular Bible translations and commentaries on Luke render δίκαιος as innocent.[124] Other scholars argue that δίκαιος should be rendered righteous. As noted above, those who see Jesus' passion and death in the light of the persecuted

---

117 Cited from Charles Talbert, *Reading the Sermon on the Mount: Character Formation and Decision Making in Matthew 5–7* (Columbia: University of South Carolina Press, 2004), 110-111.

118 D'Angelo, "*Abba* and 'Father': Imperial Theology and the Jesus Traditions," 624.

119 D'Angelo, "*Abba* and 'Father': Imperial Theology and the Jesus Traditions," 623.

120 D'Angelo, "*Abba* and 'Father': Imperial Theology and the Jesus Traditions," 628.

121 In its general sense, δίκαιος denotes obligations to man and to God. It has the legal and moral/ethical meanings. In the legal sense, δίκαιος observes the law. On the other hand, δίκαιος also has the sense of virtue. Josephus used δίκαιος to describe the heroes he praised (*Ant* 7.110; 9.216). δίκαιος in the LXX are those who fulfil their obligations towards God and the theocratic society. They are those who stand right before God. See Gottlob Schrenk, "δίκαιος," *TDNT* 2:182–185.

122 G. D. Kilpatrick, "A Theme of the Lucan Passion Story and Luke xxiii. 47," *JTS* 43 (1942): 34–36.

123 Kilpatrick, "A Theme of the Lucan Passion Story and Luke xxiii. 47," 35; Ford, *My Enemy is My Guest*, 135.

124 For instance, NAB, RSV, NRSV. Also Wilfred J. Harrington, *The Gospel According to St. Luke* (London: Chapman, 1968), 268; Frederick W. Danker, *Jesus and the New Age According to St. Luke: A Commentary on the Third Gospel* (St. Louis: Clayton, 1972, 242.

prophet, righteous sufferer and/or the suffering servant of Deutero-Isaiah translate δίκαιος as righteous. Especially Robert J. Karris argues that in Luke 23:47, "*dikaios* does not mean innocent but righteous."[125] Karris claims that the reaction of the centurion is that he "praised God," which is a soteriological phrase, and thus "the translation *dikaios* by 'innocent'—a juridical term—misses the theological thrust of the verse."[126] R. E. Brown also opines that because the word righteous might invoke Pauline ideas of righteousness, the rendering of δίκαιος as *just* is preferable since the semantic range of just includes innocence and also "reminds the readers of 'justice', a fundamental quality of a king in the OT."[127] At the end it is not necessary to drive a wedge between the translations whether it is innocent and righteous since the semantic range of δίκαιος includes both righteous and innocent.[128]

What is often neglected is the politically subversive statement of the centurion. To declare a crucified man on the cross just or innocent is to challenge the system of justice enacted by the empire. That Lukan centurion glorifying God, "Certainly this was a just man" is not a simple act of piety; it is overturning the imperial justice system as farce. Such glorifying of God places God as the ultimate dispenser of justice and not the imperial justice system, which criminalises the just. But what the Lukan centurion said is not simply a statement (εἶπεν Mark 15:39; λέγοντες Matt 27:54), but an act of declaring praise (ἐδόξαζεν) to God. This declaration implies a "*worshipping response* by people who have recognised God's presence at work in Jesus" (emphasis original).[129] In praising God at the sight of Jesus, the centurion defies the system of justice that spills the blood of an innocent victim. The centurion's declaration denies the legitimacy of the colonial penal liturgy that the colonial master conducts in order to showcase the utter foolishness of anyone who challenges the empire. In doing so, the centurion himself joins the voice of protests and dislocates the privileged meaning of colonial crucifixion. It is instructive to note that Luke articulates the voice of resistance through the centurion as though the centurion was moved by a divine revelation. It is in seeing (ἰδὼν), which is an image of revelation,[130] that the Lukan Jesus praised God. R. E. Brown noted that there is a difference between what the Markan centurion saw and what the Lukan Jesus saw before the confession. In Mark, the centurion saw Jesus died after a loud scream of abandonment. In Luke the centurion has seen "this happening" which refers to Jesus' composure in facing death, whose trustful relationship with God could not be dented even by death.

125 Robert J. Karris, "Luke 23:47 and the Lucan View of Jesus Death," *JBL* 105 (1986): 65.

126 Karris, "Luke 23:47 and the Lucan View of Jesus Death," 66.

127 Brown, *Death of the Messiah*, 2:1163. n. 56.

128 BAGD, 195–196.

129 Peter Doble, *The Paradox of Salvation: Luke's Theology of the Cross* SNTSMS 87 (Cambridge: Cambridge University Press, 1996), 25.

130 Karris, "Luke 23:47," 67.

And having seen what had happened, the centurion in Luke praised (ἐδόξαζεν) God, whereas in Mark this emphasis is absent.[131] The transformative recognition that the centurion experienced implicitly points to the activity of the Spirit of God in opening the eyes of the centurion, where-for he now glorifies God seeing the innocence/justness of Jesus and thereby challenges the illegitimacy of colonial violence. The next section takes up the role of the Spirit of God in the Lukan resurrection narrative.

6.4. Spirit and Lukan Resurrection Narrative

The resurrection of Jesus is not only a theological affirmation; it is a politically subversive claim that denies the finality of the power of the empire. Marcus J. Borg and J. D. Crossan write,

> The authors of the gospels (*sic*) do not speak of Jesus's resurrection without speaking about his crucifixion by the collusion between collaborators and imperial power. In the words of the earliest and most widespread post-Easter affirmation about Jesus in the New Testament, *Jesus is Lord*. And if Jesus is Lord, the lords of this world are not. Easter affirms that the domination systems of this world are not of God and that they do not have the final word (emphasis original).[132]

The Lukan Easter proclamation differs from the other Gospels (24:1–9 cf. Matt 28:1–8; Mark 16:1–8; John 20:1–10), but it shares the same conviction with other New Testament writers that God raised Jesus from the dead. This is clear in the use of the divine passive form ἠγέρθη (he has been raised, aorist passive indicative)[133] in the Easter proclamation like other New Testament writers: "Why do you seek the living with the dead, he is not here, but he has been raised (ἠγέρθη)" (24:5b–6a cf. Mark 16:6; Matt 28:6). Of course Luke did not say explicitly like Paul that it is the Spirit who raised Jesus from the dead (Rom 8:11), but if God raised Jesus from the dead (24:6a cf. Acts 2:32), it is naturally the work of the life giving Spirit of God. But more than this shared theological conviction of New Testament writers that (the Spirit of) God raised Jesus, Lukan resurrection narrative inscribes the active operation of the Spirit of God in empowering and instigating the frustrated band of disciples into a community of witness.

6.4.1. The Formation of the Resurrection Narratives

There are numerous variations, consisting of isolated appearances with little agreement among the Gospels on circumstances and details of the resurrection of Jesus. In all the four Gospels, it begins with the story of the women who visit

---

131 Brown, *Death of the Messiah*, vol. 2, 1161–62.

132 Borg and Crossan, *The Last Week*, 205–206.

133 Luke clearly ascribes to God's action in raising Jesus (by using the active of ἠγείρειν in Acts 3:15; 410) like other New Testament writers (Rom 4:24; 8:1; 1 Cor 6:14).

the tomb and find it empty, after which each Gospel goes its own way. There is also the ambiguity of post-resurrection appearances of Jesus.[134] Pauline account of resurrection appearance (1 Cor 15:5–8) differs greatly from the Gospels. Eventhough it is conventional wisdom that discussion of the resurrection of Jesus begins with the historicity of the account, New Testament writers provide a "testimonial rather than an evidential proof." They were not compiling "evidence that demands a verdict."[135] But resurrection was not an afterthought to come to term with the trauma of the death of Jesus (cf. Luke 24:21) but the bedrock of Christian faith firmly established in the early tradition, forcefully vocalised in 1 Cor 15:14–20:

> If Christ has not been raised, then our proclamation has been in vain and your faith has been in vain . . . If Christ has not been raised, your faith is futile and you are still in your sins . . . If for this life only we have hoped in Christ, we are of all people most to be pitied. But in fact Christ has been raised from the dead, the first fruits of those who have died.

Though the modern intellectual climate has an obsession with what actually happened, Christopher Rowland asks, "Are we justified … in reading the Resurrection stories as if they were an exact account of historical events?"[136] He contends that, the elevation of history over interpretation needs to be questioned, because as much as the contemporary readers are interpreters, the apostolic groups themselves "were making sense of their world and the confused signals of their experience by means of the Bible."[137] Evidently, the first disciples were confronted with strange encounters and diverse experiences, which were so profound that it required appropriation in profoundly theological categories, as one author puts it—"a new birth into a living hope through the resurrection of Jesus Christ from the dead" (1 Pet 1:3).[138] The apostolic claim of resurrection is not because what they have seen and heard on the first day is "rationally unassailable or psychologically comfortable" but because "the Jesus they encountered was now

134 For instance, Jesus materialises and disappears suddenly; he is mistaken as mysterious; he is thought to be a spirit or ghost; the disciples disbelieve. This suggests an apologetic tendency in the tradition, which objectified Jesus' presence by emphasizing bodily features or functions.

135 Markus Bockmuehl, "Resurrection," *The Cambridge Companion to Jesus*, ed. Markus Bockmuehl (Cambridge: Cambridge University Press, 2001), 109.

136 Christopher Rowland, "Interpreting the Resurrection," in *The Resurrection of Jesus Christ*, ed. Paul Avis (London: Longman, 1993), 68.

137 Rowland, "Interpreting the Resurrection," 69.

138 Bockmuehl, "Resurrection," 104.

emphatically the Christ, teaching, preaching and converting them to faith … [and] into empowered witnesses."[139]

N. T. Wright claims that four strange features of the resurrection stories suggest that these stories were undoubtedly told right from the start. First, unlike the passion narrative, there is the strange absence of any scriptural allusion or echo in the resurrection narrative.[140] The second strange feature is the presence of women as primary witnesses, while women's witness is simply not credible in the ancient world. Thirdly, the strange portrait of Jesus himself has no precedent, in that no biblical text predicts that resurrection would involve the kind of body Jesus had.[141] Fourthly, Wright argues that the Gospels never say, "Jesus is raised, therefore we shall be raised at last." Wright argues, "insofar as the event is interpreted in Matthew, Mark, Luke, and John, it has a very "this-worldly" meaning, relating it to what is happening here and now."[142] It claims that "Jesus is raised" and thus he is the messiah, "the true Lord of the whole world; therefore we, his followers have a job to do: we must act as his heralds, announcing his lordship to the entire world."[143]

J. D. G. Dunn claims that within the diverse traditions, there are core or key elements of the resurrection story that remain consistent despite the diversities in the tradition: empty tomb, third day, seeing, and commissioning. Dunn writes, "These key elements (core) probably go back to the (several) beginnings of the traditioning process. As consistently in the Jesus tradition, it was the *impact* made by discovery that the burial place of Jesus was empty, and by different experiences of seeing and hearing Jesus, which was embodied from the first telling in the

139 Bockmuehl, "Resurrection," 111.

140 The passion narrative has plenty of allusions to the Old Testament, but it is not the case with the Easter story. The two disciples in John went and saw the empty tomb but "yet they did not understand the scripture, that he must rise from the dead" (John 20:9). Luke has Jesus expounded the Scripture to the two travellers on the way to Emmaus, but he never mentions or quotes one of them. Wright argues that though Paul has provided a sophisticated hermeneutic of several biblical texts firmly embedded in early Christian theology (e.g. 1 Corinthians 15), the absence of any mention or particular passages or an echo of the Old Testament in the Gospel narratives suggest that the stories "go back to very early oral tradition fixed in that form." N. T. Wright, "The Surprise of Resurrection," in *Jesus, the Final Days: What Really Happened*, ed. Troy A. Miller (London: SPCK, 2008), 96.

141 The risen Jesus is mistaken as a gardener or a traveller; his body is clearly physical, but it comes and goes through the locked doors; he is not always recognised, and eventually disappears when one recognised. If Luke and John were trying to show that Jesus really was a physical person (eating broiled fish or Thomas touching the risen Jesus), they themselves disconfirm such assertion, as Jesus disappears and finally ascends into heaven. Wright writes, "These stories are extremely peculiar, and the type of peculiarity they possess is not one that would have been invented. It looks as though the Gospel writers are struggling to describe a reality for which they did not really have adequate language." Wright, "Surprise of Resurrection," 99.

142 Wright, "Surprise of Resurrection," 100.

143 Wright, "Surprise of Resurrection," 100.

tradition and gave the tradition its essential shape (emphasis original)."[144] As Dunn has noted, the forcefulness of the impact of seeing and hearing the risen Christ led to the forming of traditions. Lüdemann states, "We may reckon that the appearances of Jesus were talked about *immediately* after they happened" (emphasis original).[145]

6.4.2. Lukan Resurrection Narrative

Luke 24 reports the resurrection of Jesus and his appearances in five episodes. But in all of these reports, there is no actual description of the resurrection, and Jesus appeared only in Jerusalem and its vicinity, and at last parted by ascension.[146] The first episode, Luke 23:56b–24:12 is regarded as a redacted form of Mark 16:1–8 by some scholars.[147] However, a few interpreters think that Luke had an independent source to which Markan elements were inserted.[148] Notably there are major differences between Luke and Mark.[149] In any case, Lukan redaction on the emptiness of the tomb is visible.[150] It is noted that v. 12 which is similar to John 20:6–7 is missing in some of the manuscripts such as D and some manuscripts of the Old Latin version. Some scholars think that a later redactor added it.[151] It is likely that Luke and John had drawn from a common source on this. The most significant aspect of the empty tomb story is the attestation of women as the first witness to the resurrection of Jesus in all the four Gospels.[152] When the two men announced to the perplexed Lukan women (v. 4) the Easter proclamation

144 J. D. G. Dunn, *Jesus Remembered: Christianity in the Making*, vol. 1 (Grand Rapids: Eerdmans, 2003), 865.

145 Gerd Lüdemann, *The Resurrection of Jesus: History, Experience, Theology.* Translated by John Bowden (Minneapolis: Fortress, 1994), 38.

146 Fitzmyer, *Luke X–XXIV*, 1536.

147 Bultman *History of Synoptic Gospels*, 287; Fitzmyer, *Luke X–XIV*, 1541.

148 Taylor, *Passion Narrative*, 103–109; Marshall, *Gospel of Luke*, 882–883; M. D. Goulder, "Mark xvi. 1–8 and Parallel, *NTS* 24 (1977–1978): 235–240.

149 Luke noted that the women rested on the Sabbath according to the commandment (23:56b), which is missing in Mark. In Luke there is no mention of worry of the women about who will roll away the stones (cf. Mark 16:3). Luke mentions two men instead of one young man (24:4 cf. Mark 16:5). Easter proclamation is reformulated. Luke mentioned the women's name only in the later part of the empty tomb story, while Mark mentioned their names from the beginning. Luke 24:12 mentions Peter's verification of the tomb, which is not reported in Mark.

150 Marshall, *Gospel of Luke*, 882; G. R. Osborne, "Resurrection," in *Dictionary of Jesus and the Gospels*, ed. Joel B. Green, Scot McKnight and I. Howard Marshall (Downers Grove, IL: InterVarsity, 1992), 681.

151 Creed, *Gospel According to St. Luke*, 294; R. E. Brown, *John XIII–XXI*, 969, 1000.

152 When it comes to Paul, women's witness is already submerged and silence (cf. 1 Cor 15:3–7). In Luke the role of the women as witnesses is expanded; they saw not only the tomb but "how his body was laid" (23:55) and then were witnesses to the empty tomb on the first day of the week. Cf. Osborne, "Resurrection," 681.

(vv. 5b–6) and charged the women to "remember" what Jesus told them while he was in Galilee, they "remembered" his words, and returning from the tomb they narrated what they saw to the eleven.[153] What is significant in Luke is the *politics of memory*, which issues the beginning of bold witness.

The Walk to Emmaus (Luke 24:13–35) is unique to Luke's Gospel but certain features of the episode suggest that a tradition lies behind this episode. The name Emmaus, the destination of the two travellers could hardly be a Lukan invention though one cannot solve the text-critical problem how far Emmaus is from Jerusalem.[154] The name Cleopas must also be reckoned as traditional, because if it were Lukan invention, he would have done the same for the disciples as well. Verse 34 ("It is really true! The Lord has been raised and he has appeared to Simon") not only resonate the kerygma of 1 Cor 15:4–5, but also if Luke wrote it one would expect here Peter as in 24:12 (So also see 22:31 cf. 6:14; Acts 10:5, 18, 32). Verse 30 also contains four verbs of traditional formulation such as "take," "utter a blessing," "broke," and "offered," though it may also resonate Lukan formulation elsewhere (cf. 9:16).[155] R. H. Fuller opines that the earliest form of the story must have been shorter: "The risen one appears to the traveller incognito, encounters the disciples, and manifests his identity to them in the course of a meal, after which he vanishes."[156] Vincent Taylor has analysed this text in detail noting the peculiar Lukan constructions, vocabulary, theological motif and concluded that, "Luke has embellished an existing tradition with unusual freedom."[157]

The form critic Bultmann opines that this episode "has the character of a true legend."[158] But J. M. Creed counters, "there seems to be no good reason why the story should not be founded on fact."[159] C. H. Dodd's form-critical study of resurrection narrative identifies two classes of appearance-stories such as (1) concise narratives, and (2) circumstantial narratives, and noted that some pericopae as having a (3) mixed character.[160] He identifies Emmaus story as a

153 In Mark, terror and amazement seized the women on hearing the Easter proclamation and they said nothing to anyone (Mark 16:8). In Matthew, the women run to tell the disciples the resurrection of Jesus (28:8). Similarly, in the Fourth Gospel, Mary Magdalene went and announced to the disciples, "I have seen the Lord" (John 20:18).

154 For a discussion on probable site of Emmaus (of Luke) and its distance from Jerusalem, see Antonine Deguglielmo, "Emmaus," *CBQ* 3 (1941): 293–301.

155 Fitzmyer, *Luke X–XXIV*, 1555.

156 R. H. Fuller, *The Resurrection Narrative in Luke-Acts* (London: SPCK, 1972), 106.

157 Taylor, *Passion Narrative*, 109–112.

158 Bultmann, *History of Synoptic Tradition*, 286.

159 Creed, *Gospel According to St. Luke*, 290.

160 C. H. Dodd, "The Appearances of the Risen Christ: An Essay in Form-Criticism of the Gospels," *More New Testament Studies* (Manchester: Manchester University Press, 1968), 102–133.

circumstantial narrative. Marshall thinks that Mark 16:12–13 is probably based on Luke, but Fitzmyer counters that such a possibility is far from certain, but the episode may be "a kind of snippet of pre-Lukan tradition that enables this evangelist to build it into his dramatic story."[161] He concurs with Dodd and writes that Emmaus story is "a circumstantial narrative, an appearance-story, yet one devoid of apologetic concerns."[162] Notwithstanding Lukan artistic tapestry laden in the Emmaus pericope, it must be emphasised that, underneath this lies a tradition of the strange encounter of two travellers with the risen Jesus. Despite the fact that Emmaus story is richly theological, the political overtones of the aspiration of the frustrated disciples and their resurgence cannot be missed. This story narrates how the frustrated disciples through their encounter with the risen Jesus experienced a transformation of their subjecthood that catalyses their return to Jerusalem—the main arena of politics. Luke narrates this transformation as the work of divine activity by noting how the two disciples experienced "burning of their hearts" and "opening of their eyes" in the unfolding narrative of Emmaus story.

The third appearance account (24:36–49) has a mixed character according to Dodd, in that the concise narrative pattern reappears but it is greatly modified especially in the process of recognition (which required demonstration of the reality of resurrection) and the issuing of the word of command.[163] This third appearance is often treated as having two episodes: appearance to the disciples (24:36–43) and the commissioning (24:44–49). This appearance story happened in Jerusalem (not in Galilee) and centres on the physical reality of the resurrection. Structurally, it is closely connected to 24:13–35, for Jesus appears while the eleven are discussing the report of Cleopas and his companion. Again, a pre-Lukan tradition lies behind the story. This is evident in the appearance itself (witnessed by three other disparate sources—1 Cor 15:5; Mark 16:14–15; John 20:19–21). Especially, some common features between Luke and John can be detected. The risen Jesus "stood in their midst" (24:36b // John 20:19c) and said to them "peace be with you" (24:36c // John 20:19d), and also showed the disciples his hands and feet (24:40 // John 20:20a).[164] However, the thrust of these stories is not just the physicality of Jesus' risen body or that some people can have a certain type of

161 Fitzmyer, *Luke X–XXIV*, 1554–1555.

162 Fitzmyer, *Luke X–XXIV*, 1557.

163 Dodd, "The Appearances of the Risen Christ, 111, maintains that the word of command is longer in this account consisting of "(a) instruction regarding the use of testimonies from Old Testament (cf. Lk. xxiv. 26–7), (b) a commission to preach (cf. Matt. xxviii. 19), and (c) the assurance of the help of the Spirit (cf. Jn. xx. 22–3, Matt. xxviii. 20, where the presence of Christ is equivalent)."

164 The Lukan Jesus challenge, "Touch me and see" (24:39) is similar to Johannine Jesus offering himself to the doubtful Thomas (John 20:27) and the fish that is offered to the risen Christ in Luke 24:42 also resonates the fish that Johannine Jesus offers to the seven disciples (John 20:9–12). See, Fitzmyer, *Luke X–XXIV*, 1574; Osborne, "Resurrection," 683.

spiritual existence hereafter. For Luke, resurrection of Jesus is a "one-off" unique event. In the words of N. T. Wright, "It is a picture of the risen Jesus as a firmly embodied human being whose body possessed new, unexpected and unexplained characteristics ... a transformed physicality."[165]

Lukan resurrection narrative concludes with a mission command (24:44–49) that is (somewhat) related to the other Gospels' mission command (Matthew 28:16–20; Mark 16:15–16; John 20:21–23),[166] and the ascension of Jesus. The most significant emphasis in the Lukan mission command is the theme of testimony/witness "to all nations" (24:28) which will begin from Jerusalem.[167] But the disciples were told to wait in the city until they are "clothed with power from on high" (v. 49). In all of Lukan resurrection narratives, Luke shows the formation of a community of witness that annuls the power of crucifixion with a new narrative of the resurrection of Jesus.

6.4.3. Traditional Interpretations

Generally speaking, the rationalistic/liberal criticism of the nineteenth century discredits the resurrection stories as impossible. But, such a case against the claim of resurrection was already current in the first century and has left their marks on the later layers of the resurrection accounts that sought to answer the attacks apologetically (Matt 28:11–15; Luke 24:41–43; Acts 10:41). Nonetheless, it must be emphasised that a rational explanation that limits reality to time and space is in itself a colonial determinism as it precludes the mystical and transcendental encounter that human experiences. A majority of the historical-critical biblical scholars claim that the resurrection of Jesus is beyond empirical investigation, not that the resurrection is not real, but that resurrection itself transcends time and space.[168] However, while scholars emphasise the real-ness of the resurrection account, often it is theological explanation that dominates the interpretation.

For instance, Willi Marxsen argues that the resurrection of Jesus was simply a way of saying that the significance of Jesus' teaching or mission could never die; the purpose of Jesus is continued.[169] However, from the earliest days the apostolic

165 N. T. Wright, *Christian Origin and the Question of God*, vol. 3. *The Resurrection of the Son of God* (London: SPCK, 2003), 661.

166 Marshall, *Gospel of Luke*, 903; Fitzmyer, *Luke X–XXIV*, 1578.

167 But it is notable that Lukan mission command is strikingly different from Mark and Matthew. In the Markan appendix, the risen Lord commands the disciples "to preach the gospel" with baptism of the one who believes as an implicit instruction (Mark 16:15–16). These emphases are entirely missing from Luke. Matthew does not express mission in terms of the "gospel." The major missionary emphasis in Matthew is "to make disciples of all nations" with baptising all who believe as an additional command (Matt 28:19).

168 Meier, "Jesus," 1328.

169 Willi Marxsen, "The Significance of the Message of Resurrection," in *The Significance of the Message of the Resurrection Faith for Faith in Jesus Christ*, ed. C. F. D. Moule (London: SCM, 1968), 49–50.

kerygma was not a re-preaching of Jesus message; it was the proclamation of the resurrection, a new narrative that counters the imperial discourse about reality. Wolfhart Pannenberg argues that resurrection is a "symbolic and metaphorical expression of the hope beyond death, the resurrection from the death," because the disciples were confronted by a reality/experience that cannot be expressed otherwise than in the hope of resurrection. And it is in this sense, "the resurrection of Jesus is an historical event, an event that really happened at that time."[170] However, he claims, "[t]he appearances reported in the Gospels, which are not mentioned by Paul, have such a strongly legendary character that one can scarcely find a historical kernel of their own in them."[171] But it is the Gospel traditions that describe the reality of the disciples' encounter with the risen Jesus. It appears that "[t]he judgement of historical-critical biblical scholars like Pannenberg are neither sufficiently historical nor critical."[172]

John J. Pilch argues, traditional analyses of the resurrection appearances fail to take into account the socio-scientific information about such experiences. Pilch insists that the appearances are precisely "altered state of consciousness" (ASC) experiences. He argues that the resurrection appearance follows a pattern: The visionaries saw someone who they do not recognise. That someone assuages the visionary's concern (do not fear) and then presents his identity (it is I). In other words they saw Jesus in alternate reality, and thus the risen Jesus from an alternate reality can eat grilled fish in material reality. The appearances convinced the disciples that God has raised Jesus from the dead despite the shameful death. Pilch concludes, "[T]he appearances offer new information or a commission to the visionaries. In either case, the visionaries' doubts are removed, resolve strengthened, and each visionary can return to undisturbed, normal life."[173] It is true that "Mediterranean culture's consensus reality" may be different from "modern culture's consensus reality,"[174] it is difficult to see whether altered state of consciousness experience of some visionaries would really stir the formation of a die-hard witnessing community; the disciples did *not* return to undisturbed, normal life as Pilch contends but took Jesus' movement to the main arena of the empire. Moreover, the diverse appearance accounts plainly made the sense that the risen Jesus was seen, not "visualised" as personally present.[175]

---

170 Wolfhart Pannenberg, "Did Jesus Really Rise from the Death," *Dialog* 4 (1964): 135 cited by R. E. Brown, "The Resurrection of Jesus," *NJBC* (Bangalore: TPI, 2007), 1374.

171 Wolfhart Pannenberg, *Jesus—God and Man*, trans. Lewis L. Wilkins and Duane A. Priebe (London: SCM, 1968), 89.

172 John J. Pilch, "Altered State Consciousness in the Synoptics," in *The Social Setting of Jesus and the Gospels*, 112.

173 Pilch, "Altered State Consciousness in the Synoptics," 113.

174 Pilch, "Altered State Consciousness in the Synoptics," 105.

175 Marcus Bockmuehl, "Resurrection," *The Cambridge Companion to Jesus*, ed. Markus Bockmuehl (Cambridge: Cambridge University Press, 2001), 113.

With regard to Lukan resurrection account, traditional interpretations emphasise the theological motifs of Luke but lack attention to the language of resistance to colonial discourse of power and domination embedded in the Lukan ideological retelling of Jesus' resurrection and the formation of Easter community. To begin with, Fitzmyer claims that, the Lukan empty tomb account (24:1–12), which centres on the Easter proclamation, is to present Jesus as victor over death. Through suffering and death the risen Jesus has passed from being an earthly teacher healer to the exalted Son, who will now dispense the father's promise on all who will join him in the breaking of the bread.[176] But the Easter proclamation is not only a theological statement that the crucified Jesus has become the exalted Son of God. It is also an ideological discourse that emphasises the failure of colonial crucifixion to make its intended impact. It sends out the message that colonial violence has failed to silence the critical voice of the margins. And since the Easter proclamation transforms the women's subjecthood to become witnesses to the resurrection of Jesus, it is tenuous to emphasise their incredulity.[177] The politics of remembering what Jesus said (v. 8), and the countercultural nature of the women's witness (v. 9) in an imperial culture that is steeply patriarchal are politically subversive.

With regards to the Emmaus story (24:13–35), the motif of the scriptural fulfillment and the breaking of the bread as the location of revelation dominates traditional interpretations. R. H. Fuller asserts that scriptural fulfillment motif "must be regarded as the principal motif of the story" since Luke stressed it not less than three times (24:25, 26, 27).[178] For, Hermann Hendrickx, "[t]he account is rooted in a double situation: on the one hand the proclamation of the Christological fulfilment of the scriptures and on the other hand, the celebration of the Eucharist."[179] Green opines that, for Luke, Jesus' death has to be understood within the matrix of the scriptures (24:25–27, 32), in that, revelation comes through "a hermeneutical process of comprehending the purpose of God in the correlation of Jesus' career with the Scriptures of Israel."[180] However, the scriptural fulfillment reading of this story neglects the political dimension of Lukan reference to the law and the prophets. They signal that Jesus was one

176 Fitzmyer, *Luke X–XXIV*, 1543.

177 According to Marxsen, what the two men said to the women (in Luke 24: 5b-7) sounds like a reproach for their unbelief of what Jesus had already prophesied about his resurrection while he was in Galilee. Subsequently, they brought the message to the apostles, but they too were met with unbelief. Thus, he concludes that the finding of the empty tomb therefore does not produce faith. Willi Marxsen, *The Resurrection of Jesus of Nazareth* (London: SCM, 1970), 49–50.

178 Fuller, *Resurrection Narrative in Luke-Acts*, 111.

179 Hermann Hendrickx, *Resurrection Narratives of the Synoptic Gospels* (London: Geoffrey Chapman, 1984), 83.

180 Green, *Gospel of Luke*, 844.

like them who challenged the oppressive empire/kingdom. Lukan ideological narration seems to suggest that listening to the voice of the stranger about Jesus' death in the light of the law and the prophets rapturously evokes a consciousness that impels the two disciples to return to Jerusalem.

Moreover, given the noticeable eucharistic language in the Emmaus story, a sacramental interpretation finds much resonance among scholars. For Craddock, Luke is telling "the living Christ is both the key to our understanding the Scriptures and the very present Lord who is revealed to us in the breaking of the bread. His presence at the table makes all believers first-generation Christians and every meeting place Emmaus."[181] Fitzmyer argues, "Christ reclining at table with the disciples of Emmaus, taking bread, uttering a blessing, breaking the bread, and offering it to them (v. 30), not only recalls the Last Supper (22:19ab) but becomes the classic Lukan way of referring to the Eucharist. The lesson in the story is that henceforth the risen Christ will be present to his assembled disciples, not visibly ... but in the breaking of the bread."[182] In a similar manner H. D. Betz observes that the opening of the eyes, the recognition of the risen Jesus, and the sudden disappearance of Jesus in the breaking of the bread points to the presence of Jesus "in the act of Christian interpretation of the Scriptures and in the act of the Lord's Supper."[183] But Robert Karris contends that the meal has more to do with hospitality than the narrow interpretation of it as the Eucharist.[184] By being hospitable to the stranger, the two disciples eyes were opened.[185] In a similar line, Green maintains that, the meal scene points to the revelatory significance of the act of hospitality and table-fellowship (cf. 9:7–20).[186] Probably both ways of reading is possible. But there is something very political about the table-fellowship with the stranger. The recognition of the risen Jesus did not come as a cold knowledge. It has a pneumatic character that impelled the two disciples to go back to Jerusalem (vv. 32–33). A postcolonial viewpoint that attends to the experience of the subordinate groups who bore the wound of colonial violence will shed better light on the implications of the Emmaus story.

Thirdly, Luke 24:36–53 narrates the second appearance (vv. 36–49) and the ascension (vv. 50–53). There are many Lukan theological themes amalgamated in this final section.[187] But while attending to these themes, traditional interpretations

181 Fred B. Craddock, *Luke*, Interpretation: A Bible Commentary for Teaching and Preaching (Louisville: John Knox, 1990), 287.

182 Fitzmyer, *Luke X–XXIV*, 1559.

183 H. D. Betz, "The Origin and Nature of Christian Faith According to the Emmaus Legend (Luke 24:13–35)," *Int* 23 (1969): 37–38.

184 Robert J. Karris, "Luke 24:13–35," *Int* 41 (1987): 58.

185 Karris, "The Gospel According to Luke," 721.

186 Green, *Gospel of Luke*, 843.

187 Karris, "The Gospel According to Luke," 721, notes the theme of peace (v. 36), table fellowship (vv. 41–44), promise fulfillment (vv. 44–47), forgiveness of sins (v. 47), Jerusalem

fail to appreciate adequately that Luke is telling the story of the formation of a community of witness that would begin from Jerusalem. An appraisal of the traditional interpretation of Jesus' appearance to the disciples (vv. 36–43), the commissioning (vv. 44–49) and the ascension (vv. 50–53) are in order.

Traditional interpretations have rightly identified the theological themes such as scriptural/prophecy fulfillment, forgiveness of sins, witness, Jerusalem, Holy Spirit and so on in the commissioning pericope (vv. 44–49). Luke once again emphasises the scriptural fulfillment, associated with the necessity of Jesus' death (vv. 44–46). Notably, the theme becomes more explicit in each example. The women at the tomb were reminded that Jesus prophesied the death and resurrection of the Son of Man while he was still in Galilee (v. 7). The two wayfarers were told on the road that Moses and the prophets had prophesied that it was necessary for the messiah to suffer and to enter his glory (vv. 25–27). In the Jerusalem appearance, the disciples are told that Jesus had previously taught them that Moses, the prophets and the psalms have predicted the suffering, death and resurrection on the third day (vv. 44–46).[188] Here, Lukan Jesus cites no specific text from the scripture, and Lukan wide-ranging interpretation of the scripture takes over.[189] What is notable here is one finds a unique Lukan "emphasis on the scriptures and on making them an 'open book' in an altogether new way."[190]

What is significant for this study here is the way in which Luke narrates how the disciples came to understand with the use of the verb διανοίγω (to open) in the passive form. Luke used the verb "to open" three times in ch. 24: firstly, "their eyes were opened" (v. 31), secondly, "while he opened to us the scriptures" (v. 32), and thirdly the two motifs were brought together when "he opened their minds to understand the scriptures" (v. 45).[191] In all these three, the verb is used in the passive form indicating that it was not the disciples by their own ability they were able to open their eyes and mind to see and understand, but that it was divine intervention which enabled them to do so. Plummer notes that "[i]t was by the gift of the Spirit that their minds were opened to understand."[192] A majority of scholars do not recognise the role of the Spirit in enabling the disciples to experience this transformative recognition. Fitzmyer contends that since the Spirit was not yet given, faith in the risen Christ seems to be the hermeneutical key.[193] However, work of the Spirit of God is implicit in the opening of the minds that leads to the formation of a new community of witness.

(vv. 42, 52), witness (v. 48), Holy Spirit (v. 49), Jesus' journey to God (v. 51), and temple (53) being amalgamated in this last section of the Gospel.

188 Pheme Perkins, *Resurrection*, 165.

189 Fitzmyer, *Luke X–XXIV*, 1581.

190 Hendrickx Hermann, Resurrection Narrative, 123.

191 Hendrickx Hermann, Resurrection Narrative, 123.

192 Plummer, *The Gospel According to S. Luke*, 562.

193 Fitzmyer, *Luke X–XXIV*, 1583.

Osborne maintains that the terms the evangelist uses in the commission of the risen Christ such as "repentance" (cf. 5:32; 13:3–4; 15:7–8; 16:30; 17:3–4), "forgiveness of sins" (cf. 1:77; 3:3; 5:17–18; Acts 2:38; 5:31; 10:43) and 'preach' (3:3; 4:18–19, 43–44; 8:39; 9:2; 12:3) virtually sum up Lukan soteriology.[194] Green also opines "repentance" and "forgiveness" are important terms that express the experience of salvation in Acts. Since salvation is offered in the name of Jesus in Acts (Acts 2:21, 36, 38), it is not surprising that the disciples are to proclaim the salvific message in Jesus' name.[195] It is here, the evangelist introduces the role of the disciples as witnesses which they have to take on and play in the third phase of salvation-history.[196] However, there are political overtones in this commissioning that must be noted. To preach repentance and forgiveness of sin "in his name" is to begin a new discourse of power in the name of the one who was crucified by the empire. The commissioning envisions thus a worldwide mission "to all the nations," which implicitly mimics the dominant discourse of the empire. But for Luke, such a mission will be undertaken with the empowerment of the Holy Spirit.[197] Luke draws a direct connection between the role of the disciples as witnesses and their clothing with the Holy Spirit.[198] It is the Holy Spirit who will empower the disciples to witness.[199] Thus, it is equally important to bring out Lukan pneumatology underpinning the ideological position of Luke in the commissioning pericope.

6.4.4. Postcolonial Reading of the Lukan Resurrection Narrative

Lukan resurrection story has to be set in the context of the Roman Empire, as it tells a story of the "strange encounter" of the silenced/supressed group with the crucified Jesus who they hoped was the "prophet messiah" of Israel. A hermeneutical key may perhaps lie in reading or rather listening to this story from the vantage point of postcolonial subjects' struggle for social formation in the context of colonialism and imperialism who rememorates the life and work of those whose life was foreclosed by the violence of the empire. Spivak's notion of "listening to that which lies beyond—that which, from the past affects, the present"—a ghostly encounter which can be called "haunting," as developed by

194 This mission is to be done "in his name" (a Lukan phrase denoting power and authority in mission) "to all nations" (the universal mission) "beginning at Jerusalem" (the origin of the mission, looking forward to Acts 1–5). Each phrase prepares for the launching of the church's mission in Acts (note that the concatenation of "Jerusalem," "witnesses" and "power" occurs again in Acts 1:8, the table of contents for that book). Osborne, "Resurrection," 681.

195 Green, *Gospel of Luke*, 858.

196 Fitzmyer, *Luke X–XXIV*, 1584.

197 A majority of scholars agree that the promise of the Father and the power from on high is unambiguously referring to the Holy Spirit Fitzmyer, *Luke X–XXIV*, 1585; Johnson, *Gospel of Luke*, 403.

198 Shelton, *Mighty in Word*, 116–117.

199 Green, *Gospel of Luke*, 859.

Mayra Rivera in her work *The Touch of Transcendence: A Postcolonial Theology of God*, suggests a possible direction to read the resurrection story from the experience of the suppressed communities.[200] Rivera writes,

> The living victims of totalitarianism have for a long time sought to speak of, to, and with ghosts—of, to, and with those who are no longer—in an effort to welcome a different *porvenir*. They have prayed to be haunted by the ghosts of those who were silenced too soon, whose transcendence was violated, their possible contributions foreclosed. Images of ghosts haunt the literature of subaltern peoples.... These ghosts mark the irruption of the social conscience into the individual and also the call for decisions—for a '*politics of memory*.' These writings depict a peculiar kind of knowledge obtained through unusual kind of perceptions—neither properly seeing nor touching, but somewhat related to both.[201]

Rivera used Derrida's and Spivak's notion of "haunting" which allude to "encounters with 'certain others who are not present, nor presently living, either to us, in us, or outside of us' or 'not yet there ... whether they are already death or not yet born.'"[202] Haunting takes place in a ghostly encounter. Those who are haunted by and speak to the ghost/spirit "recover the things not seen" and lead to transformative recognition. It "disrupts the stability between the 'there' and the 'not there,' between the past and present. By witnessing to the space of the no-longer-living Other, a haunting signals to a not yet. To attend to a possibility not realized is simultaneously to contemplate the possibility of a different future."[203]

Lukan resurrection narrative has a haunting character, in that it destabilises the present by the past opening a future as the disciples encountered the risen Jesus on the third day. However, while Spivak and Rivera speak of haunting in terms of a ghostly encounter, in the case of Lukan narrative, the evangelist tried to dispel the ghostly or spirit's character of Jesus by emphasising the corporeal character of the risen Jesus, although the evangelist seems to fail terribly in this as the risen Jesus appears from nowhere and disappears into the thin air. The corporeal character of the risen Jesus has to be understood as the evangelist's struggle to depict the reality of encounter. Therefore, while the evangelist speaks of the risen Jesus showing himself corporeally, one can also read Lukan appearance-stories as ghostly/spirit's encounter as a "haunting" which seeks to "allow what cannot be voiced or spoken in the present, *to be opened, or reopened*, as that which

200 Mayra Rivera, *The Touch of Transcendence: A Postcolonial Theology of God* (Louisville: Westminster John Knox, 2007).

201 Rivera, *Touch of Transcendence*, 120.

202 Rivera, *Touch of Transcendence*, 119–120.

203 Rivera, *Touch of Transcendence*, 121.

remains ungrasped and unrealized, an approach that is always *yet to be taken*."[204] The third day encounter of the disciples shows "unusual kind of perceptions—neither properly seeing nor touching, but somewhat related to both."[205] Luke apparently insinuates the role of the Spirit in the haunting experience of the disciples, instigating the disciples to remember, burning their hearts within, opening the past to understand the present for future action. Employing "haunt" (of encountering the spirit of colonial victims who refuse to go away from the resistant community) as a hermeneutical lens, a postcolonial reading of Lukan resurrection narrative is offered in the discussion below.

6.4.4.1. The Politics of Remembering in the Story of the Empty Tomb (Luke 24:6, 8)

Lukan story of the empty tomb reports that, on the first day of the week at early dawn some women went with spices to the tomb where Jesus was laid (cf. 23:55) and found the tomb empty. While they were confused with what happened, two men in dazzling clothes stood beside them and announced the Easter proclamation: "Why do you look for the living among the dead? He is not here, but has been raised" (vv. 5b–6).[206] These men charged the women to "remember" (μνήσθητε, v. 6) what Jesus told them while he was in Galilee. They "remembered" his words, and returning from the tomb narrated what they saw to the eleven (v. 9). Some scholars have noted that here what was remembered was Jesus' own prediction of his passion, death and resurrection.[207] μιμνήσκομαι (to remember) is not exclusively a mental process but in a theological sense it calls to mind the saving action of God.[208] Luke uses the word to describe God's saving action (1:54, 72; 23:42). Furthermore, it should be noted that the use of the aorist passive form μιμνήσθητε (v. 6 cf. εμνήσθησαν v. 8) indicates that the women are divinely enabled to remember. Their remembering was then a kind of divine revelation.[209] In the act of remembering, their present frustration/perplexity at the death of their Lord was destabilised by the past memories of what happened to the prophets of old. For Luke this "politics of memory"[210]

---

204 Sara Ahmed, *Strange Encounters: Embodied Others in Post-Coloniality* (London; New York: Routlegde, 2000), 121.

205 Rivera, *Touch of Transcendence*, 120.

206 Markan Easter proclamation goes like this: "Do not be alarmed; you are looking for Jesus of Nazareth, who was crucified. He has been raised; he is not here" (Mark 16:6).

207 Stien, *Luke*, 605. John Nolland, *Luke 18:35–24:53*, WBC 35C (Dallas: Word, 1993), 1190; Green, *Gospel of Luke*, 838.

208 Michel, "μιμνήσκομαι," *TDNT* 4:676.

209 K. H. Bartels, "Remember," *NIDNTT* 3:242; Michel, *TDNT* 4:677. In John 14:26 "reminding" is the work of the Holy Spirit, the paraclete.

210 Memory is constituted by the tension between the past and the present; it is never the past itself. Thus, rememorating is an activity in the present whereby the past is continously modified. Writing about dis/continuities in the cultural memory of colonialism Jeannette Marie Mageo writes, "Much has been forgotten in the memories of colonized and colonizing

awakened the perplexed (v. 4) and terrified (v. 5) women to move to the future witness of a new narrative—the Easter narrative, which concomitantly breaks the cultural stereotyping disdain for women's witness in the first century.[211] This divine transformation of consciousness and the formation of a new subjecthood to witness what they saw points to the work of the Spirit of God.

6.4.4.2. The Haunt of Colonial Victim and the Formation of the Resistant Community

Lukan resurrection narrative has to be read from the vantage point of the community of victims who experience the silencing violence of the empire. Emmaus story is one that narrates the encounter of the two disheartened disciples with the colonial victim Jesus on their way to Emmaus from Jerusalem. They were retreating from the city where Passover festival was celebrated yet ironically with frustration discussing the death of the mighty prophet who they hoped was to redeem Israel. The strange encounter took place on the way to Emmaus where Jesus came near them and went with them (v. 15). But this story has the character of a ghostly haunt or talking with the spirit of the victim(s). Rivera writes, "Those experiences of being faced by something for which there is no concept within our system of thought, or of encountering someone or something out of its proper place or time, have the quality of haunting."[212] While Luke narrates that it was Jesus himself who joined the two wayfarers, they did not see him—"their eyes were kept from recognizing him" (v. 16); when they finally recognised him, he disappeared from their sight (v. 31). Jesus' presence has the character of a ghostly

societies: values, violence, lifeways, personal stories. But colonialism also compelled both parties to this historical experience to construct memories about what had been lost. Everyone involved had a multitude of reasons for redeeming their past in memory, reasons at once moral, political, practical, and personal.... [C]olonial contexts have created discontinuities in cultural memory but also continuities of living tradition." Jeannette Marie Mageo, "Introduction," in *Cultural Memory: Reconfiguring History and Identity in the Postcolonial Pacific* (Honolulu: University of Hawai'i Press, 2001), 8. It is also important to note that postcolonial criticism counteracts the totallising Western view of history with the submerged memory of the colonised that lie beneath the hegemonic narratives of the empire. As Graham Huggan writes, "This postcolonial memory work is by no means necessarily celebratory; rather, much of it involves a sense of deep hurt, resentment, even despair." Graham Huggan, *Interdisciplinary Measures: Literature and the Future of Postcolonial Studies* (Liverpool: Liverpool University Press, 2008), 191. But they are like a Foucauldian counter-memory that counteracts colonial representations "in which the literary text emerges as a powerful medium for the exploration of cultural memory constructed in tension with the hegemonic narrative of the imperial past." Also see Richard Werbner ed., *Memory and the Postcolony: African Anthropology and the Critique of Power* (London: Zed Books, 1998).

211 Cf. Nolland, *Luke 18:35–24:53*, 1193.

212 Rivera, *Touch of Transcendence*, 119.

presence or spirit's presence; it "demands a peculiar perception—not only a way of seeing, but also a way of feeling."[213]

This strange encounter is highly political and ideological, in that it destabilises the present by the past, and opens up a future. The frustrated disciples who were retreating from Jerusalem with a sense of defeat, met the colonial victim Jesus, who emerged from nowhere, burned the hearts, opened the eyes, opened the Scripture to the two disciples, with the stories of the victimised, assuring and empowering them that while the empire still remains, they are not to be disheartened. Luke narrates, "beginning with Moses and all the prophets, he [Jesus] interpreted to them the things about himself in all the scriptures" (v. 27). The mention of Moses and the prophets points to the figures who resisted the empires. "Was it not necessary" (24:26), is not only a Lukan way of pointing to scriptural necessity of the suffering messiah but points to the fate of every prophet who challenges the empire. Listening to the voice of the no longer living draws the two disciples affectively to come to experience "our hearts burning within us" (v. 32). But their affective experience and their decision to go back to Jerusalem did not come as a cold knowledge, but as transformative recognition. As the disciples rememorate the past in their third day encounter with the risen Jesus, their fear, doubt, and indecidability gives way to return to Jerusalem, the place where prophets were killed, to form a resistant community to witness the resurrection of the crucified Jesus.

The third day strange encounter has a pneumatic character, in that it demands not only a way of seeing but also a way of feeling affectively. The haunt of the colonial victim Jesus that burned the hearts of the disciples, opened the Scriptures for understanding, and opened the eyes of the disciples which led to recognising the risen Jesus who was no more but present in their midst can be construed only in terms of the work of the Spirit of God. In describing the process of coming to know the risen Jesus, Luke used the verb *διανοίγω* (to open) in the passive form—*διηνοίχθησαν* (their eyes were opened, v. 31). The use of divine passive indicates not the disciples' abilities to see and understand but the divine enabling them to recognise the risen Jesus. The statement *Οὐχι ἡ καρδία ἡμων καιομένη ἦν ἐν ἡμιν ... ὡς διήνοιγεν ἡμῖν γραφάς*; (Were not our hearts burning ... while he opened the scripture to us? v. 32) is also theologically significant. The use of the divine passive *καίω* (to burn) and *διανοίγω* (to open) points to the work of the Spirit in revealing the meaning of the Scripture. This burning of hearts and opening of the scripture rapturously enables the two disciples to recuperate from their doubts and fears to a new orientation that Jesus is raised. The two disciples returned to Jerusalem and found that the disciples have already gathered. The colonial cross did not have the final say. The coloniser's construction of the colonised subjectivity that the colonial cross would silence them was rendered

213 Rivera, *Touch of Transcendence*, 121.

futile when the disciples' community came out with new a narrative "the Lord had risen indeed" (24:23), and began to signal the continuity of faithful resistance.

6.4.4.3. Clothed with Power: A New Phase of Resistance

The most significant ideological and pneumatological statement in the Lukan resurrection narrative is found in Jesus' words commissioning the disciples: "And that repentance and forgiveness of sins is to be proclaimed in his name to all nations. Beginning from Jerusalem, you are witnesses of these things. And see, I am sending upon you what my father promised; so stay here in the city until you have been clothed with power from on high" (24:47–49). These verses correspond to Acts 1:8 which states, "But you will receive power when the Holy Spirit comes upon you; you will be my witnesses in Jerusalem, in all Judea and Samaria, and to the end of the earth." Here one notes the "universality of the mission" to all the nations beginning from Jerusalem. In the infancy narratives Simeon has already hinted at a worldwide programme of the messiah and told Mary about the coming sufferings and crisis within the chosen people.[214] Now a worldwide mission is explicitly stated to begin from Jerusalem. Lukan emphasis "beginning from Jerusalem" involves a subtle way of a vital transformation of normal orientation about Jerusalem. Luke did not present a centripetal orientation for the universal mission, which actually was the way Jerusalem thought of—the centre to which all nations would come.[215] Lukan mission cartography reversed the centripetal orientation and envisioned instead a centrifugal movement from the centre.[216]

The disciples are instructed to wait in the city until they are clothed with power from on high. The word δύναμις (power) here unmistakably refers to the power of the Holy Spirit as noted earlier (cf. 4:14), and especially in the sequel Acts 1:8 makes clear.[217] The phrase "power from on high" is exegetical to the "promise of the Father" which in Acts 2:33 refers to the Holy Spirit. That the phrase "power from on high" refers to the Holy Spirit can also be inferred from the annunciation scene where the angel said to Mary, "the Holy Spirit will come upon you and the power of the most high will overshadow you" (1:35).[218] For the new phase of resistance, the disciples' community will be empowered by the Spirit of God for the work against the empire. Just as the Spirit of God anointed Jesus for the liberating resistance, the community that formed around Jesus will be clothed with the power of the Spirit of God.

214 Benoit, *Passion and Resurrection*, 331.

215 Cf. Joachim Jeremias, *Jesus' Promise to the Nations* (Philadelphia: Fortress, 1982), 57–62.

216 Green, *Gospel of Luke*, 857.

217 Johnson, *Gospel of Luke*, 403.

218 Johnson, *Gospel of Luke*, 403.

6.5. Conclusion

This chapter attempted to bring out the pneumatological significance of Lukan passion and resurrection narratives. Firstly, it explored the relationship between the Spirit and suffering. And having established the relationship between the Spirit and suffering in the context of Luke's Gospel, an attempt was made to bring out the subversive function of the Spirit in the passion of Lukan Jesus. From the vantage point of postcolonial analysis, it was argued that the Lukan passion narrative is a subversive narrative, which tells the story of a political victim Jesus who defies the rulers and powers and turned the colonial torture into a site of resistance in the power of the Spirit, and thus subverts the validity of the colonial penal liturgy of crucifixion. A pneumatological exploration of this politically subversive narrative reveals that, though Luke did not explicitly mention the Spirit of God in the passion narrative, the empowering presence of the Spirit is implicit in Jesus' resilience in enduring the suffering of colonial torture and execution. This is especially evident in his confident calling on God as "Father" while he was crucified on the cross. Thus, the empowering role of the Spirit should not be solely understood as inspiring prophetic speech or empowering mission. It must be emphasised that the Spirit empowers the suffering ones and victims of the empire to persist with resilience in their engagement with the powers and rulers. It is also noteworthy that calling on God as "Father" is a subversive act that denies the validity of Caesar's claim to fatherhood. But for Luke it is the Spirit that enables Jesus to take such subversive stance. The centurion's declaration adds substance to the subversive story of the passion and death of Jesus.

Secondly, the chapter argues that Lukan resurrection narrative is a subversive narrative that displaces the colonial deterministic construction of reality that places death as the ultimate power. The new narrative of the disciples, "the Lord has risen indeed" (24:34) first announced by two men (angels) at the empty tomb (cf. 24:5), become the counter-narrative to the death-dealing colonial narrative of the crucifixion. For Luke, the formation of this new subjecthood and the concomitant formation of a witnessing community were instigated by divine intervention. In the empty tomb story, the women "remembered" what Jesus told them before and became witnesses to what they saw and heard; in the Emmaus story, the two disciples experienced the divine opening of their mind and eyes and they became witness to the resurrection of Jesus in Jerusalem; and in the Jerusalem appearance, Jesus commissioned the gathered community to become the witnessing community clothed with the Holy Spirit. Just as Jesus was anointed with the Spirit of the Lord at the outset of his public activities, for Luke, the witnessing community will be clothed with power of the Spirit in the new phase of resistance to the empire. In the following chapter, the resistance movement among the Zeliangrong Nagas against the British rule is studied in the light of the Lukan Spirit of resistance against domination and oppression.

Chapter 7

The Spirit in Luke's Gospel and the Resistance Movement Among Zeliangrong Nagas

7.1. Introduction

A postcolonial cultural reading of the Spirit-inspired voices from the margins, the acts of the Spirit-anointed Jesus, and the defiance of the Spirit-anointed Jesus even in the face of the colonial cross illustrate that, it is the Spirit of God that empowers the Spirit of resistance to the people to fight for an alternate world order for survival and representation in the context of colonial domination. This chapter argues that the Spirit of God, that empowers the formation of a community of resistance in Luke's Gospel is active in enabling the social formation of any marginalised groups that stood up against the imperial power for survival and representation. The resistance movement of the Zeliangrong Nagas that emerged in the second quarter[1] of the twentieth century against the British Raj in Nagalim is taken as a case to study the spirit of resistance in the light of Lukan Spirit studied above. The chapter begins with a note on the British imperial formation in the Naga Hills with special attention to how it dislocated the land and the people of Zeliangrong Nagas. It is followed by an historical analysis of the resistance movement and an appraisal of the resistance movement in the light of the Spirit in Luke's Gospel.

1 The resistance movement among the Zeliangrong Nagas that emerged in the second quarter of the twentieth century has a long historical trajectory. This study is limited to the British colonial period, that is, the beginning of the movement with Jadonang in the mid 1920s to the arrest and imprisonment of Gaidinliu in the early 1930s.

7.2. The British Empire and the Zeliangrong Nagas

7.2.1. Native Settings, Colonial Realpolitik and Manoeuverings

The Zeliangrong Nagas,[2] (also called the Luangdimai) which included the Rongmei, Liangmei, and Zeme Nagas, under the leadership of Jadonang and, later Gaidinliu until the latter's arrest in 1932, made an attempt to assert the identity of the people as a politically independent people during the British colonial rule in the second quarter of the twentieth century. The movement has to be seen in the light of the wider colonial formations in Assam, Manipur, and Nagaland, since the Zeliangrongs are fragmented into these three political adminstration by the colonial cartography.

The First Anglo-Burmese War that ended with the Treaty of Yandaboo (1826) was a milestone for British gradual consolidation of its power over Assam, Manipur, and the Naga Hills.[3] The Manipur State and the British Empire forged closely from 1762 to 1891 for their own imperialistic interests,[4] including the joint

2 Zeliangrong is an acronym of the first syllables of Zeme, Liangmai and Rongmei (Ze+Liang+Rong) coined in 1947. See Gangmumei Kamei, *The History of Zeliangrong Nagas: From Makhel to Rani Gaidinliu* (Guwahati: Spectrum Publications, 2004), 10–11. However, it is important to note that in the archives of Zeliangrong history, British writers and later writers have dominantly employed "Kacha Nagas" to mean the Zeme and Liangmai (Zeliang) and "Kabui" to refer to the Rongmei and Inpui (Puimei). J. H. Hutton, *The Angami Nagas with Some Notes on Neighbouring Tribes* (London: Macmillan, 1921; repr, The Government of Nagaland, 1969), 351–352; Robert Reid, *History of the Frontier Areas Bordering on Assam: From 1883–1941* (Delhi: Eastern Publishing House, 1983); C. A. Soppitt, "A Short Account of the Kachcha Naga (Empeo) Tribe in the North Chachar Hills, 1885," in *The Nagas in the Nineteenth Century*, ed. Verrier Elwin (London: Oxford University Press, 1969). Also see Kamei, *Zeliangrong Nagas*, 10–13. It is noted that some early British writers used the term "Koupooes/Koupui/Kowpoi" to refer to Zeme, Rongmei and Inpui. For instance, R. Boileau Pemberton, *Report on the Eastern Frontier of British India* (Guahati: Department of Historical and Antiquarian Studies in Assam, [1935] 1966), 17 cf. Elungkiebe Zeliang, *Charismatic Movements in the Baptist Churches in North East India: A Zeliangrong Perspective* (Delhi: ISPCK), 3. The Zeliangrongs Nagas inhabits in a geographically contiguous area but are politically divided into three states such as Assam, Manipur and Nagaland. The land of the Zeliangrongs includes the present Peren district Nagaland, Tamenlong district and part of Senapati district Manipur, and part of Dima-Hasao (Halflong) district Assam.

3 Asoso Yonuo, *The Rising Nagas: A Historical and Political Study* (Delhi: Vivek Publishing House, 1974), 69.

4 Konthoujam Indrakumar, "Colonialism and Movement for Democracy in Manipur," in *Colonialism and Resistance: Society and State in Manipur*, eds. Arambam Noni and Kangujam Sanatomba (New Delhi: Routledge, 2016), 57 writes "Manipur needed friendly diplomatic relations with the British to protect its sovereignty against Burmese invasion and to keep itself in good with the British. On the other side, British alliance with Manipur was essential to advance and protect her imperial interests, both political and commercial in her colonies in Burma and Assam."

expedition into the Naga Hills in the 1830s.[5] However, owing to the truncated initial expeditions into the Naga Hills, the British largely followed a policy of non-interference till 1866 except setting up an administrative headquarter at Asalu/Asaloo (a Zeme village, situated in the North Cachar Hills) sub-division under Nowgong district in 1852 to look after the Naga administered areas.[6] Strictly speaking, the British considered the annexation of the Naga Hills to the empire as a "civilising mission." But this civilising scheme was bent on cultural imperialism and the exploitation of natural resources from the Naga Hills.[7]

Civilising mission was strongly intended by the colonisers particularly to tackle the menace of Angami Nagas who continuously raided the British subjects in North Cachar Hills. In 1866, it was proposed that the British assert its hegemony over the Angami Nagas and "gradually reclaim them from habits of lawlessness to those of order and civilization."[8] Thus, in 1866 the British shifted the administrative headquarter at Asalu to Chumukedima (then called Sumagooting) and created the Naga Hills district. The British made headway into the heartland of Angami Nagas and in 1881 Kohima was made the new chief administrative centre and Naga Hills came under the direct control of the British.[9] After the British established the Naga Hills headquarter in Kohima, it was a matter of time to bring the other Naga tribes under its control. It is striking how the American Baptist missionaries viewed *pax Britannica* in the Naga Hills as preparing the way for a favourable mission era.[10] When Ao area was annexed to the Naga Hills district of Assam in 1890, Mary Mead Clark wrote, "From 1876 we had lived in this land of hostilities without the protection of a Christian government.... Now, earnest prayers of years were answered, and these mountain

---

5 For a brief account of the joint military expeditions of the British and Manipur into the Naga Hills and the subsequent British annexation of Naga Hills see Yonuo, *Rising Nagas*, 70–106.

6 Hokishe Sema, *Emergence of Nagaland: Socio-Economic and Political transformation and the Future* (New Delhi: Vikas Publishing House, 1986), 241.

7 John Thomas, *Evangelising the Nations: Religion and the Formation of Naga Political Identity* (New Delhi: Routledge, 2016), 20.

8 Alexander Mackenzie, *History of the Relations of the Government with the Hill Tribes of the North-East Frontier of Bengal* (New Delhi: Mittal Publications, [1884] 2007), 119.

9 Mackenzie, *North-East Frontier*, 122–144.

10 Sydney Rivenburg, an American Baptist missionary who came and settled in Kohima in 1886 wrote: "After a generation of warfare and savage strife, the government of India unfurled the peace commanding British flag over this Angami country and established a cantonment and civil government in the heart of the tribe at Kohima. The presence of a regiment of infantry and five hundred armed police indicated that the day of peace was at hand and of all points among the Nagas this appeared the most favourable for missionary labour." See S. W. Rivenburg, "Historical Sketch of Angami Naga Mission," Papers and Discussions of Jubilee Conference Held in Nowgong, 18–19 December 1886:85 cited by Thomas, *Evangelising the Nations*, 22–23.

paths, so long tracked by cruelty and blood, were open for the coming of the messengers of the prince of peace."[11]

The Nagas colonial encounter also involved the relations between the British Empire and Manipur state. The First Anglo-Burmese War enabled the liberation of Manipur from the Burmese force. Following the Treaty of Yandaboo (1826), the British Political Agent to the Manipur state was appointed in 1835 that marked the beginning of British control over Manipur.[12] The initial alliance of the British and Manipur resulted in the former manoeuvring the internal affairs of the latter through the Political Agent. Owing to an internal dissension among the ruling house, there was a "palace revolution" in September 1890.[13] The British tried to take advantage of this situation and called for a state "*Darbar*" (conference) with the punitive intention to arrest the rebel leader and appoint the Political Agent as the chief advisor to the king.[14] When the *Darbar* failed, the British troops made a vain attempt to capture the royal palace in which many British officers succumbed.[15] Subsequently, in March 1981 there was a full scale Anglo-Manipuri War in which the Manipuri state was defeated. But the "British kept the state under its suzerainty without directly annexing it."[16] Thus, the Naga Hills in Manipur came under the direct control of the British Empire.

As the real power shifted to the British, the missionaries became the civilising agents who not only converted the Nagas but also helped the colonial government to collect census and recruit the Nagas and Kukis for labour corps in the wake of the First World War.[17] In the aftermath of the First World War (1914–1918) and the Kuki Revolt (1917–1919),[18] the British created more sub-divisions to rule effectively the Nagas areas.[19] In 1919, Tamenglong (the biggest Zeliangrong village in Manipur) was made the Headquarter of the North West

11 Mary Mead Clark, *A Corner in India* (Philadelphia: American Baptist Publication Society, 1907), 126–127.

12 Indrakumar, "Colonialism and Movement for Democracy," 57.

13 Md. Badar Ruddin, "Anglo-Manipuri War, 1891," in *Manipur: Past and Present*, vol. 1, *History Polity and Law*, ed. Naorem Sanajaoba (Delhi: Mittal Publications, 1988), 113–124.

14 Jyotirmoy Roy, *The History of Manipur* (Calcutta: K. L. Mukhopadhayay, 1958), 128.

15 Roy, *History of Manipur*, 134–137; Ruddin, "Anglo-Manipuri War, 1891," 124–126.

16 Indrakumar, "Colonialism and Movement for Democracy," 58.

17 Thomas, *Evangelising the Nations*, 26.

18 The Kuki rebellion was an initial symptom of anti-colonial resistance against the British rule. In the wake of World War I, when the British government orders the recruitment of Labour Corps for France, the Kukis stirred a rebellion against the British in Manipur and Burma. The government took more than a year to crush the rebellion. Roy, *History of Manipur*, 150–151; Yonuo, *The Rising Nagas*, 124.

19 The Northeast Sub-division at Ukhrul, North-West Sub-division at Tamenlong, and the South-West Sub-division at Churachandpur. Gangmumei Kamei, *Zeliangrong Nagas*, 125.

Sub-Division to administer the Zeliangrongs with William Shaw as the first Sub-Divisional Officer (SDO).[20]

Gangmumei Kamei writes, "The British did not have a separate policy towards the Zeliangrongs as such; but their general policy greatly affected them as the Zeliangrong constituted major segments of the territory and population of North Cachar, Naga Hills and Manipur, a tract, a district, and a kingdom."[21] The colonial cartography greatly fragmented the Zeliangrongs. When the Naga Hills district was created in 1866, twenty-three Zeliangrong villages were parcelled out to the Naga Hills district Samagooting, while a major portion of Asalu region was merged with Cachar district administered from Silchar.[22] When the British superseded the Manipur state, the Zeliangrongs in Manipur came under the British rule in Manipur. The annexation of North Cachar Hills in 1854, Naga Hills in 1866, and Manipur in 1891 to the British rule brought all the Zeliangrongs under the British rule but in three different administrative headquarters making the Zeliangrong a minority in all these three political administration.[23]

While the colonial settlement in the Naga Hills was an afterthought of political expediency to end the Naga raids against the British subjects in the plains, the colonial maneuverings in the Zeliangrong lands had already begun by the second quarter of the nineteenth century when the British and the Manipur kings took advantage of the Kukis migrations towards the North Cachar Hills, Manipur, and Naga Hills. In the 1830s, the British Captain Pemberton also wrote about the Kukis migration towards the North Cachar Hills, north-west Manipur, and Naga Hills.

> From the account of Kupooee [Zeliangrong] tribe it appears certain that, the Kookies [Kukis] had been gradually advancing for years in the northerly direction, and have hitherto established themselves on the ranges which were originally occupied by more northern tribes, or committed such fearful aggressions upon the latter, as to compel them to retire and leave an unoccupied tract between themselves and these formidable opponents.[24]

Vibha J. Patel quotes a 1929 observation of William Shaw of the Assam Civil Service: "The Thadous (Kukis) who moved up most of the Barak river were utilised by the Sirkar against the Angamis. Those who came up along the hills between the Barak river [*sic*] and the valley of Manipur were similarly used by

20 Gangmumei Kamei, *Zeliangrong Nagas*, 139. Elungkiebe Zeliang, *Charismatic Movements*, 15.

21 Gangmumei Kamei, *Zeliangrong Nagas*, 71.

22 Gangmumei Kamei, *Zeliangrong Nagas*, 73, 124.

23 Hokishe Sema, *Emergence of Nagaland*, 242.

24 Pemberton, *Report on the Eastern Frontier of British India*, 17.

the Raja of Manipur placing them among the Kacha Nagas, while those on the hills were used as a barrier against the Burmese."[25] Jyotirmoy Roy claims that the British political agent McCulloh even extended monetary help to the Kukis from "his own pocket."[26] During the year 1851–1852, about 8000 Kukis invaded the Zeliangrong lands with the British sponsoring firearms and ammunitions to ward off the Nagas and the Lushais who often raided the tax paying subjects in the valley.[27] The Kukis' migration towards Cachar, Manipur and Naga Hills and later, sponsored by the colonial realpolitik over the nineteenth century created much tension over the land between the Kukis and Nagas. However, the colonial state took advantage of this conflict to enhance its control over the hill tracts and the people. The British used the Kukis against the Nagas when they rebelled and vice versa. Thomas writes, "Kukis were used to suppress the rebellion of 1879–80 among the Angamis, and many of the Nagas who had just returned after serving as labour corps in France during the First World War were used to suppress the Kuki rebellion of 1917–19."[28] Thomas continued, "Located within this larger history of conflict, the Kuki rebellion, while being against the British rule and the Manipuri kingdom, also the attack on Nagas, especially the Zeliangrongs."[29] But the Manipur colonial administration did not come to defend the Zeliangrongs but ignored the request of the people for protection as though it was a tribal war between the Zeliangrong Nagas and the Kukis. It was only with the intervention of the Assam Rifles the Kuki Revolt was suppressed in the Zeliangrong area.[30] The time was ripe for any agitation or even a movement. In the mid 1920s Jadonang came to the scene with the idea of an alternative kingdom.

7.2.2. Land Crisis, Imperial Taxation, and Colonisation of the Commons

Zeliangrong economy is land based and dominantly agricultural. The entire village area is demarcated into three categories: family land, clan land and the land that belong to the commons. Accordingly, apart from the household plots in the village, each household owns a field for cultivation and forestry for firewood.[31] Thus, when the British and Manipur state-sponsored Kuki settlement contracted

25 Cited by Vibha J. Patel, "Naga and Kuki? Who is to be Blamed?" *Economic and Political Weekly* 29 (1994): 1331. http://www.jstor.org/stable/4401261?seq=1#page_scan_tab_contents access on 7 November 2016. (1331–1332).

26 Roy, *History of Manipur*, 89.

27 Asoso Yonuo, *Nagas Struggle Against the British Rule Under Jadonang and Rani Gaidinliu 1925–1947* (Kohima: Leno Printing Press, 1982), 11.

28 Thomas, *Evangelising Nations*, 64.

29 Thomas, *Evangelising Nations*, 64. Gangmumei Kamei, *Zeliangrong Nagas*, 133 writes, "The Kuki Rebellion was anti imperial and anti monarchical. But their anti Naga military operation opened up a new front to fight and it proved to be disastrous for them."

30 Gangmumei Kamei, *Zeliangrong Nagas*, 138–139.

31 Elungkiebe Zeliang, *Charismatic Movements*, 12.

available land for cultivation in the Zeliangrong areas, it created tension between the Zeliangrongs and Kukis and also resentment against the colonial powers. Gangmumei Kamei writes,

> The land and forest which was once used by the Zeliangrong only now become shared by two the other being the Kuki settlers. The productivity of the land also decreased, and the rotation of the *jhum* cycle also decreased. Moreover, the Kuki polity controlled by their hereditary chiefs was autocratic. Their attachment was transitory while the Zeliangrong attachment to their village was deep, strong and emotional. There was not enough land for the two. The Zeliangrong Nagas blamed the Meitei kings and the British for this land encroachment.[32]

The imposition of heavy monetary imperial taxation and the demand for free and forced labour constituted the harsher physical experience of the Zeliangrong Nagas' colonial encounter. According to Gangmumei Kamei, prior to the coming of the British rule, in 1735 the Manipuri kings had already started imposing a tribute or feudal service known as *lallup* service upon the hill tribes.[33] In 1892, the Political Agent of Manipur abolished the *lallup* service and introduced a house tax of rupees three for the hills.[34] Gangmumei Kamei writes, "The *Lallup* service was abolished and replaced by the hill house tax of Rupee [*sic*] three per house. But during the colonial period, forced labour, and compulsory financial contribution to give hospitality to the touring official of the State were imposed and they were more troublesome than the *Lallup*."[35] This means that there were three forms of taxation. Firstly, the hills house tax of rupees three.[36] Secondly, forced labour that required the villagers to render free labour service for the construction and maintenance of road.[37] Thirdly, a subscription fee was collected to meet the cost of feeding colonial officials (*Pothan Senkhai*) who passed through the villages.[38] Furthermore, the British colonial masters imposed free porterage service (*Pothang Bekari*) upon the people for the transportation of all colonial agents. Since the road that connects various British colonial headquarters passed through the Zeliangrong villages, the people living beside the road were the victims of forced

32 Gangmumei Kamei, Zeliangrong Nagas, 146.

33 Gangmumei Kamei, *Zeliangrong Nagas*, 125.

34 Reid, *History of the Frontier Areas Bordering on Assam*, 73.

35 Gangmumei Kamei, *Zeliangrong Nagas*, 125–126.

36 D. P. Mukherjee, P. Gupta and N. K. Das, "The Zeliangrong or Haomei Movement," in *Tribal Movements in India*, vol. 1, ed. K. S. Singh (New Delhi Manohar, 1982), 69.

37 Mukherjee, Gupta and Das, "The Zeliangrong or Haomei Movement," 68–69.

38 Yonuo, *Naga Struggle Against British Rule*, 59.

labour.[39] The British employed colonial agents called the *dobashis/lambus*[40] who were basically peons or bearers in status but gained a lot of power as they collected taxes, by force if necessary from the villagers.[41] The *lambus/dobashis* and road *muhorrirs* at the village level represented the colonial rule. They were oppressive in their dealing with the people and abused the people subjecting them to flogging during road repairs.[42]

To add to the woes of the people there was also colonisation of the commons. The colonial administration regulated forest laws so that the people can no longer exploit the bamboos and trees from the forest regulated by the colonial authorities.[43] Forest laws also negatively impacted the customary hunting and fishing rights. The colonisation of the commons put a severe constraint on the rights of the people for use of common land for cultivation. Thus, the colonial land policy that contracted the land of the commons created resentment all over the hills of Manipur and especially in Zeliangrong lands.

7.2.3. Civilising Discourse, Religion, and Hybridity

Colonialism and Christianity went hand in hand in the Naga Hills. Evidences from the colonial archives as early as 1840 suggest both the British and the American Baptist missionaries took interest to civilise the Nagas with Christianity.[44] Based on the colonial archives, Piketo Sema argues that the early introduction of Christianity in the Naga Hills was aimed at forestalling the onslaught of Hinduism in the Naga Hills, which had already got a foothold in Assam and Manipur.[45]

39 The Cachar road that connects the Manipur valley and Cachar via Bishnupur, Khaupum, Nungba, Kala Naga (Oinamlong) and Jirighat was a highway crucial to the interests of Manipur and British. After 1891, the British impose their rule over the hills and did not allow the Raja and Manipur State Darbar to extend their rule over the hills. Gangmumei Kamei, *Zeliangrong Nagas*, 124.

40 Dobashis/lambus are interpreters or translators who acts as intermediaries between the government and the villages.

41 Mukherjee, Gupta and Das, "The Zeliangrong or Haomei Movement," 68.

42 John Thomas, *Evangelising the Nation*, 63.

43 Gangmumei Kamei, *Zeliangrong Nagas*, 146.

44 For instance, Miles Bronson (an American Baptist missionary to the Nocte Nagas who in 1840 established a mission centre in the low hills south to Sibsagar district in Assam) wholeheartedly supported the British to bring the Nocte Nagas under the direct control of the British. He suggested that the colonial government should initiate "to get hold of the Nagas and to make them feel a sort of dependence upon them for livelihood, and particularly for the administration of all their internal affairs. I see nothing that is likely to prevent their improvement in civilization at least as their perfect independence of feeling." Letter from Miles Bronson to Francis Jenkins, 22 July 1840, Foreign Department, Political, No 82, 9 November 1840, National Archives of India, New Delhi cited by John Thomas, *Evangelising the Nation*, 19.

45 Piketo Sema, *British Policy and Administration in Nagaland 1881–1947* (New Delhi: Scholars' Publishing House, 1992), 65.

Piketo Sema quotes a letter from a certain Captain Gordon to Captain Jenkins, agent to the Governor General, North-East Frontier Agency dated to 1940.

> *The establishment of the Thanah will afford a favourable opportunity for the introduction of missionaries who will probably, soon after-wards, be able to commence their labours in adjoining village, I think it of consequence that the missionaries should be early in the field as the hill tribes in this part of the world are apt to follow Hidoo [sic] customs and observances.* (*For. Deptt. Pol-A*, August 1840, no. 93).[46]

It can also be noted that John Butler who entered the Naga areas in Assam (i.e. among the Kacha Nagas) in 1845 commented that Christianity would fast dispel the "darkness and ignorance that now overshadow the land," and "our rule will prove a blessing to these benighted tribes, who henceforth enjoy the fruit of their labours in peace and prosperity."[47] In 1890s James Johnstone, the British officer stationed at Samagooting considered Chritianising the Nagas a boon for the British interest. He thought that the Angami "Nagas had no religion" and that making them a "Christian tribe" would "occupy a most useful position on our Eastern Frontier," but failing which they might follow Hinduism or Islam and become "a constant source of trouble and annoyance."[48]

Notably, Edward Clark, the American Baptist Missionary at Sibsagar had already taken up residence in Ao area in 1876 following his first visit to the area in 1872, which was largely made possible with the aid of the British. In 1880, the American Baptist missionary C. D. King opened a mission field in Kohima following the crushing of Angami revolt against the British and the establishment of Kohima as the British new headquarter. So also in the Naga Hills of Manipur, in 1895 the British allowed William Pettigrew to set up a mission station in Ukhrul who was later supported by the American Baptist Missionary Union. Following the crushing of the Kuki revolt (1917–1919), the Christian missionaries were given land to set up a mission centre at Kangpokpi. It is from the noted mission stations, Christianity penetrated into the interior areas of the Nagas. But, it must be noted that from the beginning the collusion of British colonialism and Christian mission had an ethnographic prejudice, in that the introduction of Christianity was seen by the British "to be a *sine-quo-non* for the upliftment of the Nagas, a society which they considered to be not only backward but also uncivilized."[49]

---

46 Piketo Sema, *British Policy and Administration in Nagaland 1881–1947*, 65.

47 John Butler, "Travels and Adventures in the Province of Assam, 1855, pages 66–70" in *The Nagas in the Nineteenth Century*, ed. Verrier Elwin (Oxford: Oxford University Press, 1969), 594–595.

48 James Johnstone, *My Experiences in Manipur and the Naga Hills* (London: Sampson Law, Marston & Company, 1896), 43.

49 Piketo Sema, *British Policy and Administration in Nagaland 1881–1947*, 67.

The interface of Christianity and the Zeliangrong traditional religion did not go very well with strong resistance from the latter against the former. But the inroad of Christianity in the Zeliangrong land fomented not only the clash of two religions but propelled the reformation of the Zeliangrong traditional religion, which unlike Christianity was plagued by many superstitious beliefs and practices. The growth of Christianity was apparently slow among the Zeliangrong Nagas, but it had come to stay.[50] The question was how to respond to this colonial religion?

According to John Thomas, Baptist Christianity was not the only religion pitching up its tent in the hill tract of Manipur; the Manipur kings had also sent Hindu missionaries to the hills to which the political agent of British administration complied with certain conditions.[51] He observes that it is not clear "to what extent the Hindu missionary activities were effective at all in the hill tracts. However, the fact that there were attempts towards this direction from the part of the Manipur Rajah during this period cannot be denied."[52] And based on this position he argues that Christianity and Hinduism with its canons of doctrine ready to evangelise the hill tribes threatened the existing traditional religion.

> The effects that the coming of Christianity had on villages and tribes where there has been conversions was all too familiar, and the pressing question for many would have been how one was to protect and reform the existing indigenous belief system and ceremonial practices as per the necessities of the changing material and cultural circumstances.[53]

On the other hand, it is not only the threat of an invading foreign religion that was a matter of concern; the traditional religion as practiced at that time had become a burden for the people with many superstitious beliefs and practices. Commenting on the Zeliangrong traditional religion of Jadonang's time Gangmumei Kamei writes, "Religion became a mere performances of sacrifices and propitiation of spirits and observance of gennas[54] [*sic*] ranging from the birth

---

50 From the early 1920's conversion to Christianity among the Zeliangrong in Manipur had begun in and around Tamenglong. Through the evangelism of local missionaries, Kaikao Baptist Church was established in 1924, which became the first Zeliangrong church in Tamenglong district, Manipur. However the people reacted negatively to the intrusion of a new religion and the then SDO of Tamenglong ordered the Christians to leave the village. Elungkiebe Zeliang, *Charismatic Movements*, 48. In Tamenglong, the number of Christians grew and they constructed their own village, which although remain a part of the village and built the church in 1930. However, there was much opposition and the church was destroyed. F. S. Downs, *The Mighty Works of God* (Guwahati: Christian Literature Centre, 1971), 176–177.

51 Thomas, *Evangelising the Nation*, 66.

52 Thomas, *Evangelising the Nation*, 66.

53 Thomas, *Evangelising the Nation*, 67.

54 *Genna* means taboo. The word is popularly used in the literature of/about the Nagas.

of a child, a piglet, puppy, or hatching of chicken, a kite and crow sitting over the roof, a dog climbing the low roofs, burning of house, earthquake, a still born child, death of women who died at delivery, dead by drowning, hanging etc."[55] The people were also aware of the tensions and conflicts Christianity was causing among the other tribes and villages around.

It was in this religio-cultural upheaval, Jadonang a seer from Puilan (Kambiron) undertook the project of reforming religious beliefs system, culture and "integrating it with the immediate material and political need of the (Zeliangrong) Nagas."[56] But the reform was a hybridisation of Christianity and Hinduism into the mould of Zeliangrong Nagas. Looking at the larger canvas of the intrusion of imperial religion and political power over the land and the people, the religious reformation was undertaken a means for the religio-political formation of the people. Jadonang's life was foreclosed too soon and the mantle of leadership of the movement fell on the young girl Gaidinliu. The historical trajectories of the movement under Jadonang and Gaidinliu are in order.

7.3. The Resistance Movement Among Zeliangrong Nagas Against the British Empire

7.3.1. Resistance Movement Under Jadonang (1905–1931)

Jadonang was born in an ordinary peasant family at Puiluan village (called Kambiron by the Meiteis) in 1905.[57] In his formative years, he was much exposed to the changing contours of economic, political and cultural landscape of his people under the colonial administration. As his village lay on the Cachar-Imphal road, he had seen large numbers of travellers, sepoys, colonial agents, and *coolies* who carried the baggage of colonial agents passing through his village.[58] He had witnessed his own brother carrying the baggage of the Manipur and the British officials. The Kuki Revolt (1917–1919) did not affect Puiluan village but Jadonang would have certainly seen the movement of sepoys during the Kuki revolt when he was in his teens.[59] The experience of seeing the subservience and powerlessness of his people to colonial authorities would have deeply impacted the young Jadonang to mobilise his people for freedom.

From his adolescent life, Jadonang was acknowledged as a dream interpreter and mystic healer-physician. He is said to have often gone into trance and talked with God, and it was during such occasions he received a revelation to heal the

55 Gangmumei Kamei, *Zeliangrong Nagas*, 148.

56 Thomas, *Evangelising the Nation*, 67.

57 Gangmumei Kamei, *Zeliangrong Nagas*, 147, dates Jadonang birth in 1905 but John Thomas, *Evangelising the Nations*, 67 has dated Jadonang's birth in 1895. John Thomas is dependent on Gangmumei Kamei's work, but he did not give the reason why Jadonang's birth should be dated ten years earlier.

58 Gangmumei Kamei, *Zeliangrong Nagas*, 147; Thomas, *Evangelising the Nation*, 67.

59 Gangmumei Kamei, *Zeliangrong Nagas*, 147.

various sicknesses and problems people faced. Subsequently, he became recognised by the people as a *muh* (a spiritual guide and healer).[60] The political agent J. C. Higgins called him a *Maiba* (shamans). Ursula Graham Bower described him as the "seer of Kambiron" and this seemed the most appropriate one.[61] In one of his dream divinations, he was taken to the cave of Bhuban hills of North Cachar and there the God Bisnu appeared to him.[62] Bhuban caves then became a sacred place for Jadonang (and his followers) and he made frequent pilgrimages to the cave. Jadonang then travelled extensively to the Zeliangrong villages, healing the sick, interpreting dreams and so on. Soon he became very popular among the people.[63]

During his extensive travels to the North Cachar Hills, the western hill tracts of Manipur and the south-east areas of the Naga Hills, Jadonang become more conscious of the numerous problems the people faced under the colonial rule: heavy taxation, forced labour, the ill-attitude of the British and Meitei government officials, and the growing insecurity over the land.[64] By the mid-1920s, Jadonang began preparations to launch a religious, cultural and political campaign to counter the project of colonialism that "either tended to freeze the culture and religion of the colonised, and reduce it to museum pieces as many colonial officials and anthropologists were prone to do; or to undermine it, and subject it to the 'civilising' instincts of the coloniser as many missionaries were eager to do."[65] Jadonang often visited the Bhuban caves as the sacred place of revelation that provided him legitimation to his activities. His initial activity was reforming the Zeliangrong religious practices. It is striking that the reformed religion was a hybridization of Christianity and Hinduism into the traditional religious universe of the Zeliangrongs.[66] While the reformed religion contained traces of the tenets of Christianity and Hinduism, the resistant adaptation shifted the authority of colonial religion, creating a space for the Zeliangrong to re-present its own faith and practices. The reformed religion placed a central importance to the worship of the Supreme creator and dissuaded the people from giving too much emphasis to the lesser gods and spirits.[67] The reformed religion abolished trivial taboos, sacrifices and *genna*-ridden observances and emphasised on worship

60 Gangmumei Kamei, *Zeliangrong Nagas*, 147–148.

61 Ursula Graham Bower, *Naga Path* (London: Readers Union, 1952), 41.

62 The Zeliangrong God Bisnu is not the Hindu God Vishnu. He is also known as Munchanu, Bonchanu, Buisnu, Bisnu. In the Bhuban hills there is also a temple of Hindu God Mahadev constructed by the Rajas of Tripura. Gangmumei Kamei, *Zeliangrong Nagas*, 148.

63 Yunuo, *Naga Struggle Against British Rule*, 56–57; Gangmumei Kamei, *Zeliangrong Nagas*, 147–149.

64 Thomas, *Evangelising the Nation*, 68.

65 Thomas, *Evangelising the Nation*, 68.

66 For a concise descriptive account of Jadonang's reform see, Elungkiebe Zeliang, *Charismatic Movements*, 33.

67 Yunuo, *Naga Struggle Against British Rule*, 46–47.

and prayer. To this end he constructed temples (four altogether) at Kambiron, Kekru, Nungkao (Gaidinliu's village) and Bikanandi. He also composed hymns and dances.[68] Jadonang even invented a new script and used it to write down songs and his thoughts. And he had written once to the then Sub-Divisional Officer S. J. Duncan but the latter tore it into pieces as nonsense with contempt.[69]

While to the colonisers it looked as though Jadonang was fooling the superstitious minds of his people for his self-aggrandizement, the ultimate aim of Jadonang was to form a counter discourse to the colonial discourse of power that would enable the people to drive out the colonisers and carve out a political space that the people can call their own—the Naga Raj or *Makam Gwangdi*.[70] John Thomas writes,

> In this new political space, people would neither have to pay house tax nor provide free labour and food to the visiting government officers; all the *lambus*, the government officers and others who took advantage of the people would be expelled from the region; none would have to shut their opened umbrellas or remove their headgear or caps before a British official as a show of subservience and respect; and Nagas would once again be free to decide upon their destiny.

Beginning in the mid 1920s Jadonang begin to mobilise a resistance movement from among the common people to resist the colonial rule. To construct an alternative political narrative to colonial rule, Jadonang made use of an age-old prophecy that was prominent among the Angamis about a "king" who is sleeping in a cave in North Cachar, and who would return one day to oust the British rule and rule over "all who eat from the wooden platter" (referring to the Nagas). J. H. Hutton had already documented this prophecy in a chapter "Folklore—Angami Superstitions, Traditions, Legends 'Contes'—Songs" in his work *The Angami Nagas with Some Notes on Neighbouring Tribes* (1921),[71] much earlier to the emergence of the resistance movement among the Zeliangrong Nagas. In the words of Hutton, "There is a belief in Khonoma and other Angami villages in the return of a king who will drive out the British and rule over 'all who eat from the wooden platter,' i.e., all Nagas. This king is believed to be sleeping, as Barbarossa sleeps, in a cave in Kacha Naga country (North Cachar)."[72] Hutton maintains that the origin of this prophecy is to be traced to either the Kacha Nagas (Zeliangrong Nagas) or the Kacharis.[73]

68 Gangmumei Kamei, *Zeliangrong Nagas*, 149.

69 Yunuo, *Naga Struggle Against British Rule*, 58.

70 Thomas, *Evangelising the Nation*, 72.

71 Hutton, *The Angami Nagas*.

72 Hutton, *The Angami Nagas*, 252. This prophecy is cited in many scholars who have studied or written about the resistance movement among the Zeliangrong Nagas.

73 Hutton, *The Angami Nagas*, 252.

In 1928, Jadonang popularised this prophecy.[74] He proclaimed that the British colonial rule will soon come to an end and a new kingdom *Makam Gwangdi* or Naga Raj (as understood by the colonial officials) will be established where the people will no longer be subjected to colonial rule but live in perpetual prosperity.[75] In the context where other nationalities had their own kings and kingdoms Jadonang popularised the concept of *Makam Gwangdi* in a nationalistic fervour. He said to the people, as accounted by Gangmumei Kamei,

> The Meiteis have their king, the Indian (Tajongmai) have their rulers, why should we not have our own king? The white men and we are all human beings. Why should we be afraid of them? All men are equal. We are blessed people. Our days have come. Our powerful weapons are kept hidden by God at Zeilad. We shall pray and worship God. With his grace we shall become the rulers.[76]

According to Gangmumei Kamei, though the concept of the Raj was new to the Nagas, it was "a fresh idea and attractive to his people who had been oppressed, persecuted and victimised by the alien rulers."[77] Apparently, Jadonang became restive towards the colonial officials and the agents such as the *lambus* and the *muhorrirs*. The *lambus* and the *muhorrirs* reported to the colonial administrative headquarter about the rumours of Jadonang's claim as king. Jadonang was then arrested (on 6 December, 1928) and the SDO interrogated and also ordered that he be imprisoned for a week. However, because of the pressure and restlessness of the people, he was released after three days on the condition that Jadonang would stop seditious political activities and limit himself to religious activities.[78] The imprisonment and release provided an aura of Jadonang's popularity since it showed the helplessness colonial officials against him. His name spread across the Zeliangrong country and even beyond.

74 Some scholars claim that, Jadonang appropriated the prophecy and claimed for himself as the promised messiah. Bower, *Naga Path*, 42; Yunuo, *The Rising Nagas*, 127; Elungkiebe, *Charismatic Movements*, 151. But it is not clear whether he really claimed himself to be the messiah king of the prophecy. Any claim to kingship by anyone would not find receptive ears to the Zeliangrong who were accustomed to a democratic village polity of gerontocracy. Moreover, according to Gangmumei Kamei, *Zeliangrong Nagas*, 152, 155, Jadonang denied any claim to kingship or demand of tributes when the British colonial officers interrogated him after his arrest, although he noted that the Angamis considered Jadonang's appeal to the forge alliance against the British Raj but refused to join Jadonang on the basis that it would make no sense of freedom if they come under the suzerainty of Jadonang (152) cf. John Thomas, *Evangelisng the Nations*, 80. But this could still be the perception of the others about Jadonang rather than an actual claim made by Jadonang himself.

75 Gangmumei Kamei, *Jadonang*, 31.

76 Gangmuei Kamei, *Zeliangrong Nagas*, 150; John Thomas, *Evangelising the Nation*, 73.

77 Gangmumei Kamei, *Zeliangrong Nagas*, 150.

78 Thomas, *Evangelising the Nation*, 74.

Jadonang then started recruiting *riphen* (soldiers both men and women) from Zeliangrong villages to give a concrete shape to his political agenda with military training.[79] The young Gaidinliu from Nungkao (Longkao) village, who become a follower (and latter successor) of Jadonang, was incharge of training the women.[80] The movement led by Jadonang is said to have mobilised about 500 *riphen* at its height.[81] As the movement took concrete shape, Jadonang sent out spears to the villages to forge alliance or allegiance against the mighty empire. On accepting the spears, the villages sent *mithuns* to Jadonang as their contribution to the movement.[82] Jadonang also reached out to other Naga tribes such as Angamis, Rengmas, Maos, and Marams to forge together to fight against the British.[83] Spears acceptance by villages implied joining the movement. However, Jadonang's *Makam Gwangdi* was soon to clash with the British Raj.

In 1930, the colonial administrative office North-West Sub-Division shifted from Tamenglong to Imphal. This provided Jadonang a free space to invigorate the resistance movement. Jadonang told the villages not to co-operate with the *lambus* and *dobashis* who were the support base of the colonial rule. The resistance movement took on a strategy of non-cooperation by refusing to pay house tax, subscription to entertain colonial officers, refusing to render forced labour and so on. Not Tamenglong but Kambiron soon became the centre of political gravity.[84] According to Gangmumei, in the absence of colonial administrative headquarter in Tamenglong, the people looked up to Jadonang as the real ruler, "blessed and ordained by Tingkao Ragwang."[85] Undoubtedly, Jadonang became the undisputed charismatic leader upon whom the people pledged their allegiance, though it was unlikely that the Zeliangrong Nagas who barely conceded absolute power to a single person (village chief) even in their village polity would consider Jadonang an absolute ruler. The villages' material support to Jadonang must be seen as contribution towards the resistance movement against the British Empire.

Before Jadonang could confront the colonial power with his *riphen*, he was arrested in 1931 while he was returning from his last pilgrimage to Bhuban cave in the Cachar Hills. Jadonang's arrest was a well-planned operation. The Political

---

79 The activities of the *riphen* involve grazing cattle, cultivation, pounding of paddy, collection of firewood for fuel. Military training involves handling of spears, *daos* (dagger) and muzzle-loader gun. The *riphen* conducts military drill with words coined by Jadonang. Spying and intelligence training of the *riphen* consisted of sending secret messages, counting people in secrecy, calling names by code words. Gangmumei Kamei, *Zeliangrong Nagas*, 151; Yunuo, *Naga Struggle Against British Rule*, 60.

80 Gangmumei Kamei, *Zeliangrong Nagas*, 151.

81 Gangmumei Kamei, *Jadonang*, 33.

82 Yunuo, *Naga Struggle Against British Rule*, 60.

83 Yunuo, *Naga Struggle Against British Rule*, 63, Thomas, *Evangelising the Nation*, 79.

84 Gangmumei Kamei, *Zeliangrong Nagas*, 153.

85 Gangmumei Kamei, *Zeliangrong Nagas*, 153.

Agent, J. C. Higgins sent three *lambus* to arrest Jadonang. Jadonang was arrested at Lakhipur and put into Silchar Jail, while Gaidinliu and other followers managed to escape to the mountains. After the arrest of Jadonang, Higgins marched to Kambiron on 2 March 1931, demolished Jadonang's temple and proceeded to Nungkao and met Gaidinliu who he described as "rather little unmarried girl of 17."[86] Jadonang was paraded across the Zeliangrong country while escorting him from Silchar Jail to Imphal. Gangmumei Kamei writes, "the people saw Jadonang in chains and were sympathetic to him. Thousands of market women went to see him, the rebel leader."[87] The colonial officers on several counts interrogated Jadonang whether he claimed to be king; whether he prevented census work; whether he had declared war against the colonial regime; and whether he had collected *mithuns* as tribute. Jadonang effectively denied all these charges that rendered the colonial officers helpless to prosecute him.[88] However, the murder of Manipuri traders in April 1930 at Kambiron, in which Jadonang was not directly involved, provided a good case to prosecute Jadonang on the charge of murder. He was hanged on 29 August 1931. The colonial penal liturgy extinguished the rising flame of Jadonang who in his twenties garnered a large support of the villages and challenged an empire with a new vision of freedom beyond the pale subservience to the empire of the day. It is notable that the colonial authorities on several counts wrote about Jadonang as messiah king.

7.3.2. Resistance Movement Under Gaidinliu

The actual revolt against the colonial authorities occurred after the martyrdom of Jadonang. The mantle of leadership of the resistance movement fell upon the sixteen (or seventeen) years old Gaidinliu, the charismatic spiritual and political successor of Jadonang. Gangmumei Kamei writes, "Success or failure, she did not care, Fight [*sic*] she must; she was determined to put the master's (Jadonang's) ideology to practice."[89] Gaidinliu, who became a living legend in her own lifetime, was born in Nungkao (Longkao) village. She grew up as a mystic girl with a resistive lifestyle who demanded even girls' entry into boys' dormitory. She is said to have had association with her spirit partner, the daughter of God Bisnu of the Bhuban caves, something that would not find a place among the people today.

Gaidinliu heard about the activities of Jadonang and visited him at Kambiron around 1926 or 1927. Her meeting was the beginning of master–disciple relationship that lasted for about four years. But during these years, Gaidinliu proved herself and became the second in command of the resistance movement. Gaidinliu was the main trainer of women who join the *riphen*. Jadonang would often visit Nungkao as Gaidinliu would visit Kambiron as

86 Robert Reid, *History of the Frontier Areas Bordering on Assam*, 169.

87 Gangmumei Kamei, *Zeliangrong Nagas*, 155.

88 Gangmumei Kamei, *Zeliangrong Nagas*, 156.

89 Gangmunei Kamei, *Zeliangrong Nagas*, 157.

well. Gaidinliu constructed a temple at Nungkao where people could worship Tingwang or Tingkao Ragwang. She participated in Jadonang's reformation of the traditional religion, abolition of *gennas*, mobilsation of religious congregations and the innovation and performance of dancing and singing.[90]

The decisive moment for Gaidinliu came when Jadonang was imprisoned with little hope of release. When the trial against Jadonang was under way, the colonial agents made attempts to woo Gaidinliu to turn against Jadonang with the offer to exculpate her from the murder charge of Manipuri traders at Kambiron. But Gaidinliu went into hiding accompanied by loyal followers of the movement. After the execution of Jadonang, Gaidinliu took up the leadership and stepped-up the resistance movement. Though Gaidinliu was previously ignored owing to her juvenile age,[91] after Jadonang she became the target of colonial authorities. Gangmumei writes, "From April 1931 to October, 1932 Gaidinliu was in the whirlpool of action in rebellion. She visited the villages in the Trans Barak Basin in Western Tamenglong Subdivision and set ablaze the whole area into rebellion."[92]

The people believed in the charismatic leadership of Gaidinliu and rallied behind her against the British Empire with the hope of attaining a better future—freedom from foreign rule. The hunt for Gaidinliu was even more intense than that of Jadonang. For the arrest of Gaidinliu, an initial award of two hundred rupees was announced which was later enhanced to five hundred rupees.[93] Ursula Bower gives an interesting description about the hunt of Gaidinliu by the colonial authorities.

> Troops were sent out to all the three districts in which the Kacha Naga country fell—Manipur, Naga Hills and North Cachar. Outposts were set up at strategic points; searches were instituted; patrols went out; and local movement between villages were sternly restricted. But Gaidinliu, piloted by her North Cachar agent, Masang of Kepelo, remained at large. The bulk of Zemi were on her side, and those who were not were afraid to speak. The country was a warren of game trails, field-tracks, paths caves, forests and ravines. Every settlement had its own private ways, its back entrances revealed to none, its secret hideouts. Abetting movement villages signaled, by beacon, the movement of patrols. She came and went like a ghost. To make things worse, she was often present only in spirit, and panting sepoys, sent out on the best information, found Nagas dancing solemnly before an empty throne. To crown it all, she was—on the principle of 'darkest

90 Gangmumei Kamei, *Zeliangrong Nagas*, 157–158.

91 Bower, *Naga Path*, 43.

92 Gangmumei Kamei, *Zeliangrong Nagas*, 159.

93 Gangmumei, *Zeliangrong Nagas*, 160.

below the lamp'—concealed for three months within sight of the out post of Hangrum.[94]

The patrols of the colonial soldiers and the hunt for Gaidinliu grew so intense that Gaidinliu decided to attack the Assam Rifles outpost at Hangrum village. The Assam Rifles had superior firearms while the rebels had only *daos* and spears, but they dared to attack the colonisers. The empire struck back with burning down villages, torturing people and imposing huge fines.[95] However, the Battle of Hangrum 1932 sent a message to the colonial authorities the people's defiance against the colonial presence. After the Hangrum battle, Gaidinliu escorted by her agents left Hangrum and went on to other Zeme villages and engulfed them with the spirit of resistance. Nari Rustomji writes, "An elaborate saga had meanwhile grown around her name to the extent that she had become a supernatural being and could elude her captors through her magical power, appearing in several places at the same time."[96] However, it is questionable to romanticise the movement as though it was Gaidinliu's (supernatural) magical charm that engulfed the movement and belittle the people's fight for liberation. As Gangmumei Kamei observes, "She had no magical power but the popular support of the people and the secret paths saved her."[97] In a note in June 1932 J. P. Mills describes the movement thus:

> The real danger of the movement is the spirit of defiance now aboard. Nagas who are ordinarily truthful and friendly have been taught that officers are to be lied to as deprival of information. These lessons will not be quickly forgotten. The capture of Gaidinliu will not end the agitation. There is a warrant of murder out against her and she can be dealt with when caught. She will be succeeded by one or more "medium." To be a medium is not offence under any law. Yet they will continue to keep the people in a state of constant excitement, and Nagas will continue to be set over against the Government and Kukis. The result from the administrative point of view will be serious. Once she is in our hands, we must aim at gradually suppressing the movement by punishment, persuasion and personal influences. This will be a long task.[98]

As the search continued, Gaidinliu moved through the Zeme villages in the Naga Hills and took her last stand at Poilwa (Pulomi/Populongmai). Poilwa,

94 Bower, *Naga Path*, 43.

95 Gangmumei, *Zeliangrong Nagas*, 163.

96 Nari Rustomji, *Enchanted Frontiers* (Bombay: Oxford University Press, 1971), 102–106 cited by Gangmumei Kamei, *Zeliangrong Nagas*, 162.

97 Gangmumei Kamei, *Zeliangrong Nagas*, 162.

98 Reid, *History of the Frontier Areas Bordering on Assam*, 170.

a village that asserted its independence from colonial intrusion since 1832, welcomed Gaidinliu and her followers. A major preparation of the resistance movement was underway to challenge any attack from outside. However, a medical practitioner, Harielungbe (Haralu), who himself hailed from Poilwa village understood the possible large scale violence and loss of lives that may transpire if a full scale combat ensued between the resistance movement and the colonial army, helped the colonial authorities to arrest Gaidinliu at Poilwa on 19 October 1932. Gaidinliu was taken to Kohima and then sent to Imphal for trial. She was given a life term of imprisonment and was first locked in Guwahati jail, then taken to Shillong, to Aizwal and finally to Tura jail. As J. P. Mills predicted, the movement continued. However it was a matter of time for the colonial authorities to capture all the rebel leaders and sentence them. Nevertheless, the people believed that a leader like Gaidinliu would rise again to lead them to fight against the foreign rulers.[99]

7.3.3. Political Analysis of the Resistance Movement Among Zeliangrong Nagas

Many writers from various fields of scholarships have (studied and) written about the movement with varying opinions about the resistance movement among the Zeliangrong Nagas against the British Raj. To begin with, it is striking that the colonial officials who suppressed the movement ended up calling the movement as "Naga Raj" though they clearly wanted to describe the movement as a Zeliangrong phenomenon.[100] Colonial anthropologists found this movement "odd and interesting," which was termed more a "money-spinning God-racket,"[101] made up of "ruffians" whose activity was extortion.[102] Even the church historian Frederick S. Downs considers the movement as anti-Christian,[103] though the movement never took on an anti-Christian campaign in its own time.[104] Joykumar Singh thinks that the movement emerged as a classic millenarism "with an objective to regenerate the old religion of the Zeliangrong people against formidable approaching force of the Christian religion."[105] On the other hand, native writers differ greatly in how they perceived the movement. Asoso Yonuo describes the movement led by Jadonang and Gaidinliu as "the Naga Struggle against the British rule" on the basis of the causes, the scope of mobilisation of the movement, and the goal of the movement that was aimed at establishing the

---

99 Bower, *Naga Path*, 45.

100 Cf. Reid, *History of the Frontier Areas Bordering on Assam*, 167, 169.

101 Bower, *Naga Path*, 41, 43 cf. Stephen Fuchs, *Rebellious Prophets: A Study of Messianic Movement in Indian Religions* (Bombay: Asia Publishing House, 1965), 151.

102 Fuchs, *Rebellious Prophets*, 151.

103 Downs, *The Mighty Works of God*, 147, 179.

104 Thomas, *Evangelising the Nation*, 89.

105 N. Joykumar Singh, *Social Movements in Manipur*, 2nd ed. (New Delhi: Mittal Publications, 2005), 59.

Makam Kingdom (or Naga Kingdom).[106] Gangmumei Kamei claims that it was a "Zeliangrong Revolt," though he cannot excuse himself from explaining *Makam Gwangdi* as either referring to either Zeliangrong Kingdom or Naga Kingdom.[107] But it is not uncommon among writers to consider this movement as a purely Kabui or Zeliangrong movement that too, as though it emerged as an anti-Kuki movement. However, to trivialise the movement of the people that took shape in the context of colonial oppression would miss the most important point, that it was a resistance movement against the overarching hegemony of the empire.

There is also a fallacy that confuses the resistance movement among the Zeliangrong Nagas led by Jadonang with Heraka movement.[108] Asoso Yunuo anachronistically attributes the reform movement led by Jadonang as Heraka movement. Yunuo claims that Jadonang gave the name to the reformed religion as "Haraka."[109] Undoubtedly, Jadonang is held in high honour as one of the reformer by the Heraka movement, but the name Heraka itself was coined only in 1974.[110] Some studies done by historians tends to maintain a predominant assumption that the Zeliangrong movement led by Jadonang is a precursor of the Heraka movement, and was mostly concerned with the pan-ethnic unity and identity of the Zeliangrong.[111] However, in his anthropological work on Zeme Nagas, *Reform, Identity and Narratives of Belonging: The Heraka Movement of Northeast India*, Arkotong Longkumer provides an informed observation that distinguishes the resistance movement of the Zeliangrong Nagas led by Jadonang during the colonial era and the Heraka movement of the post-independent India.

> The connection between the two mentioned movements is tenuous at best because the 'Jadonang movement' as we know it, exists largely in the pages of colonial reports, while the Heraka movement has dispersed into two geographical regions, reflecting different sets of conditions that have influenced and perpetuated its existence. Therefore, though it is sometimes assumed as 'knowledge' among historians of Northeast India that the Heraka and the 'Jadonang movement' are connected, forming a continuous chain of events since its inception in the late

---

106 Yuono, *Naga Struggle against British Rule.*

107 Gangmumei Kamei, *Zeliangrong Nagas*, 145 cf. 150.

108 Yonuo, *Naga Struggle Against the British Rule*, 53. 1982. Mukherjee, Gupta and Das, "The Zeliangrong or Haomei Movement," 70.

109 Yuono, *Naga Struggle Against the British Rule*, 53.

110 Arkotong Longkumer, *Reform, Identity and Narratives of Belonging: The Heraka Movement of Northeast India* (London: Continuum, 2010), 2. Cf. Haireiwangbe Zeliang, *A Brief History of Zeliangrong Heraka Movement and Its Impact in North East India* (Dimapur: Zeme Council North East India, 2015), 84.

111 Gangmumei Kabui, "The Zeliangrong Movement: An Historical Study," in K. S. Singh *Tribal Movements in India*, 53–66; Mukherjee, Gupta and Das, "The Zeliangrong or Haomei Movement," 67–95.

1920s to its current form, I am not quite convinced that such is the case.[112]

The study of this movement continues in the academia from different vantage points. But this study is limited to the analysis of the movement as a resistance movement against the British Empire in the light of the Lukan Spirit.

7.4. The Spirit and the Resistance Movement Among Zeliangrong Nagas

The major research question in this section is "can the resistance movement of the Zeliangrong Nagas be seen as the activity of the Spirit of God in the light of Lukan Spirit?" The Spirit in Luke's Gospel is definitely the driving force in enabling the victims of empire to find their socio-religious and political space in the context of Roman imperial hegemony. In Luke's Gospel, it is the Spirit of God that inspired emancipatory resistant discourses against the dominant imperial discourse of power. The Spirit-anointed Jesus, who was the leader of the mass movement, showed its contempt against the status quo of the empire and dared to defy the colonial penal liturgy in the Spirit-anointing power of God. So also, the resurrected Lukan Jesus assured the gathered community of disciples in Jerusalem that they would be clothed with power from on high meaning that the Spirit of God will empower the disciples' community to continue the works of resistance against the empire. One cannot take any movement at random and equate it to Jesus' movement and claim the same theological legitimacy. However, if Jesus movement was a resistance movement par excellence against the empire, and as the biblical exegete of the Holy Spirit Richard Tholin asserts, "If at the heart of the work of the Spirit in the biblical record is action to proclaim release to the captives... to set at liberty those who are oppressed (Isa 61:1–2; Luke 4:18) it should come as no surprise that Christians are confronted with the possibility that the spirit is at work in the midst of movement for human liberation,"[113] and in the present case, the resistance movement among Zeliangrong Nagas. In other words, if the Spirit of God is thought to be at work in the midst of movement for liberation, the challenge at this point is to discover and translate the sense of the Spirit of God as the driving force of the movement enabling the victims of empire to fight for their own liberation. One way of discovering the divine impulse in the resistance movement among the oppressed group would be to analyse their resistant discourse that was produced in their engagement with the empire. Such a task will involve revisiting their archive from the vantage point of the margins to reclaim and re-inscribe the indigenous subjecthood.

On several counts, the resistance movement among the Zeliangrong Nagas betrays the social formation on the fringes of the society in the context of the

112 Longkumer, *Reform, Identity and Narratives of Belonging*, 16.

113 Richard Tholin, "The Holy Spirit and Liberation Movement the Response of the Church," in *The Holy Spirit*, ed. Kirkpatrick (Nashville: Tidings, 1974), 55.

empire in many ways similar to the resistance movements in biblical records. Firstly, the charismatic leaders Jadonang and Gaidinliu were clearly seen by the followers as divinely endowed authoritative figures who rose up to lead the people with an inspired vision of liberation. Secondly, the movement produced a counter discourse with resistant adaptation of the imperial discourse of power. Thirdly, the movement challenged the empire by influencing the villages to stop paying colonial taxation. In order to bring out the activity of the Spirit in the resistance movement among the Zeliangrong Nagas, the discursive and non-discursive practices of the movement is taken into conversation with the activity of the Spirit in Luke's Gospel.

7.4.1. The Spirit and the Prophetic Protest

The Lukan Jesus movement find its resource for counter social formation by reinventing ancient promises and prophecies with the inspiration of the Spirit of God. In the previous chapters, this study has contended that the Spirit of God inspired the prophetic voices of Mary, Zechariah and Jesus who appropriated ancient promises and prophecies to construct an alternative vision of the future that counters the dominant narrative of the empire. The resistance movement among the Zeliangrong Nagas led by Jadonang and later by Gaidinliu also raised a prophetic protest in the colonial context of economic hardship and physical oppression by evoking the coming kingdom of "all who eat from the wooden platter" (that is the Nagas), a popular *belief* documented by J. H. Hutton much earlier to the emergence of the resistance movement among the Zeliangrong Nagas. In the words of Hutton, "There is a belief in Khonoma and other Angami villages in the return of a king who will drive out the British and rule over 'all who eat from the wooden platter,' i.e., all Nagas. This king is believed to be sleeping, as Barbarossa sleeps, in a cave in Kacha Naga country (North Cachar)."[114]

Ursula Bower, rather derogatively notes, "Their programme was an attractive one, the very blue-print of a Naga heaven—the millennium was at hand, the faithful were to spend everything in one stupendous feast ... and live in plenty ever after on their God's miraculous bounty."[115] But it is not an illusory millenarian vision. It encapsulates both political and economic freedom. The native resistance movement engaged the British Empire with counter imagination of a new kingdom that would displace the alien rule in the land. In this new political space, the natives would no longer pay house tax, nor provide forced labour; the natives will no longer live in subservience to an alien rule. Added to this political liberation is the construction of a liberated economy in which the people will have plenty. This emancipatory prophetic voice challenged the British colonial control of the natives with census, house tax, and free and forced labour that coloured the daily lives of the colonised. This counter discourse points to the forming of

114 Hutton, *The Angami Nagas*, 252.

115 Bower, *Naga Path*, 42 cf. Fuchs, *Rebellious Prophets*, 151.

political consciousness of the colonised, that refused to put up with the status quo of the empire.

As any resistance voice against colonial domination that emerged from the colonised world concerns primarily with power and material relations, there is an essential correspondence between the resistant discourse of the Zeliangrong movement noted above and the Lukan prophetic voices. The political and economic freedom envisioned in the native discourse essentially corresponds to Mary's song that celebrates bringing down the mighty from their thrones, lifting up the lowly, and filling the hungry with good things (1:52–53). Similarly, the discourse of freedom from the British rule for all who eat from the wooden platter is like a Jubilee discourse that proclaims the favourable year of the Lord for the oppressed and the victims of the empire. In the light of Spirit-inspired emancipatory discourses in Luke's Gospel such as the canticles and the Nazareth proclamation, it is legitimate to claim that it is the Spirit of God that inspired the emancipatory native discourse of the oppressed Zeliangrong Nagas.

7.4.2. The Spirit and Counter Discourse Production

Jadonang's call for a new kingdom, the *Makam Gwangdi*[116] is an oppositional discourse to the existing exploitative rule of the British. In the words of Gangmumei Kamei, Jadonang made a clarion call saying,

> The Meiteis have their king, the Indian (Tajongmai) have their rulers, why should we not have our own king? The white men and we are all human beings. Why should we be afraid of them? All men are equal. We are blessed people. Our days have come. Our powerful weapons are kept hidden by God at Zeilad. We shall pray and worship God. With his grace we shall become the rulers.[117]

The symbolic appropriation of *kingdom* for the construction of a new political space suggests that the movement led by Jadonang was not a retreat to the traditional pristine tribal polity. Rather, it made use of the colonial symbol of power with a resistant adaptation to carve out a political space for the people native to the land. What is significant here is that, mimicry here did not only

---

116 According to Gangmumei Kamei, *Zeliangrong Nagas*, 150, *Makam Gwangdi* simply means the kingdom of the *Makam*. But he is ambiguous whether *Makam* means Zeliangrong or the Nagas though he concedes that the British colonial rule described it as Naga Raj. Given that he sees the movement led by Jadonang and Gaidinliu as the "Zeliangrong Revolt," Kamei is conservative to attribute the movement as a Naga movement (145). On the other hand, John Thomas, *Evangelising the Nations*, 91 n. 15 claims that though "Gwangdi referred to Kingdom in Rongmei, Makam was used as a generic term for Nagas and may been derived from Makhel, which is also known as Makhan or Makhiang .... By evoking the word makam, Jadonang hope to forge unity among the Naga tribes and create a kingdom outside the control of British and the plains people."

117 G. Kamei, *Zeliangrong Nagas*, 150; John Thomas, *Evangelising the Nations*, 73.

involve a resistant adaptation of colonial symbol of kingdom, but the invocation of divine agency for emancipation from the colonial yoke. Jadonang spoke like a prophet and the people believed his charismatic leadership. He made a bold assertion of the equality of all humankind and stood up to challenge the empire with a new political subjecthood. The voice of freedom became a galvanising weapon to inspire the enthusiasm of the people to come forward in support of the new political vision. In the light of the Lukan Spirit that give voices to the oppressed to voice out their deep longings and aspirations with new subjecthood for an alternate kingdom of God in the context of imperial situation, one can legitimately claim that the same Spirit of God was breathing powerfully in the voice of the victimised and oppressed Zeliangrong Nagas empowering them to resist the empire for a new political space. Gangmumei Kamei contends that Jadonang's "political dream of a Kingdom was a natural response to the British colonialism. It was always resisted and never compromised by him or by his people in the past."[118] In the light of the Lukan Spirit, such a power of resistance to the empire that oppressed and suppressed the people can be translated as the work of the Spirit of God.

Jadonang also composed many songs to inspire the people. One of his songs expresses the deep longing of a colonised people for liberation:[119]

<table>
<tr><td>Damloumei Ragwang Zuk hei tangputhe
Kandih chaogum kanmei juk tei tio Ragwang gaimei
Azuk tang thao puethei bui bangta samaknga

Amuang rui daopunithe Ngampui hiak hio
Atta sumit titha tingpuk kaothu

Tingkao Ragwangta ngammei thounaicho
Apu Ragwang pan khouruina meita ai pinglakkhe</td><td>Creator God! The time is here.
Grant us the age buried under the earth, good God.
When my time comes mouth and mouth fight will be.
There will be no more dao and spear.
Write the victorious scripts when I am put out.
Who can defeat the God of heaven?
In God my father, I shall not fear!</td></tr>
</table>

This song is a song of resistance that invoked the creator God as the ultimate power as no power on earth is above God. The anti-imperial tone of the song would not be missed by those who heard the song in the context of the pervasive power of the British Raj. There is a strong martial tone in this song that speaks

118 Gangmumei Kamei, *Zeliangrong Nagas*, 150.

119 Namthiubuiyang Pamei, *The Trail from Makuilongdi: The Continuing Saga of the Zeliangrong People* (Tamenglong: Gironta Charitable Foundation, 2001), 40-41.

of the inevitable violent confrontation with the "power that be" in the search for a new political space. However, the song of Jadonang attests a deep commitment to God. Like the Lukan Jesus, he used familial language to call God as Father. He used a language as though he was entrusted by God to lead the people in the fight against foreign rule. Such a conviction could not have been possible without divine inspiration. But, one may ask how does one derive any sense of divine empowerment in a movement that prepares for violent confrontation with the empire? In the case of Jesus' movement, non-violent active resistance was the main mode of confrontation with the "power that be" to usher in the kingdom of God. Jesus' movement did not subscribe to taking up arms to fight against the Roman Empire! But like many of the violent resistance movements attested by both biblical traditions and contemporary history, the resistance movement among the Zeliangrong Nagas was not an exception. The resistance movement among the Zeliangrong Nagas led by Jadonang and Gaidinliu against the British Raj took on a militaristic colour.

However, the vision of the resistance movement reflected in their song of liberation is noteworthy. Jadonang's song constructs a new socio-political space of the age to come that is till then buried under the earth. The novelty of his vision lies in constructing a new socio-political relationship where there would be no more use for *dao* (dagger) and spear for warfare. It is significant to note that how Jadonang constructs a new political space where there would be no war, considering the fact that he hailed from a cultural background where inter-village and inter-tribal feuds was dominant in the past, and at the same time his formative years were exposed to colonial oppression, the sounds of war and military operations. It is his testament that though his life may be put out, the victory for the age to come should be inaugurated. Most significantly, the song invokes the power of God as the ultimate one. The song reflects not the human confidence of a political revolutionary, but a trust in the power of God that would lead the people to freedom. But it is not simply the song of the individual Jadonang; it is the song of the community of resistance, who pledged their confidence in God and work for their liberation. Such a profound theology of resistance and a vision for a better world could only be attributed to the inspiration of the Spirit of God. Thus, one can say that the same Spirit that inspired the ancient Israelites, the Spirit that was embodied in the Spirit-anointed Jesus, is the Spirit that is always at work in the midst of people's movement for liberation.

7.4.3. The Spirit and the Community of Resistance

In the context of black experience in America, the black theologian James Cone writes, "In America, the Holy Spirit is black people making decisions about their togertherness, which makes preparation for an encounter with white people."[120]

120 James Cone, A Black Theology of Liberation (Philadelphia: J. B. Lippincott Co., 1977), 122.

It is already noted that in Luke's Gospel the actvity of the Spirit is located in the community's resistance to the empire, and in this light the Zeliangrong community's resistance to the British Empire can be appreciated as the activity of the Spirit of God. The formation of the resistance force *riphen* is an expression of collective endeavour to resist the British Raj. The mobilisation and the response of the Zeliangrong villages to form a dynamic force show the collective preparation of the people to challenge the empire under the leadership of Jadonang and Gaidinliu. It must be emphasised that the formation of the *riphen* was not a vain glorious enterprise of Jadonang nor could the formation of such a force be possible without the mass support of the people. The *sending of spears* to other Naga tribes to forge a united front also points to the collective endeavour of the people. The movement garnered enough strength to resist the empire by banning imperial house tax, forced labour and other colonial impositions and asked the villages to support the resistance movement instead. As the non-cooperation movement got underway, it naturally invited the empire to strike the leader Jadonang to serve as a detterent for the followers. But the movement did not die, as expected by the colonial state, but took on a robust stance under the leadership of Gaidinliu with the support of the villages. It is in this collective unity of the community to resist their oppressor that one must appreciate the activity of the Spirit of God.

Like many other subordinate group resistances against the empire, the Zeliangrongs responded to the British imperial rule under the leadership of Jadonang and Gaidinliu in order to assert their independence. The leadership of Jadonang and Gaidinliu gave the people both hope and vision to construct a new socio-political order in the context of oppressive and exploitative British rule. But since the vibrancy of the resistance movement depends on the participation of the mass, this study has consciously maintained the movement was not simply as Jadonang's or Gaidinliu's movement *per se* but a collective resistance of the people. From a theological point of view, the study has noted that the prophetic voice from the margins that calls for a new socio-political order over against the British rule evokes the inspiration of the Spirit of God. Especially, reading the discourse of this movement, such as the appropriation of ancient prophecy to awaken the political consciousness of the people and the production of counter discourse for self-formation with a profound political theology, in the light of Lukan Spirit of resistance betrays the activity of the Spirit of God.

7.5. Conclusion

In this chapter, the resistance movement among the Zeliangrong Nagas was studied as a case in point in order to explicate as to what extent contemporary resistance movements for freedom from colonial power can be seen in the light of the activity of the Lukan Spirit. In order to discover or translate the divine impulses that fermented the resistance movement among the Zeliangrong Nagas, the movement and its resistant discourses were analysed by revisiting their archives.

A postcolonial analysis of the movement has shown that the movement actively resisted the British Empire by challenging the legitimacy of house tax, force labour and other forms of control, at the same time produced hybrid resistant discourses adopting the colonial language of power but shifting the authority of colonial discourse with theopolitical imagination of power. And noting this theology of resistance, the study argues that the Spirit of God that empowers the struggle of the marginalised towards an alternative socio-political space in Luke's Gospel can be located in the resistance movement among Zeliangrong Nagas.

Conclusion

This study on the Spirit and community formation in Luke's Gospel is based on the assumption that the Spirit in Luke's Gospel is the driving force for the social formation of the Jesus' movement to resist the domination system of the empire. It is shown that Lukan pneumatology is a pneumatology of resistance that engenders counter social formation at the margins in the context of colonialism and imperialism. This general conclusion provides the gist of the study, its implications, its limitations and direction for further research in this line.

The study has considered afresh the pneumatology of Luke's Gospel from a postcolonial viewpoint with the help of postcolonial and socio-cultural criticism. This study has noted that Luke's Gospel takes a detour from the Synoptics' eschatological colouring of the Spirit's activity and presents the Spirit as the driving force in the life and work of Jesus' movement that challenges and subverts the status quo of the empire. Luke's Gospel begins with the Spirit-inspired bold proclamations of God's liberative work and God's favour for the marginalised through the voices from the margins of the Roman Empire. At the same time, the Gospel is set within the larger political landscape of the Roman Empire and narrates the subversive activities of the Spirit anointed-Jesus that attracted the opposition from client rulers of Rome. But noting the apparent lack of adequate attention among interpreters to study the political dimension of the Spirit of God in Luke's Gospel, this study has attempted to fill this gap.

The exploration of the background of Lukan pneumatology (Chapter two) through the Old Testament and Second Temple literary repertoire has shown that there is a consistent characteristic feature of the Spirit of God that envisages the role of the Spirit in the formation of a new community in the various historical contexts of Israel's history. And this community-forming Spirit of God is always resistive to the socio-political status quo and constructs an alternative socio-political space in which God's people will experience justice and freedom. This Spirit of resistance is operative in the Jewish socio-political formations (Chapter three) in the contexts of Hellenistic Empires and Roman Empire. It is also clear that Jesus' movement emerged within these wider Jewish social formations as one of the movements that resisted the Roman Empire with an alternative vision of the kingdom of God.

A brief analysis of the Luke's Gospel highlights how conflict and resistance went hand in hand in forging a new community in a world dominated by the Roman Empire. Luke draws Jesus' traditions from Mark, Q, and his own special traditions to narrate the life and work of Jesus and the community formed around him. It is noted that, Luke carefully underlines the colonial experience of the subordinate groups such as census, taxation, and military presence of the empire. Luke's accounts of the Spirit-messiah Jesus' open commensality, breach of Jewish purity map, exorcisms and healings with a deliberate concern for the outcasts, reflects how the Lukan community engages with the empire system of domination and the hierarchical status quo that colours the daily life of the people. It is also shown that, as any piece of art would reflect the world of its composition, Luke's Gospel betrays a Hellenistic city setting of the Mediterranean East (the cities of Asia Minor and Greece), wherein the audience is a mixed group of people in terms of race, gender, and class.

A postcolonial cultural analysis of the Spirit-inspired Lukan canticles (the Magnificat and the Benedictus) and the Spirit-anointed Jesus' Nazareth proclamation (Chapter four) highlighted that these texts are resistant voices from the colonised world, which appropriate the imperial language with "resistant adaptation" of the dominant discourse for justice and re-presentation. In Luke's scheme, the Spirit is the driving force behind the formation of such new subjecthood and the formation of a resistant community. The Spirit that cries out through the voices of the margins proclaim something new, that is God's favourable status for all, and not only for those born in a particular situation. Their voices do not validate the established status quo of the empire but unsettles the fixity of status quo with new a set of values. The Spirit-inspired Lukan canticles overturn the metanarrative of Caesar by proclaiming God's mighty acts in bringing down the mighty and powerful and lifting up the lowly. It hybridises the claim of Caesar by elevating Jesus as the saviour and subverts the imperial meaning of peace and salvation. So also the Nazareth proclamation notifies the situation of poverty, sickness, bondage which charaterise the imperial order and declares the Jubilee Year from all bondages. The voice of justice and freedom that cried out in the Nazareth proclamation is the voice of the Spirit (Luke 4:18–19) challenging the colonial system of injustice and oppression. The liberating messages that are sounded in the canticles and the Nazareth proclamation enable the readers of Luke's Gospel, especially for those in a postcolonial situation, to rediscover not only the liberative voice of the Spirit, but also the Spirit of God that is active in the resistant community in the contemporary times.

The exorcism of the Capernaum demoniac (chapter five) demonstrates that Luke locates the work of the Spirit in the liberating activities of the oppressed. In the Galilean colonial context where the experience of marginality mystified the harsh reality of Roman domination into demon possession as a means of coping oppression, the Spirit-messiah Jesus intervenes and exorcises demonic domination from the place and transmits power to the people to resist the forces of domination towards the future of God's domination-free order. This politics of exorcism engenders the social formation of the oppressed community that resists the system of domination. However, the Spirit works among the oppressed not with instruments of power that were available to the mighty empires, but with affective power of the Spirit to build an inclusive free community. The healing of the unclean paralytic demonstrates how the community of resistance identifies with the oppressed and engages in social healing contravening the social boundary maintaining purity system of the religion of cultural and religious elites. The wider implications of the Spirit-anointed Jesus' healing of the paralytic are that the outcast and the unclean are incorporated into the community, the oppressed are released from social ostracism, and an inclusive community is formed.

A study on the Lukan passion and resurrection narrative (chapter six) elucidates the empowering role of the Spirit in the suffering of the oppressed who resists the empire. It noted that for Luke, Spirit's anointing does not only empower radical prophetic voices and liberative actions but necessarily involves the vocation of suffering and experiencing opposition from the authorities. Though the relationship between the Spirit and suffering is conspicuously a neglected area in the study of Lukan pneumatology, it is shown that there are many hints that the empowering of the Spirit for the mission of the good news of the kingdom of God involves opposition from earthly authorities. A postcolonial analysis of the Lukan passion narrative suggests that it is a subversive narrative that retells the story of a colonial victim Jesus who defies the colonial authorities and their penal liturgy of crucifixion that forecloses the lives of those who challenge the empire. In his defiance against the colonial liturgy of crucifixion, Lukan Jesus turns his tortured body into a site of struggle for justice, showing the nakedness of colonial violence. The powerful voice from the abyss of suffering that cries out "Father," is the voice of the Spirit that denies the legitimacy of crucifixion by appealing to an authority higher than Caesar who is God. The centurion's confession that a just man was crucified reiterates the invalidity of the colonial justice system. But the Spirit's empowering provides Jesus the power of resilience to withstand the silencing violence of the empire that is opposed to the kingdom of God. Luke's own audience will understand that it is the Spirit of God that empowers the oppressed in their struggle for a just socio-political space even while the empire remains a reality.

A postcolonial analysis of the resurrection narrative (chapter six) indicates that the colonial cross did not have the final say. The Spirit empowers the disciples' community for the continuity of faithful resistance to the empire. Lukan resurrection narrative shows that the Spirit of God plays a key role in enabling the formation of the new subjecthood—"the Lord is risen"—and renders futile the colonial deterministic construction of the colonised subjectivity that violence would silence the colonised. Though it is noted that Luke himself struggles to find a fitting language to express how real the third day encounter of the risen Jesus was, without resorting to stating that Jesus appeared in the Spirit, the third day strange encounter has a pneumatic character that demands not only a way of seeing but also a way of feeling affectively that leads to transformative recognition. The *haunting* or the *pneumatic* character of the risen Jesus' elusive appearance and disappearance, that burnt the disciples' hearts, opened the vision of their eyes, and opened their minds to understand the Scripture, destabilises their present by the past memory of all who were victims to the violence of the empire, and opens up the future course of faithful resistance. This affective encounter with the risen Jesus enabled the disciples a transformative recognition that while the empire still remains, the disciples' community should not be disheartened but continue its faithful resistance. The community of resistance has to witness to all nations the death and resurrection of the colonial victim Jesus. But the witnessing community is to be "clothed with power from on high,"—meaning that the community will witness with the empowerment of the Spirit of God.

The analysis of the resistance movement among the Zeliangrong Nagas in the light of Lukan Spirit (chapter seven) has shown that peoples' resistance movement from the margins against the empire evokes the activity of the Spirit of God. Like resistance movements of any other subordinate groups against the empire, the Zeliangrongs responded to the British imperial rule under the leadership of Jadonang and Gaidinliu in order to assert their independence. The leadership of Jadonang and Gaidinliu gave the people both hope and vision to construct a new socio-political order in the context of oppressive and exploitative British rule. From a theological point of view, the study has noted that the prophetic voice from the margins that calls for a new socio-political order over against the British rule, and their active resistance activities evoke the inspiration of the Spirit of God. Especially, reading the discourse of this movement, such as the appropriation of ancient prophecy to awaken the political consciousness of the people and the production of counter discourse for self-formation with a deep confidence that God will stand by their site of struggle, in the light of the Lukan Spirit of resistance betrays the activity of the Spirit of God.

This study has paid close attention to the political dimension of Lukan pneumatology and has brought out that the Lukan Spirit is the Spirit of resistance that engenders the social formation of the marginalised. This Lukan pneumatological paradigm is important for a postcolonial context like India. The practical implications of Lukan pneumatology of resistance that engenders the social formation of the marginalised includes the need to translate the presence of God's Spirit in the numerous contemporary movements of people's struggle for identity, justice, and liberation whether they are political, socio-economic, religious, or ideological. Such a pneumatology of resistance proffers a holistic understanding of the Spirit of God as the Spirit that is not limited to established ecclesiastical circles but is active in the socio-political struggle of the marginalised communities. Lukan pneumatological paradigm is relevant to transform the struggles of the marginalised as the prophetic site of resistance to challenge injustice, institutionalised violence, and marginalisation of the minorities and the powerless. Lukan pneumatological paradigm of resistance would enable the church and society to listen and understand the groans and cries of the marginalised as the voice of the Spirit breathing in the midst of suffering communities that struggle for identity, re-presentation, justice, and liberation.

The limitation of this study lies in two areas. Firstly, from the methodological point of view, the use of postcolonial criticism and socio-cultural criticism has its limitations. Postcolonial criticism as it has gained currency in biblical studies centres prominently on the imperial-colonial formations of the West from the eighteenth century through the twentieth centuries and lacks attention to the realm of antiquity from which the biblical texts originated. It also overlooks religious matters as though religious texts and expressions did not form part of the cultural production and as though religious institutions and practices did not belong to the social matrix of the imperial-colonial frameworks. Nonetheless, its critical activity, which dislodges and destabilises the totalising, eurocentric, individualistic, patriarchal orientation of western biblical interpretation provides space for the voices of those in the margins past and present. Similarly the use of modern socio-cultural and anthropological models that were developed in the modern period may have the risk of reductionism. Nevertheless when used cautiously, they function as a heuristic tool that allows the researcher to analyse how socio-cultural interactions might play out in a given context.

Secondly, this study is limited to the first volume of Luke's writing (Luke's Gospel), and the second volume (Acts of the Apostles) is left unexplored. Since Luke-Acts is considered as one single work with two volumes, it can be legitimately questioned how far one could arrive at a conclusion concerning Lukan pneumatology by studying only one volume? The researcher is fully aware of this lacuna. However, on the one hand, the constraint of space does not allow adequate treatment of the text if one were to take the whole of Luke-Acts. Thus, this study has limited itself to a few selected texts from the Gospel. The practical advantage of limiting the study to the Gospel also allows locating Jesus' movement alongside many other Jewish movements in historical, theological, and postcolonial perspective. On the other hand, the supposition that Luke-Acts is a single work also supposes that the two volumes are not incongruent in theology/pneumatology. It is hoped that this study would also open further the field of research in Lukan pneumatology.

Bibliography

Primary Works

Biblia Hebraica Stuttgartensia. Edited by Karl Elliger and Wilhelm Rudolph. Stuttgart: Deutsche Bibelgesellschaft, 1983.

Eusebius, *Ecclesiastical History: According to the Text of Burton*. Clarendon, 1872.

Josephus. Translated by Henry St. J. Thakeray et al. 10 vols, LCL. Cambridge: Harvard University Press, 1926–1965

New Testament Apocrypha. 2 vols. Edited by Wilhelm Schneemelcher. English trans. ed. R. McL. Wilson. Philadelphia: Westminster, 1963–1965.

Orientis Graeci Inscriptiones Selectae. Edited by Wilhelm Dittenberger. 2 vols. Leipzig: Hirzel, 1903–1905.

Tacitus, *The Complete Works of Tacitus: The Annals, The History, The Life of Gnaeus Julius Agricola, Germany and Its Tribes, A Dialogue on Oratory*. Translated by Alfred John Church and William Jackson Brodribb. New York: Random House Inc., 1942.

The Bible. New Revised Standard Version: Catholic Edition. Bangalore: TPI, 2003.

The Greek New Testament. Edited by Barbara Aland, *et al.* Fourth Revised Edition. Fifth Printing. Stuttgart: United Bible Societies, 2001.

The Mishṇah: A New Translation. Translated by Jacob Neusner et al. New Haven: Yale University Press, 1988.

Secondary Works

Achtemeier, Elisabeth. *The Community and Message of Isaiah 56–66: A Theological Commentary*. Minneapolis: Augsburg, 1982.

Ackroyd, Peter R. *Israel under Babylon and Persia*. Oxford: Oxford University Press, 1970.

Ahmed, Sara. *Strange Encounters: Embodied Others in Post-Coloniality*. London: Routlegde, 2000.

Albertz, R. and C. Westermann. "רוח ruah spirit." Pages 1202–1220 in vol. 3 of *TLOT*. 3 vols. Edited by Ernst Jenni, with assistance from Claus Westermann. Translated by Mark E. Biddle. 3 vols. Peabody, MA: Hendrickson, 1997.

Albright, William F. "Samuel and the Beginning of the Prophetic Movement." in *Interpreting the Prophetic Tradition*. Edited by Harry M. Orlinsky. New York: Ktav, 1969.

Alexander, Loveday. "Ancient Book Production and the Circulation of the Gospels." Pages 71–112 in *The Gospels for all Christian: Rethinking the Gospel Audiences*. Edited by Richard Bauckham. Grand Rapids: Eerdmans, 1998.

______. *The Preface of Luke's Gospel: Literary Conventions and Social Context in Luke 1.1–4 and Acts 1.1*. SNTSMS 78. Cambridge: Cambridge University Press, 1993.

Anderson, A. A. "The Use of 'Ruah' in 1QS, 1QH and 1QM." *JSS* 7 (1962): 293–303.

Anderson, Hugh. "Broadening Horizons: The Rejection of Nazareth Pericope of Luke 4:16–30 in the Light of Recent Critical Trends." *Int* 18 (1964): 259–275.

Applebaum, S. "Economic Life in Palestine." Pages 631–700 in *The Jewish People in the First Century: Historical Geography, Political History, Social, Cultural Life and Institutions*. Vol. 2. *Compendia rerum Iudaicarum ad Novum Testamentum: Section 1*. Edited by S. Safrai and M. Stern. Philadelphia: Fortress, 1976.

Atkinson, Kenneth, and Jodi Magness. "Josephus Essenes and the Qumran Community." *JBL* 129 (2010): 317–342.

Aulén, Gustaf. *Jesus in Contemporary Historical Research*. Translated by Ingalill H. Hjelm. Philadelphia: Fortress, 1976.

Aune, David E. *Apocalypticism, Prophecy, and Magic in Early Christianity*. Grand Rapids: Baker Academic, 2008.

Bagnall, Roger and Bruce Frier. *The Demography of Roman Egypt*. Cambridge: Cambridge University Press, 1994.

Bailey, John Amedee. *The Traditions Common to the Gospels of Luke and John*. Leiden: Brill, 1963.

Barclay, John M. G. "The Empire Writes Back: Josephan Rhetoric in Flavian Rome." Pages 315–332 in *Flavius Josephus and Flavian Rome*. Edited by Jonathan Edmondson, Steve Mason and James Rives. Oxford: Oxford University Press, 2005.

Barnett, P. W. "The Jewish Sign Prophets—A.D. 40–70—Their Intentions and Origins." *NTS* 27 (1980–81): 679–697.

Baron, S. W. *A Social and Religious History of the Jews*. Vol. 2. *Christian Era: The First Five Centuries*. New York: Columbia University Press, 1952.

Barrett, C. K. *The Holy Spirit and the Gospel Tradition*. London: SPCK, 1958.

Bartchy, S. Scott. "The Historical Jesus and Honor Reversal at the Table." Pages 175–183 in *The Social Setting of Jesus and the Gospels*. Edited by Wolfgang Stegemann, Bruce J. Malina and Gerd Theissen. Minneapolis: Fortress, 2002.

Bartels, K. H. "Remember." Pages 230–247 in vol. 3 of *NIDNTT*. Edited by Colin Brown. 3 vols. Exeter: Paternoster, 1975–1978.

Baslez, Marie-F. "The Origin of the Martyrdom Images: From the Book of Maccabees to the First Christians." Pages 113–130 in *The Books of the Maccabees: History, Theology, Ideology: Papers of the Second International Conference on the Deuterocanonical Books, Pápa, Hungary, 9–11 June, 2005*, Géza G. Xeravits and József Zsengellér eds. JSJSup 118. Leiden: Brill, 2007.

Beck, Brian E. "Imitatio Christi and the Lucan Passion Narrative." Pages 28–47 in *Suffering and Martyrdom in the New Testament: Studies Presented to G. M. Styler*. Edited by William Horbury and Brian McNeil. Cambridge: Cambridge University Press, 1981.

Bemile, Paul. *The Magnificat within the Context and Framework of Lukan Theology: An Exegetical Theological Study of Lk 1:46–55*. Regensburger Studien zur Theologie 34. Frankfurt am Main: Lang, 1986.

Benoit, P. *The Passion and Resurrection of Jesus Christ*. Translated by Benet Weatherhead. London: Darton, Longman & Todd, 1969.

Berquist, Jon L. "Resistance and Accommodation in the Persian Empire." Pages 41–58 in *In The Shadow of Empire: Reclaiming the Bible as History of Faithful Resistance*. Edited by Richard A. Horsley. Louisville: Westminster John Knox, 2008.

Betz, H. D. "The Origin and Nature of Christian Faith According to the Emmaus Legend (Luke 24:13–35)." *Int* 23 (1969): 32–46.

Black, M. *The Book of Enoch*. Leiden: Brill, 1985.

Blenkinsopp, Joseph. *A History of Prophecy in Israel*. Louisville: Westminster John Knox, 1996.

______. *Isaiah 1–39: A New Translation with an Introduction and Commentary*, AYB 19. New Haven: Yale University Press, 2000.

______. *Isaiah 56–66: A New Translation with an Introduction and Commentary*, AYB 19B. New Haven: Yale University Press, 2011.

Block, Daniel I. "Empowered by the Spirit of God: The Holy Spirit in the Historiographic Writings of the Old Testament." *SBJT* 1 (1997): 42–61.

______. "The Prophet of the Spirit: The Use of *RWH* in the Book of Ezekiel." *JETS* 32 (1989): 27–49.

______. *The Book of Ezekiel Chapters 1–24*. Grand Rapids: Eerdmans, 1997.

Bock, Darrel L. *Luke 1–9:50*, BECNT 3A. Grand Rapids: Baker Books, 1994.

Boff, Leonardo. *The Maternal Face of God: The Feminine and its Religious Expressions*. Translated by Robert R. Barr and John W. Diercksmeier. San Francisco: Harper & Row, 1987.

Boobyer, George H. "Mark II, 10a and the Interpretation of the Healing of the Paralytic." *HTR* 47 (1954): 115–120.

Borg, Marcus J. and J. D. Crossan. *The Last Week: The Day-by-Day Account of Jesus's Final Week in Jerusalem*. San Francisco: HaperSanFrancisco, 2006.

______. *Conflict, Holiness and Politics in the Teachings of Jesus*. New York: Edwin Mellen, 1984.

______. *Jesus: Uncovering the Life, Teachings, and Relevance of a Religious Revolutionary*. San Francisco: Harper San Francisco, 2006.

Boring, M. Eugene. *Sayings of the Risen Jesus: Christian Prophecy in the Synoptic Tradition*. Cambridge: Cambridge University Press, 1982.

Botterweck, G. Johannes and Helmer Ringgren, eds. *TDOT.* Translated by John T. Willis et al. 15 vols. Grand Rapids: Eerdmans, 1974–2006.

Bovon, Francois. *Luke 1*, Hermeia. Translated by Christine M. Thomas. Minneapolis: Fortress, 2000.

______. *Luke The Theologian: Thirty-Three Years of Research (1950–1983).* Translated by Ken McKinney. Allison Park, PN: Pickwick, 1987.

Bower, Ursula Graham. *Naga Path*. London: Readers Union, 1952.

Bowker, John. *Jesus and the Pharisees*. Cambridge: Cambridge University Press, 1973.

Brent, Allen. "Luke-Acts and Imperial Cult in Asia Minor." *JTS* 48 (1997): 427–433.

______. *Imperial Cult and the Development of Church* Order. Brill: Leiden, 1999.

Briggs, Charles. "The Use of רוח in the Old Testament." *JBL* 19 (1900): 132–145.

Brown, Francis, ed. *The New Brown, Driver and Briggs Hebrew and English Lexicon of the Old Testament*. Lafayette, Indiana: Associated Publishers and Authors, 1981.

Brown, R. E. "The Resurrection of Jesus." *NJBC*. Bangalore: TPI, 2007.

______. *The Birth of the Messiah: A Commentary on the Infancy Narratives in Matthew and Luke*. Garden City, NY: Double Day, 1977.

______. *The Death of the Messiah: A Commentary on the Passion Narratives in the Four Gospels*. 2 vols. New York: Doubleday, 1994.

______. *The Gospel According to John*. AB 29A. Garden City, NY: Doubleday, 1970.

Brown, Robert McAfee. *Unexpected News: Reading the Bible with Third World Eyes*. Philadelphia: Westminster, 1984.

Brueggemann, Walter. *Isaiah 1–39*. Westminster Bible Companion. Louisville: Westminster John Knox, 1998.

Bultmann, Rudolf. *Jesus and the Word*. New York: Charles Schribner's Sons, 1934.

______. *The History of Synoptic Tradition*. Translated by John Marsh. Oxford: Basil Blackwell, 1963.

______. *Theology of the New Testament*. Translated by Kendrik Grobel. New York: Charles Scribner's Sons, 1954.

Burrus, Virginia. "The Gospel of Luke and Acts of the Apostles." Pages 133–155 in *A Commentary on the New Testament Writings*. Edited by Fernando F. Segovia and R. S. Sugirtharajah. London: T&T Clark, 2007.

Butler, John. "*Travels and Adventures in the Province of Assam*, 1855, pages 66–70." Pages 594–595 in *The Nagas in the Nineteenth Century*. Edited by Verrier Elwin. Oxford: Oxford University Press, 1969.

Cadbury, Henry J. *The Making of Luke-Acts*. 2nd ed. New York: Macmillan, 1927.

Caponi, Livia. *Augustan Egypt: The Creation of a Roman Province*. New York: Routledge, 2016.

Caroll, Robert P. *Jeremiah: A Commentary*. Philadelphia: Westminster Press, 1986.

Carter, Warren. "Singing in the Reign: Performing Luke's Song and Negotiating the Roman Empire (Luke 1–2)." Pages 23–43 in *Luke-Acts and Empire: Essays in Honor of Robert L. Brawley*. PTMS 151. Edited by David Rhoads, David Esterline, and Jae Won Lee. Eugene, OR: Pickwick, 2011.

Casey, Maurice. *The Solution to the 'Son of Man' Problem*. London: T&T Clark, 2007.

Cassidy, Richard J. *Jesus, Politics, and Society: A Study of Luke's Gospel*. Maryknoll, NY: Orbis Books, 1978.

Catchpole, David R. "The Anointed One in Nazareth." *From Jesus to John* ed. Martinus C. de Boer, JSNTSup 84. Sheffield: JSOT Press, 1993.

Chancey, Mark A. *The Myth of a Gentile Galilee*. Cambridge: Cambridge University Press, 2002.

Childs, B. S. *The Book of Exodus*. OTL. Philadelphia: Westminster, 1974.

______. *Isaiah: A Commentary*. Louisville, Kentucky: Westminster John Knox, 2001.

Chilton, Bruce and Jacob Neusner. *Types of Authority in Formative Christianity and Judaism*. New York: Routledge, 1999.

______. "Announcement in Nazara: An Analysis of Luke 4:16–21." Pages 147–172 in *Gospel Perspectives*. Vol. 2. Edited by R. T. France and D. Wenham. Sheffield: JSOT Press, 1981.

Cho, Youngmo. *The Spirit and the Kingdom in the Writings of Luke and Paul: An Attempt to Reconcile these Concepts*. Milton Keynes: Paternoster, 2005.

Clark, Mary Mead. *A Corner in India*. Philadelphia: American Baptist Publication Society, 1907.

Clements, R. E. *Isaiah 1–39*. NCBC. Grand Rapids: Eerdmans, 1980.

Cogan, Mordechai. *1 Kings*. AYB 10. New Haven: Yale University Press, 2008.

Cohen, Shaye J. D. *From the Maccabees to the Mishnah*. Philadelphia: Westminster Press, 1987.

Collins, J. J. "Introduction: Towards the Morphology of a Genre." *Semeia* 14 (1979): 1–19.

Conzelmann, Hans. *An Outline of the Theology of New Testament*. New York: Harper & Row, 1969.

______. *Theology of St. Luke*. Translated by Geoffrey Buswell. Philadelphia: Fortress, 1982.

Cook, Joan E. "The Magnificat: Program for a New Era in the Spirit of the Song of Hannah." *Proceedings EGL & WMBS* 15 (1995): 35–43.

Craddock, Fred B. *Luke. Interpretation: A Bible Commentary for Teaching and Preaching*. Louisville: John Knox, 1990.

Craigie, Peter C., Page H. Kelly and Joel F. Drinkard. *Jeremiah 1–25*. WBC 26. Dallas: Word Books, 1992.

Craoto, José Saverino. "From the Leviticus Jubilee Year to the Prophetic Liberation Time: Exegetical Reflections on Isaiah 61 and 68 in Relation to the Jubilee." Pages 89–111 in *God's Economy: Biblical Studies fro Latin America*. Edited by Rose Kinsler and Gloria Kinsler. Maryknoll, NY: Orbis, 2005.

Crapanzano, Vincent. "Spirit Possession." Pages 12–19 in vol. 14 of *Encyclopedia of Religion*. Edited by Mircea Eliade et al. 16 vols. New York: MacMillan, 1987.

Crawford, Barry. Review of *Jesus the Magician*, by Morton Smith. *JAAR* 47 (1979): 321–322.

Creed, J. M. "'L' and the Structure of the Lucan Gospel: A Study of Proto-Luke Hypothesis." *ExpTim* 46 (1934–1935): 101–107.

______. *The Gospel According to St. Luke: The Greek Text with Introduction, Notes, and Indices*. London: MacMillan, 1930.

Crenshaw, James L. *Prophetic Conflict: Its Effect Upon Israelite Religion*. Berlin: Walter de Gruyter, 1971.

Crockett, Larrimore C. "Luke 4:25–27 and Jewish-Gentile Relations in Luke Acts." *JBL* 88 (1969): 177–183.

Cross, Frank Moore. *Canaanite Myth and Hebrew Epic*. Cambridge: Harvard University Press, 1973.

Crossan, J. D. *The Cross that Spoke: The Origins of the Passion Narrative*. San Francisco: Harper & Row, 1988.

Crossan, J. D. "Roman Imperial Theology." Pages 59–73 in *In the Shadow of Empire: Reclaiming the Bible as History of Faithful Resistance*. Edited by Richard A. Horsley. Louisville: Westminster John Knox, 2008.

______. *God and Empire: Jesus Against Rome, Then and Now*. New York: Harper Collins, 2007.

______. *Jesus: A Revolutionary Biography*. San Francisco: HaperSanFrancisco, 1994.

______. *The Birth of Christianity: Discovering What Happened in the Years Immediately After the Execution of Jesus*. New York: HarperCollins, 1998.

______. *The Historical Jesus: The Life of A Mediterranean Jewish Peasant*. New York: HarperSanFrancisco, 1991.

Culpepper, R. Alan. "The Gospel of Luke." Pages 3–490 in vol. 9 of *NIB*. Edited by Leander E. Keck. 12 vols. Nashville: Abingdon, 1995.

Cunningham, Scott. '*Through Many Tribulations*': *The Theology of Persecutions of Luke-Acts*. JSNTSup 142. Sheffield: Sheffield Academic Press, 1997.

Danker, Frederick W. *Jesus and the New Age According to St. Luke: A Commentary on the Third Gospel*. St. Louis: Clayton, 1972.

Daube, David. *The New Testament and Rabbinic Judaism*. London: Athlone Press, 1956.

Davies, Stevan L. *Jesus the Healer*. London: SCM Press, 1975.

Davies, W. D. *Introduction to Pharisaism*. Philadelphia: Fortress, 1967.

Davis, James A. *Spirit and Wisdom: An Investigation of 1 Corinthians 1.18–3.20 Against the Background of Jewish Sapiential Traditions in the Greco-Roman Period*. Lanham, MD: University Press of America, 1984.

Dawsey, James M. "Confrontation in the Temple: Luke 19:45–20:47." *PRSt* 11 (1984): 153–165.

Deane, W. J. *Samuel and Saul: Their Lives and Times*. London: James Nibet and Co., 1886.

Deasley, Alex R. G. "The Holy Spirit if the Death Sea Scrolls." *WTJ* 21 (1986): 48–51.

Deguglielmo, Antonine. "Emmaus." *CBQ* 3 (1941): 293–301.

Deissmann, Adolf. *Light From the Ancient East*. Translated by Lionel R. M. Strachan. 2nd ed. London: Hoder & Stoughton, 1909.

Delling, D. Gerhard. *Worship in the New Testament*. Translated by Percy Scott. London: Darton, Longman & Todd, 1962.

Derrenbacker, Robert A. Review of *The Story of Jesus According to L*, by Kim Paffenforth. *CBQ* 61 (1999): 375–376.

deSilva, David A. "Jewish Martyrology and the Death of Jesus." Pages 51–67 in *Pseudepigrapha and Christian Origins: Essays from the Studiorum Novi Testamentis Societas*. Edited by Gerbern S. Oegema and James H. Charlesworth. New York: T&T Clark, 2008.

Destro, A. and M. Pesce. "Forgiveness of Sins without a Victim: Jesus and the Levitical Jubilee." in *Sacrifice in Religious Experience*. Edited by Albert I. Baumgarten. Leiden: Brill, 2002.

DeVries, Simon J. *1 Kings*, WBC 12. Waco: Word Books, 1985.

Dibelius, Martin. *From Tradition to Gospel*. London: Ivor Nicholson and Ivor, 1934.

Doble, Peter. "Luke 24.26, 44—Songs of God's Servant: David and His Psalms in Luke-Acts." *JSNT* 28 (2006): 267–283.

______. *The Paradox of Salvation: Luke's Theology of the Cross*. SNTSMS 87. Cambridge: Cambridge University Press, 1996.

Dodd, C. H. *Apostolic Preaching and Its Developments*. London: Hodder & Stoughton, 1936.

______. *Historical Tradition in the Fourth Gospel*. Cambridge: Cambridge University Press, 1963.

______. *More New Testament Studies*. Manchester: Manchester University Press, 1968.

Donaldson, Laura E. "Postcolonialism and Biblical Reading: An Introduction." *Semeia* 75 (1996): 1–12.

______. ed. Postcolonialism and Biblical Reading. *Semeia* 75 (1996).

Downing, F. G. "A Genre for Q and a Socio-cultural Context for Q: Comparing Sets of Similarities with Sets of Differences." *JSNT* 55 (1994): 3–26.

______. "Theophilus's First Reading of Luke-Acts." Pages 91–109 in *Luke's Literary Achievement: Collected Essays*. Edited by C. M. Tuckett, JSNTSup. Sheffield: Sheffield Academic Press, 1995.

Downing, John. "Jesus and Martyrdom." *JTS* 14 (1963): 279–93.

Downs, F. S. *The Mighty Works of God*. Guwahati: Christian Literature Centre, 1971.

Duhm, Bernhard. *Das Buch Jesaja: Übersetzt und eklärt*, HKAT 3. Göttingen: Vanderhoeck & Ruprecht, 1902.

Dumbrell, W. J. "Spirit and Kingdom of God in the Old Testament." *RTR* 33 (1974): 1–10.

Dunn, J. D. G. *Christology in the Making: A New Testament Inquiry into the Origins of the Doctrine of Incarnation*. London: SCM, 1980.

______. *Jesus Remembered: Christianity in the Making*. Vol. 1. Grand Rapids: Eerdmans, 2003.

______. *Baptism in the Holy Spirit: A Re-examination of the New Testament Teaching on the Gift of the Spirit in Relation to Pentecostalism Today*. London: SCM Press, 1970.

______. *Christ and the Spirit*. Grand Rapids: Eerdmans, 1998.

______. *Jesus and the Spirit: A Study of the Religious and Charismatic Experience of Jesus and the First Christians as Reflected in the New Testament*. London: SCM Press, 1975.

______. *Jesus, Paul and the Law: Studies in Mark and Galatians*. London: 1990.

Easton, Burton Scott. *The Gospel According to Luke: A Critical and Exegetical Commentary*. Edinburgh: T&T Clark, 1926.

Edersheim, Alfred. *The Life and Times of Jesus the Messiah*. Grand Rapids: Eerdmans, 1956.

Ehrman, Bart D. and Mark A. Plunkett, "The Angel and the Agony: Textual Problem in Luke 22:43–44." *CBQ* 45 (1983): 401–416.

Eichrodt, Walther. *Ezekiel: A Commentary*. Translated by Cosslett Quin. London: SCM, 1970. 137–138.

______. *Theology of the Old Testament*. Translated by J. A. Baker. 2 vols. London: SCM, 1961.

Elliott, John H. "Social Scientific Criticism of a Biblical Text: 1 Peter as an Example." Pages 339–358 in *Social Scientific Approaches to New Testament Interpretation*. Edited by David G. Horrell. Edinburgh: T&T Clark, 1999.

______. *What is Social-Scientific Criticism?* Minneapolis: Fortress, 1993.

______. "Temple Versus Household in Luke-Acts: A Contrast in Social Institution." Pages 211–240 in *The Social World of Luke-Acts: Models for Interpretation*. Edited by Jerome H. Neyrey. Peabody: Hendrickson, 1991.

Ellis, E. Earle. *The Gospel of Luke*. London: Nelson, 1966.

Elwin, Verrier, ed. *The Nagas in the Nineteenth Century*. Oxford: Oxford University Press, 1969.

Esler, Philip F. *The First Christian World*. New York: Routledge, 2000.

______. *Community and Gospel in Luke-Acts: The Social and Political Motivations of Lucan Theology*. Cambridge: Cambridge University Press, 1987.

______. "Rome in Apocalyptic and Rabbinic Literature." Pages 9–33 in *The Gospel of Matthew in Its Roman Imperial Context*. JSNTSup 276. Edited by John Riches and David C. Sim. London: Continuum, 2005.

Evans, C. F. *Saint Luke*. London: SCM, 1990.

Evans, Craig A. "The Shout of Death." Pages 1–38 in *Jesus, the Final Days*. Edited by Troy A. Miller. London: SPCK, 2008.

Eve, Eric. *The Healer from Nazareth: Jesus' Miracles in Historical Context*. London: SPCK, 2009.

______. *The Jewish Context of Jesus' Miracles*. JSNTSup 231. Sheffield: Sheffield Academic Press, 2002.

Farmer, William R. "Modern Development of Griesbach's Hypothesis." *NTS* 23 (1976–1977): 283–289.

Farris, Stephen. *The Hymns of Luke's Infancy Narrative: Their Origin, Meaning and Significance,* JSNTSup 9. Sheffield: JSOT Press, 1985.

Feldman, Louis H. and Meyer Reinhold. *Jewish Life and Thought among Greeks and Romans: Primary Readings.* Minneapolis: Fortress, 1996.

Fitzmyer, Joseph. *The Gospel According to Luke I–IX: Introduction, Translation, and Notes.* AB 28. Garden City, NY: Doubleday, 1981.

______. *The Gospel According to Luke X–XXIV: Introduction, Translation, and Notes.* AB 28A. Garden City, NY: Double Day, 1985.

Flusser, David. *Judaism and the Origins of Christianity.* Jerusalem: Magnes, 1988.

Ford, J. Massyngbaerde. *My Enemy is My Guest: Jesus and Violence in Luke.* Maryknoll: Orbis Books, 1984.

______. "Zealotism and the Lukan Infancy Narratives." *NovT* 18 (1976): 280–292.

Foucault, Michel. *Discipline and Punish: The Birth of the Prison.* New York: Pantheon, 1977.

Franklin, E. *Christ the Lord: A Study in the Purpose and Theology of Luke-Acts.* Philadelphia: Westminster, 1975.

Freedman, David Noel, ed. *ABD.* 6 vols. New York: Doubleday, 1992.

Freyne, Sean. "The Galileans in the Light of Josephus' VITA." *NTS* 26 (1980): 400– 412.

______. "The Geography of Restoration: Galilee–Jerusalem Relations in Early Jewish and Christian Experience." *NTS* 47 (2001): 293.

______. *Galilee: From Alexander the Great to Hadrian 323 BCE to135 BCE.* Edinburgh: T&T Clark, 1980.

______. *Jesus, a Jewish Galilean: A New Reading of the Jesus Story.* London: T&T Clark, 2004.

______. Review of *Jesus the Magician*, by Morton Smith. *JBL* 41 (1979): 658–661.

Fuchs, Stephen. *Rebellious Prophets: A Study of Messianic Movement in Indian Religions.* Bombay: Asia Publishing House, 1965.

Fuller, R. H. *The Resurrection Narrative in Luke-Acts.* London: SPCK, 1972.

Funk, Robert W. and the Jesus Seminar. *The Acts of Jesus: The Search for the Authentic Deeds of Jesus.* New York; San Francisco: HarperCollins Publishers, 1998.

Gallagher, Susan VanZanten, ed. *Postcolonial Literature and Biblical Call for Justice.* Mississippi: University Press of Mississippi, 1994.

Gaston, Llyod. *No Stone on Another: Studies in the Significance of the Fall of Jerusalem in the Synoptic Gospels.* Leiden: Brill, 1970.

Geertz, Clifford. *The Interpretation of Culture.* 1972. Repr., London: Fontana Press, 1993.

Gilbert, Gary. "Luke-Acts and Negotiation of Authority and Identity in the Roman World." Pages 83–104 in *The Multivalence of Biblical Texts and Theological Meanings*. SBLSS 37. Edited by Christine Helmer and Charlene T. Higbe. Atlanta: Society of Biblical Literature, 2006.

______. "Roman Propaganda and Christian Identity in the Worldview of Luke-Acts." Pages 233–256 in *Contextualizing Acts: Lukan Narrative and Greco-Roman Discourse*. Edited by Todd Penner and Caroline Vander Stichele. Atlanta: Society for Biblical Literature, 2003.

Gilmour, S. M. "A Critical Examination of Proto-Luke." *JBL* 67 (1948): 143–152.

Godet, F. *A Commentary on St. Luke's Gospel*. Vol. 1. London: T&T Clark, 1870.

Goldstein, Jonathan A. *II Maccabees: A New Translation With Introduction and Commentary*. AB 41A. Garden City, NY: Doubleday, 1983.

Goodman, Martin. "Opponents of Rome: Jews and Others." Pages 222–238 in *Images of Empire*. JSOTSup 122. Edited by Loveday Alexander. Sheffield: JSOT Press, 1991.

Gottwald, Norman K. *The Hebrew Bible: A Socio-Literary Introduction*. Philadelphia: Fortress, 1985.

______. *The Tribes of Yahweh: A Sociology of the Religion of Liberated Israel 1250–1050 B.C.E.* Maryknoll, NY: Orbis Books, 1979.

Goulder, M. D. "Mark xvi. 1–8 and Parallel." *NTS* 24 (1977–1978): 235–240.

______. *Luke: A New Paradigm*. Vol. 1. JSNTSup 20. Sheffield: Sheffield Academic Press, 1989.

Grabbe, Lester L. "Sadducees and Pharisees." Pages 35–62 in *Judaism in Late Antiquity*. Vol. 2. Edited by Jacob Neusner and Allan J. Avery-Peck. Boston: Brill Academic Publishing, 2001.

Grant, F. C. *The Economic Background of the Gospels*. London: Oxford University Press, 1926.

Grau, Marion. "Divine Commerce: A Postcolonial Christology for the Times of Neocolonial Empire." Pages 164–184 in *Postcolonial Theologies: Divinity and Empire*. Edited by Catherine Keller, Michael Nausner and Mayra Rivera. St. Luois, Missouri: Chalice, 2004.

Green, Joel B. *The Gospel of Luke*, NICNT. Grand Rapids: Eerdmans, 1997.

______. *The Theology of the Gospel of Luke*. Cambridge: Cambridge University Press, 1995.

Greenberg, Moshe. *Ezekiel 1–20*, AB 22. New York: Doubleday, 1983.

Grimshaw, Jim. "Luke's Market Exchange District: Decentering Luke's Rich Urban Center." *Semeia* 86 (1999): 33–51.

Guelich, Robert A. *Mark 1–8:26*. WBC 34A. Dallas: Word Books, 1989.

Guijaro, Santiago. "The Politics of Exorcism." Pages 159–174 in *Social Setting of Jesus* and the Gospels. Edited by Wolfgang Stegemann, Bruce J. Malina and Gerd Theissen. Minneapolis: Fortress, 2002.

Gunkel, Herman. *The Influence of the Holy Spirit: The Popular Teaching of the Apostolic Age and the Teaching of the Apostle Paul.* Translated by Roy A. Harrisville and Philip A Quanbeck II. Philadelphia: Fortress, 1979.

Gutiérrez, Gustavo. *A Theology of Liberation: History, Politics and Salvation.* Translated by Caridad Inda and John Eagleson. Maryknoll, NY: Orbis Books, 1973.

Haber, Susan. *"They Shall Purify Themselves": Essays on Early Judaism.* Atlanta: Society for Biblical Literature, 2008.

Hahn, Frances Hickson. "Performing the Sacred: Prayers and Hymns." Pages 235–248 in *A Companion to Roman Religion*, Blackwell Companion to the Ancient World. Edited by Jörg Rüpke. Malden, MA: Blackwell, 2007.

Hamerton-Kelly, Robert G. "A Note on Matthew 12:28 Par. Luke 11:20." *NTS* 11 (1965): 167–169.

Hanson, K. C. "Kinship." Pages 62–79 in *The Social Sciences and New Testament Interpretation.* Edited by Richard Rohrbough. Peabody, MA: Hendrickson, 1996.

______. and Douglas E. Oakman, *Palestine in the Time of Jesus: Social Structure and Social Conflict.* 2nd ed. Minneapolis: Fortress, 2008.

Hanson, P. D. *The Dawn of Apocalyptic.* Philadelphia: Fortress, 1965.

Harrington, Jay M. *The Lukan Passion Narrative. The Markan Material in Luke 22:54–23:25: A Historical Survey:* 1891–1997. Leiden: Brill, 2000.

Harrington, Wilfred J. *The Gospel According to St. Luke.* London: Chapman, 1968.

______. Review of *Jesus the Liberator: Nazareth Liberation Theology, Luke 4:16–30,* by Michael Prior. *CBQ* 59 (1997): 169–171.

Hendrickx, Herman. *The Miracle Stories of the Synoptic Gospels.* London: Geoffrey Chapman: 1987.

______. *Third Gospel for the Third World: Preface and Infancy Narrative (Luke 1:1–2:52).* Collegeville, MN: Liturgical. 1996.

______. *Resurrection Narratives of the Synoptic Gospels.* London: Geoffrey Chapman, 1984.

Hengel, Martin. *Crucifixion.* Philadelphia: Fortress, 1977.

______. *Judaism and Hellenism: Studies in their Encounter in Palestine during the Early Hellenistic Period.* Vol. 1. Translated by John Bowden. Philadelphia: Fortress, 1974.

______. *The Zealots: Investigation into the Jewish Reform Movement in the Period from Herod I Until 70 A.D.* Translated by David Smith. Edinburgh: T&T Clark, 1989.

Herzog II, William R. *Parables as Subversive Speech: Jesus as Pedagogue of the Oppressed*. Louisville, Kentucky: Westminster/John Knox Press, 1994.

Heskett, Randall. *Messianism within the Scriptural Scrolls of Isaiah.* New York: T&T Clark, 2007.

Hildebrandt, Wilf. *An Old Testament Theology of the Spirit of God*. Peabody, MA: Hendrickson, 1995.

Hill, David. "The Rejection of Jesus at Nazareth (Luke iv: 16–30)." *NovT* 13 (1971): 161–180.

______. *Greek Words and Hebrew Meanings: Studies in the Semantics of Soteriological Terms*. Cambridge: Cambridge University Press, 1967.

______. *New Testament Prophecy*. London: Marshall, Morgan & Scott, 1979.

Hollenbach, Paul W. "Jesus, Demoniacs, and Public Authorities: A Socio-Historical Study." *JAAR* 49 (1981): 568–588.

______. "John the Baptist." Pages 887–898 in vol. 3 of *ABD*. Edited by David Noel Freedman. 6 vols. New York: Doubleday, 1992.

Hope, Valerie. "Status and Identity in the Roman World." Pages 125–152 in *Experiencing Rome: Culture, Identity and Power in the Roman Empire*. Edited by Janet Huskinson. Milton Keynes: Open University, 2009.

Horn, F. W. "Holy Spirit." Pages 260–280 in vol. 3 of *ABD*. Edited by David Noel Freedman. 6 vols. New York: Doubleday 1992.

Horsley, A. Richard. *Jesus and the Powers: Conflict, Covenant, and the Hope of the Poor*. Minneapolis: Fortress, 2011.

______. "Menahem in Jerusalem: A brief Messianic Episode among the Sicarii—Not 'Zealot Messianism,'" *NovT* 27 (1985): 334–348.

______. "Popular Messianic Movement Around the Time of Jesus." *CBQ* 46 (1984): 471–495.

______. "Popular Prophetic Movements at the Time of Jesus: Their Principal Features and Social Origins." Pages 124–148 in *New Testament Background: A Sheffield Reader*. Edited by Craig A. Evans and Stanley E. Porters. Sheffield: Sheffiled Academic, 1997.

______. "The Imperial Situation of Palestinian Jewish Society." Pages 395–407 in *The Bible and Liberation: Political and Social Hermeneutics*. Edited by Norman K. Gottwald and Richard A. Horsley. Maryknoll, NY: Orbis Books, 1993.

______. and John S. Hanson, *Bandits, Prophets, and Messiahs: Popular Movements in the Time of Jesus*. San Francisco: Harper & Row, 1985.

______. *Jesus and Empire: The Kingdom of God and the World Disorder*. Minneapolis: Fortress, 2003.

______. *Jesus in Context: Power, People, and Performance*. Minneapolis: Fortress, 2008.

______. *The Liberation of Christmas: The Infancy Narratives in Social Context*. New York: Crossroad, 1989.

______. *Galilee: Politics, History, People*. Valley Forge, PA.: Trinity Press International, 1995.

Huggan, Graham. *Interdisciplinary Measures: Literature and the Future of Postcolonial Studies*. Liverpool: Liverpool University Press, 2008.

Hur, Ju. *A Dynamic Reading of the Holy Spirit in Luke-Acts*. Sheffield: Sheffield Academic Press, 2001.

Hutton, J. H. *The Angami Nagas with Some Notes on Neighbouring Tribes*. London: Macmillan, 1921. Repr., The Government of Nagaland, 1969.

Indrakumar, Konthoujam. "Colonialism and Movement for Democracy in Manipur." Pages 56–74 in *Colonialism and Resistance: Society and State in Manipur*. Edited by Arambam Noni and Kangujam Sanatomba. New Delhi: Routledge, 2016.

Isaacs, Marie E. *The Concept of the Spirit: A Study of Pneuma in Hellenistric Judaism and its Bearing on the New Testament*. Heythorp Monographs. London: Heythorp College, 1976.

Jacob, Edmond. *Theology of the Old Testament*. Translated by A. W. Heathcote and P. J. Allock. London: Hodder & Stoughton, 1958.

Jagersma, H. *A History of Israel from Alexander the Great to Bar Kochba*. Translated by John Bowden. London: SCM, 1985.

James, Paula. "The Language of Dissent." Pages 277–303 in *Experiencing Rome: Culture, Identity and Power in the Roman Empire*. Edited by Janet Huskinson. Milton Keyes: Open University, 2009.

Janowitz, Naomi. *Magic in the Roman World: Pagans, Jews and Christians*. London: Routledge, 2001.

Jeremias, Joachim. *Jerusalem in the Time of Jesus*. Translated by F. H. Cave and C. H. Cave. Philadelphia: Fortress, 1969.

Jeremias, Joachim. *Jesus' Promise to the Nations*. Philadelphia: Fortress, 1982.

______. *New Testament Theology: The Proclamation of Jesus*. Translated by John Bowden. New York: Charles Scribner's Sons, 1971.

______. *The Eucharistic Words of Jesus*. Translated by Norman Perrin. New York: Charles Scribner's Sons, 1966.

______. *The Prayers of Jesus*. London: SCM, 1967.

Jervell, Jacob. *The Theology of the Acts of the Apostles*. Cambridge: Cambridge Academic Press, 1996.

Jipp, Joshua W. "Luke's Scriptural Suffering Messiah: A Search for Precedent, a Search for Identity." *CBQ* 72 (2010): 255–274.

Joel, Marcus. "Crucifixion as Parodic Exaltation." *JBL* 125 (2006): 78–79.

John H. Kautsky, *The Politics of Aristocratic Empires*. Chapel Hill: University of North Carolina, 1982.

Johnson, Aubrey R. *Cultic Prophet in Ancient Israel*. Cardiff: University of Welsh Press, 1962.

Johnson, L. T. *The Gospel of Luke*, Sacra Pagina. Vol. 3. Collegeville, Minnesota: Liturgical, 1991.

Johnson, Luke Timothy. "Luke-Acts, Book of." Pages 403–420 in vol. 4 of *ABD*. Edited by David Noel Freedman. 6 vols. New York: Doubleday, 1992.

______. *The Gospel of Luke*, Sacra Pagina. Vol. 3. Grand Rapids: Eerdmans, 1991.

______. *The Writings of New Testament: An Interpretation*. Bangalore: TPI, 2009.

Johnstone, James. *My Experiences in Manipur and the Naga Hills*. London: Sampson Law, Marston & Company, 1896.

Jones, Douglas R. "The Background and Character of Lukan Psalms." *JTS* 19 (1968): 19–50.

Joy, C. I. David. *Mark and Its Subaltern: A Hermeneutical Paradigm for a Postcolonial Context*. London: Equinox, 2008.

______. *Overlooked Voices*. Borderless Press, 2015.

Kabui, Gangmumei. "The Zeliangrong Movement: An Historical Study." Pages 53–56 in vol. 1 of *Tribal Movements in India*. Edited by K. S. Singh. New Delhi: Manohar, 1982.

Kähler, Martin. *The So-Called Historical Jesus and the Historic Biblical Christ*. Translated by Carl E. Braaten. Philadelphia: Fortress, 1964.

Kaiser, Otto. *Isaiah 1–12*, OTL. Translated by John Bowden. Philadelphia: Westminster, 1983.

______. *Isaiah 13–39: A Commentary*. Translated by R. A. Wilson. London: SCM Press, 1974.

Kamei, Gangmumei. *The History of Zeliangrong Nagas: From Makhel to Rani Gaidinliu*. Guwahati: Spectrum Publications, 2004.

Kampen, John *The Hasideans and the Origin of Pharisaim*. SCS 24. Atlanta: Scholars Press, 1988.

Kapelrud, Arvid S. "The Spirit and the Word in the Prophets." *ASTI* 11 (1977–78): 41–47.

Karris, Robert J. "Luke 23:47 and the Lucan View of Jesus Death." *JBL* 105 (1986): 65–74.

______. "Luke 24:13–35." *Int* 41 (1987): 57–61.

______. "Poor and Rich: The Lukan Sitz im Leben." Pages 112–125 in *Perspectives in Luke-Acts*. Edited by C. H. Talbert. Edinburgh: T&T Clark, 1978.

______. "The Gospel According to Luke." Pages 675–721 in *New Jerome Bible Commentary*. Bangalore: TPI, 1992.

Keener, Craig. S. *Miracles: The Credibility of the New Testament Accounts*. Vol. 1. Grand Rapids: Baker Academics, 2011.

Keil, C. F. and F. Delitzsch. *Biblical Commentary on the Books of Samuel.* Grand Rapids: Eerdmans, 1950.

Kelber, Werner H. *The Oral and Written Gospel: The Hermeneutics of Speaking and Writing in the Synoptic Tradition, Mark, Paul and Q*. Philadelphia: Fortress, 1983.

Kelly, Christopher. *Roman Empire: A Very Short Introduction*. Oxford: Oxford University Press, 2006.

Kendall, D. J. "The Use of *Mispat* in Isaiah 59." *ZAW* 96 (1984): 404

Kilpatrick, G. D. "A Theme of the Lucan Passion Story and Luke xxiii. 47." *JTS* 43 (1942): 34–36.

Kingsbury, J. D. *Conflict in Luke: Jesus, Authorities, Disciples*. Minneapolis: Fortress, 1991.

Kinman, Brent. *Jesus' Entry into Jerusalem: In the Context of Lukan Theology and the Politics of His Day.* Leiden: Brill, 1995.

Kinsler, Ross and Gloria Kinsler. *The Biblical Jubilee and the Struggle for Life*. Maryknoll, NY: Orbis, 2000.

Kittel, Gerhard, and Gerhard Friedrich, eds. *TDNT*. Translated by Geoffrey W. Bromiley. 10 vols. Grand Rapids: Eerdmans, 1964–1976.

Kleinman, Arthur. *Patients and Healers in the Context of Culture: An Exploration of Borderland Between Anthropology, Medicine, and Psychiatry*. Berkeley and Los Angeles: University of California Press, 1980.

______. *The Illness Narratives: Suffering, Healing and the Human Condition* .New York: Basic Books, 1988.

Kloppenborg, John S. et al., *Q-Thomas Reader*. Sonoma, CA: Polebridge, 1990.

Klutz, Todd. *The Exorcism Stories in Luke-Acts: A Sociostylistic Reading*. Cambridge: Cambridge University Press, 2004.

Knight, George A. F. *Servant Theology: A Commentary on the Book of Isaiah 40–55*. Edinburgh: Handsel, 1984.

Knight, Jonathan. *Luke's Gospel*. London: Routlegde, 1998.

Knudson, Albert C. *The Prophetic Movement in Israel.* New York: The Methodist Church Book Concern, 1921.

Koch, Robert. *Der Geist Gottes im Alten Testament*. Frankfurt: Lang, 1991.

Koester, Helmut. "Apocryphal and Canonical Gospel." *HTR* 73 (1980): 105–130.

______. *Ancient Christian Gospels: Their History and Development.* London: SCM, 1990.

______. *Introduction to New Testament*. Vol. 1. *History, Culture, and Religion of the Hellenistic Age*. Philadelphia: Fortress, 1980.

Kuecker, Aaron. *The Spirit and the "Other": Social Identity, Ethnicity and Intergroup Reconciliation in Luke-Acts*. LNTS 444. London: Bloomsbury, 2011.

Kümmel, W. G. *Introduction to the New Testament*. Translated by A. J. Mattill, Jr. Nashville: Abingdon, 1966.

Lampe, G. W. H. "Holy Spirit." Pages 626–639 in vol. 2 of *IDB*. Edited by George A. Buttrick. 4 vols. New York: Abingdon, 1962.

______. "The Holy Spirit in the Writings of St. Luke." Pages 159–200 in *Studies in the Gospels: Essays in Memory of R.H. Lightfoot*. Edited by D. E. Nineham. Oxford: Blackwell, 1957.

Latourelle, René. *The Miracles of Jesus and the Theology of Miracles*. Translated by Matthew J. O'Connell. New York: Paulist Press, 1988.

Leclerc, Thomas L. *Yahweh is Exalted in Justice: Solidarity and Conflict in Isaiah*. Minneapolis: Fortress, 2001.

Legrand, Lucian. *The Bible on Culture: Belonging or Dissenting*. Bangalore: TPI, 2008.

Lenski, Gerhard E. *Power and Privilege: A Theory of Social Stratification*. New York: McGraw-Hill Book Company, 1966.

Levine, Baruch A. "Religion in the Heroic Spirit: Themes in the Book of Judges." Pages 27–42 in *Thus Says the Lord: Essays on the Former and Later Prophets in Honor of Robert R. Wilson*. Edited by John J. Ahn and Stephen L. Cook. London: T&T Clark, 2009.

Levison, John R. "Did the Spirit Withdraw from Israel? An Evaluation of the Earliest Jewish Data." *NTS* 43 (1997): 35–57.

______. "Prophecy in Ancient Israel: The Case of the Ecstatic Elders." *CBQ* 65 (2003): 503–521.

Lewis, Iaon. *Ecstatic Religion, A Study on Shamanism and Spirit Possession*. 2nd. ed. London: Routledge, 1989.

Lincoln, Andrew T. "'Born of the Virgin Mary': Creedal Affirmation and Critical Reading." Pages 84–103 in *Christology and Scripture: Interdisciplinary Perspective*. Edited by Andrew T. Lincoln and Angus Paddison. London: T&T Clark, 2008.

Lindblom, Johannes. *Prophecy in Ancient Israel*. Oxford: Blackwell, 1962.

Longkumer, Arkotong. *Reform, Identity and Narratives of Belonging: The Heraka Movement of Northeast India*. London: Continuum, 2010.

Loshe, Eduard. *The New Testament Environment*. Translated by John E. Steely. Nashville: Abingdon, 1976.

Love, Stuart L. "Jesus Heals the Hemorrhaging Woman." Pages 85–101 in *The Social Setting of Jesus and the Gospels*. Edited by Wolfgang Stegemann, Bruce J. Malina and Gerd Theissen. Minneapolis: Fortress, 2002.

Lüdemann, Gerd. *The Resurrection of Jesus: History, Experience, Theology.* Translated by John Bowden. Minneapolis: Fortress, 1994.

Ma, Wonsuk. *Until the Spirit Comes: The Spirit of God in the Book of Isaiah*, JSOTSup 271. Sheffield: Sheffield Academic Press, 1999.

Mackenzie, Alexander. *History of the Relations of the Government with the Hill Tribes of the North-East Frontier of Bengal.* 1884. Repr., New Delhi: Mittal Publications, 2007.

MacMullen, Ramsay. *Romanization in the Time of Augustus*. New Haven: Yale University Press, 2003.

Maddox, Robert. *The Purpose of Luke-Acts*. Edinburgh: T&T Clark, 1982.

Mageo, Jeannette Marie. "Introduction." Pages 1–10 in *Cultural Memory: Reconfiguring History and Identity in the Postcolonial Pacific.* Honolulu: University of Hawaiʻi Press, 2001.

Malbon, Elisabeth Struthers. "Galilee and Jerusalem: History and Literature in Marcan Interpretation." *CBQ* 42 (1982): 242–255.

Malina, Bruce J. "Criteria for Assessing the Authentic Words of Jesus: Some Specifications." Pages 27–45 in *Authenticating the Words of Jesus*. Edited by Bruce Chilton and Craig A. Evans. Leiden: Brill, 2002.

______. and Richard Rohrbough. *Social-Science Commentary on the Synoptic Gospels*. Minneapolis: Fortress, 1992.

Manson, T. W. *Studies in the Gospels and Epistles*. Philadelphia: Westminster, 1962. 143.

Marshall, I. Howard. *The Gospel of Luke: A Commentary on the Greek Text*. Grand Rapids: Eerdmans, 1978.

Martínez, Florentino García. *The Dead Sea Scrolls Translated: The Qumran Text in English*. Translated by Wilfred G. E. Watson. 2nd ed. Leiden: Brill, 1996.

Marvin L. Chaney. "Systemic Study of the Israelite Monarchy." *Semeia* 37 (1986): 53–76.

Marxsen, Willi. *The Resurrection of Jesus of Nazareth*. London: SCM, 1970.

______. "The Significance of the Message of Resurrection." Pages in 15–50 in *The Significance of the Message of the Resurrection Faith for Faith in Jesus Christ*. Edited by C. F. D. Moule. London: SCM, 1968.

Massey, James. *The Gospel According to Luke*. Dalit Bible Commentary. Vol. 3. New Delhi: Centre for Dalit/Subaltern Studies, 2007. 72.

Matera, F. J. "The Death of Jesus According to Luke: A Question of Sources." *CBQ* 47 (1985): 469–485.

McKay, Niall. "A Political Reading of Luke 1:51–52 and 3:8–9 in the Light of Ezekiel 17—Inspired by John Howard Yoder and a Poststructural Intertextuality." *Neotestamentica* 47 (2013): 25–45.

McKenzie, John L. *Second Isaiah*. AB 20. New York: Doubleday, 1968.

McKenzie, Steven J. *The Trouble With Kings: The Composition of the Book of Kings in the Deutoronomistic History*. VTSup 42. Leiden: Brill, 1991.

Mead, Richard T. "The Healing of the Paralytic—A Unit." *JBL*, 80 (1961): 348–354.

Meeks, Wayne A. *The First Urban Christians*. New Haven: Yale University Press, 1983.

Meier, John P. "Jesus in Josephus: A Modest Proposal." *CBQ* 52 (1990): 84–87.

______. "Jesus." Pages 1316–1328 in *New Jerome Bible Commentary*. Bangalore: TPI, 1991.

______. *A Marginal Jew: Rethinking the Historical Jesus*. Vol. 2. *Mentor Message and Miracles*. New York: Doubleday, 1994.

Meier, Samuel A. *Speaking of Speaking: Making Direct Discourse in the Hebrew Bible*. VTSup 46. Leiden: Brill, 1992.

Menzies, Robert P. *Empowered for Witness: The Spirit in Luke-Acts*. JPTSup 6. Sheffield: Sheffield Academic Press, 1994.

______. *The Development of Early Christian Pneumatology with Special Reference to Luke-Acts*. Sheffield: Sheffield Academic Press, 1991.

Metzger, Bruce M. *A Textual Commentary on the Greek New Testament*, 2nd ed. Stuttgart: Deutche Bibelgesellschaft, 2002.

Meyer, Ben. *The Aims of Jesus*. Eugene, OR: Pickwick, 2002.

Meyers, Carol L. and Eric M. Meyers. *Haggai, Zechariah 1–8: A New Translation with Introduction and Commentary*. AB 25B. New York: Doubleday, 1987.

Miller, Amanda C. *Rumors of Resistance: Status Reversal and Hidden Transcripts in the Gospel of Luke*. Minneapolis: Fortress, 2014.

Miller, P. D. "Luke 4:16–21." *Int* 29 (1975): 417–421.

Minear, Paul S. "Dear Theo: The Kerygmatic Intention and Claim of the Book of Acts." *Int* 27 (1973): 132.

Mittlestadt, Martin William. *The Spirit and Suffering in Luke-Acts: Implications for a Pentecostal Pneumatology*. London: T&T Clark, 2004.

Moffatt, James. *Introduction to the Literature of the New Testament*, 3rd ed. 1918. Repr., Edinburgh: T&T Clark, 1961.

Montague, G. T. *The Holy Spirit: The Growth of Biblical Tradition*. New York: Paulist, 1976.

Montifiore, H. W. "Does 'L' Hold Water?" *JTS* 12 (1961): 59–60.

Moore, Stephen D. and Fernando F. Segovia, eds. *Postcolonial Biblical Criticism: Interdisciplinary Intersections*. London: T&T Clark, 2005.

Moreland, Milton. "The Jerusalem Community in Acts: Mythmaking and the Sociorhetorical Function of a Lukan Setting." Pages 285–310 in *Contextualizing Acts: Lukan Narrative and Greco-Roman Discourse*. Edited by Todd Penner and Caroline Vander Stichele, SBLSymS. Atlanta: Society of Biblical Literature, 2003.

Mowinckel, Sigmund. "The 'Spirit' and the 'Word' in the Pre-exilic Reforming Prophets." *JBL* 53 (1934): 199–227.

______. *He that Cometh*. Translated by G. W. Anderson. New York: Abingdon, 1954.

Moxnes, Halvor. "Ethnography and Historical Imagination in Reading Jesus as an Exorcist." *Neotestmantica* 44 (2010): 327–341.

______. "The Social Context of Luke's Community." *Int* 48 (1994): 381–387.

Mukherjee, D. P. P. Gupta and N. K. Das. "The Zeliangrong or Haomei Movement." Pages 67–95 in *Tribal Movements in India*. Vol. 1. Edited by K. S. Singh. New Delhi: Manohar, 1982.

Mulholland, M. Robert. "Sociological Criticism." Pages 296–316 in *New Testament Criticism and Interpretation*. Edited by David Alan Black and David S. Dockery. Grand Rapids: Zondervan, 1991.

Murphy-O'Connor, Jerome. "The Judean Desert." Pages 119–156 in *Early Judaism and Its Modern Interpreters*. Edited by R. A. Kraft and George W. E. Nickelsburg. Philadelphia: Scholars, 1986.

Myers, Ched. *Binding the Strong Man: A Political Reading of Mark's Story of Jesus*. Maryknoll, NY: Orbis Books, 1988.

Neusner, Jacob. *From Politics to Piety: The Emergence of Pharisaic Judaism*. New Jersey: Prentice-Hall, 1973.

______. *The Idea of Purity in Ancient Judaism*. Eugene, OR: Wipf & Stock, 1973.

______. *Tosefta: An Introduction*. Atlanta: Scholars Press, 1992.

Neve, Llyod. *The Spirit of God in the Old Testament*. Tokyo: Seibunsha, 1972.

Neyrey, Jerome H. "Clean/Unclean, Pure/Polluted, and Holy/Profane: The Idea and the System of Purity." Pages 80–104 in *The Social Science and the New Testament Interpretations*. Edited by Richard L. Rohrbaugh. Peabody, MA: Hendrickson, 1996.

______. "The Absence of Jesus' Emotions: The Lucan Redaction of Luke 22, 39–46." *Bib* 61 (1980): 153–171.

______. "The Symbolic Universe of Luke-Acts." Pages 274–285 in *The Social World of Luke-Acts: Models for Interpretation*. Edited by Jerome H. Neyrey. Peabody, Massachusetts: Hendrickson Publishers, 1991.

Nickelsburg, George W. E. "1 and 2 Maccabees – Same Story, Different Meaning." Pages 659–674 in *George W. E. Nickelsburg in Perspective: An Ongoing*

Dialogue of Learning. Vol. 2. JSTJSup 80. Edited by Jacob Neusner and Alan J. Avery-Peck. Leiden: Brill, 2003.

______. *Ancient Judaism and Christian Origins: Diversity, Continuity, and Transformation*. Minneapolis: Fortress, 2003.

______. *Jewish Literature Between the Bible and the Mishnah: A Historical and Literary Introduction*. Philadelphia: Fortress, 1981.

Nolland, John. *Luke 1–9:20*. WBC 35A. Dallas: Word, 1989.

Nolland, John. *Luke 18:35–24:53*. WBC 35C. Dallas: Word, 1993.

North, C. R. *The Suffering Servant in Deutero-Isaiah*. London: Oxford University Press, 1948.

North, Robert. "Maccabean Sabbatical Years." *Bib* 34 (1953): 503–506.

O'Neill, J. C. *The Theology of Acts in Its Historical Setting*. London: SPCK, 1961.

Oakes, Peter, ed. *Rome in the Bible and Early Church*. Carlisle: Paternoster, 2002.

Oakman, Douglas E. "The Countryside in Luke-Acts." Pages 151–179 in *The Social World of Luke-Acts: Models for Interpretation*. Edited by Jerome H. Neyrey. Peabody: Hendrikson Publishers, 1991.

______. *Jesus and the Economic Questions of His Day*. Lewiston: Mellen, 1986.

Osborne, G. R. "Resurrection." Pages 673–688 in *Dictionary of Jesus and the Gospels*. Edited by Joel B. Green, Scot McKnight and I. Howard Marshall. Downers Grove, IL: InterVarsity, 1992.

Oswalt, John N. *The Book of Isaiah Chapters 1–39*. NICOT. Grand Rapids: Eerdmans, 1986.

Paffenroth, Kim. *The Story of Jesus According to L*. JSNTSup 147. Sheffield: Sheffeild Academic, 1996.

Pamei, Namthiubuiyang. *The Trail from Makuilongdi: The Continuing Saga of the Zeliangrong People*. Tamenglong: Gironta Charitable Foundation, 2001.

Pannenberg, Wolfhart. *Jesus—God and Man*. Translated by Lewis L. Wilkins and Duane A. Priebe. London: SCM, 1968.

Patel, Vibha J. "Naga and Kuki? Who is to be Blamed?" *Economic and Political Weekly* 29 (1994): 1331–1332. http://www.jstor.org/stable/4401261?seq=1#page_scan_t ab_contents accessed on 7 November 2016.

Pearson, Brook W. R. "Lucan Censuses, Revisited." *CBQ* 61 (1999): 262–282.

Pemberton, R. Boileau. *Report on the Eastern Frontier of British India*. 1935. Repr., Guahati: Department of Historical and Antiquarian Studies in Assam, 1966.

Perkins, Pheme. *Introduction to the Synoptic Gospel.* Grand Rapids: Eerdmans, 2007.

Perkins, Phil and Lisa Nevett. "Urbanism and Urbanisation in the Roman World." Pages 213–244 in *Experiencing Rome: Culture, Identity and Power in the*

Roman Empire. Edited by Janet Huskinson. Milton Keyes: Open University, 2009.

Perrin, Nicholas. *Jesus the Temple*. London: SPCK, 2010.

______. *A Modern Pilgrimage in New Testament Christology*. Philadelphia: Fortress, 1974.

______. *Rediscovering the Teachings of Jesus*. London: SCM, 1967.

Pfeiderer, O. *Paulinism: A Contribution to the History of Primitive Christian Theology*. Vol. 1. Translated by E Peters. London: William & Norgate, 1877.

Philip, Finny. *The Origins of Pauline Pneumatology*. WUNT 194. Tübingen: Mohr Siebeck, 2005.

Philip, Mary (Joy). "Majestic at the Margins." Pages 104–113 in *Still at the Margins: Biblical Scholarship Fifteen Years after the Voices from the Margins*. Edited by R. S. Sugirtharajah. London: T&T Clark, 2008.

Pilch, John J. "Altered State Consciousness in the Synoptics." Pages 103–115 in *The Social Setting of Jesus and the Gospels*. Edited by Wolfgang Stegemann, Bruce J. Malina and Gerd Theissen. Minneapolis: Fortress, 2002.

______. "Sickness and Healing in Luke-Acts." Pages 181–209 in *The Social World of Luke-Acts: Models for Interpretation*. Edited by Jerome H. Neyrey. Peabody: Hendrickson, 1991.

Pilgrim, Walter E. *Good News to the Poor: Wealth and Poverty in Luke-Acts*. Minneapolis: Augsburg Publishing House, 1981.

Pixley, George V. "God's Kingdom in First Century Palestine." Pages 378–393 in *The Bible and Liberation: Political and Social Hermeneutics*. Edited by Norman K. Gottwald. Maryknoll NY: Orbis Books, 1989.

Plöger, Otto. *Theocracy and Eschatology*. Translated by S. Rudman. Richmond: John Knox Press, 1968.

Plummer, Alfred. *The Gospel According to S. Luke*, ICC, 5th ed. Edinburgh: T&T Clark, 1922, 1960.

Poirier, John C. "Purity beyond the Temple in the Second Temple Era." *JBL* 122 (2003): 247–265.

Porton, Gary G. "Diversity in Postbiblical Judaism." Pages 57–80 in *Early Judaism and its Modern Interpreters*. Edited by Robert A. Kraft and George W. E. Nickelsburg. Atlanta: Scholars, 1986.

Price, S. R. F. *Rituals and Power: The Roman Imperial Cult in Asia Minor*. Cambridge: Cambridge University Press, 1984.

Prior, Michael. "Isaiah, Jesus and the Liberation of the Poor (Luke 4.16–30)." *Scripture Bulletin* 24 (1994): 36–46.

______. *Jesus the Liberator: Nazareth Liberation Theology* (Luke 4:16–30). Sheffield: Sheffield Academic Press, 1995.

Purvis, James D. *The Samaritan Pentateuch and the Origin of the Samaritan Sect.* Cambridge: Harvard University Press, 1968.

Putnam, Michael. *Horace's Carmen Saeculare: Ritual Magic and Poet's Art.* New Haven: Yale University Press, 2001.

Reddittt, Paul L. "The Vitality of Apocalyptic Vision." Pages 77–118 in *Passion Vitality, and Foment: The Dynamics of Second Temple Judaism.* Edited by Lamontte M. Luker. Harrisburg, PA: Trinity Press International, 2001.

Reed, Jonathan. *Archaeology and the Galilean Jesus: A Re-examination of the Evidence.* Harrisburg: Trinity Press International, 2000.

Reid, Robert. *History of the Frontier Areas Bordering on Assam: From 1883–1941.* Delhi: Eastern Publishing House, 1983.

Revkin, Ellis. *A Hidden Revolution.* Nashville: Abingdon, 1978.

Richardson, Allan. *The Miracle Stories of the Gospels.* London: SCM, 1941. Repr., 1963.

Ringe, Sharon H. *Jesus, Liberation and the Biblical Jubilee: Images for Ethics and Christology.* OBT. Philadelphia: Fortress, 1985.

Rivera, Mayra. *The Touch of Transcendence: A Postcolonial Theology of God.* Louisville: Westminster John Knox, 2007.

Robbins, Vernon K. "The Social Location of the Implied Author of Luke-Acts." Pages 305–333 in *The Social World of Luke-Acts: Models for Interpretation.* Edited by Jerome H. Neyrey. Peabody, MA: Hendrickson, 1993.

Robinson, J. A. T. *Redating the New Testament.* London: SCM, 1976.

Robson, James. *Word and Spirit in Ezekiel.* New York, London: T&T Clark, 2006.

Rohrbaugh, Richard L. "The Pre-Industrial City in Luke-Acts: Urban Social Relations." Pages 125–149 in *The Social World of Luke-Acts.* Edited by Jerome H. Neyrey. Peabody, MA: Hendrickson, 1991.

Rose D'Angelo, Mary. "*Abba* and "Father": Imperial Theology and the Jesus Traditions." *JBL* 111 (1992): 611–630.

Rostovtzeff, M. *The Social and Economic History of the Hellenistic World.* Vol. 2. Oxford: Clarendon, 1941.

Roth, Wolfgang. "The Story of the Prophet Micaiah (1 Kings 22) in Historical-Critical Interpretation." Pages 105–137 in *The Biblical Mosaic Changing Perspectives.* Edited by Robert. M. Polzin and Eugene Rothman. Philadelphia: Fortress, 1982.

Rowland, Christopher. "Interpreting the Resurrection." Pages 68–84 in *The Resurrection of Jesus Christ.* Edited by Paul Avis. London: Longman, 1993.

Rowley, H. H. *The Relevance of Apocalyptic.* 2nd ed. London: Lutherworth Press, 1952.

______. *The Servant of the Lord and Other Essays on the Old Testament.* Oxford: Basil Blackwell, 1965.

Roy, Jyotirmoy. *The History of Manipur*. Calcutta: K. L. Mukhopadhayay, 1958.

Ruddin, Md. Badar. "Anglo-Manipuri War, 1891." Pages 113–134 in *Manipur: Past and Present*. Vol. 1. *History Polity and Law*. Edited by Naorem Sanajaoba. Delhi: Mittal Publications, 1988.

Russell, D. S. *The Method and Message of Jewish Apocalyptic*. London: SCM, 1964.

Saldarini, Anthony J. "Pharisees." Pages 289–303 in vol. 5 of *ABD*. Edited by David Noel Freedman. 6 vols. New York: Doubleday, 1992.

______. *Pharisees, Scribes and Sadducees in Palestinian Society: A Sociological Approach*. Grand Rapids: Eerdmans, 2001.

Samuel, Simon. *A Postcolonial Reading of Mark's Story of Jesus*. London: T&T Clark, 2007.

Sanders, E. P. *Jesus and Judaism*. London: SCM, 1985.

Sanders, James A. "From Isaiah 61 to Luke 4." Pages 46–69 in *Luke and Scripture, The Function of Sacred Tradition in Luke-Acts.* Edited by Craig A. Evans and James A. Sanders. Minneapolis: Fortress, 1993.

Sandmel, Samuel. *The First Christian Century in Judaism and Christianity: Certainties and Uncertainties.* New York: Oxford University Press, 1969.

Sawicki, Marianne. *Crossing Galilee: Architecture of Contact in the Occupied Land of Jesus*. London: Continuum, 2000.

Schaberg, Jane. *The Illegitimacy of Jesus: A Feminist Theological Interpretation of the Infancy Narratives*. New York: Crossroad, 1990.

Schmidt, John J. "Preexilic Hebrew Prophecy." Pages 482–489 in vol. 5 of *ABD*. Edited by David Noel Freedman. 6 vols. New York: Doubleday, 1992.

Schnabel, Eckhard J. *Law and Wisdom from Ben Sira to Paul: A Tradition Historical Enquiry into the Relation of Law, Wisdom, and Ethics*. Tübingen: Mohr Siebeck, 1985.

Schoemaker, William Ross. "The Use of רוח in the Old Testament, and of πνεῦμα in the New Testament." *JBL* 23 (1904): 13–67.

Schüngel-Straumann, Helen. *Rûah bewegt die Welt: Gottes schöpferische Lebenskraft in der Krisenzeit des Exils*, Stuttgarter Bibelstudien 151. Stuttgart: Katholisches Biblewerk, 1992.

Schürmann, Heinz. *Das Lukasevangelium*. Part 1. *Kommentar zu Kap. 1,1–9,50* 3rd ed. Frieburg: Herder, 1984.

Schweizer, Eduard. *The Good News According to Luke*. Translated by David E. Green. Atlanta: John Knox, 1984.

Scobie, Charles H. *John the Baptist*. Philadelphia: Fortress, 1964.

Scroggs, Robin. "Paul: ΣΟΦΟΕ and ΠΝΕΥΜΑΤΙΚΟΕ." *NTS* 14 (1967): 33-55.

Segovia, Fernando F. "Postcolonial Criticism and the Gospel of Matthew." Pages 194–237 in *Methods for Matthew*. Edited by Mark Allan Powell. Cambridge: Cambridge University Press, 2009.

______. "Mapping the Postcolonial Optic in Biblical Crticism: Meaning and Scope." Pages 23–78 in *Postcolonial Biblical Criticism: Interdisciplinary Intersections*. Edited by Stephen D. Moore and Fernando F. Segovia. London: T&T Clark, 2005.

Sema, Hokishe. *Emergence of Nagaland: Socio-Economic and Political transformation and the Future.* New Delhi: Vikas Publishing House, 1986.

Sema, Piketo. *British Policy and Administration in Nagaland 1881–1947*. New Delhi: Scholars' Publishing House, 1992.

Seo, Pyung Soo. *Luke's Jesus in the Roman Empire and the Emperor in Luke's Gospel.* Eugene, OR: Pickwick Publishers, 2015.

Shelton, James B. *Mighty in Words and Deeds: The Role of the Holy-Spirit in Luke-Acts*. Peabody, MA: Hendrickson, 1991.

Shepherd, W. H. *The Narrative Function of the Holy Spirit as a Character in Luke-Acts*, SBLDS 147. Atlanta: Scholar Press, 1994.

Sherwin-White, A. N. *Roman Law and Roman Society in the New Testament*. Oxford University Press, 1963. Repr., Grand Rapids: Baker Books, 1992.

Sicker, Jeffrey S. "'First to the Gentile': A Literary Analysis of Luke 4:16–30." *JBL* 111 (1992): 73–90.

Simon, M. *Jewish Sect at the Time of Jesus*. Translated by J. H. Farley. Philadelphia: Fortress, 1967.

Singh, N. Joykumar. *Social Movements in Manipur*. 2nd ed. New Delhi: Mittal Publications, 2005.

Sjoberg, Gideon. *The Preindustrial City*. New York: Free Press of Glencoe, 1960.

Sklba, Richard J. "Until the Spirit from on High is Poured Out on Us (Isa 32:15): Reflections on the Role of the Spirit in the Exile." *CBQ* (1984): 1–17.

Sloan, R. B. *The Favorable Year of the Lord: A Study of Jubilary Theology in the Gospel of Luke*. Austin: Schola, 1977.

Smallwood, E. Mary. *The Jews Under the Roman Rule: From Pompey to Diocletian*. Leiden: Brill, 1981.

Smend, R. *Yahweh War and Tribal Confederation*. Translated by Max Gray Rogers. Nashville: Abingdon, 1970.

Smith, Gary V. *Isaiah 1–39*. NAC 15A. Nashville: Broadman & Holman, 2007.

______. *Isaiah 40–66*. NAC 15B. Nashville: B&H Publishing Group, 2009.

Smith, Mark S. "What is Prologue is Past: Composing Israelite Identity in Judges 5." Pages 43–58 in *Thus Says the Lord: Essays on the Former and Later Prophets in Honor of Robert R. Wilson*. Edited by John J. Ahn and Stephen L. Cook. London: T&T Clark, 2009.

Smith, Morton. "Zealots and Sicarii, their Origins and Relation." *HTR* 64 (1971): 1–19.

______. *Jesus the Magician*. New York: Harper & Row, 1978.

Soares-Prabhu, George M. "Class in the Bible: The Biblical Poor as a Social Class?" Pages 147–171 in *Voices from the Margins: Interpreting Bible from the Third World*. Edited by R. S. Sugirtharajah. Maryknoll, NY: Orbis Books, 1991.

Society for Biblical Literature Handbook of Style. 2nd ed. Atlanta, GA: SBL, 2014.

Soppitt, C. A. "A Short Account of the Kachcha Naga (Empeo) Tribe in the North Chachar Hills, 1885." In *The Nagas in the Nineteenth Century*. Edited by Verrier Elwin. London: Oxford University Press, 1969.

Sorensen, Eric. *Possession and Exorcism in the New Testament and Early Christianity*, WUNT 2/157. Tübingen: Mohr Siebeck, 2002.

Spicq. C. "σωτήρ." Pages 351–356 in vol. 3 of *TLNT*. Translated and edited by J. D. Ernest. 3 vols. Peabody, MA: Hendrickson, 1994.

Stambaugh, John and David Balch. *The Social World of the First Christians*. London: SPCK, 1994.

Stanton, Graham. "Message and Miracles." Pages 56–71 in *The Cambridge Companion to Jesus*. Cambridge: Cambridge University Press, 2001.

Stauffer, E. "Messias oder Menschensohn." *NovT* 1 (1956): 81–102.

______. *Christ and Caesars: Historical Sketches*. Translated by K. and R. Gregor Smith. Philadelphia: Westminster, 1955.

Stegemann, Ekkehard W. and Wolfgang Stegemann. *The Jesus Movement: A Social History of Its Frist Century*. Translated by O. C. Dean, Jr. Minneapolis: Fortress, 1999.

Stein, Robert H. *Luke*, NAC 24. Nashville: Broadman, 1992.

______. *Mark*. BECNT. Grand Rapids: Baker Academic, 2008.

Sterling, Greg. "*Mors philosophi*": The Death of Jesus in Luke." *HTR* 94 (2001): 383–402.

Strauss, David Friedrich. *The Life of Jesus Critically Examined*, trans. G. Eliot, Life of Jesus Series. Philadelphia Fortress, 1972.

Strecker, Christian. "Jesus and the Demoniacs." Pages 117–133 in *The Social Setting of Jesus and the Gospels*. Edited by Wolfgang Stegemann, Bruce Malina and Gerd Theissen. Minneapolis: Fortress, 2002.

Streeter, B. H. *The Four Gospels: A Study of Origins, Treating of the Manuscript Tradition, Sources, Authorship, and Dates*. London: Macmillan, 1924.

Stronstad, Roger. *The Charismatic Theology of St. Luke*. Peabody: Hendrickson, 1984.

Sugirtharajah, R. S. "A Brief Memorandum on Postcolonialism and Biblical Studies." in *Postcolonial Perspectives on the New Testament and Its Interpretation*. Special Issue *JSNT* 73 (1999): 3–5.

______. "Biblical Studies after the Empire: From a Colonial to a Postcolonial Mode of Interpretation." Page 12–22 in *The Postcolonial Bible*. Edited by R. S. Sugirtharajah. Sheffield: Sheffield Academic Press, 1998.

______. *Asian Biblical Hermeneutics and Postcolonialism: Contesting the Interpretations*. Sheffield: Sheffield Academic Press, 1998.

______. *Postcolonial Criticism and Biblical Interpretation*. Oxford: Oxford University Press, 2002.

______. ed. *The Postcolonial Bible*. Sheffield: Sheffield Academic Press, 1998.

Sweeney, Marvin A. *Isaiah 1–39: With an Introduction to Prophetic Literature*. FOTL 16. Grand Rapids: Eerdmans, 1996.

Tabb, Brian J. "Is Lucan Jesus a 'Martyr'?: A Critical Assessment of a Scholarly Consensus." *CBQ* 77 (2015): 280–301.

Talbert, Charles H. *Reading the Sermon on the Mount: Character Formation and Decision Making in Matthew 5–7*. Columbia: University of South Carolina Press, 2004.

______. "Martyrdom in Luke-Acts and the Lukan Social Ethics." Pages 99–110 in *Political Issues in Luke-Acts*. Edited by Richard Cassidy and Phillip J. Sharper. Maryknoll, NY: Orbis Books, 1983.

______. *Reading Luke: A Literary and Theology Commentary on the Third Gospel*. New York: Crossroad, 1982.

Tamez, Elsa. *Bible of the Oppressed*. Translated by Matthew O'Connell. Maryknoll, NY: Orbis Books, 1982.

Tannehill, Robert C. "The Magnificat as Poem." *JBL* 93 (1974): 263–275.

______. *Luke*, Abingdon New Testament Commentaries. Nashville: Abingdon, 1996.

______. *The Narrative Unity of Luke-Acts: A Literary Interpretation,* vol. Philadelphia: Fortress, 1986.

Taylor, Mark Lewis. "Spirit and Liberation: Achieving Postcolonial Theologies in the Untied States." Pages 39–55 in *Postcolonial Theologies: Divinity and Empire*. Edited by Catherine Keller, Michael Nausner and Mayra Rivera. St. Luois, Missouri: Chalice, 2004.

Taylor, Vincent. *Formation of Gospel Traditions*. London: Macmillan, 1933.

______. *Behind the Third Gospel: A Study of the Proto-Luke Hypothesis*. Oxford: Clarendon, 1926.

______. *The Gospel According to St. Mark: The Greek Text with Introduction, Notes, and Indexes*. London: Macmillan, 1953.

______. *The Passion Narrative of Luke*. Cambridge: Cambridge University Press, 1972.

Tcherikover, Victor. *Hellenistic Civilization and the Jews*. Philadelphia: Jewish Publication Co., 1959.

Theissen, Gerd and Annette Merz, *The Historical Jesus: A Comprehensive Guide*. Translated by John Bowden. London: SCM, 1998.

Thiering, B. E. "Inner and Outer Cleansing as a Background to New Testament Baptism." *NTS* 26 (1980): 266–277.

Thiselton, Anthony C. *New Horizons in Hermeneutics*. Grand Rapids: Zondervan Publishing House, 1992.

Tholin, Richard. "The Holy Spirit and Liberation Movement the Response of the Church." Pages 40–75 in *The Holy Spirit*. Edited by Kirkpatrick. Nashville: Tidings, 1974.

Thomas, John. *Evangelising the Nations: Religion and the Formation of Naga Political Identity*. New Delhi: Routledge, 2016.

Tiede, David L. *Luke*, ACNT. Minneapolis: Augsburg Publishing House, 1988.

______. *Prophecy and History in Luke-Acts*. Philadelphia: Fortress, 1980.

Toner, Jerry. *Popular Culture in Ancient Rome*. Cambridge: Polity Press, 2009.

Treves, M. The Two Spirit of the Rule of the Community." *RevQ* 3 (1961): 449–452.

Tribelco, Paul R. *Jewish Communities in Asia Minor*. Cambridge: Cambridge University Press, 1991.

Trocmé, André. *Jesus and the Nonviolent Revolution*. Translated by Michael H. Shank and Marlin E. Miller. Scottdale, PA: Herald Press, 1973.

Trocmé, Etienne. *Jesus as Seen by His Contemporaries*. Philadelphia: Westminster, 1973.

Tuckett, Christopher. Review of *The Story of Jesus According to L* by Kim Paffenforth. *NovT* 91 (1999): 191–192.

Turner, Max. *Power from on High: The Spirit in Israel's Restoration and Witness in Luke-Acts*. Sheffield: Sheffield Academic Press, 1996.

Twelftree, Graham H. *Jesus the Exorcist: A Contribution to the Study of Historical Jesus*. Eugene, OR: Wipf and Stock, 2010.

______. *Jesus the Miracle Worker*. Downers Grove, Illinois: InterVarsity Press, 1999.

Tyson, Joseph B. "The Jewish Public in Luke-Acts." *NTS* 30 (1984): 574–583.

______. "The Lukan Version of the Trial of Jesus." *NovT* 3 (1959): 249–258.

Verbin, J. S. K. *Excavating Q: The History and Setting of the Q Gospel*. Edinburgh: T&T Clark, 2000.

Vermes, Geza. "The Qumran Interpretation of Scripture in Its Historical Setting." Pages 37–49 in *Post-Biblical Jewish Studies*. Edited by Geza Vermes. Leiden: E.J. Brill, 1975.

______. "Use of the נשא בר/נש בר in Jewish Aramaic." Pages 310–330 in *An Aramaic Approach to the Gospels and Acts*. Edited by Matthew Black, 3rd ed. Oxford: Clarendon, 1967.

______. *Jesus the Jew: A Historian's Reading of the Gospels*. Philadelphia: Fortress, 1973.

______. *The Dead Sea Scrolls: Qumran in Perspective*. Revised ed. London: SCM, 1994.

Via, E. Jane. "According to Luke, Who Put Jesus to Death?" Pages 122–145 in *Political Issues in Luke-Acts*. Edited by Richard J. Cassidy and Philip J. Scharper. Maryknoll, NY: Orbis Books, 1983.

von Rad, Gerard. *Old Testament Theology*. Vol. 2. Translated by D. M. G. Stalker. Edinburgh: Oliver and Boyd 1965.

Wacker, Marie-Theres. "The Spirit of God in the Public Sphere of Christian Communities: The Inspiration of the Hebrew Bible." *Concilium*, 2011/4 (2011): 32–42.

Walaskay, Paul W. *"And So We Came to Rome": The Political Perspective of St. Luke*, SNTSMS 49. Cambridge: Cambridge University Press, 1983.

Walsh, Jerome T. "Elijah." Pages 463–466 in vol. 2 of *ABD*. Edited by David Noel Freedman. 6 vols. New York: Doubleday, 1992.

Walton, Steve "The State They Were in: Luke's View of the Roman Empire." Pages 1–50 in *Rome in the Bible and Early Church*. Edited by Peter Oakes. Carlisle: Paternoster, 2002.

Warrington, Keith. "Suffering and the Spirit in Luke-Acts." *JBPR* 1 (2009): 15–32.

Watts, John D. W. *Isaiah 34–66*. WBC 25. Waco: Word Books, 1987.

Weatherly, Jon A. *Jewish Responsibility for the Death of Jesus in Luke-Acts*, JSNTSup 106. Sheffield: Sheffiled Academic Press, 1994.

Webb, Robert L. *John the Baptizer and Prophet: A Socio-Historical Study*. JSNTSup 62. Sheffield: Sheffield Academic, 1991.

Weisman, Ze'ev. "The Personal Spirit as Imparting Authority." *ZAW* 93 (1981): 225–234.

Welker, Michael. *God the Spirit*. Translated by John F. Hoffmeyer. Minneapolis: Fortress, 1994.

Wenk, Matthias. *Community Forming Power: The Socio-Ethical Role of the Spirit in Luke-Acts*. Sheffield: Sheffield Academic Press, 2000.

Werbner, Richard, ed. *Memory and the Postcolony: African Anthropology and the Critique of Power*. London: Zed Books, 1998.

Wernberg-Møller, P. "A Reconsideration of the Two Spirits in the Rule of the Community (1 Q Serek III, 13–IV, 26)." *RevQ* 3 (1961): 413–441.

Westermann, Claus. *Isaiah 40–66*, OTL. Translated by D. M. G. Stalker. London: SCM, 1969.

Whybray, R. N. *Isaiah 40–66*. London: Oliphants, 1975.

Wigoder, Geoffrey et al. eds. "Sadducees." Pages 618–619 in *The Encyclopedia of Judaism*. New York: MacMillan, 1989.

Wilcox, Peter and David Patton-Williams. "The Servant Songs in Deutero-Isaiah." *JSOT* 42 (1988): 79–102.

Williams, Maraget. "Jews and Jewish Communities in the Roman Empire." Pages 305–334 in *Experiencing Rome: Culture, Identity and Power in the Roman Empire*. Edited by Janet Huskinson. Milton Keynes: Open University, 2009.

Willoughby, Robert. "The Concept of Jubilee and Luke 4:18–30." Pages 41–55 in *Mission and Meaning: Essays Presented to Peter Cotterell*. Edited by Antony Billington, Tony Lane and Max Turner. Carlisle: Paternoster, 1995.

Wilson, Emily. *Death of Socrates: Hero, Villain, Chatter Box, Saint*. London: Profile Books, 2007.

Wilson, Gerald H. "The Use of Royal Psalms at the 'Seams' of the Hebrew Psalter." *JSOT* 35 (1986): 85–94.

Wilson, Robert R. "From Prophecy to Apocalyptic: Reflection on the Shape of Israelite Religion." *Semeia* 21 (1981): 79–95.

Wilson, Robert R. *Prophecy and Society in Ancient Israel.* Philadelphia: Fortress, 1980.

Wink, Walter. *Naming the Powers: The Language of Power in the New Testament.* Philadelphia: Fortress Press, 1984.

Wink, Walter. *Unmasking the Powers: The Invisible Force that Determine our Existence.* Philadelphia: Fortress Press, 1986.

Winter, Paul. "Magnificat and Benedictus: Maccabean Psalms?" *BJRL* 37 (1954): 328–347.

Witherington III, Ben. *The Acts of the Apostles: A Socio-Rhetorical Commentary.* Grand Rapids: Eerdmans, 1998.

Witmer, Amanda. *Jesus, the Galilean Exorcist: His Exorcism in Social and Political Context.* London: Bloomsbury, 2012.

Wolff, Hans Walter. *A Commentary on the Book of the Prophet Hosea.* Translated by Gary Stansell. Hermeia. Philadelphia: Fortress, 1974.

______. *Joel and Amos: A Commentary on the Books of the Prophets Joel and Amos.* Translated by W. Janzen, S. D. Macbride, Jr. and C. A Muenchaw. Hermeia. Philadelphia: Fortress, 1977.

Wolfson, Harry Austryn. *Philo: Foundations of Religious Philosophy in Judaism, Christianity, and Islam.* Vol. 2. Cambridge: Harvard University Press, 1948.

Wright, N. T. "The Surprise of Resurrection." Pages 75–108 in *Jesus, the Final Days: What Really Happened.* Edited by Troy A. Miller. London: SPCK, 2008.

______. *Christian Origin and the Question of God.* Vol. 3. *The Resurrection of the Son of God.* London: SPCK, 2003.

Yamazaki-Ransom, Kazuhiko. *The Roman Empire in Luke's Narrative*. London T&T Clark, 2008.

Yoder, John Howard. *The Politics of Jesus*. Grand Rapids: Eerdmans, 1972.

Yonuo, Asoso. *Nagas Struggle Against the British Rule Under Jadonang and Rani Gaidinliu 1925–1947*. Kohima: Leno Printing Press, 1982.

______. *The Rising Nagas: A Historical and Political Study*. Delhi: Vivek Publishing House, 1974.

Zeitlin, S. "The Pharisees: A Historical Study." *JQR* 52 (1961): 97–128.

Zeliang, Elungkiebe. *Charismatic Movements in the Baptist Churches in North East India: A Zeliangrong Perspective*. New Delhi: ISPCK, 2014.

Zeliang, Haireiwangbe. *A Brief History of Zeliangrong Heraka Movement and Its Impact in North East India*. Dimapur: Zeme Council North East India, 2015.

Zimmerli, Walther. *Ezekiel 2: A Commentary on the Book of the Prophet Ezekiel Chapters 25–48*. Translated by J. D. Martin. Hermeia. Philadelphia: Fortress, 1983.

______. *Old Testament Theology* in Outline. Translated by D. E. Green. Edinburgh: T&T Clark, 1978.